Generative AI for Everyone

Deep learning, NLP, and LLMs for creative and practical applications

Karthikeyan Sabesan

Sivagamisundari

Nilip Dutta

bpb

www.bpbonline.com

First Edition 2025

Copyright © BPB Publications, India

ISBN: 978-93-65897-388

To View Complete
BPB Publications Catalogue
Scan the QR Code:

Dedicated to

To the innovators, generative AI practitioners, and visionaries who boldly ask, "What's next?"

And to ourselves—who had the courage to start and are dedicated to growing with every new challenge.

About the Authors

- **Karthikeyan Sabesan** is a business consultant and innovation enthusiast with over 17 years of experience across various roles, including project management, business development, strategy consulting, sales, and leading a Center of Excellence. Karthikeyan specializes in innovation and business strategy building, and currently, Karthikeyan spearheads Edge computing and generative AI initiatives for enterprise businesses. He is passionate about sharing knowledge and exploring new frontiers in generative AI through his continuous blog writing. Additionally, he enjoys mentoring emerging talent and strives to make complex concepts accessible to everyone.

- **Sivagamisundari** has over 19 years of experience across multiple domains: banking, oil & gas, retail, and telecom. She handled multiple roles: cloud solution architect, Siebel consultant, test automation engineer, business analyst, and developer. She is involved in providing solutions and guiding the team to develop complete Cloud Solutions Design and deployment of Azure/AWS solutions considering sizing, infrastructure, data protection, disaster recovery, and application requirements for hybrid enterprise systems. Participated in Microsoft Hackathon around AI and was among the top 10 contestants by Techdig.

- **Nilip Dutta** is a seasoned technology professional with over 19 years of leadership experience, specializing in delivering cutting-edge solutions for clients ranging from small businesses to large enterprises. With experience in cloud computing, networking, telephony and a robust background in SRE (Site Reliability Engineering), virtualization, SAN storage, and Unix systems, Nilip has consistently demonstrated a proven ability to design innovative, scalable solutions tailored to business needs. His leadership extends across pre and post-sales processes, leveraging methodologies to meet evolving business requirements. A natural mentor and trainer, he excels at fostering collaboration among cross-functional teams and driving common goals, all while championing a customer-first approach. A thought leader and technology visionary, Nilip is passionate about exploring the forefront of emerging technologies like generative AI and quantum computing while also prioritizing sustainability and enterprise architecture.

About the Reviewers

❖ **Rajiv Avacharmal** is a leading expert in the field of AI/ML risk management, with a particular focus on generative AI. With a distinguished career spanning over 13 years, Rajiv has held senior leadership roles at several multinational banks and currently serves as the Corporate Vice President of AI and Model Risk at a leading Life Insurance Company. Rajiv's research interests lie at the intersection of AI/ML, risk management, and explainable AI.

❖ **Aqsa** is an award-winning AI/ML product manager with expertise in the enterprise domain. An author, international speaker, and judge, she has been recognized on several forums for her product management outcomes and influence.

She has 7+ years of experience and a proven track record in achieving business outcomes in products across Ads measurement, Recommendation systems, Content Management, Business intelligence platforms, and Data Analytics from her time across Google Ads, Cloud, and Assistant.

She is passionate about building world-class innovative and AI product experiences and is energized working with motivated and humble teammates. Outside work, she enjoys beaches, brunches, and learning languages.

Acknowledgements

We would like to express our gratitude to our colleagues and co-workers in the tech industry, whose valuable contributions over the years have taught us so much and encouraged us to think beyond our daily routines. We would like to extend a special thank you to Lekha Menon for her active role in shaping the book's content.

We are deeply thankful to our families for their patience, motivation, and encouragement at every step of our journey, constantly pushing us to pursue our ambitions and goals. We appreciate our teamwork and the mutual support that helped us stay committed to completing this book.

As one of the authors of this book, I, Karthikeyan Sabesan, would like to take a moment to convey my deepest gratitude to my family—Jayaraman Rukmani, Narayanaswamy Sabesan, T.S.Rajeshwari, Vaishnavi Sabesan, and my kids. Their unwavering support, love, and encouragement have been instrumental in the creation of this book.

As one of the authors of this book, I, Nilip Dutta, would like to express my heartfelt gratitude to my family—my daughter Nimisha, wife Soumi, brother Nibir and parents Smt Rita and Mr Nisith Kumar Dutta. Their unwavering support, love, and encouragement have been invaluable in bringing this book to life.

As one of the authors of this book, I, Sivagamisundari, want to extend my deepest gratitude to my family for their patience, encouragement, and understanding throughout this challenging process that involved countless revisions and late nights.

I want to thank my co-authors for their expertise and collaborative spirit, their openness to explore ideas, and their dedication towards making this book a reality that I truly believe the readers will enjoy.

We extend our gratitude to BPB Publications for their guidance and expertise in bringing this book to life. The process of revising the book was lengthy, but it was enriched by the valuable input and collaboration of reviewers, technical experts, and editors.

Most importantly, we want to thank all the readers who have shown interest in our book and supported us in making it a reality. Your encouragement has been truly invaluable.

Preface

Generative AI, a branch of artificial intelligence, has made remarkable strides in recent years. These advancements have enabled a variety of applications, including the creation of lifelike images, videos, text, and music. The many benefits of generative AI can help different industries improve their processes and boost efficiency. This technology has the potential to automate and enhance human and machine tasks, as well as autonomously execute business and IT processes. However, it is important to remain aware of the risks and limitations associated with generative AI. Therefore, understanding its evolution, techniques, architecture, and potential risks is essential.

This book is designed for readers of all levels, from beginners to experienced professionals. It covers fundamental concepts, practical applications, advanced topics, and includes hands-on coding examples.

Chapter 1: AI Fundamentals – The chapter introduces **artificial intelligence** (**AI**) technology, its terminologies, and its significance across industries. It explains the concepts of machine learning and various ML techniques, such as supervised, unsupervised, semi-supervised and reinforced learning, highlighting their benefits and challenges. The chapter also focuses on the concept of design patterns, explaining its importance in AI applications.

Chapter 2: GenAI Foundation – The chapter is to provides a foundation for generative AI technology that is deep neural network and its significance. It aims to explain the concepts of deep learning and various **deep learning** (**DL**) techniques such as deep neural network elements, gradient descent, backpropagation, hyper-parameters, performance metrics and highlighting their significance and options. The chapter includes coded examples for supervised deep learning regression and classification problems .

Chapter 3: GenAI for Images – This chapter provides an overview of computer vision, CNN architectures, and image processing techniques. It covers the basics of image processing, computer vision tasks, real-world applications, and the evolution of deep learning architectures. Additionally, it explores representation learning, including autoencoders and variational autoencoders, for computer vision tasks. The chapter discusses encoder-decoder architectures, encoding and decoding mechanisms, and coded examples such as U-Net for image segmentation and VAE for image generation

Chapter 4: Transforming Images with GenAI – The chapter provides an overview of generative modeling, covering different types of explicit and implicit modeling methods. It delves into **generative adversarial networks** (**GANs**), discussing their architecture, variations, and applications including example for VQGAN and CLIP. Diffusion processes and diffusion models are explained, including their architecture, training process, and the latent diffusion model for image processing (MNST example).

Chapter 5: GenAI for Text – The chapter provides an overview of NLP technology, its key concepts, and its applications in various industries. It explains text pre-processing and post-processing techniques, and discusses different deep learning architectures for NLP tasks, including traditional models like RNN and LSTM, and more recent transformer architectures. The chapter focuses on different types of transformer architectures, their components in details, and their applications in tasks like summarization, question answering, and speech-to-text recognition. The chapter includes coded examples to fine tune GPT model for new tasks and Text summarization task.

Chapter 6: ChatGPT – In this chapter, we will look into ChatGPT essentials, its features, integrations and addons along with image generation and speech to text examples. Further, we will understand the importance of prompts, their types, frameworks, and examples, and delve into the prompt engineering process. Finally, we will create a prompt Playground application for enterprises.

Chapter 7: Large Language Model Frameworks – The objective of this chapter is to provide a overview of LangChain framework, its components, and examples. We will build three prototypes 1.) use llms to chat with your excel documents 2.) Retrieve contextual information using Retrieval Augmented generation (RAG) from customer knowledge base 3.) create a chat application that can query medical research journals and extract property graph out of it

Chapter 8: Large Language Model Operations – The objective of this chapter is to go through complete LLM system lifecycle, starting from data preparation, pre-training, benchmarking, experimentation, AI alignment, model experimentation, model serving, validation, security and monitoring. This chapter aims to explain the concepts of LLMOps, including various optimization techniques to improve the performance and efficiency of the LLM system as a whole.

Chapter 9: Generative AI for Enterprise – The chapter provides an overview of how GenAI technology is leveraged by enterprises for their business improvements. This chapter covers various enterprise use cases, GenAI products and their capabilities. It also focusses on risks related to AI models, GenAI model vulnerabilities and factors that enterprise must consider while implementing GenAI projects. It also gives foundation to responsible AI, Its applicability in enterprise systems and the examples.

Chapter 10: Advances and Sustainability in Generative AI – The chapter helps to understand the advancements happening in generative AI in terms of business, technology and regulation. We will also look into the types of business strategy that an enterprise must adopt to leverage GenAI's potential to their competitive advantage. Further we will look into the environmental impact due to training & inferencing of GenAI models, way to measure and mitigate the same.

Code Bundle and Coloured Images

Please follow the link to download the
Code Bundle and the *Coloured Images* of the book:

https://rebrand.ly/1fdc32

The code bundle for the book is also hosted on GitHub at
https://github.com/bpbpublications/Generative-AI-for-Everyone.
In case there's an update to the code, it will be updated on the existing GitHub repository.

We have code bundles from our rich catalogue of books and videos available at **https://github.com/bpbpublications**. Check them out!

Errata

We take immense pride in our work at BPB Publications and follow best practices to ensure the accuracy of our content to provide with an indulging reading experience to our subscribers. Our readers are our mirrors, and we use their inputs to reflect and improve upon human errors, if any, that may have occurred during the publishing processes involved. To let us maintain the quality and help us reach out to any readers who might be having difficulties due to any unforeseen errors, please write to us at :

errata@bpbonline.com

Your support, suggestions and feedbacks are highly appreciated by the BPB Publications' Family.

Piracy

If you come across any illegal copies of our works in any form on the internet, we would be grateful if you would provide us with the location address or website name. Please contact us at **business@bpbonline.com** with a link to the material.

If you are interested in becoming an author

If there is a topic that you have expertise in, and you are interested in either writing or contributing to a book, please visit **www.bpbonline.com**. We have worked with thousands of developers and tech professionals, just like you, to help them share their insights with the global tech community. You can make a general application, apply for a specific hot topic that we are recruiting an author for, or submit your own idea.

Reviews

Please leave a review. Once you have read and used this book, why not leave a review on the site that you purchased it from? Potential readers can then see and use your unbiased opinion to make purchase decisions. We at BPB can understand what you think about our products, and our authors can see your feedback on their book. Thank you!

For more information about BPB, please visit **www.bpbonline.com**.

Join our book's Discord space

Join the book's Discord Workspace for Latest updates, Offers, Tech happenings around the world, New Release and Sessions with the Authors:

https://discord.bpbonline.com

Table of Contents

CHAPTER 1
AI Fundamentals

Introduction

Generative AI (GenAI) has become a catalyst for any business. Though it does not seem to be disrupting industries immediately, the advances in GenAI is making it move from current state of collaborator to disruptor. AI has been a while since 1950's and **machine learning (ML)** sub-domain of AI has been successful in many industry domains. So, understanding its evolution, techniques, and underlying architecture is a must. Before delving into GenAI, this chapter gives an introduction to AI; it is methods and design features. In upcoming chapters, we will detail GenAI concepts of deep learning, generative modeling techniques, various GenAI examples, ChatGPT essentials, and GenAI use cases, and conclude with enterprise risks and responsibility. Throughout the book, we will understand the AI concepts, specific techniques, mathematical briefings, and examples. Though we were not able to provide examples of all techniques, we have carefully chosen the ones that are needed to understand GenAI concepts holistically.

Structure

In this chapter, we will learn the following topics:

- Introduction to AI
- Supervised and unsupervised learning

- Semi-supervised learning and reinforcement learning
- Design patterns

Objectives

The objective of this chapter is to introduce **artificial intelligence** (**AI**) technology, its terminologies, and its significance across industries. It aims to explain the concepts of machine learning (ML) and various ML techniques, such as supervised and unsupervised learning, highlighting their benefits and challenges. The content also focuses on the advanced ML methods of semi-supervised and **reinforcement learning** (**RL**). Furthermore, the content introduces the concept of design patterns, explaining its importance in AI applications.

Introduction to AI

Welcome to the world of AI, a term that might sound complex but holds a simple and very interesting idea at its core. AI is all about infusing intelligence into things that are not alive, making them smart in a way that even surpasses human intelligence. This concept envisions achieving super-intelligence, where non-living entities become smarter than the brightest human minds. Now, you might wonder, should we be worried? The answer is no. History has shown that with every technological leap, there has been disruption, but it has been a disruption for the better. Think about the transition from calculators to computers or from steam engines to electric trains—each change has transformed our lives, opening new opportunities and enhancing our lifestyles.

What exactly is AI? Why do we believe AI is necessary? Are there any challenges or concerns hidden in the AI landscape? In this chapter, we will delve into all these questions, exploring the depths of AI and uncovering the mechanisms that power it. We will navigate through the various categories of AI, observing its remarkable progress. You might be surprised to learn that AI has already found its way into our lives, subtly weaving its benefits into our routines. You might be using AI and its applications without even realizing it. Ignorance causes fear, but knowledge and awareness help us to be more creative by utilizing the powerful tool.

Acquiring knowledge about this tool and understanding how to hold and use it properly is crucial, especially when the tool possesses intelligence. Extreme caution is required. As we learn more about AI, we must approach it with responsibility, guided by appropriate governance, policies, and guardrails.

Moving on, let us explore a specific example that is familiar to many: self-driving cars. The reason why we do not see self-driving cars dominating the roads as expected is not just about technology; it is about regulations, rules, and the allocation of responsibility in case of mishaps.

From these scenarios, we draw a key message: leveraging AI tools and technologies demands not only the right resources but also a deep understanding of their application and a well-crafted governance plan. This combination ensures that we can fully harness AI's potential, reaping its benefits while minimizing risks.

Now, let us further understand the world of AI.

Defining AI

Imagine teaching computers to be smart, just like we teach our friends. AI is like giving computers brains to think, learn, solve problems, and talk like humans do. It is like having a new friend who is good at understanding and helping us.

AI is already reshaping various fields like education, research, healthcare, and transportation. However, the recent goal is to develop **artificial general intelligence (AGI)**, which would empower computers to perform any cognitive task that a human can. This concept might sound like science fiction, but it is becoming a reality. AI's primary aim is to enhance computer intelligence significantly, making them exceptionally intelligent and helpful. In the future, these machines could surpass human intelligence, a state known as **super-intelligence**. This journey in AI is all about creating incredibly advanced and friendly technology. Take a look at the following figure:

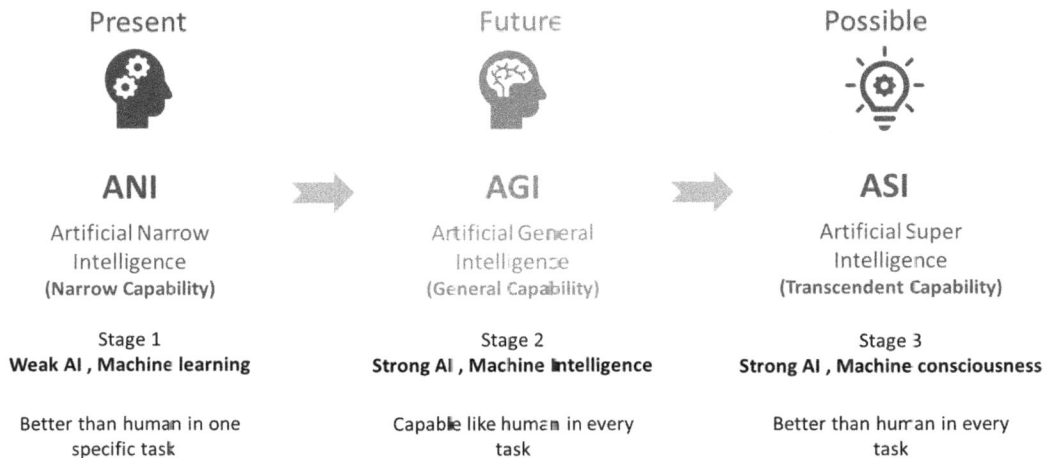

Present	Future	Possible
ANI	**AGI**	**ASI**
Artificial Narrow Intelligence (Narrow Capability)	Artificial General Intelligence (General Capability)	Artificial Super Intelligence (Transcendent Capability)
Stage 1 **Weak AI , Machine learning**	Stage 2 **Strong AI , Machine Intelligence**	Stage 3 **Strong AI , Machine consciousness**
Better than human in one specific task	Capable like human in every task	Better than human in every task

Figure 1.1: Current and future of AI

Artificial Narrow Intelligence

Just like the name suggests, Narrow AI has a limited scope. It is designed for a particular job within a specific field or area. Think of it as a specialist AI that is trained for a particular industry or situation, and it cannot handle tasks beyond its specialized training. That is why it is also called **Weak AI**.

For instance, imagine a chatbot working as a customer service representative for a bank. This chatbot is only trained to handle questions related to that specific bank's customer service. It would not be able to chat about anything else or perform tasks outside of banking inquiries. Similarly, let us consider a predictive maintenance model used to prevent failures in a system. However, this model is limited to predicting issues within the specific system it is designed for. So, if it is created for a car engine, it would not be able to predict problems in an entirely different type of machinery. In a nutshell, Narrow AI or Weak AI is like a highly focused expert—it is great at what it is trained for, but it cannot handle tasks that fall outside its narrow area of expertise.

Artificial General Intelligence

Strong AI's purpose is to build human-like intelligence to think and give general answers like a human. Strong AI, or AGI, aims to create intelligence in machines that is like human thinking. Imagine a computer that can understand and respond to things just like a human can. An example could be the future multi-modal **Generative Pre-trained Transformer (GPT)**. The goal, arguably, is to have super-intelligence.

Artificial Super-intelligence

In AI, the idea of super-intelligence sparks varied opinions due to different levels of understanding. Some believe that achieving super-intelligence is both possible and beneficial, while others hold the view that it is neither attainable nor desirable.

In his enlightening book *SUPERINTELLIGENCE*, *Nick Bostrom* puts forth a definition for super-intelligence. He describes it as any intellect that substantially exceeds the cognitive performance of humans in practically all categories of interest. *Bostrom* categorizes super-intelligence into three types, each with its own unique characteristics, as follows:

- **Speed super-intelligence**: A system that can do all that a human intellect can do, but much faster.
- **Quality super-intelligence**: A system that is at least as fast as a human mind and vastly qualitatively smarter.
- **Collective super-intelligence**: A system composed of a large number of smaller intellects such that the system's overall performance across many very general domains vastly outscripts that of any current cognitive system.

Exploring Artificial Narrow Intelligence

Well, AI has different ways to work its magic, but two of the coolest ANI ones are **machine learning (ML)** and deep learning. These are like training programs for computers. You know how we learn from books, experiences, and practice? Computers learn from lots of information too, just like we teach them. Deep learning uses something special called

neural networks (**NN**). These networks are like the computer's brain cells that help them learn from a ton of information. Then, using what they have learned, computers can make clever choices, almost like how you make smart decisions after learning from your experiences. Take a look at the following figure that showcases the artificial narrow intelligence sub-domains:

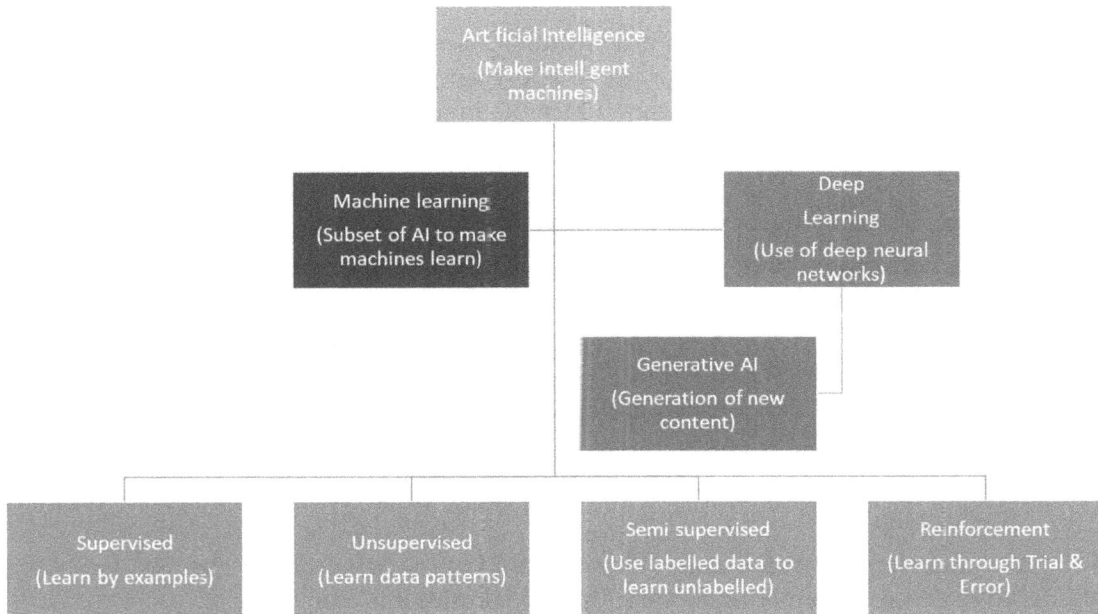

Figure 1.2: Artificial narrow intelligence and its sub-domain

Here are some definitions from text by *Professor Christopher Manning*, September 2020:

AI, a term coined by emeritus *Stanford Professor John McCarthy* in 1955, was defined by him as the science and engineering of making intelligent machines. Much research in the past was to program machines that can behave in a clever way, like playing chess, but today, we emphasize machines that can learn, at least somewhat like human beings do.

ML is the part of AI studying how computer agents can improve their perception, knowledge, thinking, or actions based on experience or data. For this, ML draws from computer science, statistics, psychology, neuroscience, economics, and control theory. ML allows machines to learn without programming.

Deep learning is the use of large multi-layer **artificial neural networks** (**ANN**) that compute with continuous (real number) representations, a little like the hierarchically organized neurons in human brains It is currently the most successful ML approach, usable for all types of ML, with better generalization from small data and better scaling to big data and compute budgets.

Machine learning

We all have different ways of teaching, and avail them based on the needs of students; the same principle applies when we teach machines. Imagine teaching kids or even pets—each requires a unique approach. Similarly, we have different methods to teach machines, and it is important to find a suitable one.

The concept behind teaching machines is similar. We provide the machine with existing data that contains input and output pairs, and then we ask the machine to convert the underlying pattern, logic, or algorithm. Once the machine figures out the algorithm, we can build a model based on it. This model becomes capable of performing similar tasks in the future with the knowledge it has gained.

The machine's learning journey can be broken down into the following steps:

1. **Data collection**: First, we gather the data that will be used to train the machine. This data holds the key to help the machine understand and learn from examples.

2. **Data exploration**: Think of this step as getting to know the data. We thoroughly study it to ensure it is the right fit for the specific use case. By understanding the data, we are better equipped to harness its potential.

3. **Data preparation**: Here, we clean and organize the data, getting it ready for the machine to learn from. It is like preparing the ingredients before cooking a delicious meal.

The preceding steps consume a significant portion of the ML process. The next two steps are iterative processes aimed at refining the model until it is at its best:

1. **Modeling**: This is where the magic begins. We feed the historical input and output data into the machine, allowing it to figure out the hidden algorithm. This step might need to be repeated a few times to ensure the model is as accurate as possible.

2. **Evaluation**: Using the newly constructed model, we compare its outputs to the previously evaluated ones. This helps us determine how accurate the model is. Think of it as checking the model's homework—the percentage of accuracy reveals how well the model has learned and how mature it has become.

Following these steps, we guide machines through their learning process, from data collection to model evaluation. The journey might involve a bit of trial and error, but it is this process that empowers machines to assist us in incredible ways. So, as we continue this journey, remember that just like teaching a pet a new trick, teaching machines is all about patience, exploration, and discovery.

Understanding different learning approaches in machine learning

In ML, there are four primary types of algorithms used to train models. These algorithms determine how machines learn from data and enable them to perform tasks. Let us explore these types:

- **Supervised ML**: Imagine having a teacher guiding you at every step. Similarly, in supervised learning, the training data comes with labels or annotations, acting as a guide for the machine. These labels show the machine the correct answers, allowing it to learn patterns and associations. This type of learning is like teaching a student answers to questions, helping the machine to make accurate predictions or decisions when faced with new, unseen data.

- **Unsupervised ML**: Now, consider a scenario where you are exploring a new city without a tour guide. Unsupervised learning is somewhat similar. Here, the training data is not labeled or categorized. The machine is presented with a heap of data, and its task is to find patterns, groupings, or relationships within the data. It is like discovering hidden themes or connections in a collection of information without predefined supervision.

- **Semi-supervised ML**: This type of learning lies between supervised and unsupervised learning, where we have a small amount of labeled data and a large amount of unlabeled data. Here, machines try to learn the information from labeled data and use it to predict or classify the unlabeled data. It is more like experimentation, where we do lab experiments with known facts and generalize the observation to unknown scenarios.

- **Reinforcement ML**: Think of this type of learning as training a pet to perform tricks. In RL, the machine interacts with its environment and receives continuous feedback through rewards or penalties based on its actions. This constant feedback loop helps the machine learn to make better decisions over time. Like a dog learning to fetch a ball through trial-and-error with the reward given for correct action, the machine refines its actions with feedback to achieve a goal.

In summary, these four learning approaches each have their unique strengths. Supervised learning guides machines with labeled data; unsupervised learning lets machines uncover hidden structures, **semi-supervised learning** (SSL) leverages supervised data to learn unlabeled ones, and RL nurtures learning through continuous feedback. As we learn further into this section, we will unlock the intricacies of supervised learning and see how it empowers machines to become insightful learners.

We want to highlight one crucial factor that holds utmost importance for any AI application is the aspect of risk and governance, as well as the level of knowledge and awareness about the technology. Ensuring responsible use of AI and taking on the associated responsibilities are vital considerations that should be given the highest priority in any AI use case.

Supervised and unsupervised learning

In this section we will go into brief on supervised and unsupervised learning. Both these approaches played a pivotal role in the advancement of ML and data-driven decision making. The availability of label and preprocessing of data is the key difference between the two. In practical AI applications, a complex training process involves multiple steps that include different approaches like supervised, unsupervised and RL. In this chapter, we will look into supervised and unsupervised learning techniques and their pros and cons.

Supervised learning

In the world of ML, one of the key methods we use is called supervised learning. This approach involves using data that is already labeled or supervised. Think of it like having a teacher beside you, guiding you every step as you learn. In this section, we will delve into the logic of supervised learning to explore how it works. There are various supervised learning algorithms and are majorly categorized at high levels into regression and classification:

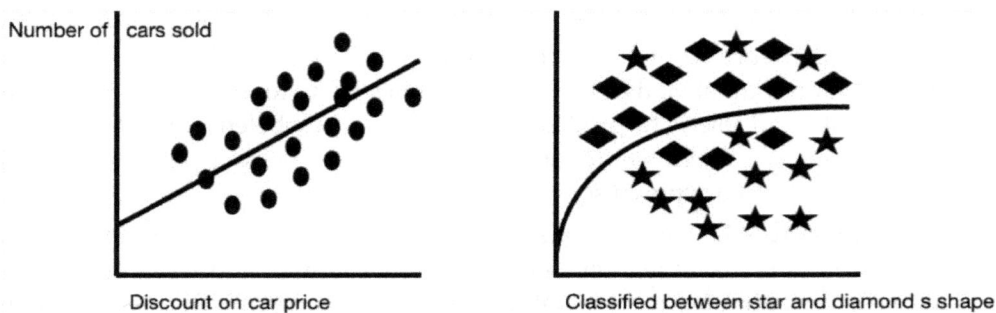

Figure 1.3: Regression (left) vs classification (right)

At its core, supervised learning is about understanding the relationship between two types of variables: the independent variable, which serves as the input, and the dependent variable, which is the output. This relationship is what we aim the machine to learn. Let us break down the process:

1. **Training the model**: In supervised learning, we present the machine with pairs of input and output data. The machine's task is to understand the connection between these two variables. It is like showing a student various math problem and their solutions so they can learn the rules and logic behind solving similar problems in the future.

2. **Creating a trained model**: Once the machine understands the relationship between inputs and outputs from the training data, it is like the student grasping the concepts. We then use this understanding to create a model. This model encapsulates the knowledge the machine has gained and allows it to predict outputs for new inputs.

3. **Testing and accuracy**: Now comes the interesting part. We feed the model with new sets of input data, just like giving the student new problems to solve. The model generates outputs based on its learning. But here is the catch—we already know the correct answers for this new data. We compare the model's outputs

to the actual outputs, and this comparison tells us how accurate the model's predictions are.

Imagine the student mastering math problems to the point where they are perfect at every test. Similarly, if the model's accuracy percentage is close to 100%, it is a sign that the machine has learned the relationship between input and output and is making accurate predictions.

Remember, just as a teacher nurtures a student's growth, supervised learning nurtures the growth of machines into insightful learners. In the following figures, we will bring a simple illustration of the supervised ML process, like training, validation and calculate the performance. Take a look at the following figure:

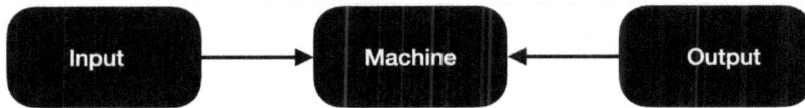

Figure 1.4: *Train machine with past input and output data*

Take a look at the following figure:

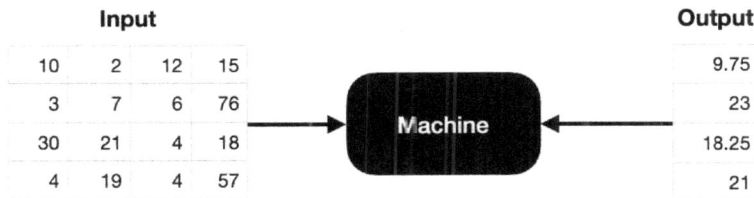

Figure 1.5: *AI model is built by a machine to understand the relationship between input and output*

Take a look at the following figure:

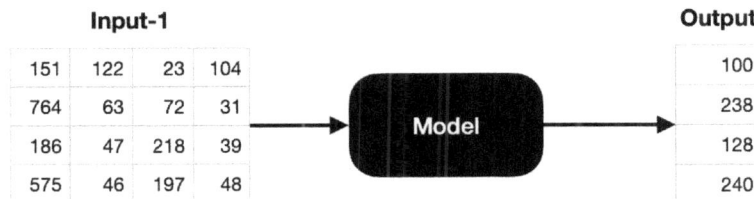

Figure 1.6: *AI model is tuned to give the correct output and the difference in prediction determine the performance*

With more training data, the model is expected to give more accurate results, which can ensure that the machine is learning. From the insights given in the above depiction, it is evident that supervised ML is meant to craft predictive models. By understanding historical data, it gains the skill to anticipate future outputs based on provided inputs. Consider a scenario where a model is fed data of customer's income, miles driven, location, previous cab booking records, and the type of car they purchased before—be it luxury, sedan, suv, hatchback, electric, etc. Through learning from these labeled examples, the model becomes proficient at forecasting the customer's subsequent car purchase, thereby helping car sellers target customers effectively.

Supervised learning methods

Supervised ML majorly has two primary categories of algorithms, as follows:

- **Regression**: This model is designed to predict continuous future values by analyzing the relationships within the historical independent/input and dependent/output data that have trained the model. Regression is predominantly utilized when dealing with continuous data.

- **Classification**: In classification, the ML model segregates data based on their distinct independent features. This method is particularly effective for dealing with discrete data, where the goal is to classify inputs into specific categories or classes.

The below figure depicts the categorization of various supervised learning algorithms:

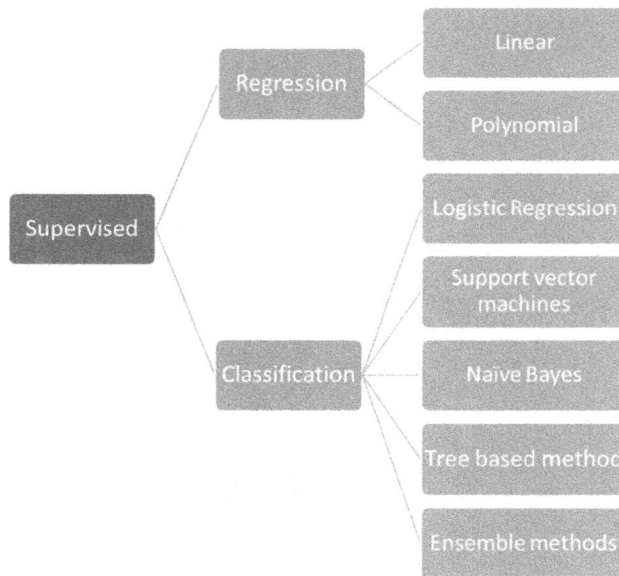

Figure 1.7: Supervised learning algorithm categories

Let us take a look at advantages and disadvantages of supervised ML:

Advantages

The advantages of supervised ML are as follows:

- **Knowledge amplification**: Supervised learning generates new insights by learning from past experiences, allowing machines to make informed predictions.

- **Guided learning**: Leveraging labeled data provides initial context and understanding of the underlying patterns, expediting the learning process and optimize performance.
- **Simplicity and interpretability**: Compared to unsupervised learning, supervised learning is often less complex to interpret.
- **Practical problem solving**: Well-suited for addressing real world computational challenges.
- **Validation and control**: Validation using established training data ensures reliable performance, while customizing the training data allows class selection from the training data.

Disadvantages

The disadvantages of supervised ML are as follows

- **Big data complexity**: Handling large datasets for classification.
- **Data preparation**: Preparing the dataset for training demands effort.
- **Incomplete values**: Dealing with missing or incomplete data points.
- **Bias handling**: Addressing bias in input data is crucial to ensure fair and unbiased predictions.
- **Resource-intensive training**: Training the model demands substantial time and resources, incurring costs.
- **Complexity limitations**: While effective. supervised learning has its boundaries in handling highly complex tasks.
- **Label dependency**: Labeled data requirement can be a limitation, as obtaining accurate labels may not always be feasible.

As we conclude this section, you should have gained a good grasp of supervised ML its essence, underlying principles, strengths, and weaknesses. This foundational knowledge equips to give a thought on the next steps in the learning journey, considering the complexities of any context and specific needs. Delving into real-life applications of supervised ML, we find its relevance in diverse areas, including the following:

- Predicting prices for cars, stocks, real estate and so on
- Detecting spam
- Fraud detection
- Sentiment analysis

Unsupervised learning

Unsupervised learning is a ML technique that enables machines learn data patterns without external interventions. In this learning the training data has input vectors without label or target. Unlabeled data input makes this learning attractive as labeling datasets is challenging (costly, resource intensive, error-prone, scarce, or unavailable). The objective of this learning is to learn the underlying pattern of input data set without any human intervention (without labeling). These learned patterns are often used for downstream processing and prediction. There are various unsupervised methods and at high level they are categorized into clustering, dimensionality reduction and association techniques.

Unsupervised learning methods

In this chapter, we will discuss some of clustering and dimensionality reduction techniques. The following shows some of the clustering techniques:

Clustering

Take a look at the following figure:

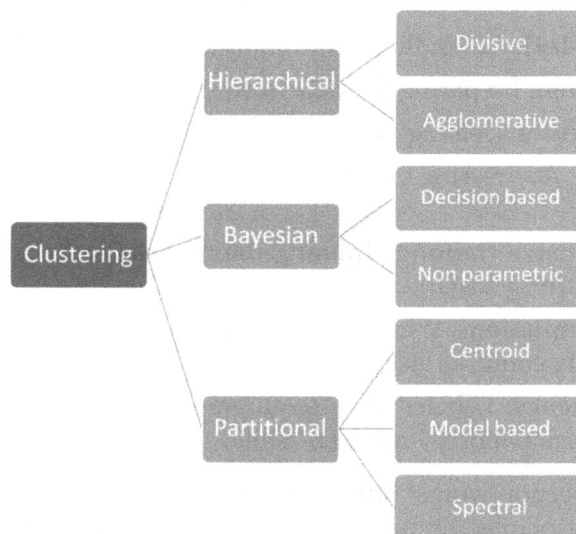

Figure 1.8: Clustering techniques categorization

Hierarchical clustering

It is a method based on the hierarchy representation of clusters, where each parent cluster node is made of multiple child cluster nodes, and each node represents the data points in one cluster. The two hierarchical techniques are agglomerative (a bottom-up approach) and divisive (a top-down approach). In the divisive method, entire data points in an input data set are considered as a single cluster, and further splitting is carried out iteratively until each data point becomes an isolated cluster representation. In the agglomerative approach, each data point in the input data set is considered an individual cluster, and a merge is carried out iteratively by a linkage process until a single cluster is formed for the entire data set.

Agglomerative clustering is a popular method of choice with various linkage techniques such as min linkage, max linkage, average linkage, centroid linkage, and ward linkage for merging clusters. The clusters are visually presented as hierarchical tree called **dendrograms**. Some applications of hierarchical clustering are a phylogenetic tree of animal evolution, customer segmentation based on purchase attributes, document analysis, and document mining. Take a look at the following figure:

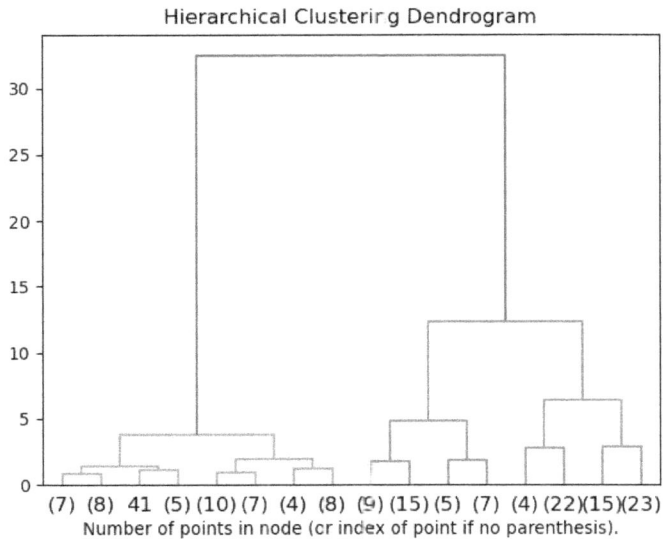

Figure 1.9: Dendrogram view of hierarchical clustering[1]

K-means clustering

It is a popular clustering technique with numerous variations, such as K++ and K-medoids based on different ways of cluster centroid initialization and update. K-means is computationally efficient and simple to perform. The objective of K-means is to partition a given dataset into K-clusters such that the data points within the clusters are highly similar; that is, intra-cluster variation is minimal. The optimization problem is to find the best set of centroids $C = \{c_1, c_2, \ldots, c_k\}$ for the given input data set of n data points $\{x_1, x_2, \ldots, x_n\} \varepsilon R^d$ that minimizes $\sum_{i=1}^{n} \sum_{k=1}^{k} w_{ik} ||x_i - c_k||^2$ for k clusters. The objective function is optimized through *Lloyd's* heuristic method, which iteratively follows the steps of centroid initialization, assignment of data points to centroids based on distance metrics, and updating the centroid with the mean of newly assigned data points. Selection of optimal k is done through the empirical elbow method, and validation of cluster is done by external measures using a dataset with class labels or done internally through silhouette coefficient, which defines compactness (closeness of data points within the clusters) and connectedness (separation between the clusters). The disadvantage of K-means is

---

its dependency on centroid initialization, selection of predefined k values, sensitivity to outliers, and scalability with a number of dimensions.

Gaussian mixture model

It is a probabilistic model where data can be represented as multiple Gaussian distributions with its own mean and variance. Each distribution is considered as a cluster of data. Mixture weights are assigned to each cluster, which represent the probability of selecting the cluster when generating data. Take a look at the following figure:

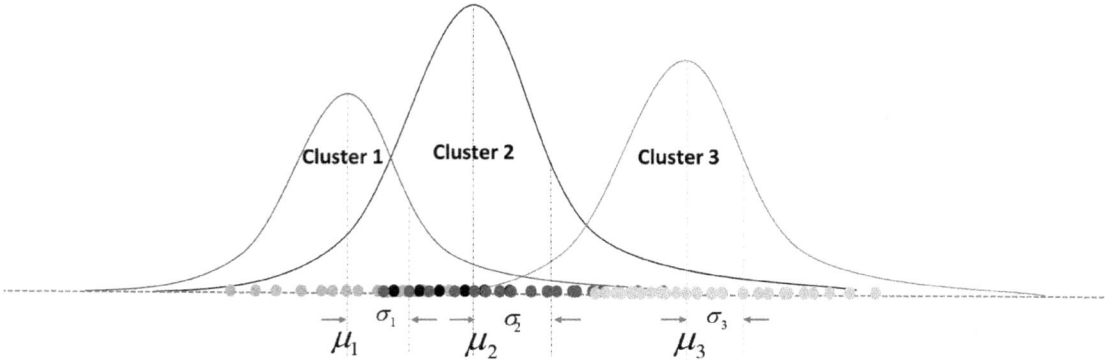

Figure 1.10: GMM cluster view

Gaussian density function for a probability distribution $P(X)$ of random variable $X \varepsilon R^d$ is given by $P(X) = \sum_{k=1}^{K} w_k \eta_k (X, \mu_k, \sigma_k)$

where $\sum_{k=1}^{K} w_k = 1$; $\eta(X, \mu, \sigma) = \frac{1}{(2\pi)^{D/2}|\sigma|^{1/2}} e^{-1/2(X-\mu)^T(\sigma)^{-1}(X-\mu)}$;

mean $\mu = \begin{bmatrix} \mu_1 \\ \mu_2 \\ \mu_d \end{bmatrix}$ and covariance matrix $\sigma = \begin{pmatrix} \sigma^2_1 & & 0 \\ & \ddots & \\ 0 & & \sigma^2_n \end{pmatrix}$.

So parameters $\theta = \{\mu_1, \sigma_1, w_1, \ldots, \mu_d, \sigma_d, w_d\}$ are learned to maximize the log likelihood of the dataset i.e., $\max_{\theta} \log P(X|\theta) = \max_{w_i, \mu_i, \sigma_i,} \sum_i \ln[\sum_{k=1}^{K} w_k \eta (X_n|\mu_k, \sigma_k)]$.

Instead of direct optimization or gradient descent, **expectation maximization (EM)** algorithms are used to solve the maximum likelihood of the **Gaussian mixture model (GMM)** due to the feasibility and the harder constraint issue in the prior techniques. EM algorithm is an iterative approach that cycles between the estimation step that estimates the latent variables and the maximization step that optimizes the parameters to explain the data.

GMM is flexible in terms of cluster shape, where K-means are limited to spherical clusters, and GMM can handle missing data. GMM is used in many applications, such as density estimation, clustering, image segmentation, etc.

Distance metrics

The popular distance metric used in clustering is the Euclidean distance method (*L2* and *L1* norms), and the other few non-Euclidean methods are Jaccard distance, cosine distance, Mahalanobis distance. These metrics are used to measure the proximity of vectors in the vector space. In this section, we will look into Euclidean and cosine distance.

Eucledian measures the distance between the ends of the vectors and mathematically given by $x = (x_1, x_2....x_n)$, $y = (y_1, y_2....y_n)$ is L_2 *norm* $||x - y||_2 = \sqrt{(x_1 - y_1)^2 + ... + (x_n - y_n)^2}$

Euclidean distance is scale-dependent, ignores the relationship between measurement and is sensitive to outliers. Cosine similarity is the cosine of the angle between the non-zero vectors of an inner product space which is bound to range between 0 (vectors are orthogonal) and 1 (Vectors are oriented in the same direction). $cos(\theta) = \frac{x^T y}{|x|.|y|}$. The vector magnitude information is not considered in the cosine similarity metric. The other metric is a dot product $x.y = |x|.|y| \cos \theta$. The dot product is proportional to both the cosine and the lengths of vectors. The choice of distance metric is critical when it comes to clustering and it is done based on multiple factors like scale and type of data (continuous, categorical), task (clustering, information retrieval, recommendation systems). To summarize, Euclidean metric is used when we have dense vectors, and magnitude is critical, cosine similarity is used when vector is space and the angle between the vector is important. The dot product is used when the direction of the vector is critical. There are other heterogeneous distance metrics, such as **Heterogeneous Euclidean Overlap Metric** (**HEOM**), and **Heterogeneous Value Difference Metric** (**HVDM**) to handle data with both continuous and nominal attributes.

Dimensionality reduction

It is a method to reduce the number of dimensions in an input dataset while retaining the relevant information. With a larger number of dimensions, that is, a dataset with a greater number of input variables, it becomes difficult to generalize the model as the model has to face the curse of dimensionality issues. Larger dimensions increase the volume of feature space, and the data becomes sparser and affects model performance.

Dimensionality reduction techniques

There are vast methods for dimensionality reduction, which are categorized at a high level into feature selection and feature reduction. Further feature reduction has linear and non-linear methods . Some linear methods are **principal component analysis** (**PCA**), LDA, SVD, . Some non-linear methods are t-Kernel PCA, **t-Distributed Stochastic Neighbor Embedding** (**t-SNE**), ISOMAP, UMAP, and Autoencoder. In this section, we will discuss on feature reduction technique of linear PCA and non-linear method t- SNE.

Principal component analysis

PCA is a popular dimensionality reduction technique. It defines the direction of maximum variance and projects it onto a smaller dimensional subspace while retaining most of the information. Eigenvectors (the direction) and eigenvalues (variance magnitude) of covariance matrix is the core of PCA. Given a set of features, PCA will construct principal components that are linear combination of original set of features.

$PC_1 = w_{11} x_1 + w_{12} x_2 + ... + w_{1d} x_{d'}....., PC_n = w_{n1} x_1 + w_{n2} x_2 + ... + w_{nd} x_{d'}$ where the principal components $PC_1...PC_n$ are orthogonal eigenvectors of the data covariance matrix. Eigenvectors of the covariance matrix reflect the proportionality of variability captured by corresponding principal components. The components are uncorrelated, that is, orthogonal to each other and with the first component (PC_1) explaining the most variability, each successive component (PC_n) explains the variability that is left with its preceding ones (PC_{n-1}). The components are chosen in an ordered way according to the cumulative variability they explain. Take a look at the following figure:

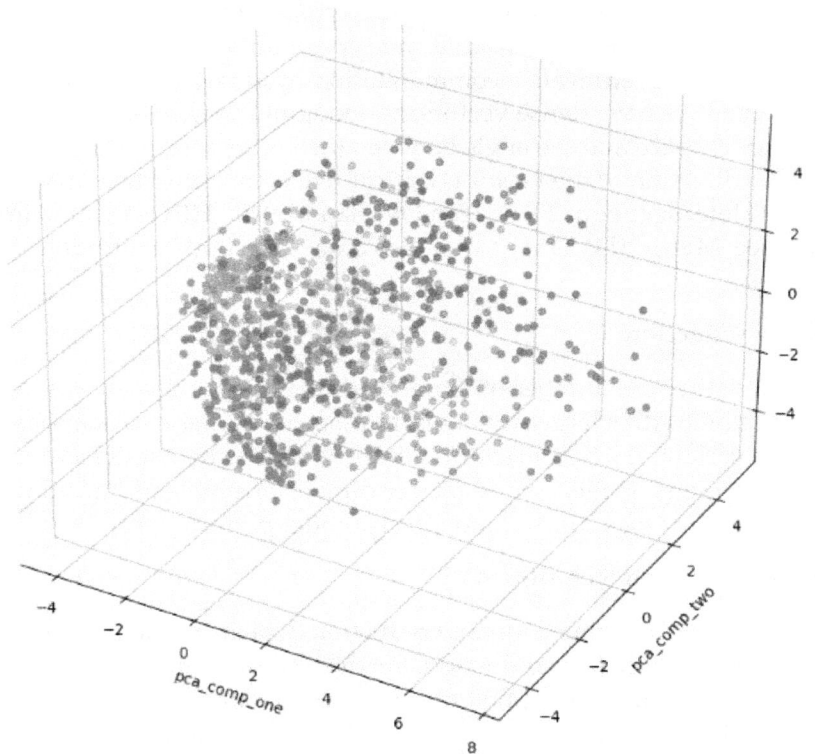

Figure 1.11: *PCA Component view of MNIST dataset (1000 samples)*

Apart from dimensionality reduction, PCA is used for variables categorization and noise elimination. Some of the cons of PCA are: PCA assumes correlation and linear relationship among features, need for numerical input variables, is sensitive to the scale, not robust against outliers, the trade-off between information loss and dimensionality reduction, and the interpretability of principal component is difficult.

T-Distributed Stochastic Neighbor Embedding

Real-life application data generally have a large number of dimensions and are non-linear in nature. Non-linear dimensionality technique also called **manifold learning** aim to project a higher dimensional data to lower dimensional latent manifolds. Latent manifolds is defined as mathematical space where items that are similar to each other will be positioned closer. Unlike PCA, t-SNE is a non-linear dimensionality reduction. Non-linear dimensionality reduction means that the algorithm allows us to separate data that cannot be separated by a straight line. It first models a data point i to be a neighbor of another data point j based on pairwise similarity calculated using Gaussian kernel (similar to GMM discuss above) cantered at i in higher dimensional space. Probability density of (i, j) is proportional to its similarity density.

Higher dimensional affinity $p_{j|i} = \frac{exp(-||x_i-x_j||^2/2\sigma_i^2)}{\sum_{k\neq i} exp(-||x_i-x_k||^2/2\sigma_i^2)}$. The variance s_i is indirectly given as an input through the perplexity parameter, which specifies the expected number of neighbors. The joint probability p that represents the high dimensional data is given by $p_{ji} = \frac{p_{j|i}+p_{i|j}}{2n}$. Similarly, the distribution for lower dimensional space q using heavy-tailed student t-distribution to address the crowding and optimization problems is given by $q_{ij} = \frac{(1+||y_i-y_j||^2)^{-1}}{\sum_{k\neq j}(1+||y_k-y_l||^2)^{-1}}$. So, the objective function is represented as the closeness of joint probability distributions P_{ij} (Higher dimension) and Q_{ij} (Lower dimension) using Kullback-Leibler divergence $(KL(P|Q) = \sum_{i=1}^{n}\sum_{j=1}^{n} p_{ij} log \frac{p_{ij}}{q_{ij}})$ which is optimized using gradient descent algorithms. Major cons with t-SNE is, it is computationally intensive due to joint probability estimation, dependency on perplexity.

Applications

Unsupervised learning is majorly used in recommending systems, image classifications, anomaly detection, customer segmentation, and document categorization. Even state-of-art **large language models** (**LLMs**) typically start with unsupervised learning to learn the relationship between different words and concepts, which are used by downstream tasks or models.

Semi-supervised learning and reinforcement learning

We have learned about the models that handle input data sets with labels (supervised) or without labels (semi-supervised). In real world, the scenario could be different, where we have a mix of data. Few of them are labeled and most of them unlabeled. There are various sources from which the data get acquired. For example, data sources for ML project can be publicly available, web content, books, articles, Wikipedia, journals, code repositories, blogs etc. So, we can observe that most of the data from public sources will be unlabeled and a few that are from paid sources can be labeled. A supervised or unsupervised way of learning on such mixed data is not an optimal way. Henceforth SSL is field of ML that fuse both supervised and unsupervised learning by taking advantage of labeled datasets to learn the unlabeled ones. In this chapter, we will discuss about SSL.

Semi-supervised learning

Unlike supervised learning, which is inductive, SSL is transductive learning, which learns Points of interest (unlabeled data) from the given data set (labeled data). In contrast to inductive learning where the model is exposed to training to create generalized rules and applied to testing data set. In transductive learning, model is exposed to both trained and testing sets. For an SSL to generalize a model from a finite training set to a set of infinitely unseen data sets, certain assumptions will have to hold. Some of the assumptions are as follows:

Assumptions:

- **Continuity assumption**: If two input data points are closer in higher density regions, then they like to share the corresponding labels. Based on this assumption, SSL sets decision boundaries on low-density region.

- **Cluster assumption**: If the data points are from same cluster, then they are likely to share the same labels. This is just to mean that objects of distinct classes are likely to be in the same cluster.

- **Manifold assumption**: The input high dimensional data can be represented roughly on a low dimensional space called a **manifold**. This assumption avoids the high dimensional complexity and allows the use of density estimates and distance metrics defined on manifold.

Semi-supervised algorithms

There are broad categories of techniques for SSL, and they can be cataloged into 5 methods (Generative, pseudo labeling, consistency regularization, graph based, hybrid) as shown in the *Figure 1.12*. Some of these methods have further classifications and each has its own tree of algorithms. In this section, we will discuss some of them—pseudo labeling method (Pseudo label), consistency regularization method (Π-model, temporal ensembling, and mean teacher), and hybrid method (MixMatch learning). Generative methods will be discussed in upcoming chapters. Take a look at the following figure:

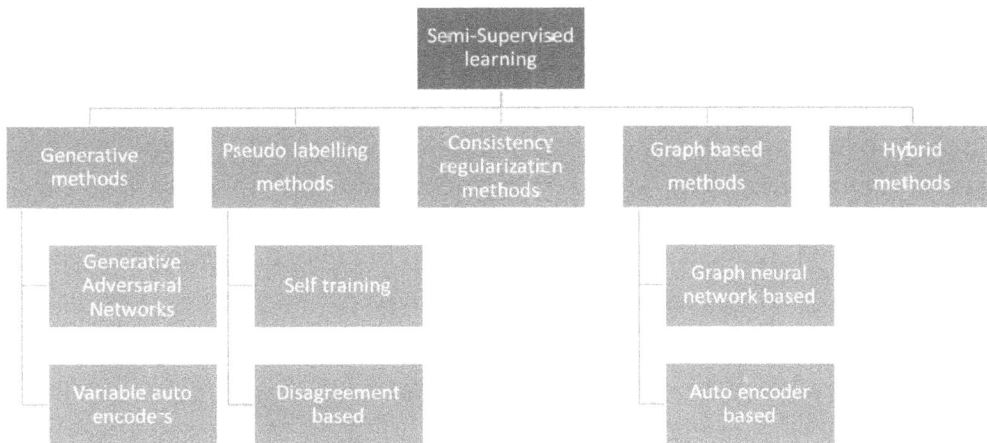

Figure 1.12: SSL techniques categorization

Pseudo labeling methods

In this section, we will discuss on pseudo label a popular method of self-training. In this method the model is a classifier that is trained (supervised manner) with labeled data, and the same model is used iteratively to identify the pseudo labels of unlabeled data based on the maximum confidence class. The new classifier then gets trained simultaneously with predicted pseudo and original labels. The overall loss function for this method is a weighted sum of labeled and unlabeled loss terms (cross-entropy). The primary challenges of this method are its dependency on model performance on unlabeled data, as it may become bad feedback to new classifiers, the dependency on a small volume of labeled data to represent the cluster of larger unlabeled ones, and its sensitivity to the outliers.

Co-training is the modified version of self-training where two independent classifiers are trained on different views of the input data set. The most confident predicted label from one classifier is used as pseudo-labeled data for the other classifier. Beyond this multi-view form of co-training, there is single-view co-training, which is used for data sets where no natural split is known **prior**. The challenges with the co-training method are an appropriate division of views, estimation of confidence, and the choice of classifiers that can affect performance.

Consistency regularization method

The objective of this method is to make the model learn consistent representation of unlabeled data even if they are perturbated. The main assumption of this method is that input perturbations must not affect the class semantics. Π-model, temporal ensembling and mean teacher are popular consistency regularization techniques. In all these techniques, the final loss will be time dependent weighted sum of supervised and unsupervised loss after

perturbation that is $L = \frac{1}{m}\sum_{k=1}^{m}\sum_{i=1}^{n} L$ (output,label) + a(t)$\frac{1}{m^{\boxtimes}}\sum_{k=1}^{m^{\boxtimes}}\sum_{i=1}^{n} L$ (output,Pseudo-label) where m is number of labeled data input and m' is the number of unlabeled data input with n number of classes. $\alpha(t)$ is the weight coefficient that is optimized by increasing the same during the training for achieving better local minima.

In Π model, input data x_i is augmented and version of labeled/unlabeled input is passed to the drop-out network model along with augmented data. The final loss function is time dependent weighted sum ($\mu(t)$) of supervised loss (cross-entropy for labeled data Y_i) and unsupervised loss (Consistency loss is mean square difference between predicted outputs Z_i and $\tilde{Z}_i$ given same original input x_i). Take a look at the following figure: Π model of SSL:

π model

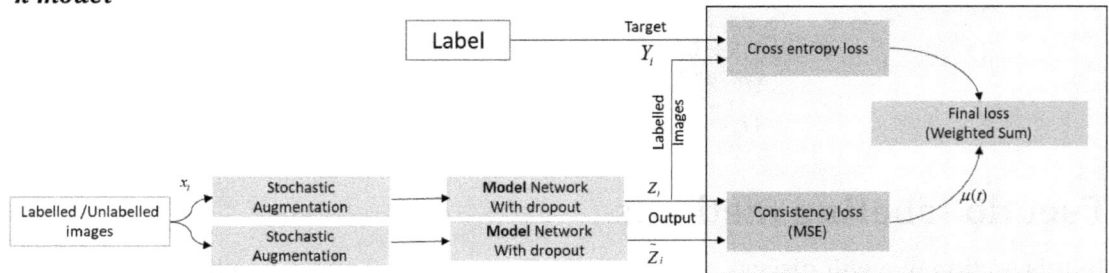

Figure 1.13: SSL—Π model

Temporal ensembling is a modified version of Π model which leverages **exponential moving average (EMA)** of past predictions instead of running two passer per sample. The only difference is the consistency loss, which is calculated as the mean square difference between the expected moving average of the model prediction in time and the current prediction from the augmented data. In temporal ensembling EMA model prediction in time is evaluated and updated only once per epoch. Take a look at the following figure: Temporal ensembling model of SSL. Find the following figure that depicts the temporal ensemble model flow:

Temporal Ensembling *model*

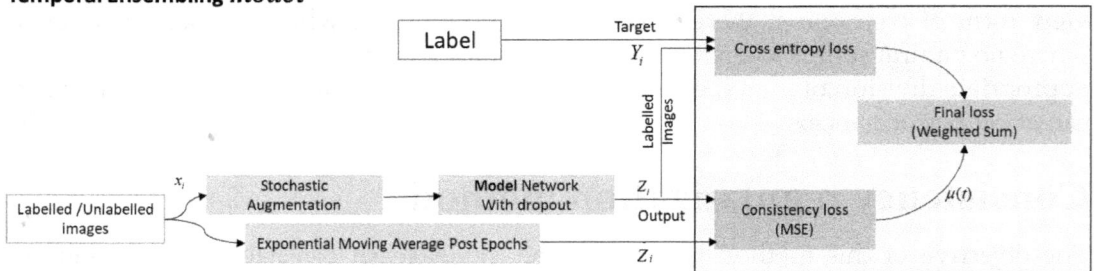

Figure 1.14: SSL—temporal ensembling

Mean teacher model is similar to temporal ensembling where the consistency loss is calculated between the predicted outputs of student and teacher models. The objective is to minimize the distribution difference between the student and teacher model. Unlike

Π model, mean teacher uses two different models, student x (regular network with drop-out) and teacher y (network with updated EMA weights of student model). Mean teacher model tracks the moving average of model weights instead of model predictions, that is, during training portion EMA weights of student model are set to teacher model at every step. Take a look at the following figure, show mean teacher model of SSL:

Mean Master model

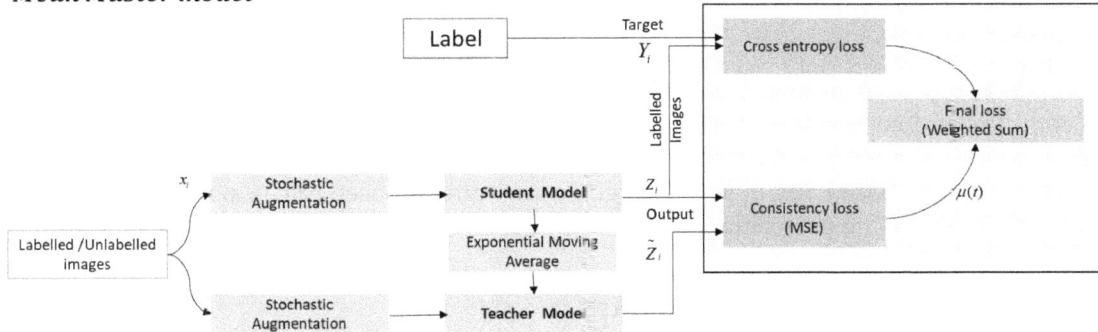

Figure 1.15: *SSL—mean master model*

Hybrid method

MixMatch: It is a hybrid approach of having both pseudo labeling and consistency regularization technique. In MixMatch both labeled input data (x_i) and unlabeled input data (u_j) are augmented. But for each of unlabeled (u_j) MixMatch generate k augmentations, that is $(\tilde{u}_{j,k} = Augment(u_j) \, for \, (k = 1 .... k))$ and pseudo labels are assigned based on the average and temperature scaling of the predictions on k augmentation, that is $\left(\tilde{y}_k = \frac{1}{k}\sum_{k=1}^{k} p(y| \tilde{u}_{j,k}; \theta)\right)$. Temperature scaling is a technique to tune the sharpness of a model distribution, that is, $\left(Sharpern(p,T)_i = (\frac{p_i^{1,T}}{\sum_1^L p_j^{1/T}})\right)$ where p is average class predictions over augmentations, temperature is a hyperparameter that needs to be tuned to control the sharpness or flatness of predicted probability distribution. After augmentation, a batch of augmented labeled data $\left(\hat{X} = (\tilde{x}_i, \tilde{y}_i)\right)$ and a batch of augmented unlabeled data with predicted labels $\left(\hat{U} = (\tilde{u}_{j,k}, \tilde{y}_k)\right)$ are shuffled to form $W = shuffle(concat(\hat{X}, \hat{U}))$.

After *MixUp* the labeled X', that is, $\left(MixUp(\hat{X}_i, W_i)\right)$ and unlabeled U', that is, $\left(MixUp(\hat{U}_i, W_{i+|\hat{X}|})\right)$ we calculate $\left(X', U' = MixMatch(X, U, T, K, a)\right)$ and final loss function.

MixUp is a simple data augmentation method that mixes data points (labeled and unlabeled) randomly in a linear interpolation manner in order to improve the generalization of SSL as weighted summation of cross-entropy loss, that is, $\left(L_x = \frac{1}{|X'|}\Sigma_{x,p\in X'}\, H(p, p_{mod\,el}(y|x; \theta)) \right)$ for labeled and $L2$ loss of predictions and guessed labels. That is, $\left(L_u = \frac{1}{|U'|}\Sigma_{u,q\in U'}\, ||q - p_{mod\,el}(y|u; \theta))||_2^2 \right)$. FixMatch is another SSL technique similar to MixMatch where weak augmentation and strong augmentation are used to predict the pseudo label.

Applications

SSL is majorly used in image and audio analysis and classification, where labeling data is complex and costly. The other applications include: In life science domain for protein sequencing, in healthcare domain for medical imaging, in banking domain for fraud detection, graph based SSL in search engines, co-training based SSL is also used in current LLMs to improve the performance of prompt-based learning by using unlabeled data.

Reinforcement learning

RL is a type of ML, where the models learn dynamic environments to make optimal sequences of decisions without human intervention. Models learn in a trial-and-error method using agents and feedback loops to maximize the positive outcome of actions. At a high level, RL mimics human learning. For example, in the field of sports, players will undergo rigorous training under supervision and certain qualities will improve based on the supervision feedback. This helps the players to take suitable action to maximize reward in a particular game situation.

Reinforcement learning components

The components of RL are as follows:

- **Agent**: It is a model or trainer that interacts with the environment to act, observe, and collect data.
- **Actions (a_t)**: The decisions that the agent takes for each state (s_t) inside the environment and set of actions in an environment is called action space.
- **State (s_t)**: The available information with the agent about the environments at a particular point in time. Action taken on any state (s_t) will lead to future states (s_{t+1}).
- **Environment**: This is the dynamic simulated system of interest. The agent interacts with the environment by its action. Observation is how the environment responds to agents. The environment in a RL algorithm is commonly expressed as a **Markov Decision Process (MDP)**, and almost all RL problems are formalized using MDPs.
- **Rewards (r_t)**: A feedback measure that illustrates the success or failure of agent action. Rewards can be immediate or long-term.

- **Policy**: The policy is the strategy which dictates the agent's actions to maximize the reward r_t based on the state s_t in a particular environment. Policy can be probabilistic. Take a look at the following figure:

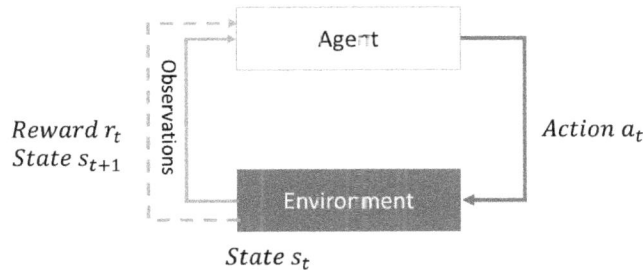

Figure 1.16: *RL components*

The above figure Agent repeatedly takes action a_t at time t to receive rewards r_t is from an environment state s_t that is partially observed.

Algorithms

Broadly RL algorithms are classified into model-based and model-free. Model-free is further categorized into value-based and policy-based methods. Take a look at the following figure that shows various reinforcement algorithms and categorizations:

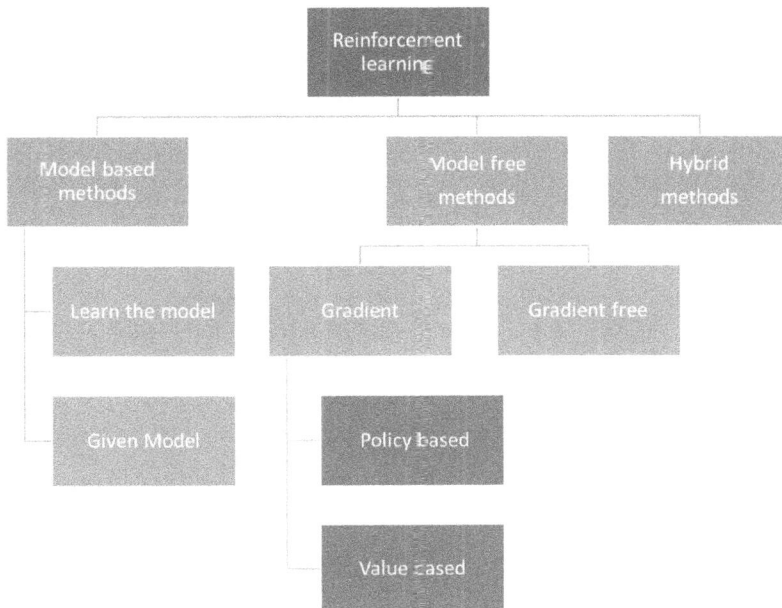

Figure 1.17: *RL methods*

Model-based algorithms build an explicit model of the environment. Model-based system has a transition probability that defines the state transitions based on the agent's actions. In model-based system, agents interact with the environment, learn the model, and use the model for making decisions. In this method, models can be defined as the GMM, Gaussian process, or deep neural networks and trained using the supervised learning method. A few examples of model-based algorithms are **Monte Carlo Tree Search** (**MCTS**) in games, **probabilistic inference for learning control** (**PILCO**), model-based RL with **model-free fine-tuning** (**MBMF**), **model-based value expansion** (**MBVE**) and world models.

Model-free algorithms do not build an explicit model. The model directly learns the optimal policy by interacting with the environment. The two main approaches are policy iteration and value-based. Value-based on-policy **state-action-reward-state-action** (**SARSA**) or off-policy (Q-learning) method finds the optimal policy implicitly by training the value function. The policy iteration method is a gradient-based method where arbitrary policy is iteratively evaluated and improved. Some of value-based techniques are (off-policy (Q-learning), **Deep Q-Networks** (**DQN**), SARSA (on-policy)) and policy-based techniques are (Reinforce, actor-critic, **Asynchronous Advantage Actor-Critic** (**A3C**), A2C).

Value-based

Q-learning is an off-policy temporal difference algorithm to find the optimal policy by updating the state-action value function(Q). Q-learning decide on optimal action based on its current state. Here policy is implicitly updated through Q-value. The Q-values are the expected total future reward for action and are stored in the Q-table. Q-value function is

given by $Q_\pi(s) = E\left(R_t = \sum_{i=t} \gamma^i r_i \mid s_0 = s \right)$ where g is the discount factor which makes future

reward less significance compared to immediate ones. The objective is to optimize the policy to make the maximum rewards. The optimal state function is given by high possible value function compared to other value function for all states.

Q-table helps us to find the best action for each state. We use the Bellman equation at each state to get the expected future state and reward and save it in a table to compare with other states. We use the Bellman equation at each state to get the expected future state and reward and save it in a table to compare with other states. Bellman optimality equation is given by New $Q(S_t, A_t) \boxtimes Q(S_t, A_t) + \alpha (R_{t+1} + \gamma \, max \, Q(S_{t+1}), a) - Q(S_t, A_t)))$ where action A_t = arg max $Q(S_t, a)$ is picked according to Q-value.

One of the major Q-learning challenge is exploration and exploitation trade-off where the agent has find the balance to exploit what it has already experienced in order to obtain reward, but it also has to explore in order to make better action selections in the future.

Deep Q-learning uses the Q-learning idea and takes it one step further. Instead of using a Q-table, we use a NN that takes a state and approximates the Q-values for each action based on that state.

Policy gradient-based

In the value-based method, we learn the state-action value function, and actions are selected accordingly. In policy gradient method, policy is learned directly with a parameterized function with respect to $\theta, \pi_\theta(a|s)$. The reward/objective function depends on the policy $\theta, \pi_\theta(a|s)$ is given by $J(\theta) = E_{\pi_\theta}[r] = \sum_s d^\pi(s) \sum_a \pi_\theta(a|s) Q^\pi(s,a)$ where $d^\pi(s)$ is stationary distribution of Markov chain of π_θ, $Q^\pi(s,a)$ is value of state action pair similar to value function, $\pi_\theta(a|s)$ is stochastic policy parameterized by q. We maximize the objective function $J(\theta)$ using gradient descent method where gradient is given by $\nabla_\theta J(\theta) = E_{\pi\theta}[Q^\pi(s,a)\nabla_\theta \ln \pi_\theta(a|s)]$ with the help of policy gradient algorithms such as reinforce, actor-critic, A3C, A2C.

State-of-art RL actor-critic algorithm such as A3C uses multiple independent agents trained simultaneously on the environment and aggregate their overall experience. The algorithm is fast and robust compared to other RL algorithms. A3C has been used to train robots to perform complex tasks, such as grasping objects and navigating through environments.

Applications

Autonomous/Self-driving vehicle is one of the primary use cases where the RL is used to learn multiple aspects of autonomous vehicle, such as driving zones, parking policies, speed limits, traffic handling, lane changing etc. The other major application is in robotics. RL enables robots to discover optimal behavior and learn tasks to be performed in real world like packaging, grasping, cleaning etc. through trial-and-error interactions in a simulated environment. The other applications include RL system to track the reader's return behaviors for news recommendations, RL system in games to determine the best moves, RL in video encoding etc. Recently **reinforcement learning from human feedback (RLHF)** has been used in LLMs to improve the model's understanding and performance by incorporating human ranking of model outputs as feedback to steer the model to prefer certain results.

Design patterns

Design patterns are generally defined as reusable solution components for commonly occurring problems. There are numerous design patterns throughout the AI lifecycle, beginning from ML problem framing, input data pre-processing, model training and testing, and operationalizing. In this chapter, we will be covering only 3 such patterns that we often come across in any AI project. One is real word data representation for training models, second one is different training strategies, and the third one is performance improvement techniques.

Real world data representation

There are different ways real world data is input into model. Below are the two common ways of converting real world non-numerical data to ML readable input. There are other forms of representations, like the graphs (nodes and edges), that are used for supply chain modeling that are not covered as part of this book. Take a look at the following figure: It shows different ways of data representation:

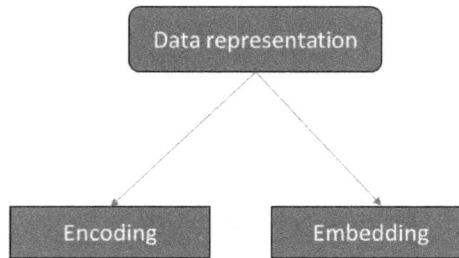

Figure 1.18: *Different ways of data representation*

Encoding

ML and deep learning models generally operate on numerical input. However, in real world, apart from continuous or discrete data, there are inputs which are categorical in nature, for example, the gender of a person, types of vehicles, etc. These variables can be categorized into nominal or ordinal data. Nominal data do not have a quantitative value and do not have any defined order or hierarchy, for example, type of vehicles. Unlike nominal data, ordinal data can be numeric and qualitative. They have defined orders, for example, customer feedback. So, if the input data column is categorical in nature, it is necessary to convert the categorical column into a numerical representation. There are various techniques to handle categorical input, but each has its own trade-offs and alternatives. Label encoding is one technique which assigns a unique numerical value to each distinct category, but it introduces an arbitrary order to the categorical value, which might be a wrong assumption. The alternative could be one-hot encoding, which is the popular technique to handle categorical variables where {**Car**, **Bike**, **Bus**} is mapped into feature vectors {**Car** = **[1.0,0.0,0.0]**}; {**Bike** =**[0.0, 1.0,0.0]**}; {**Bus** = **[0.0,0.0, 1.0]**}} and the size of the vector is length of the vocabulary. But one hot encoding technique cannot be adopted when there are:

- Incomplete vocabulary.
- Sparsity due to a large number of categories.
- Cold start issues with new or unknown category.

The alternative could be a feature hashing technique that operates by converting the category variable into a unique string using a deterministic hashing algorithm and assigning it to a fixed number of bins. The hash bin approach is a lossy operation that may not fully represent and must tolerate that multiple categorical data shall be hashed into the same bucket. Feature hashing is used on high cardinality data where the category column has many possible values. For example, Order ID in an online sales data set.

Embedding

Categorical encoding is a simple form of embedding where categorical variables are converted into numerical representation based on the ordinal and nominal characteristics. Embedding, in general, is a numerical representation of complex information like text, images, voice to a ML model readable format. In NN (Neural Network), embeddings are set to transform information-dense higher dimensional input variables into a lower dimensional space while maintaining the semantic relations. Format of embedding is a fixed size vector of floating-point numbers either scaled logarithmically or normalized between 0 and 1 values. Embeddings are generally stored in vector stores. Vector store is a type of data structure that allows embeddings to be stored in a native format and allows the performance of vector operations, such as cosine similarity, additions, etc., directly in the vector format. Embedding places the input variables that are similar in nature closer in embedding space that can be utilized to improve model performance, to do input analysis, search, comparisons and conversions.

Image embedding

Image is digitally represented as a matrix of pixels and each pixel is represented by a set of colors and depth. One way to embed an image is to use image characteristics like color, texture, and spatial profiles using computer vision techniques. These kinds of representational embeddings are then used by applications like **content-based image retrieval (CBIR)** to retrieve or classify images from databases.

The other approach used is to learn embeddings using hidden layers during training. **Convolution neural network (CNN)** is a popular deep neural network architecture choice that uses sub-sampling and convolution techniques to capture the local image features. CNN will be trained where the images with the same labels are embedded closer. The number of neurons in the final layer will be the length of the embedding. In unsupervised scenarios, autoencoders (encoder-decoder) are used to compute the latent space vector in the bottleneck layer, which is a compressed representation of images. After training the encoder-decoder model, the encoder network alone is utilized to extract the embedding from raw input data.

There is a wealth of pre-trained models available that act as a tool to create image embedding. Vision Transformer models like **BERT image transformers (BEiT)**, DINO, and **masked autoencoders (MAE)** are some image embedding models popular in creating image embeddings. The other models like, VisualBERT, are available to prepare to embed for image text pairs in case of multi-modality scenarios.

Audio embedding

The sound wave of the audio signal is typically encoded as numerical samples in the continuous space. The audio signal is generally represented as a waveform with frequency, amplitude and phase characteristics. Audio signal is a multifaceted data type that spans from noise to music. Traditionally, audio features like zero crossing rate, pitch, log-mel spectrogram, **Mel Frequency Cepstral Coefficients** (**MFCC**) are extracted using audio signal analysis techniques and used as embeddings. Speech recognition, emotion detection and speech enhancement are the typical applications built on top of these extracted features.

The other approach used is to convert the audio signal into images, that is, spectrogram signal plots and use image embedding techniques like CNN to extract the features of images as audio embedding. Spectrogram represents the distribution of audio signal strength at particular time. Audio classification and audio scene recognition use cases are developed using spectrogram image and CNN techniques. A popular method to extract **acoustic word embeddings** (**AWE**) is to use a sequence-to-sequence autoencoder model with **recurrent neural network** (**RNN**) as both encoder and decoder. The model receives the different instances of the same word form as an MFCC coefficient, where one of the wordform instances is used to construct a fixed vector and used to reconstruct the other instance sequentially. There are various applications of AWE, such as automatic speech recognition systems, speech indexing, spoken-term discovery, keyword spotting, etc.

The other approach is to use pre-trained audio neural network models that are trained on large audio data set as a feature extractor. Some of them Wav2Vec for acoustic model training, YAMNet for sound classification, **Wav2Vec+BERT** (**w2v-BERT**) for speech recognition, Whisper LLM for multilingual translation and transcription, X-LLM for multi-modalities. The other popular models in speech intelligence are convolution augmented transformer models (conformer), Wav2Vec 2.0, and HuBERT.

Text embedding

Text content are generally treated with **natural language processing** (**NLP**) techniques to create embeddings. NLP is a sub-field of AI which gives the machine the ability to interpret, manipulate, and comprehend human language. NLP techniques such as **Term Frequency-Inverse Document Frequency** (**TF-IDF**) based on the frequency and rarity of words, and bag of words based on feature counts are generally used for basic text analysis, information retrieval, stop words removal, and keyword extractions.

The other popular technique is Word2Vec uses shallow neural network architectures of either Skip-gram or continuous bag of words to create embedding, which is used for capturing semantic information. The other popular method is **Global Vectors for Word Representations** (**GloVe**) which is a pre-trained model that operates on matrix factorization (co-occurrence matrix) technique.

The other method is to use contextual word embedding using pre-trained transformer models. In transformer token-vector mapping is generally called word embedding. Pre-trained transformer models such as **Bidirectional Encoder Representations from**

Transformers (BERT), **Embeddings from Language Models (ELMo)**, GPT are trained on large corpus of data that are generalized for various task like text generation, summarization, question answering, etc. The other pre-trained models, like **Contrastive Language-Image Pre-training (CLIP)** are used for image-text multimodality scenarios.

Training strategies

Different training strategies are adopted based on the use cases, data set availability, compute capabilities and performance objective. In this section, we will cover three strategies, mainly transfer learning, **multi-task learning (MLT)**, and distribution training strategy, that are popular in the GenAI world. Strategies like batch, mini-batch, checkpoints, online learning, fine tuning, etc. will be covered in relevant sections.

Transfer learning

Training a larger model requires heavy compute and massive datasets. GenAI models like ChatGPT are trained on petabytes of data on trillions of parameters for months. It is not feasible to build such a massive AI application for all use cases. So, it will be ideal to build a custom model for individual use cases on top of a pre-trained model like ImageNet or GTP-3 instead of training a model from its base. Pre-trained models are state-of-art models that are trained on extremely large, labeled, and unlabeled data sets by tech-forward or research organizations. Transfer learning enables us to utilize these pre-trained model weights and layers on similar tasks with domain specific datasets. Pre-trained model selection is a critical factor in transfer learning, which needs to be selected based on the similarity of data and the task that needs to be solved. For example, A Dalle-2 image generation foundation model will be an ideal choice for image captioning tasks. A growing number of 100+ GenAI foundation models trained on different massive datasets for different tasks are available for custom utilization. These models capture the general patterns on larger datasets and act as knowledge base for solving specific problems on similar datasets.

There are various approaches to transfer learning based on the modality, task, and dataset availability. A simple one could be taking a pre-trained model, freeze most of the model layer weights and tune only trainable layers of pre-trained model for solving similartasks on custom data. Generally, the flattened layers or the layer before the output is removed from the pre-trained model. Another approach could be fine-tuning. In this approach, some of the top layers of the frozen model base are unfrozen, and the model is trained on the custom data set on both the top and newly added base layers. This will fine-tune the high-order feature representation relevant to the custom tasks. Take a look at the following figure that shows transfer and fine-tuning approaches:

Pretrained Model **Custom Model**

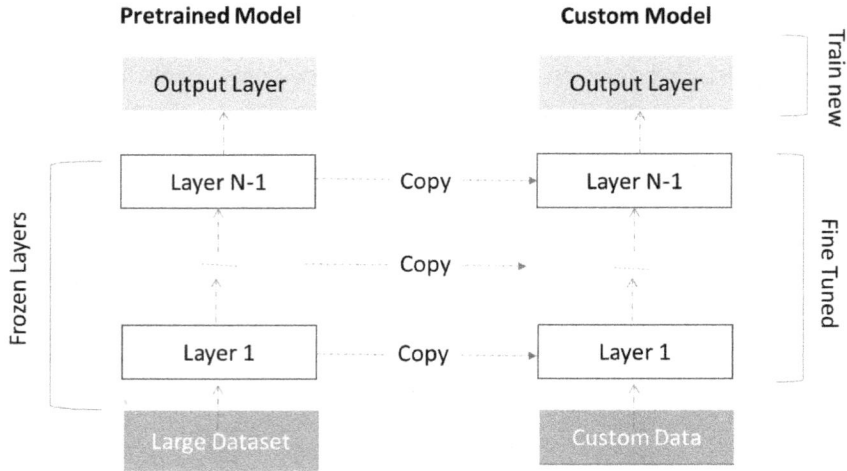

Figure 1.19: *Transfer learning and fine-tuning*

There are special cases of transfer learning techniques such as multi-task and meta learning.

Multi-task learning

Many real world scenarios require AI applications to perform different tasks simultaneously. An example could be a retail product recommender system in which a store camera has to detect the purchaser persona and a recommendation based on the instore purchase behavior. In this scenario, a model must perform a minimum of two prediction tasks prior to recommendation, that is, persona identification, and the other one is in-store behavior analysis. One way of solving this is to use an **Multi task learning (MTL)** model with camera feed input to identify persona and user behavior. The multitask model can be cascaded with product recommendation model using a pipeline method where multitask model output could be the input to the product recommendation model. MTL encapsulates multiple learned tasks in a single model and often lets those tasks learn jointly. Based on the location of task interaction happening in the neural network layer, MTL models are categorized into hard parameter sharing or soft parameter sharing. In hard parameter sharing, the hidden layers are shared between all tasks while keeping individual task specific output layers. Hard parameter sharing is composed of shared backbone network and task specific branches for learning task specific representations. This kind of neural architecture is often called multi-head architecture. Similarly, in soft parameter sharing, each task has its own model with its own parameters. These task specific backbone parameters are linked through regularization of fusion techniques. Take a look at the following figure that shows hard and soft parameter sharing approaches:

Hard Parameter Sharing   **Soft Parameter sharing**

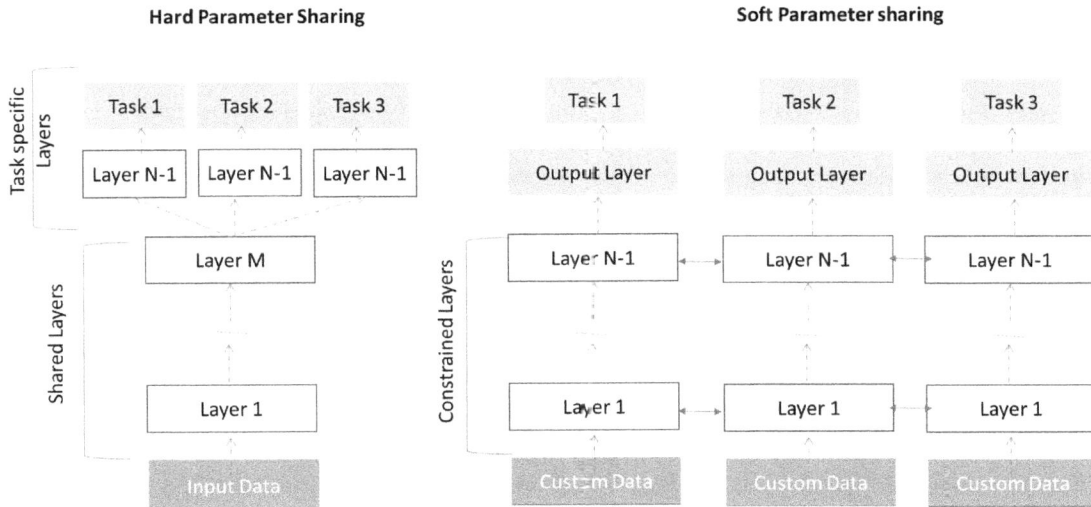

Figure 1.20: Hard and soft parameter sharing approach

In large deep neural network, like GenAI, extensive model parameters sharing among tasks affect the predictions due to inherent conflicts from tasks.

Distribution strategy

The training of large GenAI models spans over multiple days or months. Training of such large models on huge data sets needs a strategy to reduce the computation duration. One of the popular techniques is to adopt distributed training method. Distributed training method can be carried out by data parallelism and model parallelism. Data parallelism is most common where the training data is split into mini-batches and allocated to the individual compute device. Each device has a local model copy, which performs a forward pass and compute gradients on mini-batch data. These local gradients are aggregated and all-reduced to have the identical model update for synchronized training, or local gradients are updated to the parameter server to enable independent local model update for asynchronous training. In model parallelism, large model is split into multiple arrays of devices. Parallelism can happen at inter or intra layer level. In inter layer model parallelism, tensor computation at individual layers can be distributed across multiple devices. In intra layer parallelism, the model is split into layers of networks and computed across multiple devices. During the forward pass, each device passes the intermediate activation to the next stage. During the backward pass, each device passes the gradient of the input tensor back to the previous pipeline stage. This allows devices to compute simultaneously and increases the training throughput.

Performance improvement strategies

There are extensive custom performance improvement techniques, such as data improvement, hyperparameter tuning, feature selection, objective function selection, regularization techniques, neural architecture design, selecting the right performance measures, etc., that are practiced in AI projects. In this section, we cover only ensemble technique that is adopted widely to mitigate the bias-variance trade-off risk. The other techniques will be discussed in the relevant sections of deep learning and GenAI chapters.

Ensemble learning

It is a strategy in which a group of models are used to solve ML tasks. In this method, diverse learning models are combined to form a single predictive model. Unlike a single model, as an ensemble aggregate results from multiple models, it improves the accuracy of the predictions. Ensemble techniques are often adopted to mitigate bias-variance trade-off. ML models are stochastic in nature. The errors in the model predictions are classified into inherent irreducible (due to physical measurement) and reducible errors (Bias and variance). Bias is a systematic error due to the incorrect representation by mapping functions between input and output. Variance error is when the model cannot generalize beyond the training data set that it has not seen. Model with high bias results in underfitting and poor training accuracy, and a model with high variance results in overfitting. Take a look at the following figure that shows bias-variance trade-off illustration and low test accuracy:

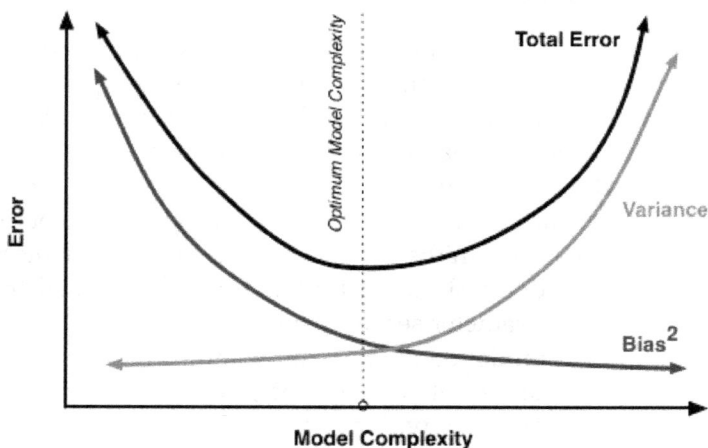

Figure 1.21: Bias and variance graph illustration

As shown in *Figure 1.21* Low bias and low variance are ideal expectations in any model. However, as shown in below *Figure 1.22* with an increase in model complexity, bias decreases but variance increases. Similarly, with simplified model variance decreases and bias increases.

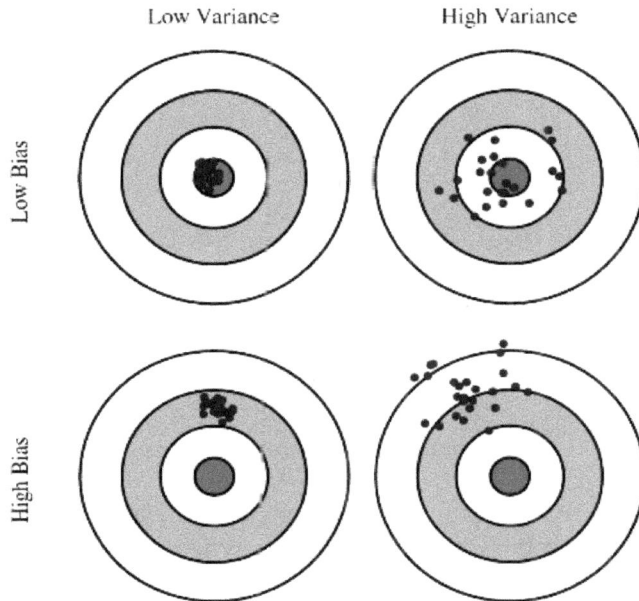

Figure 1.22: Variation of bias and variance with the model complexity[2]

Striking a balance between accuracy and the ability to generalize it for unseen data is the bias-variance trade-off. Ensemble methods of model prediction are one way to getting the bias and variance balanced. There are different techniques to ensemble methods. Bagging is an ensemble technique used to address high variance scenarios, where data is subsampled randomly and trained in parallel with different models. The ensemble model predictions are aggregated at the output either through the averaging method (for regression) or through a majority vote (for classification). Boosting is another technique used to address high bias scenarios, where ensemble of models is sequentially built that iteratively adjust the weights based on the incorrect predictions. It iteratively improves the weaker predictions to derive a stronger output by taking a weighted average of weaker ones. Stacking is another technique which combines output of different level-0 base models outputs using level-1 meta model. Meta model learns how to best combine the predictions of the base models. Unlike boosting, stacking uses a single model to learn how to best combine the predictions from base models. Some of the advanced ensemble methods include neural ensemble/architecture search sampling, which proposes ensembles of NN for the task.

The question that arises from the above discussion is how highly complex GenAI models like GPT with billion parameters perform well without over-fitting. The answer is that modern DL models encounter a surprising phenomenon called **double descent**. Double descent phenomenon does not nullify bias-variance trade-off. Take a look at the following figure: show the two regimes of the double descent risk curve:

---

2   Source: http://scott.fortmann-roe.com/docs/BiasVariance.html

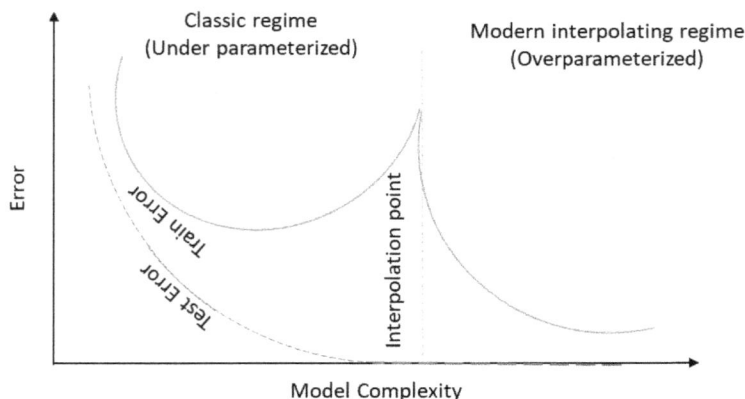

Figure 1.23: Double descent risk curve

In the above diagram, error peak occurs at the peak of the interpolation threshold. There are two regimes: an under-parameterized regime, where the model complexity is small compared to the number of samples, and the test error as a function of model complexity follows the u-like behavior predicted by the classical bias/variance trade-off. once model complexity is sufficiently large to interpolate, that is, achieve (close to) zero training error, then increasing complexity only decreases test error, following the modern intuition that bigger models are better. Double descent occurs as a function of model parameters, training duration, and dataset size. Double descent regime happens both model wise with increasing parameters and sample wise when data is increased beyond model parameters. Double descent results in super generalization of unseen data.

Mixture of experts

It is a special case of an ensemble method used in large neural networks. Unlike the earlier versions of ChatGPT with a single global model GPT-3, the future versions like GPT-4 is expected to use a mixture of expert techniques. The objective of mixture of experts (MOE) is to achieve a sublinear compute cost with respect to parameters by breaking down the ML problem into homogenous tasks and assigning an intelligent expert to solve the tasks. By doing so, only a fraction of the network is used to predict the output from one input. MOE begins with dividing a complex ML problem into sub tasks, training an expert that is multi-layer perceptron to solve these sub tasks, building a routing layer to decide on the choice of expert model based on the task, and finally pooling the predictions from the expert models to arrive a final output. There are multiple variants of MOE based on the routing logic, and some are switch transformer, expert choice, soft mixture of experts.

Conclusion

In this chapter, we understood popular ML techniques like supervised, un-supervised, semi-supervised, and reinforcement learning. We also understood the different algorithms used under each learning technique. Besides that, we understood common design patterns applicable to AI project lifecycle, like real word data representation, training strategies, and performance improvement techniques. In the next chapter, we will delve into sub-domain of ML called deep learning and apply supervised learning techniques to solve regression and classification problems.

Key terms

- Machine learning
- Deep learning
- Supervised learning
- Unsupervised learning
- Semi-supervised learning
- Reinforcement learning
- Embeddings

Questions

1. What is AI and the sub-fields of AI?
2. What are the different machine learning techniques?
3. How do calculate loss function in linear regression model?
4. What is the difference between supervised and unsupervised learning?
5. What are the benefits of semi-supervised learning?
6. What is meant by Embeddings in machine learning space?

Join our book's Discord space

Join the book's Discord Workspace for Latest updates, Offers, Tech happenings around the world, New Release and Sessions with the Authors:

https://discord.bpbonline.com

CHAPTER 2
GenAI Foundation

Introduction

In an earlier chapter, we understood the AI fundamentals and high-level concepts of deep learning techniques. In this chapter, we will understand the basic mathematics behind any neural networks and deep dive into deep learning concepts. We will understand the function of neural units, the objectives of deep learning networks, and techniques related to train and testing deep learning models. In this chapter, we will brief deep learning techniques, neural architectures, mathematical briefing and examples. We will introduce **generative AI (GenAI)** and different GenAI use cases across various industry domain.

Structure

In this chapter, we will discuss the following topics:

- Basic mathematics of artificial intelligence
- Deep learning
- Deep learning guide
- Artificial neural network: Classification problem
- Introduction to generative AI

Objectives

The objective of this chapter is to provide a foundation for GenAI technology that is deep neural network and its significance. It aims to explain the concepts of deep learning and various deep learning techniques, such as deep neural network elements, gradient descent, backpropagation, hyperparameters, performance metrics and highlighting their significance and options. The content also focuses on the DL guide for supervised deep learning regression and classification problems.

Basic mathematics of artificial intelligence

In order to understand the core theory of modern deep learning, one must be able to comprehend the **machine learning** (ML) or deep learning concepts in mathematical language. Though all models are constructed using mathematics behind, the beauty of AI is that one can sail through the AI concepts with basic mathematical knowledge. The following section covers certain basic mathematical concepts and is not exhaustive.

Scalar, vectors and matrices

Tensor is a mathematical object described by its order used to generalize high order vectors and matrices. Scalar is 0th order tensor. It defines set of values. $x \in \mathbb{R}$ where x is element of Real valued numbers (e.g.: -2, -1.5, 0, 1, 1.5). Vectors are ordered arrays of scalars with magnitude and direction. Vectors are 1st order tensors. $x = \begin{bmatrix} x_1 \\ x_2 \\ \vdots \\ x_n \end{bmatrix}$ defines value x

is n dimensional vector space of real numbers $\mathbb{R}^n$. x_i is the i the scalar element of the vector. Given two column vectors, it is possible to define the dot product (or scalar product) between them by taking the transpose of one to form a product. Take a look at the following equation: $x^T y = \sum_{i=1}^{n} x_i y_i$.

The matrix $\begin{bmatrix} a_{11} & \cdots & a_{1n} \\ \vdots & \ddots & \vdots \\ a_{m1} & \cdots & a_{mn} \end{bmatrix}$ $m \times n$ contains m n numbers with m rows and n column. Matrix

are 2nd order tensors. Matrix can be represented as $A \in \mathbb{R}^{m \times n}$ where A is a matrix with m x n dimensional real-valued vectors. Components of matrix are identified by a_{ij} where i, j represents the index to matrix row and column. Tensor encapsulates scalar, vector, matrix and higher orders. For example: 3rd order tensors are used to represent image channels (RGB) in deep learning. Tensor element is represented by a_{ijkl} where i, j, k, l are representations of multiple dimensions. A simple use case of tensor could be as solving linear equation as shown below:

Solve $\{ x + y + z = 6; 2y + 5z = -4; 2x + 5y - z = 27 \}$

$\begin{bmatrix} 1 & 1 & 1 \\ 0 & 2 & 5 \\ 2 & 5 & -1 \end{bmatrix} \begin{bmatrix} x \\ y \\ z \end{bmatrix} = \begin{bmatrix} 6 \\ -4 \\ 27 \end{bmatrix}$ gives $A X = B$

To find X we calculate $X = A^{-1} B$ and $A^{-1} = \frac{1}{|A|} \cdot Adj\ A.$

determinant $|A| = a_{11}(-1)^{1+1} \begin{bmatrix} a_{22} & a_{23} \\ a_{32} & a_{33} \end{bmatrix} + a_{12}(-1)^{1+2} \begin{bmatrix} a_{21} & a_{23} \\ a_{31} & a_{33} \end{bmatrix} + a_{13}(-1)^{1+3} \begin{bmatrix} a_{21} & a_{22} \\ a_{31} & a_{32} \end{bmatrix}$

So $|A|$ determinant for $\begin{bmatrix} 1 & 1 & 1 \\ 0 & 2 & 5 \\ 2 & 5 & -1 \end{bmatrix} = -21$

Now we calculate Adj A = Transpose of cofactor matrix.

Cofactor element $a_{ij} = (-1)^{i+j}$ *Minor of* $a_{ij}.$

So cofactor element $a_{11} = (-1)^{1+1}$ *Minor of* $a_{11} = (-1)^{1+1} * \begin{bmatrix} a_{22} & a_{23} \\ a_{32} & a_{33} \end{bmatrix}$

So cofactor matrix is given by $\begin{bmatrix} (-1)^{1+1}M_{11} & (-1)^{1+1}M_{12} & (-1)^{1+1}M_{13} \\ (-1)^{2+1}M_{21} & (-1)^{1+1}M_{22} & (-1)^{1+1}M_{23} \\ (-1)^{3+1}M_{31} & (-1)^{1+1}M_{32} & (-1)^{1+1}M_{33} \end{bmatrix}$

where *Minor of* a_{ij} is given by $M_{ij}.$

So cofactor of $\begin{bmatrix} 1 & 1 & 1 \\ 0 & 2 & 5 \\ 2 & 5 & -1 \end{bmatrix} = \begin{bmatrix} -27 & 10 & -4 \\ 6 & 3 & -3 \\ 3 & -5 & 2 \end{bmatrix}$ and its transpose is $\begin{bmatrix} -27 & 6 & 3 \\ 10 & 3 & -5 \\ -4 & -3 & 2 \end{bmatrix}.$

So the inverse is given by $\frac{1}{|A|} \cdot Adj\ A = \begin{bmatrix} \frac{9}{7} & \frac{-2}{7} & \frac{-1}{7} \\ \frac{-10}{21} & \frac{1}{7} & \frac{5}{21} \\ \frac{4}{21} & \frac{1}{7} & \frac{-2}{21} \end{bmatrix}.$

So $X = \begin{bmatrix} x \\ y \\ z \end{bmatrix} = A^{-1}B = \begin{bmatrix} 5 \\ 3 \\ -2 \end{bmatrix}$

Linear and non-linear functions

Linear equation $y = w\,x + b$ where y is the dependent and x *(real numbers)* is the independent variable with as weight and constant as the bias. Without bias term the model has a limitation in training to fit the model to pass through origin. For multiple x, we can define $y = w_1x_1 + w_2x_2 + w_3x_3 + b$ the assumption of linearity here is the variable y can be expressed as weighted sum of independent variables x with some affine transformation on adding the bias term. Linear models are linear in the parameters which have to be estimated, but not necessarily linear in the independent variables. For example, in the equation $y = w_1x_1 + w_2x_2 + w_3x_3^2 + b$, while the independent variable is squared (x_3^2), the model is still linear in the parameters. Linear models can also contain log terms and inverse terms to follow different kinds of curves and yet continue to be linear in the parameters. That is why *Figure 2.1* shows a linear discrimination though the independent variable x is non-linear.

The term non-linear refers to the parameters in the model, as opposed to the independent variables. Take a look at the following figure:

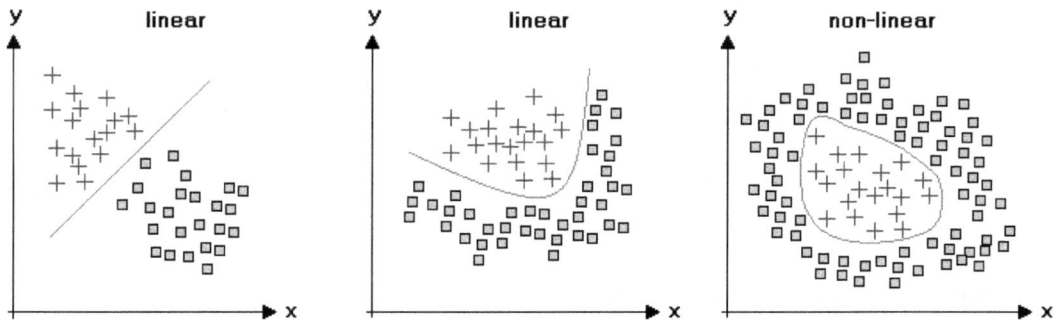

Figure 2.1: *Linear and non-linear functions*

In certain scenarios, non-linear models can be converted into linear models through transformations. Those transformable functions are generally solved through Intrinsically linear models. Before transformation $Y = w_1^2 \, x_1$ (*Non-linear in parameters*) and after transformation $\ln y = 2 \ln w1 + \ln x_1$ (*linear in parameters*). One must be cognizant of the effects that the transformation has on the distribution of the errors. Once we model the data as linear or non-linear functions, we can estimate the unknown parameters by applying methods like linear least square (Regression) or non-linear least square (Gauss-Newton).

There are various ways to build a mathematical model for the given data and some are exponential functions $y = ab^x$ for modeling investment growth, atmospheric pressure change, radioactive decay; logarithmic functions $y = a + b \ln x$ for modeling intensity of sound, production of goods, growth of infants and logistic functions $y = \frac{c}{1+ae^{-bx}}$ for modeling population growth, spread of diseases. There are many mathematical model based on the use case phenomenon. One of the popular models used in disease modeling used during pandemic is **Susceptible-Infected-Recovered (SIR)** model. Based on the dynamics of disease variants of SIR, such as including exposure period SEIR, when immunity lasts only for a short period SIRS, recovery has no immunity SIS.

Differentiable function

A function is differentiable if we can evaluate the derivative at every point on the curve. Not all functions are differentiable. Generally, the functions whose graphs have corner, discontinuity, and vertical tangent lines are non-differentiable. For example, the accuracy function is not differentiable. So, we often optimize loss functions like cross-entropy, a differentiable surrogate, considering that minimizing the proxy loss function will maximize the original accuracy metric. Some of the non-differential functions are shown in the following figure:

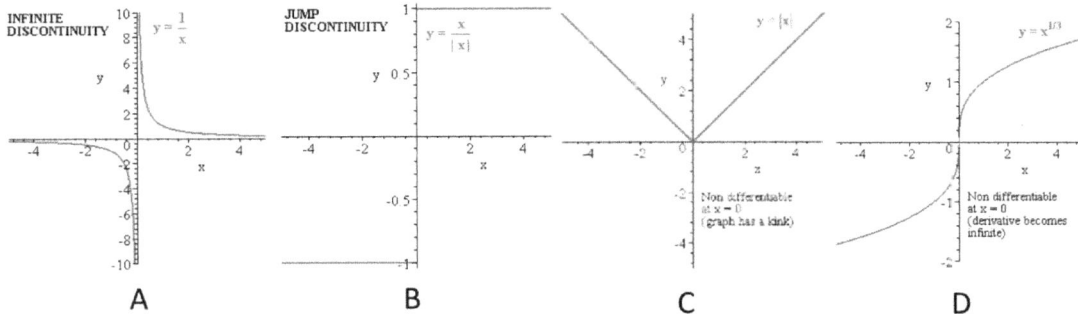

Figure 2.2: A and B are discontinuous non-differentiable; C and D are Continuous but non-differentiable functions

Derivatives, gradient and Jacobian matrix

Derivative is the rate of change in a function with respect to its inputs. We need derivatives in ML or deep learning to observe the change in loss function with respect to node weights. During training, we will backpropagate through neural network layers and tune the node weights to decrease the loss value defined by the cost function using different optimization techniques.

Derivate of function $f(x)$ and examples of derivatives are as follows:

1. $f'(x) = \lim\limits_{n \to 0} \frac{(f(x+n) - f(x))}{n}$ or $\frac{df(x)}{dx}$

2. $f(x) = x^n$ *implies* $f'(x) = nx^{n-1}$ *where* $n \neq 0$

3. $f(x) = \epsilon^x$ *implies* $f'(x) = e^x$

4. $f(x) = \ln x$ *implies* $f'(x) = \frac{1}{x}$

5. $f(x) = n \ constant \ implies \ f'(x) = 0$

In deep learning, functions we need to deal with many variables that is multi-variate functions. We briefly introduce notions of the partial derivatives that apply to such multi-variate functions. A partial derivative with respect to x is just the usual scalar derivative, simply treating any other variable in the equation as a constant. For functions of multiple parameters such as $f(x, y) = 6x^2 + 2y$, we compute derivatives with respect to one variable (x) or (y) at a time, giving us two different partial derivatives $\frac{d(f(x,y))}{dx}, \frac{d(f(x,y))}{dy}$. The gradient is the generalization of the derivative to multi-variate functions $f(x, y)$. So gradient is a vector of partial derivatives or vector gradient represented by $\boxtimes f(x,y) = \left[\frac{d(f(x,y))}{dx}, \frac{d(f(x,y))}{dy} \right]$. Derivatives of many functions are represented in matrix where each row is the vector gradient of each function. When we have two functions $f(x, y) \ g(x, y)$, we organize their gradients into a matrix by stacking the gradients to get the Jacobian matrix in numerator

layout. $J = \begin{bmatrix} \nabla f(x,y) \\ \nabla g(x,y) \end{bmatrix} = \begin{bmatrix} \frac{d(f(x,y))}{dx} & \frac{d(f(x,y))}{dy} \\ \frac{d(g(x,y))}{dx} & \frac{d(g(x,y))}{dy} \end{bmatrix}$ that is, for $f(x, y) = 6x^2 + 2y$ & $g(x, y) = 3x^2 + y$

Jacobian matrix will be:

$$J = \begin{bmatrix} 12x & 2 \\ 6x & 1 \end{bmatrix}$$

Let us consider a complicated functions like nested function $y = f(g(x))$. Computing a derivative using matrix calculus is computationally expensive. So, we use chain rule to breakdown the complex expressions into simple sub expressions and compute the derivatives in an isolated way. Isolated derivatives are used to compute the final result. Chain rules are typically defined in terms of nested functions $y = f(g(x))$. So if $n = g(x)$, the derivative of y by applying chain rule is $\frac{dy}{dx} = \frac{dy}{dn} * \frac{dn}{dx}$.

Chain rule

In deep learning, the chain rule is the way compilers construct a procedure to compute the nested function derivatives. This process of optimal procedure construction by computing programs using chain rules is called **automatic differentiation (autodiff)**. Forward and reverse mode auto-differentiation are special cases of autodiff. Reverse mode is also called **backpropagation** in neural terms that computes the gradients with specific order of operations using chain rule recursively. The node parameters of a neural network are learned through backpropagation. For example, $y = sin(x^3)$ the data flow will be $[x \boxtimes$

Cubic $\boxtimes$ Sine] so forward differentiation from $x \boxtimes y$ will be $\frac{dy}{dx} = \frac{dn}{dx} * \frac{dy}{dn}$ and the reverse

differentiation from $y \boxtimes x$ will be $\frac{dy}{dx} = \frac{dy}{dn} * \frac{dn}{dx}$. There are different chain rules applicable to function types.

The above is a simpler scalar chain rule. For deep learning, the vector chain rule, which is a product of Jacobians and will be used to find the gradient of node activation function.

Let us consider a nested function $y = f(g(x))$ that is, $y = \begin{bmatrix} f1(g) \\ f2(g) \end{bmatrix}$ where $g = \begin{bmatrix} g1(x) \\ g2(x) \end{bmatrix}$ and x is

a vector then calculating the derivative using vector chain rule is as follows:

$\frac{\partial y}{\partial x} = \frac{\partial (f(g(x)))}{\partial x} = \frac{\partial f(g)}{\partial g} \cdot \frac{\partial g(x)}{\partial x} = \begin{bmatrix} \frac{\partial f1}{\partial g1} & \frac{\partial f1}{\partial g2} \\ \frac{\partial f2}{\partial g1} & \frac{\partial f2}{\partial g2} \end{bmatrix} * \begin{bmatrix} \frac{\partial g1}{\partial x1} & \frac{\partial g1}{\partial x2} \\ \frac{\partial g2}{\partial x1} & \frac{\partial g2}{\partial x2} \end{bmatrix}$. The resulting Jacobian is $m*k$ and

$k*n$ resulting in m*n matrix. Given a fully connected neural net with 3 inputs, (x1, x2, x3), and hidden layer with two neurons (g1, g2), and a single scalar output (y). Then, the derivative of the lower layers can be decomposed and nicely computed with matrix

multiplication as $\frac{\partial y}{\partial x} = \begin{bmatrix} \frac{\partial y}{\partial g1} & \frac{\partial y}{\partial g2} \end{bmatrix} * \begin{bmatrix} \frac{\partial g1}{\partial x1} & \frac{\partial g1}{\partial x2} & \frac{\partial g1}{\partial x3} \\ \frac{\partial g2}{\partial x1} & \frac{\partial g2}{\partial x2} & \frac{\partial g2}{\partial x3} \end{bmatrix}$.

Deep learning

Deep learning is a subset of ML that uses multi-layered neural network (describe in the below section) in order to perform complex ML tasks. In this chapter, we will start with **single-layer perceptron** (**SLP**), build multi-layer perceptron and understand the neural network elements. Further, we will understand neural network training concepts like cost functions, gradient descent optimization, regularization, and performance metrics.

Single and multi-layer perceptron

The SLP is the first proposed neural model. A SLP is a feed-forward network based on a threshold transfer function. SLP is the simplest type of **artificial neural network** (**ANN**) and can only classify linearly separable cases with a binary target (1,0). The calculation of the single-layer is done by multiplying the sum of the input vectors of each value by the corresponding elements of the weight vector. Then output value Z is the input of the activation function. That is a binary step function. The function produces 1 (or true) when input passes the threshold limit, whereas it produces 0 (or false) when input does not pass the threshold. That is why they are very useful for binary classification studies.

$$Z = \sum_{j=1}^{n} x_j w_j = w_1 x_1 + w_2 x_2 - ... + w_n x_n, \text{ where } f(z) = \begin{cases} 1; if (z \geq \theta) \\ 0; others \end{cases}.$$

Take a look at the following figure:

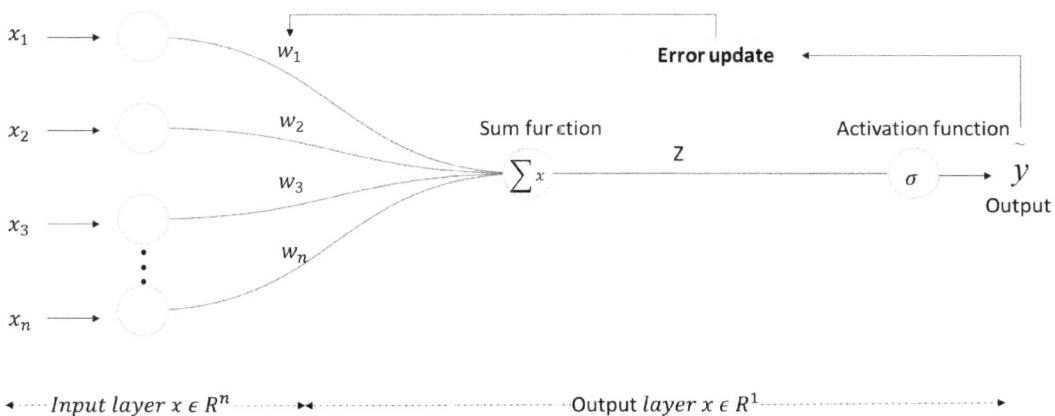

Figure 2.3: Perceptron architecture

Multi-layer perceptron

A neural unit or neuron is the building block for any neural network. At a high level, a neural network can be considered as a collection of connected neural units stacked in layers. The limitation of linearity in SLP can be addressed by stacking the neural units and by introducing hidden layers into the network. On adding hidden layers, a new set of weights is added and learned by the network. All pairwise neurons between layers are fully connected. For a simple neural network of 3 inputs and 2 hidden layers of 6 neurons each and 2 outputs , the number of learnable parameters will be 84 (weight terms (3*6 +6*6+6*2) + bias terms (1*6+1*6+1*2)). Mathematical representation can be given by where represent input layer $i * h_1 + \sum_{k=1}^{n-1}(h_k * h_{k-1}) + h_n * o + \{\sum_{k=1}^{n}(h_k) + o\}$, represent hidden layer, and h represent output layer. Take a look at the following figure:

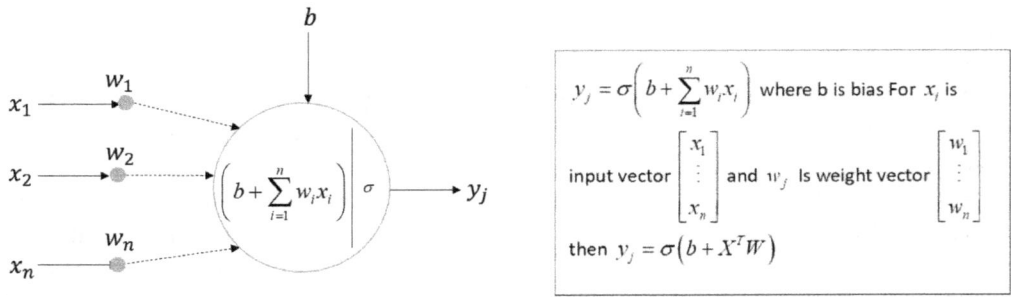

Figure 2.4: Neural unit or neuro n representation

As shown in the *Figure 2.4* the output of hidden layer is computed as $h_j^l = \sigma(w_{ok}^l + \sum_{k=1}^{n_{i-1}} w_{j,k}^l h_k^{l-1})$ where h_j^l is the output of neuron j in l^{th} hidden layer. σ is the activation function. n_i is a number of neurons in l^{th} hidden layer. $w_{j,k}^{l-1}$ is between the (neuron j in the hidden layer l) and (neuron k in the hidden layer l-1). Take a look at the following figure:

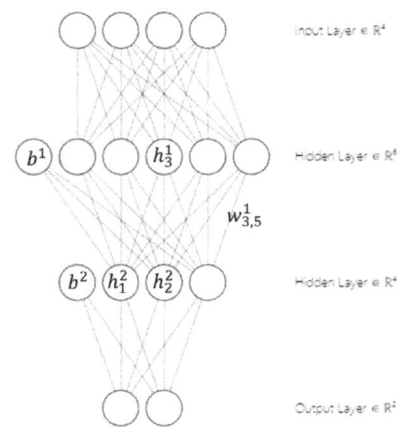

Figure 2.5: Multi-layer Perceptron architecture

The equation on entire hidden layer l can be written in vectorized form as $h^l = \sigma(z^l)$ where $z^l = W^l h^{l-1} + b^l$, W^l is the matrix of all weights between layer $l-1$ and l. h^l & b^l are vectors of outputs from neuros and biases from layer l.

By stacking more layers h^l i.e (h^l, h^2...h^{r-1}, h^r), where r is the total number of layers in the network, we get a deep neural network as shown here:

$$h_{1=} \begin{pmatrix} h_1^1 \\ \vdots \\ h_k^1 \\ \vdots \\ h_{n_1}^1 \end{pmatrix} = \begin{pmatrix} \sigma\left(\sum_{k=1}^{n_0} w_{1,k}^0 \, x_k\right) \\ \vdots \\ \sigma\left(\sum_{k=1}^{n_0} w_{j,k}^0 \, x_k\right) \\ \vdots \\ \sigma\left(\sum_{k=1}^{n_0} w_{n1,k}^0 \, x_k\right) \end{pmatrix} \quad \& \quad h_{r-1} = \begin{pmatrix} h_1^1 \\ \vdots \\ h_k^l \\ \vdots \\ h_{n_{r-1}}^l \end{pmatrix} = \begin{pmatrix} \sigma\left(\sum_{k=1}^{n_{r-2}} w_{1,k}^{r-2} \, h_k^{r-2}\right) \\ \vdots \\ \sigma\left(\sum_{k=1}^{n_{r-2}} w_{j,k}^{r-2} \, h_k^{r-2}\right) \\ \vdots \\ \sigma\left(\sum_{k=1}^{n_{r-2}} w_{n_{r-1},k}^{r-2} \, h_k^{r-2}\right) \end{pmatrix}$$

where h_1 is the first and h_{r-1} is $(r-1)^{ht}$ neural layer output.

Activation function (σ)

Activation function is a critical component of a neural network. It is a mathematical function that is applied to the output of the neuron network. The purpose of the activation function in deep learning is to introduce non-linearity into the network to make them understand the complex relationships and patterns. Activation functions are generally classified into linear or identity function, binary or step function, and non-linear function types. Activation function in deep neural network must be differentiable, continuous, non-linear, monotonic, and quickly converging. Without non-linear activation function, model creates only linear decision boundaries irrespective of the network size.

When designing a neural network, the activation function is defined individually for each hidden layer and output layer. Therefore, all elements of neural network including activation function must be differentiable in order to train the network. There are different non-linear activation functions to choose from. Some popular activation functions are sigmoid or logistic, **hyperbolic tangent activation function (Tanh), rectified linear unit (ReLU), Leaky ReLU (LReLU)**, softmax, **exponential linear units (ELU)**, and SWISH. Take a look at the following figure:

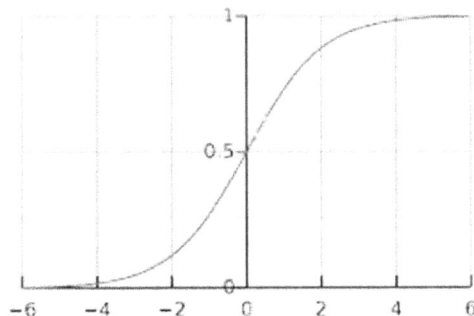

Figure 2.6: Sigmoid activation function

Mathematical formula for sigmoid is $\sigma(x) = \dfrac{1}{1+e^{-x}}$ and the derivative will be $\sigma'(z) = \sigma(z) * (1 - \sigma(z))$.

Sigmoid function is a squashing function that takes input (x) and generates bounded output between [0,1]. So, the output of the sigmoid function is often interpreted as probability and often used in the output layer. Sigmoid forms a S-curve with a strong slope in the middle and shallow slopes in the end. A neuron gets activated when the output value is close to 1, and while a value close to 0 corresponds to an inactive neuron. Vanishing gradients, slow convergence and computational expensiveness are some of the issues with sigmoid function. As backpropagation of deep network layers passes through multiple sigmoid functions, it faces the issue of gradient saturation leading to little or no learning. The sigmoid function is a non-zero-centered activation function. That is, the function is not symmetric about the origin, so the model will converge at a very slow rate due to zig-zag learning. Take a look at the following figure:

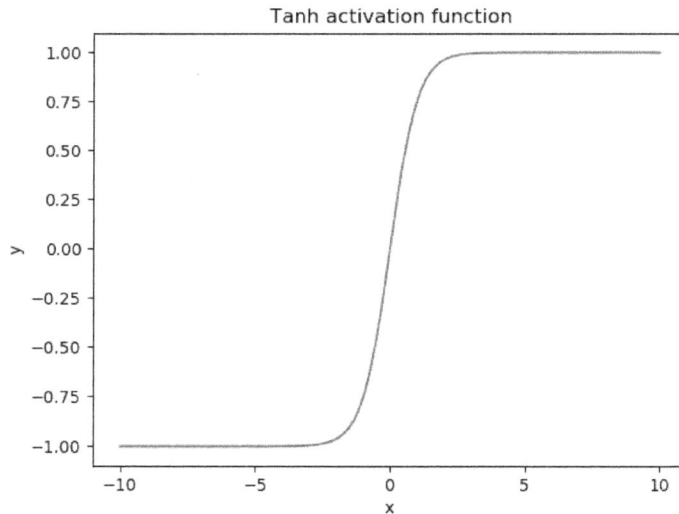

Figure 2.7: Tanh activation function

The mathematical formula for Tanh is $\sigma(x) = \dfrac{e^x - e^{-x}}{e^x + e^{-x}}$ and the derivative will be $\sigma'(z) = 1 - \sigma(z)^2$.

The output range of the Tanh function is bounded between (-1, 1). The function is mostly used in hidden layers. Unlike the sigmoid function, Tanh is zero centered activation function enabling faster convergence. The Tanh function is symmetric around the origin, that is, Tanh outputs negative values for negative input values and positive values for positive input values. Model learning with big learning steps. Tanh function still has issues of vanishing gradients, and it is computationally expensive as sigmoid. Take a look at the following figure:

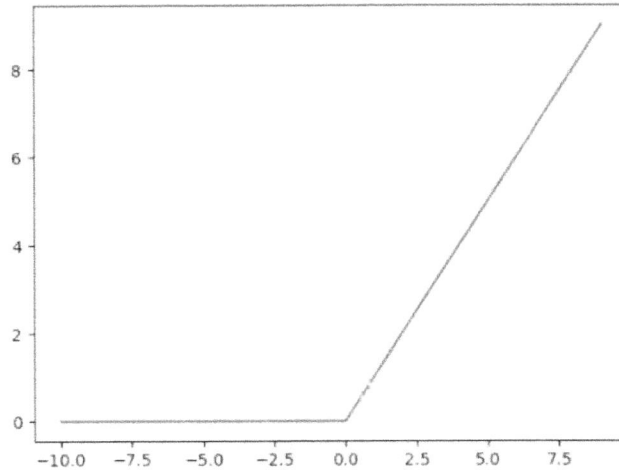

Figure 2.8: *ReLU—rectifier linear unit activation function*

Mathematical formula for ReLU is $\sigma(x) = \max(0, x)$ and the derivative will be

$$\sigma'(z) = \begin{pmatrix} 1, z > 0 \\ 0, otherwise \end{pmatrix}.$$

The output range of the ReLU function is bounded between $(0, \infty)$. ReLU function does not have asymptotic upper and lower bounds. Unlike Tanh and sigmoid, ReLU does not have a vanishing gradient issue, as the derivative $\sigma'(z)$ is either 0 or 1. So, as backpropagation passes through multiple activation functions into deep network layers, gradients will either return 1 or return nothing. This introduces neural network sparse, where certain activation is saturated. This leads to improvements in compute time efficiency and space complexity. Though the function is not differentiable at all points, that is, at $x=0$, it is still used pragmatically by setting the derivative of the function to 0 at $x=0$. ReLU faces the issue of dying ReLU; that is, when many neurons become inactive with output 0, the gradients fail to flow during backpropagation, and the model stops learning. As the slope of the function is also 0 in the negative region, it remains unrecoverable. Apart from negative inputs, larger negative bias and large learning rates could be the reason for the dying ReLU problem. There are variations of ReLU such as LReLU introducing a small non-zero constant gradient α in the negative region, **Parametric ReLU (PReLU)** same as LReLU but α is parameterized, ELUs introducing a log curve instead of a straight line in the negative region) to address the dying ReLU problem. One more important variation is the **Gaussian Error Linear Unit (GELU)**, considered to be a smoother version of ReLU, and is the popular activation function used in large-scaled language models like GPT-3, BERT, etc.

Take a look at the following figure:

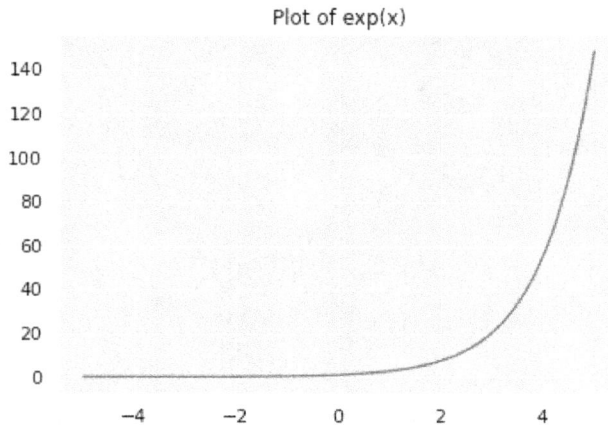

Plot of exp(x)

Figure 2.9: *Softmax activation function*

Mathematical formula for softmax is $\sigma(x)_i = \dfrac{e^{z_i}}{\sum\limits_{j=1}^{n} e^{z_j}}$ and the derivative will be

$$\sigma(x)_i = \begin{cases} \sigma(x_i) * (1 - \sigma(x_i)) & \text{if } i = j \\ -\sigma(x_i) * \sigma(x_j) & \text{if } i \neq j \end{cases}.$$

Softmax is often considered a generalized form of sigmoid function that turns input vector values into normalized probability distribution with a range between [0,1]. Softmax activation function is generally used in the output layer for multi-class classification, where it assigns decimal probabilities to each class in a multi-class problems. The softmax function assigns the highest probability to the output with the highest value and assigns zero probability to the other outputs. Softmax is sensitive to outliers, class imbalance, overlapping classes, and input scaling.

Choosing activation function

Choosing the right activation function is similar to hyperparameter tuning as it determines the efficiency of the neural network. While for hidden layer ReLU function has become the industry standard, the output layer activation function majorly depends on the problem or output type that a model expects. The following figure shows high-level choices based on the problem type:

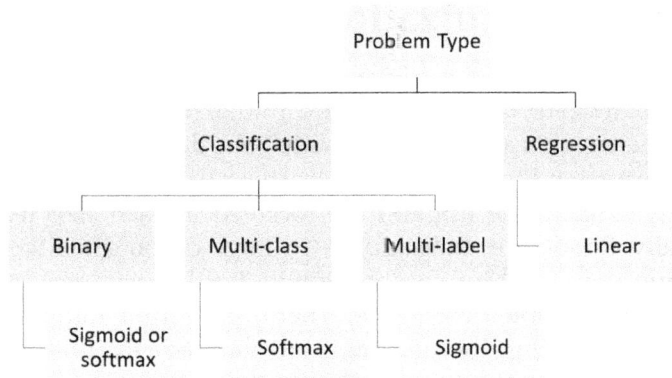

Figure 2.10: *High level Activation function choices*

As shown in *Figure 2.10*, sigmoid is computationally efficient and preferred for solving binary classification problems. Softmax for solving multi-class classification problems. A total number of classes will determine the output layer, and the output is a probability vector. sigmoid is preferred for the multi-label classification problem. Unlike softmax, the sigmoid model predicts all the labels for which the probability value is greater than a certain threshold.

Bias term

Bias is unique to every layer of the neural network. The purpose of the bias term is to shift the position of the activation curve left or right to delay or accelerate the activation of a node. As shown in *Figure 2.11*, unlike other neurons, the Bias neuron does not have previous layer inputs. They have only output connections with weights. Bias ensures activation in neurons even when neural networks have zeros as inputs. In a neural network, weight impacts the curve's steepness, while bias shifts the curve left or right without changing the shape of the curve. The bias is used to shift the result of the activation function towards the positive or negative side. Bias is the negative of the threshold. Therefore, the value of bias controls when to activate the activation function. Take a look at the following figure:

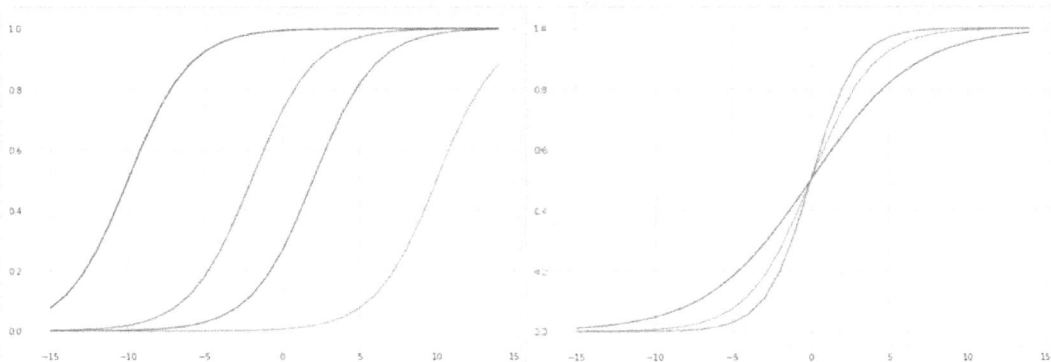

Figure 2.11: *Left: Bias varies with weights fixed, Right: Weight varies with bias fixed*

Weight and bias initialization

Weight and bias initialization play a critical role in neural network training. In practice, biases are initialized to zero, and weights are initialized randomly. Zero or constant initialization. If all the weights are initialized with 0, the derivative with respect to the loss function will be the same and lead to neurons learning the same features during training. With same initial weights, same updates are received at each step leading neurons to evolve symmetrically. Random initialization—too large or too small weight initialization can lead to exploding and vanishing gradient issues. Further random weight initialization can lead to slow learning and divergence. There are varied initialization schemes to avoid above issues by drawing the weights from the variance that is neither too large nor too small. Some are *Xavier* initialization $W \sim N(0, \frac{2}{n_{in} + n_{out}})$ for zero mean activations like sigmoid and Tanh activation, He/Kaiming initialization $W \sim N\left(0, \frac{2}{2n_{in}}\right)$ for ReLU activation that does not have zero mean. Bias can be initialized in same manner as weights where bias can be initialized at zero to allow optimizer to learn and initialize bias during first few steps or bias can empirically random like 0.01 for ReLU kind of activation or follow *Xavier* way of initialization considering bias as another weight term. Bias term is mathematically equivalent to weights. So bias updates happen along with weight terms during back propagation in similar manner. Bias terms are not regularized and do not contribute to the cost. The derivative of cost function C with respect to k^{th} *bias in layer l* is given by $\frac{\delta C}{\delta b_k^l} = \frac{\delta C}{\delta z_k^l} = \partial_k^l$ and bias update happens as $b_k^l = b_k^l - \alpha \partial_k^l$.

Cost function

It measures the model performance by quantifying the error between the expected and predicted values for a given data set. The objective of model training is to find the optimal weight parameters that either minimize the cost or, in certain cases, it can even maximize the cost, that is, reward. The cost function value represents the summation of loss errors in our model for the given data set. So for a given dataset of $X = \{x_0, x_1, x_2 .... x_n\}$ where $x_i \in \mathbb{R}^d$ and target $Y = \{y_0, y_1, y_2 .... y\}$ *where* $y_i \in \mathbb{R}^t$ the loss function for a training sample can be generally defined by $J(x_i, y_i; \theta) = J((x_i, \theta), y_i) = J(\widetilde{y}_i, y_i)$ where $\widetilde{y}_i$ is the predicted value. So, the cost function is the average of loss values across the entire training data set, that is, $\sum_{i=0}^{N} J((x_i, \theta), y_i)$. The loss function must be continuous and differentiable. Based on the problem type, there are multiple types of cost functions, as shown in the following figure:

Loss Functions

```
Loss Functions
├── Regression
│     ├── Mean squared error (MSE)
│     ├── Mean Absolute Error (MAE)
│     ├── Root Mean Square Error (RMSE)
│     ├── Mean Bias Error (MBE)
│     └── Huber Loss (HL)
├── Binary Classification
│     ├── Likelihood Loss (LHL)
│     ├── Binary Cross Entropy (BCE)
│     ├── Weight standardization
│     └── Squared Hinge loss
├── Multi Class classification
│     ├── Categorical Cross Entropy (CCE)
│     └── Kulback Leibler Divergence
└── Other loss functions
      ├── Ranking loss
      ├── Contrastive loss
      └── Cosine embedding loss
```

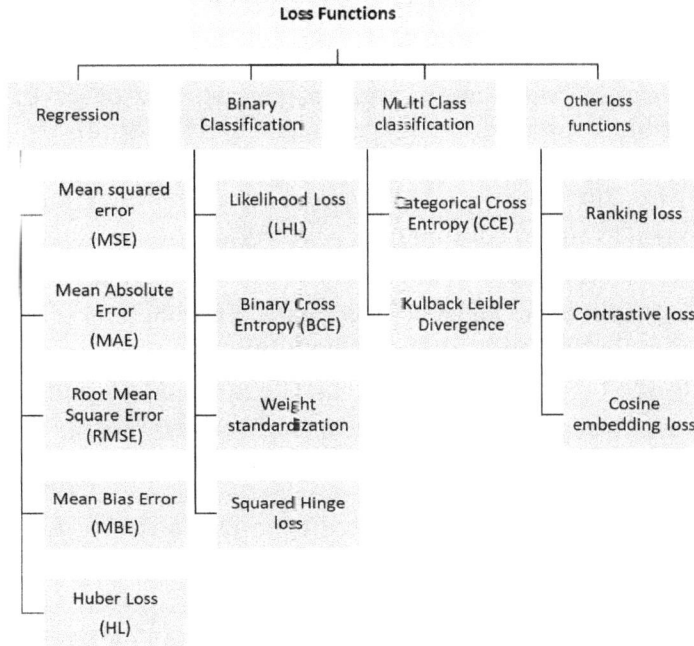

Figure 2.12: Loss functions

Mean squared loss is the common regression loss function popularly used. It measures the average squared loss value, that is, the difference between the actual and predicted target outcomes. $MSE = \frac{1}{N}\sum_{I=1}^{N-1}(\tilde{y}_i - y_i)^2$. The function is convex and differentiable at every point so that it can be optimized with gradient descent techniques like **stochastic gradient descent (SGD)**. **Mean square error (MSE)** is sensitive to outliers as it penalizes the parameter when the error is higher. MAE is similar to MSE, but instead of squared loss value, we use absolute loss value in MAE.

$$MSE = \frac{1}{N}\sum_{I=1}^{N-1}|\tilde{y}_i - y_i|.$$

The main drawback is that the function is not differentiable, so a variant of MSE like SmoothL1 loss is often used. The other drawback is the gradient of the MAE function becomes undefined as the cost value approaches the minimum. To address the shortcomings of MSE and MAE, Huber cost function is often preferred. Huber cost uses a hyperparameter ∂ which acts as a threshold that enables the cost function to be quadratic for small errors similar to MSE when the distance is less than ∂ and linear for large errors similar to MAE when distance is greater than or equal to ∂. Huber cost function is given by:

$$L(X,Y,\theta,\partial) = \begin{cases} \frac{1}{2}\sum_{I=1}^{N}(\tilde{y}_i - y_i)^2, & if\ |\tilde{y}_i - y_i| < \partial \\ \partial\sum_{I=1}^{N}|\tilde{y}_i - y_i| - \frac{\partial}{2}, & if\ |\tilde{y}_i - y_i| \geq \partial \end{cases}.$$

This is the popular loss function used in support vector machines.

Binary and multi-class classification loss functions

Maximum likelihood estimation (MLE) is an estimation method that allows us to estimate the parameters of the probability distribution that generated the observed data. (e.g., in the case of normal distribution, the parameters are mean and variance). The likelihood $p(x, \theta)$ is the joint density estimation of observed data as a function of model parameters. It is a probability density function parametrized by given as constant. The log likelihood is given by $l(X|\theta) = \sum_{x \varepsilon X} \log p_\theta(X)$ and maximum likelihood function is given by $\bar{\theta} = arg\max\limits_{\theta} l(X|\theta)$. As x_i are assumed to be independent and identically distributed, MLE can be expanded as $\bar{\theta} = arg\max\limits_{\theta} \prod_{i=1}^{m} l(x_i|\theta)$. MLE can be viewed as a way of minimizing the closeness between the training data distribution and the model distribution. In case of supervised learning with outputs (y_i) as the target variables MLE can be written as $\bar{\theta} = arg\max\limits_{\theta} \prod_{i=1}^{m} l(y_i|x_i, \theta)$. Minimizing the cross-entropy loss function that is often used in classification problems is viewed as equivalent to maximizing the log likelihood. In deep learning, cross-entropy is used in the loss function where the label represents the true probability distribution and another distribution is represented by the prediction of the model. Algorithms based on MLE principles often adopt cross-entropy as a cost function.

Cross-entropy and Kullback–Leibler divergence

Entropy is considered as average bits of information required to represent an event drawn from the probability distribution. For discrete events, entropy is defined by:

$$H(x) = -\sum_x p(x)\log(p(x))$$

Entropy increases with an increase in uncertainty. Cross-entropy is the average number of bits required to represent one distribution compared to another distribution:

$$H(P, Q) = -\sum_x p(x)\log(q(x))$$

where p is the true distribution and q is the estimated distribution. Cross-entropy is also called as **log loss**. **Kullback-Leibler (KL)** divergence is also similar to cross-entropy that quantifies how much two probability distributions differ. Unlike cross-entropy, that measures total bits to represent an event from one distribution compared to another, KL measures only the additional bits that are required to represent the event. So, KL divergence is given by:

$$KL(P||Q) = -\sum_x p(x)\log(q(x)/p(x))$$

In a deep learning classification task, each input belongs to one of the C classes. The target label will be one hot vector with a positive class and C-1 negative class. A one hot encoding as discussed in *Chapter 1 AI Fundamentals* in *Embeddings* section, is a representation of categorical variables as binary vectors. Each predicated class probability is compared with the target and the calculated loss is penalize the probability based on how far it is from expected value. Cross-entropy cost function is given by:

$$L_{CE} = - \sum_{nclasses} t_i \log(p_i)$$

Where t_i is the truth label (one hot encoded) and p_i is the softmax or sigmoid probability distribution. In case of binary cross-entropy, the number of classes is 2, that is, $t_i[0,1]$. So $L_{CE} = - \sum_2 t_i \log(p_i) = -t_1 \log(p_1) - (1 - t_1) \log(1 - p_1)$. Binary cross-entropy is built on top of sigmoid. When number of classes is more than 2, that is, multi-class we adopt **categorical cross-entropy** (**CCE**). CCE is used in multi-class classification task. It is built on top of softmax activation, so it is also called as **softmax loss**. The cross-entropy function is convex and can be optimized through gradient descent algorithms. The main disadvantage of cross-entropy is that it does not reflect the accuracy of the model in the classification task. The loss value must be used in conjunction with other accuracy metrics such as F1 score, precision, recall etc. to evaluate the model.

Gradient descent

Gradient descent is an optimization algorithm used to find weight parameters of neural network that minimizes thes cost functions discussed in the above section. It iteratively minimizes the prediction error of model by adjusting the model parameters. Deep learning optimization problem is complex and some of the challenges in gradient based optimization are local minima, saddle points and vanishing gradients. Local minima is a point where the cost function $J(\tilde{y}_i, y_i)$ is smaller compared to the neary by points. Global minima is a point where the cost function $J(\tilde{y}_i, y_i)$ is smaller over the entire domain. Generally deeplearning functions have more local minimas and often batch gradient descent algorithm converge to local minima as the gradient of the cost function approaches to zero. The other challenge for optimization is saddle point where the gradient of cost function vanishes but the point is neither local nor global minima. At saddle point the cost function local minima in one direction and local maxima in another direction. Take a look at the following figure:

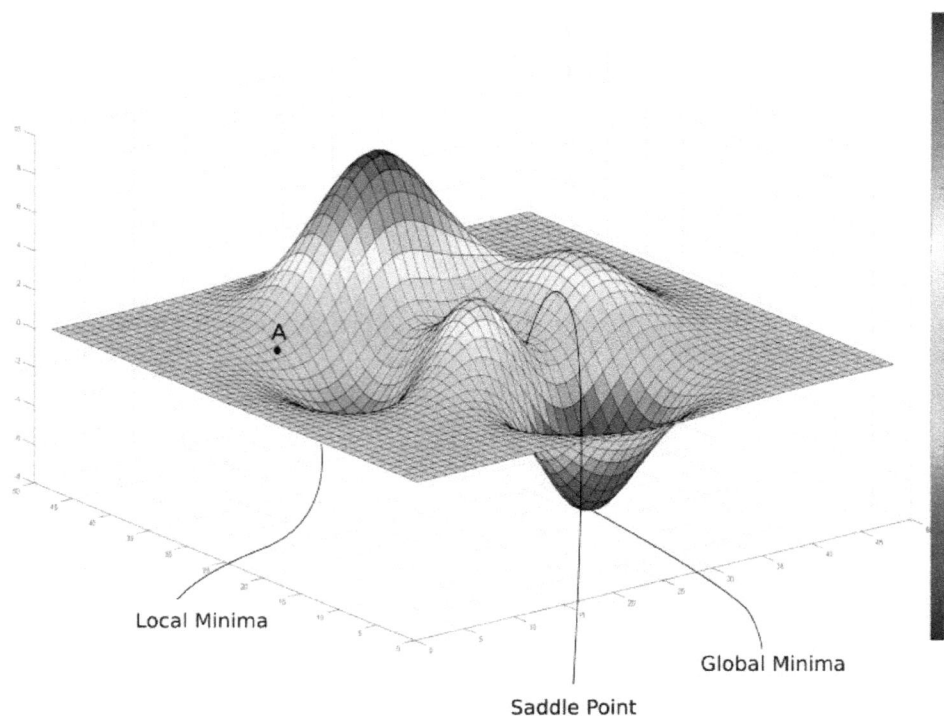

Figure 2.13: *Representative cost function*
Source: *https://imlim0813.tistory.com/16*

Gradient descent procedure

It is a first order optimization algorithm; gradients refer to the slope of a curve, and descent implies to the direction of movement to low value points. The algorithm works iteratively by calculating the gradient that is, first order derivative of cost function at the point and then perform scaled step towards the direction opposite to the gradient. As the gradient points to the direction of the steepest increase in the cost function, the movement must be in the opposite direction, that is, a negative gradient, to reduce the loss. In deep learning, gradient is vector of partial derivatives with respect to the weights.

Mathematically it is defined by $\theta = \theta - \alpha\nabla_\theta J(\theta)$ where θ model parameter, $\nabla_\theta J(\theta)$ is gradient of the cost function the **a** and is the learning rate.

The algorithm for SGD can look like the following:

For mini-batch size b, learning rate

Initialize: Parameters θ

While: Stopping criteria not met

Do: Sample b samples from training set of $\{x^1, \dots \dots x^n\}$

Compute: The gradient $\nabla_\theta J(\theta) = \frac{1}{b}\nabla_\theta \sum_{i=0}^N J((x_i, \bar{\theta}), y_i)$

Update: Model parameters $\theta = \theta - \alpha\nabla_\theta J(\theta)$

Types of gradient descent algorithm

Three major types of gradient descent algorithms are batch, stochastic and mini-batch gradient descent. In batch type gradients are calculated for entire dataset. It is slow and not suitable for larger data sets that do not fit into the memory. Mathemetically it is defined by $\theta = \theta - \alpha\nabla_\theta E[J(\theta)]$ where q model parameter, $\nabla_\theta J(\theta)$ is gradient of the cost function the and is the learning rate. The gradient for the entire data set must be calculated to perform a one-time parameters update. Another issue with batch optimization is its inabllity to update model online with new data.

Unlike batch gradient descent , SGD updates parameter for each training sample (x^i, y^i). Mathemetically, it is defined by $\theta = \theta - \alpha\nabla_\theta J(\theta, x^i, y^i)]$. SGD does frequent updates with high variance and is sensitive to the learning rate. Unlike batch gradient descent, SGD fluctuates, that enables the gradient to jump out of the local minima and find the optimal global minima. However the fluctuation induces the slowness in the convergence. Main advantage of SGD over batch is it overcomes the cost of running back propogation over the full training set. Also, SGD allows model to update online setting with new data.

Mini-batch gradient descent peform the parameter update for gradient calculated on n samples instead of whole dataset (batch gradient descent) or individual training sample SGD. The sample value n is a hyperparameter. $\theta = \theta - \alpha\nabla_\theta J(\theta, x^{i,i+n}, y^{i,i+n})]$. Performing update for every n samples, the algorithm address both the issues of cost of backprogration as well the variance in parameter updates.

Momemtum is a method adopted along with SGDs to reduce the fluctuations and enable SGD's to move in the relevant direction. The oscillations in SGDs in shallow ravines lead to slow convergenence, hence the momentum involves adding an additional hyper parameter that controls the amount of history to include in the updates. Mathematically, it is defined by:

$$v_{t-1} = \gamma v + \alpha\nabla_\theta J(\theta, x^i, y^i)] \text{ and } \theta = \theta - v_t$$

where v_t is the current velocity vector, is the model parametrs, and is the momentum usually set to 0.9.

There are various alternatives to gradient descent algorithms like **Limited-memory Broyden, Fletcher, Goldfarb, Shano (L-BFGS)** for memory constrained devices, **Levenberg-Marquardt algorithm (LMA)**, simulated annealing optimization, evolutionary algorithm optimization, particle swarm optimization, conjugate gradient and many more that can address the limitations with gradient descent like the requirement of cost functions to be convex, differentiable and the assumption of derivation of gradient is globally Lipschitz continuous.

Backpropagation

Backpropagation is a differentiation algorithm used with gradient descent algorithms to calcualte the gradients of network parameters. Together, Gradient descent and backpropogation alogrithms traing the neural network. Backpropogation involves the recursive application of the chain rule that is used to calculate the derivative of a sub-function given the derivative of the parent function for which the derivative is known. In simple terms the backpropogation objective is to compute the partial derivatives ($\frac{\partial C}{\partial w}$ & $\frac{\partial C}{\partial b}$) of cost function ($C$) with respect to weight or bias.

Backpropogation procedure

Feed forward network computes the hidden layer outputs $h^{x,l} = W^{x,l}h^{x,l-1} + b^l$ for each $l = 2, 3.....r$ where $h^{x,l} = \sigma(z^{x,l})$ and $\sigma^{x,l}$ is the activation function for input layers.

Calculate the cost function $C = \sum_{i=0}^{N} J((x_i, \theta), y_i)$

Compute the gradient of C which is given by $(\frac{\partial C}{\partial w_{jk}^l}) = \sigma_k^{l-1}\delta_j^l$ and $(\frac{\partial C}{\partial b_j^l}) = \delta_j^l$

Update the weights according to the rule $w^l = w^l - \frac{\alpha}{m}\sum_x \partial^{x,l}(h^{x,l-1})^T$ and the biases according to $b^l = b^l - \frac{\alpha}{m}\sum_x \partial^{x,l}$ and repeat the process until convergence.

Chain rule in backpropagation

In order to understand the applicability of chain rule, we will derive the chain of changes that happens when a small change happens to the model weights. The change in cost function is given by $\Delta C \approx \frac{\partial C}{\partial w_{jk}^l}\Delta w_{jk}^l$ where ΔC is the cost is related to change Δw_{jk}^l change in weight. The change in weight parameter (Δw_{jk}^l) changes activation output given by:

$$\Delta h_j^l \approx \frac{\partial h_j^l}{\partial W_{jk}^l}\Delta w_{jk}^l$$

where h_j^l in the activation of jth neuron in the lth layer. The change in activations causes changes in all the activation in next layer $\Delta h_q^{l+1} \approx \frac{\partial h_q^{l+1}}{\partial h_j^l} * \Delta h_j^l$, that is, equivalent to $\Delta h_q^{l+1} \approx \frac{\partial h_q^{l+1}}{\partial h_j^l} * \frac{\partial h_j^l}{\partial W_{jk}^l}\Delta w_{jk}^l$ which in turn causes a change in other layer following a path of $h_j^l, h_q^{l+1}, ..., h_n^{L-1}, h_m^L$ then the resulting final expression is $\Delta C \approx \frac{\partial C}{\partial h_m^L} * \frac{\partial h_m^L}{\partial h_n^{L-1}} * ...... * \frac{\partial h_q^{l+1}}{\partial h_j^l} * \frac{\partial h_j^l}{\partial h_{jk}^l} * \Delta w_{jk}^l$. This represent the change in C due to changes in activation along their particular path through the network. As changes can be influenced by many such paths, total change in cost is sum of the changes over all possible paths between weight and final cost $\Delta C \approx \sum_{m,n,p...q} \frac{\partial C}{\partial h_m^L} * \frac{\partial h_m^L}{\partial h_n^{L-1}} * \cdots \cdots * \frac{\partial h_q^{l+1}}{\partial h_j^l} * \frac{\partial h_j^l}{\partial h_{jk}^l} * \Delta w_{jk}^l$. Thus, backpropagation algorithm computes the rate of change of C with respect to model weights and biases over all possible paths using chain rule and auto-differentiation methods for the defined trained samples.

Generalization

The term generalization refers to the model's capability to adapt and react properly to previously unseen, new data, which is assumed to be drawn from the same distribution as the one used to train the model. In other words, generalization examines how well a model can fit to new data and make correct predictions. Regularization is a way to constrain a model to a small set of solutions to make the complex model simpler.

There is a set of techniques adopted to reduce the generalization error. Generalization errors are majorly due to bias-variance trade-off and model overfitting. We have already discussed in *Chapter 1, AI Fundamentals,* about the bias-variance trade-off issues in detail. *Figure 2.14* shows some of the techniques to avoid generalization errors. We will discuss a few of the popular ones. Take a look at the following figure:

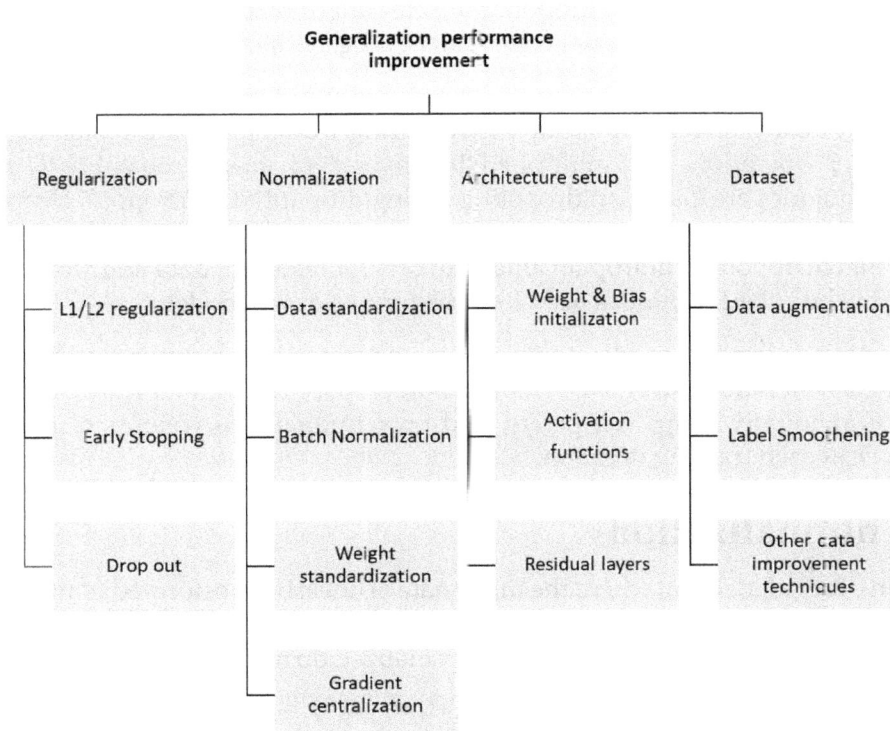

Figure 2.14: Techniques adopted to reduce the generalization error

L1/L2 regularization

This technique is also known as **weight decay** or **L2-Ridge regularization** and **L1-Lasso regularization**. The objective is to constrain the weight update by introducing a penalty term. Regularized loss function *(f'(θ, X, y) where X- input,y-output and θ- weight parameters)* is given by *(f(θ, X, y) + penalty term)*.

While for L1 regularization, the penalty is the absolute value of weights $((+ \lambda | | \theta | |))$, L2 regularization the penalty term is the sum of square of all feature weights $(+ \lambda | | \theta | |^2)$. Unlike L2, instead of reducing the magnitude of weights to near zero, L1 introduces sparsity and forces weights to be zero which make L1 suitable for feature selection.

Dropouts

Dropout refers to the dropping out of neural network nodes during training at each iteration with a dropout probability of *p* or keep the probability of *(1-p)*. The idea behind this is to train different models for each iteration by keeping a subset of neurons. During training, dropped neurons do not contribute for both forward and backward propagation. By randomly deactivating the portion of neurons, the network learns more robust and generalized features leading to an increase in the performance of unseen data. Different ways of dropouts are available. The dropout rate is typically determined manually as a hyperparameter. By varying the dropout rate, amount of regularization can be fine-tuned to optimal trade-off between model complexity and generalization.

One of the techniques is inverse dropout. In order to avoid any scaling operations during inference, we follow inverse dropout where during training, all the remaining weights after dropout operations are multiplied by inverse of keep probability *(1-p)*. Other dropout techniques are Gaussian dropout, pooling dropout, data dropout, DropConnect, DropBlock, MaxDropout, Attention dropout, dropout with RNN and more. Structured dropout, PatchDropout, Unidrop an amalgamation of featured, data and structured drop out are some popular techniques used for transformer-based models.

While dropout, is kind of an idea to drop some neuros and respective weights of certain layers at each iteration, stochastic depth another popular technique exclusively used in ResNets randomly drops full layers, and only updates the weights of the resulting subnetwork at each training iteration.

Batch normalization

It is a form of regularization where the input data is linearly transformed to fit into a space (like Gaussian) with zero mean, unit variance and decorrelated. It normalizes the input to the layers in the network. Layers that are batch normalized do not have bias. The mathematical formulation for batch norm of input $x = (x^1, x^2 .... x^n)$ is $\tilde{x}^k = \frac{x^k - \mathbb{E}[x^k]}{\sqrt{Var[x^k]}}$. Henceforth for batch $B = \{x^1, x^2 \dots x^n\}$ the mean is $\mu_B = \frac{1}{n}\sum_{i=1}^{n} x^i$ and variance is $\sigma_B^2 = \frac{1}{n}\sum_{i=1}^{n}(x^i - \mu_B)^2$. The normalized batch input $\tilde{x}^i = \frac{x^i - \mu_B}{\sqrt{\sigma_B^2 + \epsilon}}$. The output $y^i = \gamma\tilde{x}^i + \beta = BN_{\gamma,\beta}(x^i)$ where γ, β are learnable parameters. Batch norm reduces the internal covariance shift between layer, that is reducing the change in data distribution between network layers.

Gradient centralization

While batch normalization or weight normalization is based on z-score standardization applied to activation function or weight vectors, gradient centralization operates on gradients directly by centralizing the gradient vectors to zero mean. For every column of the gradient matrix, mean column value is subtracted so that each gradient of loss function is transformed to weight vector with its mean equal to zero. We have obtained the gradient through backward propagation, then for a weight vector w_i whose gradient is $\nabla_{w_i}L$ (1,2 ... n) the GC operator, denoted by Φ_{GC}, is defined as follows:

$$\Phi_{GC}(\nabla_{w_i}L) = \nabla_{w_i}L - \frac{1}{M}\sum_{j=1}^{M}\nabla_{w_{i,j}}L \;\; (Calcuale\; th\; mean\; of\; gradient\; vectors\; and\; subtact)$$

After obtaining the centralized gradient, it can be used directly to update the weight in the optimization algorithms. Apart from regularization, this method avoids gradient explosion thereby stabilizing the model.

Learning rate

Learning rate is a configurable hyperparameter that controls the step size taken towards the gradient descent direction. It is a positive scalar that generally ranges between 0.0 and 1.0. During backpropagation, the learning rate scales the amount of update on weight parameters with respect to the loss gradient. A larger learning rate enables larger step size leading to faster learning by model, but it may overshoot the minimum point and arrive on a sub-optimal set of weights. A smaller learning rate allow the model to learn a more optimal set of weights but take longer time to converge. Besides that, smaller learning rate may lead to model get stuck on local minimum rather than global minimum. The optimal configuration of learn rate depends on loss function, optimizer, regularization, weight and bias initialization and input data distribution. However, there are different ways to configure learning rate. Some methods are learning rate decay, learning rate schedule and adaptive learning rate. Learning rate decay initializes with larger values but reduces it over time. So, during backpropagation, larger weight changes happen during the beginning and slowly changes on weights decays over time as the network gets closer to loss value. There are different decay types such as step decay, exponential decay, inverse time decay and adaptive decay.

Adaptive learning rates

Adaptive gradient descent (AdaGrad) is a per parameter adaptive learning rate scheme.

In case of sparse data, the learning rate either decreases too slowly for frequent features or too quickly for infrequent ones. In order to address this, past gradient stats are observed. Learning rates are set dynamically per parameter for each iteration in such a way the parameters that correspond to large gradients are scaled down (smaller updates by setting a small learning rate), and parameters with small gradients, that is, infrequent ones are treated gently (larger updates by setting larger learning rate). A different learning rate is used for each parameter.

In previous methods, parameter (q) updates happen at once, and each parameter (θ_i) uses learning rate **a**. In AdaGrad, different learning rates are used for every parameter (θ_i) at every time step (t). The stochastic gradient descent update for an individual parameter (θ_i) at every time step (t) is given by $\theta_{t,+1,i} = \theta_{t,i} - \alpha * g_{t,i}$ where $g_{t,i} = \nabla_\theta J(\theta_{t,i})$ and $g_{t,i}$ is the partial derivative of the objective function with respect to an individual parameter (θ_i) at every time step (t). For AdaGrad, the learning rate **a** gets modified at every time step (t) for individual parameter (θ_i) based on the past gradients. So $\theta_{t,+1,i} = \theta_{t,i} - \frac{\alpha}{\sqrt{G_{t,ii}}+\epsilon} * g_{t,i}$ where $G_{t,ii}$ is diagonal matrix where i is the sum of squares of gradient with respect to (θ_i) up to timestamp (t). In expanded form is $\theta_{t,+1,i} = \theta_{t,i} - \frac{\alpha}{\sqrt{G_{t,ii}}+\epsilon} \odot g_{t,i}$

Where $\odot$ is the Hadamard product between matrices. The main negative of AdaGrad is the accumulated gradients causing the learning rate to infinitely small. Which leads to the stagnancy of model learning. AdaGrad is sensitive to initialization and global learning rates.

Unlike AdaGrad, which accumulates the past squared gradient, AdaDelta restricts the collection to a window w and squared updates are accumulated with running average parameter ρ. So, the running average $E[g^2]_t$ at time step (t) is given by fraction (ρ) of previous average and the current gradient, that is, $E[g^2]_t = \rho E[g^2]_{t-1} + (1 - \rho)g_t^2$. The SGD update is given by $\theta_{t,+1,i} = \theta_{t,i} - \frac{\alpha}{\sqrt{E[g^2]_t}+\epsilon} * g_{t,i}$. **Root Mean Square Propagation (RMS Prop)** is similar to AdaGrad method, but in AdaDelta the learning rate is replaced by root mean squared error or parameter update.

Model performance metrics

Model evaluation metrics describes the performance of the model. Regression metric includes mean absolute error, mean squared error, RMS error and others. Classification metric includes, precision, recall, accuracy, F1 score, AUC-ROC and others. Metrics related to LLMs, computer vision models and GenAI models will be discussed in the upcoming chapters.

Confusion matrix a tabular visualization of the model predictions versus the ground-truth labels.

True negative: Both prediction and actuals are negative

True positive: Both prediction and actuals are positive

False positive: (Type 1 error) prediction is positive and actual is negative

False negative: (Type 2 error) prediction is negative and actual is positive

Take a look at the following figure:

Actual

	Positive(1)	Negative (0)
Positive (1)	Ture Positive (TP)	False Positive (FP)
Negative (0)	False Negative (FN)	True Negative (TN)

Predicted

Figure 2.15: Confusion Matrix

Recall, precision and F-measure can be calculated using the following equations:

$$Re\,call = \frac{TP}{TP + FN}$$

$$Pr\,ecision = \frac{TP}{TP + FP}$$

$$F - Measure = \frac{2 * Re\,call * Pr\,ecision}{Re\,call + Pr\,ecision}$$

Classification accuracy

The ratio of number of correct predictions to the total input samples predicted using the following equation:

$$Accuracy = \frac{Number.of\ Correct.Pr\,ediction}{Total\ Pr\,edictions}$$

Receiver operating charachtestic curve

It is a plot that shows **true positive rate** (**TPR**) vs **false positive rate** (**FPR**) for various threshold values. Each point on the ROC curve represents a sensitivity/specificity pair corresponding to a particular decision threshold. Therefore the closer the ROC curve is to the upper left corner, the higher the overall accuracy. Area under the ROC curver measures two dimensional area underneath the entire ROC curve. AUC is threshold invariant and it is a evaluation metric for binary classification. The higher the AUC, F1 score, accuracy, the better the model's performance. Take a look at the following figure:

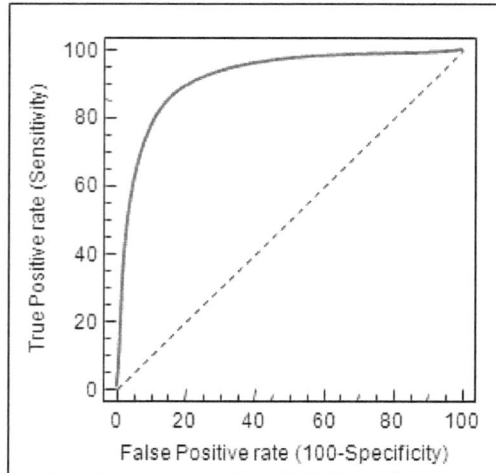

Figure 2.16: Receiver operating characteristic curve

So far We have understand the function of neural units, the objectives of deep learning networks, and techniques related to train and testing deep learning models. We will demonstrate an example in the following section.

Deep learning guide

ANN—regression problem

Objective: Build an ANN (Artificial Neural Network) for predicting the median house value of the *California* housing dataset. The problem is a supervised regression problem.

Perquisites

Python version = 3.10.12

NumPy = 1.23.5

Matplotlib = 3.7.1

TensorFlow = 2.13.0 (In colab environment follow **!pip install tensorflow**)

Loading libraries

Load the library using the following code:

```
1. import numpy as np      # Library for number operations
2. import pandas as pd     # Library for data operations
```

3. `import` seaborn `as` sb   # *Library for data visualization*

4. `import` matplotlib.pyplot `as` plt # *Library for data visualization*

5. `import` numpy `as` np

6. `from` sklearn.metrics `import` ConfusionMatrixDisplay

Loading dataset

About California housing dataset

This dataset was obtained from the **StatLib** repository.

https://www.dcc.fc.up.pt/~ltorgo/Regression/cal_housing.html This dataset was derived from the 1990 *U.S. census,* using one row per census block group. A block group is the smallest geographical unit for which the *U.S.*

Census Bureau publishes sample data (a block group typically has a population of 600 to 3,000 people).

The target variable is the median house value for California districts, expressed in hundreds of thousands of dollars ($100,000). Dataset can be loaded using the following code:

1. # *Fetching California Dataset*

2. #*skLearn software machine learning library for the Python programming language*

3. `from` sklearn.datasets `import` fetch_california_housing

4. ann_data = fetch_california_housing()

5. ann_data.feature_names # *Dataset features or columns*

Output:

```
['MedInc',
 'HouseAge',
 'AveRooms',
 'AveBedrms',
 'Population',
 'AveOccup',
 'Latitude',
 'Longitude']
```

Figure 2.17: Dataset column names

Exploratory data analysis

1. df = pd.DataFrame(data=ann_data.data,columns=ann_data.feature_names) # *store it in a datfarme python datastructure*

2. df.head()

Output:

	MedInc	HouseAge	AveRooms	AveBedrms	Population	AveOccup	Latitude	Longitude
0	8.3252	41.0	6.984127	1.023810	322.0	2.555556	37.88	-122.23
1	8.3014	21.0	6.238137	0.971880	2401.0	2.109842	37.86	-122.22
2	7.2574	52.0	8.288136	1.073446	496.0	2.802260	37.85	-122.24
3	5.6431	52.0	5.817352	1.073059	558.0	2.547945	37.85	-122.25
4	3.8462	52.0	6.281853	1.081081	565.0	2.181467	37.85	-122.25

Figure 2.18: Top 4 rows of Dataset

```
1.  ann_data.target # The column that needs to be predicted (Y)
```

Output:

```
array([4.526, 3.585, 3.521, ..., 0.923, 0.847, 0.894])
```

```
1.  df.shape # 20640 rows, 8 cols
```

Output:

```
(20640, 8)
```

```
2.  df.describe() #returns description of the data in the DataFrame
```

Output:

	MedInc	HouseAge	AveRooms	AveBedrms	Population	AveOccup	Latitude	Longitude
count	20640.000000	20640.000000	20640.000000	20640.000000	20640.000000	20640.000000	20640.000000	20640.000000
mean	3.870671	28.639486	5.429000	1.096675	1425.476744	3.070655	35.631861	-119.569704
std	1.899822	12.585558	2.474173	0.473911	1132.462122	10.386050	2.135952	2.003532
min	0.499900	1.000000	0.846154	0.333333	3.000000	0.692308	32.540000	-124.350000
25%	2.563400	18.000000	4.440716	1.006079	787.000000	2.429741	33.930000	-121.800000
50%	3.534800	29.000000	5.229129	1.048780	1166.000000	2.818116	34.260000	-118.490000
75%	4.743250	37.000000	6.052381	1.099526	1725.000000	3.282261	37.710000	-118.010000
max	15.000100	52.000000	141.909091	34.066667	35682.000000	1243.333333	41.950000	-114.310000

Figure 2.19: Statistics of data frame

Now, execute the following code:

```
1.  import seaborn as sns
2.  sns.scatterplot(
3.      data=df, # input data frame
4.      x="Longitude", # axis
```

```
5.      y="Latitude", # axis
6.      size="HouseAge", # Grouping variable that will produce points
        with different sizes
7.      hue="HouseAge", # Grouping variable that will produce points
        with different colors.
8.      alpha=0.55, # Transparency )
```

Output:

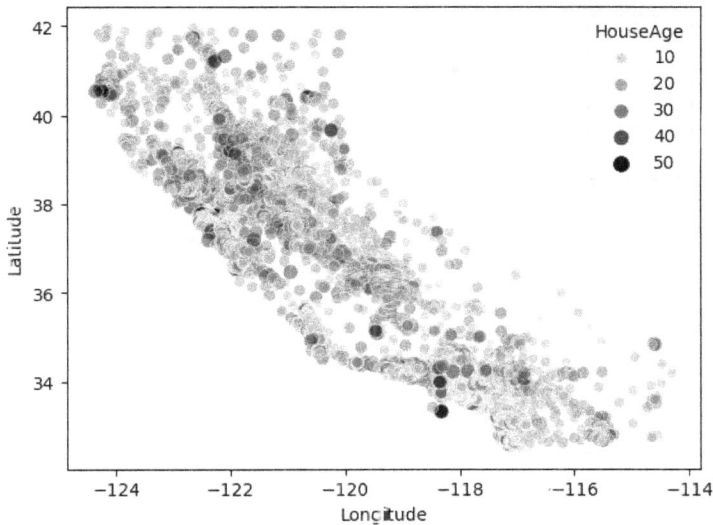

Figure 2.20: *Graph visualization of dataset*

Train and test split

Execute the following code:

```
1. from sklearn.model_selection import train_test_split # Quikc Utility
   Split arrays or matrices into random train and test subsets.
2. X, y = ann_data.data, ann_data.target
3. # train-test split for model evaluation
4. X_train, X_test, y_train, y_test = train_test_split(X, y, train_
   size=0.8, shuffle=True)
5. print(X_train.shape , y_train.shape)
6. print(X_test.shape, y_test.shape)
```

Output:

```
[➤  (16512, 8) (16512,)
    (4128, 8) (4128,)
```

Figure 2.21: Train and test dataset shape

Next, execute the following code:

1. `from` sklearn.preprocessing `import` StandardScaler `#` *Standardize features by removing the mean and scaling to unit variance*
2. `X_train = StandardScaler().fit_transform(X_train)` `# Scale train data`
3. `X_test = StandardScaler().fit_transform(X_test)` `# Scale test data`

Model building

TensorFlow is an open-source deep-learning library that is developed and maintained by *Google*. It offers dataflow programming, which performs a range of ML tasks. It was built to run on multiple CPUs or GPUs and even mobile operating systems, and it has several wrappers in several languages like Python, C++, or Java.

Keras is an open-source neural network library in Python that runs on top of Theano or TensorFlow. It is designed to be modular, fast and easy to use. It was developed by *François Chollet*, a Google engineer. It is a useful library to construct any deep learning algorithm It is an end-to-end platform that is built to be powerful and operate at a high-performance level. Execute the following code:

1. `import` tensorflow `as` tf
2. `from` tensorflow `import` keras
3. `from` tensorflow.keras `import` layers
4. `from` keras.models `import` Sequential
5. `from` keras.layers `import` Dense
6.
7. `model = Sequential()` `# Create the sequential keras model`
8.
9. `#first layer with 8 neurons, mentioning the input layer as well`
10. `model.add(Dense(`**16**`, activation='relu',input_shape=X_train.shape[`**1**`:]))`
11.
12. `#adding layers to the DL model`
13.
14. `#First hidden layer with 16 neurons`

```
15. model.add(Dense(16, activation='relu'))
16.
17. #Second hidden layer with 16 neurons
18. model.add(Dense(16, activation='relu'))
19.
20. #Second hidden layer with 16 neurons
21. model.add(Dense(16, activation='relu'))
22.
23. #output layer with 1 neuron for regression predicted value
24. model.add(Dense(1))
25. from keras.utils import plot_model
26. plot_model(model, to_file='model_plot.png', show_shapes=True, show_
    layer_names=True)
```

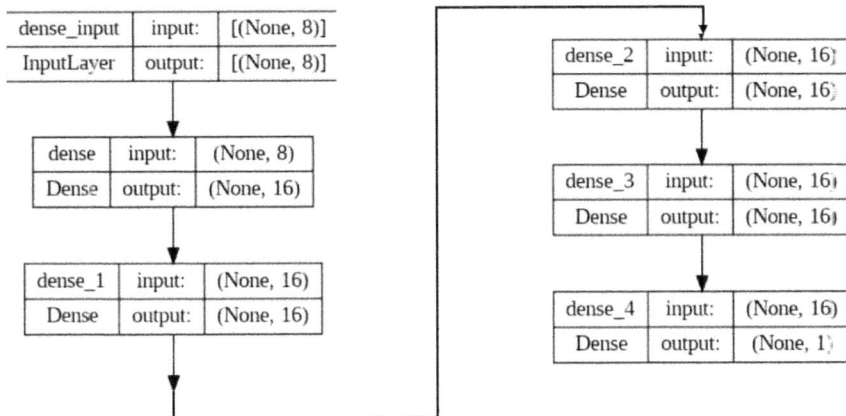

Figure 2.22: *ANN architecture*

Regression model training

Use the following code:

```
1. # Configure the model
2. model.compile(
3.     optimizer='adam',
4.     loss='mean_absolute_error',
5.     metrics=['mean_squared_error']
6. )
7. # Start model training phase
```

```
8.  history = model.fit(
9.  X_train,
10. y_train,
11. batch_size=128,
12. validation_split=0.1,
13. epochs=500,
14. verbose=1,
15. )
16. Score,mse_test = model.evaluate(X_test, y_test,batch_size=100)
17. print ('Train score',Score)
18. print ('MSE Error',mse_test)
```

Output:

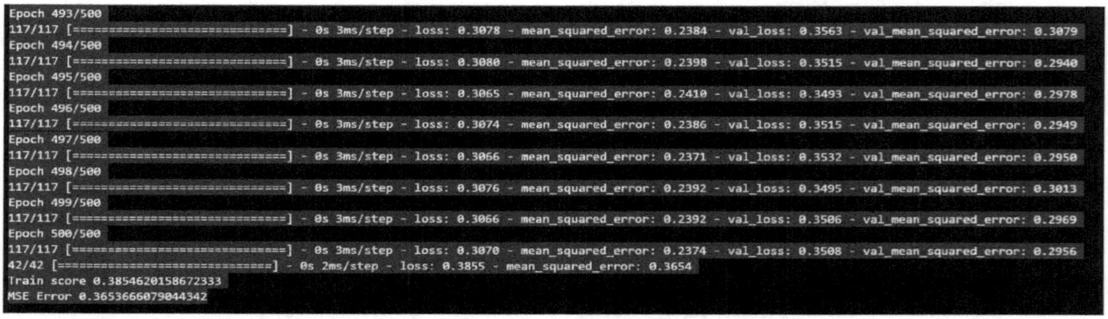

Figure 2.23: Model training output for epochs

Regression model testing

Use the following code:

```
1. plt.plot(history.history['loss'], color='g', label='Training loss')
2. plt.plot(history.history['val_loss'], color='b', label='Validation loss')
3. plt.title('Model loss progress during training the model')
4. plt.xlabel('Epochs')
5. plt.ylabel('Training loss & Validation Loss')
6. plt.legend()
7. plt.show()
```

Output:

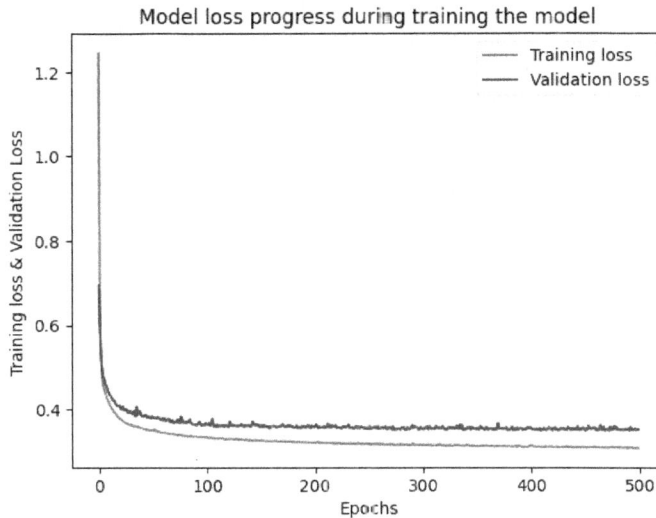

Figure 2.24: Loss curve

Now, execute the following code:

```
1.  from sklearn import metrics
2.  MAE = metrics.mean_absolute_error(y_test, y_pred)
3.  MSE = metrics.mean_squared_error(y_test, y_pred)
4.  RMSE= np.sqrt(metrics.mean_squared_error(y_test, y_pred))
5.  n = len(X_test)
6.  k = X_test.shape[1]
7.  r2 = metrics.r2_score(y_test, y_pred)
8.  adj_r2 = 1-(1-r2)*(n-1)/(n-k-1)
9.  print('RMSE =', RMSE, '\nMSE=', MSE, '\nMAE=', MAE,'\nAdjusted R2=',
    adj_r2)
10. print('Varscore:', metrics.explained_variance_score(y_test,y_pred))
```

Output:

```
RMSE = 0.6044556435909171
MSE= 0.3653666250689097
MAE= 0.3854620202028289
Adjusted R2= 0.7184635751284362
Varscore: 0.7264483504572458
```

Figure 2.25: Error metric

```
1. fig=plt.figure(figsize=(10,5))
2. plt.scatter(y_test, y_pred)
3. plt.plot(y_test,y_test,'r')
```

Output:

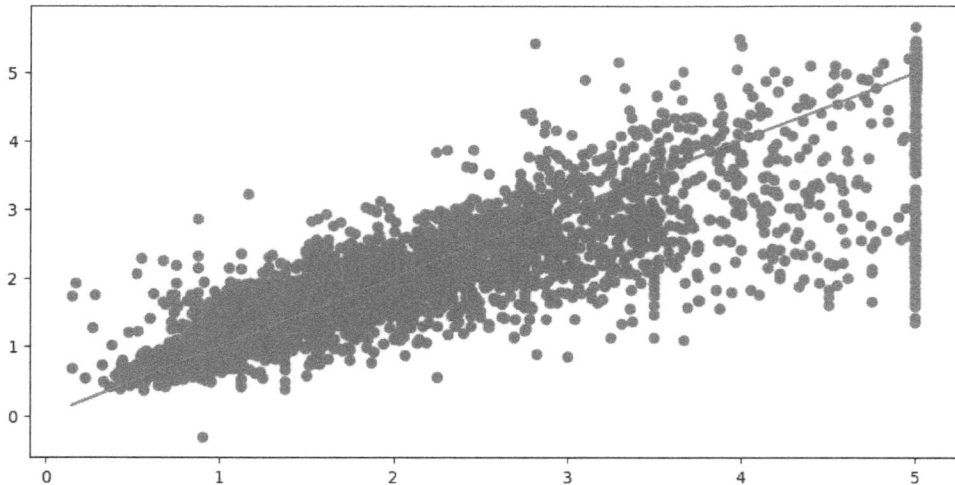

Figure 2.26: Regression line plot

Artificial neural network: Classification problem

Our business problem is a classification problem wherein we have a dataset with details of a bank's customers, and the target variable is a binary variable reflecting the fact whether the customer will leave the bank (closed his/her account) or continues to be a customer. Execute the following code:

Import libraries

```
1. import numpy as np # linear algebra
```

2. ```import``` pandas as pd # data processing, CSV file I/O (e.g. pd.read_csv)

3. ```import``` os

4. ```#try```:

5.   #   ```import``` theano

6. ```#except```:

7.   #   !pip install **Theano**

8. ```#import``` theano

9. ```import``` keras

10. ```import``` tensorflow

11. ```import``` matplotlib.pyplot as plt

12. ```import``` seaborn as sns

Loading dataset

1. # *Importing the dataset*

2. ```import``` pandas ```as``` pd

3. ```from``` google.colab ```import``` files

4. data_to_load = files.upload()

5. churn_data = pd.read_csv('**Churn_Modelling.csv**')

6. churn_data.info()

Output:

```
<class 'pandas.core.frame.DataFrame'>
RangeIndex: 10000 entries, 0 to 9999
Data columns (total 14 columns):
 #   Column           Non-Null Count  Dtype
---  ------           --------------  -----
 0   RowNumber        10000 non-null  int64
 1   CustomerId       10000 non-null  int64
 2   Surname          10000 non-null  object
 3   CreditScore      10000 non-null  int64
 4   Geography        10000 non-null  object
 5   Gender           10000 non-null  object
 6   Age              10000 non-null  int64
 7   Tenure           10000 non-null  int64
 8   Balance          10000 non-null  float64
 9   NumOfProducts    10000 non-null  int64
 10  HasCrCard        10000 non-null  int64
 11  IsActiveMember   10000 non-null  int64
 12  EstimatedSalary  10000 non-null  float64
 13  Exited           10000 non-null  int64
dtypes: float64(2), int64(9), object(3)
memory usage: 1.1+ MB
```

Figure 2.27: Churn modeling dataset columns

```
1. churn_data.describe()
```

Output:

	RowNumber	CustomerId	CreditScore	Age	Tenure	Balance	NumOfProducts	HasCrCard	IsActiveMember	EstimatedSalary	Exited
count	10000.00000	1.000000e+04	10000.000000	10000.000000	10000.000000	10000.000000	10000.000000	10000.00000	10000.000000	10000.000000	10000.000000
mean	5000.50000	1.569094e+07	650.528800	38.921800	5.012800	76485.889288	1.530200	0.70550	0.515100	100090.239881	0.203700
std	2886.89568	7.193619e+04	96.653299	10.487806	2.892174	62397.405202	0.581654	0.45584	0.499797	57510.492818	0.402769
min	1.00000	1.556570e+07	350.000000	18.000000	0.000000	0.000000	1.000000	0.00000	0.000000	11.580000	0.000000
25%	2500.75000	1.562853e+07	584.000000	32.000000	3.000000	0.000000	1.000000	0.00000	0.000000	51002.110000	0.000000
50%	5000.50000	1.569074e+07	652.000000	37.000000	5.000000	97198.540000	1.000000	1.00000	1.000000	100193.915000	0.000000
75%	7500.25000	1.575323e+07	718.000000	44.000000	7.000000	127644.240000	2.000000	1.00000	1.000000	149388.247500	0.000000
max	10000.00000	1.581569e+07	850.000000	92.000000	10.000000	250898.090000	4.000000	1.00000	1.000000	199992.480000	1.000000

Figure 2.28: Churn modeling dataset statistics

```
1. churn_data.head()
```

Output:

RowNumber	CustomerId	Surname	CreditScore	Geography	Gender	Age	Tenure	Balance	NumOfProducts	HasCrCard	IsActiveMember	EstimatedSalary	Exited
1	15634602	Hargrave	619	France	Female	42	2	0.00	1	1	1	101348.88	1
2	15647311	Hill	608	Spain	Female	41	1	83807.86	1	0	1	112542.58	0
3	15619304	Onio	502	France	Female	42	8	159660.80	3	1	0	113931.57	1
4	15701354	Boni	699	France	Female	39	1	0.00	2	0	0	93826.63	0
5	15737888	Mitchell	850	Spain	Female	43	2	125510.82	1	1	1	79084.10	0

Figure 2.29: Top 5 rows of churn dataset

```
1. # some columns are totally unproductive so let's remove them
2. churn_data.drop(['CustomerId','Surname'],axis=1,inplace=True)
3. Geography_dummies    =    pd.get_dummies(prefix='Geo',data=churn_
   data,columns=['Geography'])
4. Gender_dummies    =    Geography_dummies.replace(to_replace={'Gender':
   {'Female': 1,'Male':0}})
5. Gender_dummies.head()
```

Output:

RowNumber	CreditScore	Gender	Age	Tenure	Balance	NumOfProducts	HasCrCard	IsActiveMember	EstimatedSalary	Exited	Geo_France	Geo_Germany	Geo_Spain
1	619	1	42	2	0.00	1	1	1	101348.88	1	1	0	0
2	608	1	41	1	83807.86	1	0	1	112542.58	0	0	0	1
3	502	1	42	8	159660.80	3	1	0	113931.57	1	1	0	0
4	699	1	39	1	0.00	2	0	0	93826.63	0	1	0	0
5	850	1	43	2	125510.82	1	1	1	79084.10	0	0	0	1

Figure 2.30: Top 5 rows of Gender_dummies dataset

Exploratory data analysis

Refer the following code for reference:

```
1.  sns.countplot(y=churn_data_encoded.Exited ,data=churn_data_encoded)
2.  plt.xlabel("Count of each Target class")
3.  plt.ylabel("Target classes")
4.  plt.show()
5.
6.  churn_data_encoded.hist(figsize=(15,12),bins = 15)
7.  plt.title("Features Distribution")
8.  plt.show()
9.
10. plt.figure(figsize=(15,15))
11. p=sns.heatmap(churn_data_encoded.corr(), annot=True,cmap='RdYl-
    Gn',center=0)
12.
13.
14. #Train & Test Split
15. X = churn_data_encoded.drop(['Exited'],axis=1)
16. y = churn_data_encoded.Exited
17.
18. # Splitting the dataset into the Training set and Test set
19. from sklearn.model_selection import train_test_split
20. X_trair, X_test, y_train, y_test = train_test_split(X, y, test_size =
    0.33, random_state = 0)
21.
22.
23. # Feature Scaling because yes we don't want one independent variable
    dominating the other and it makes computations easy
24. from sklearn.preprocessing import StandardScaler
25. sc = StandardScaler()
26. X_train = sc.fit_transform(X_train)
27. X_test = sc.transform(X_test)
28.
29. #Creating Model
```

```
30. # sequential model to initialise our ann and dense module to build the
    layers
31. from keras.models import Sequential
32. from keras.layers import Dense
33. classifier = Sequential()
34. # Adding the input layer and the first hidden layer
35. classifier.add(Dense(units = 6, kernel_initializer = 'uniform',
    activation = 'relu', input_dim = 12))
36.
37. # Adding the second hidden layer
38. classifier.add(Dense(units = 6, kernel_initializer = 'uniform',
    activation = 'relu'))
39.
40. # Adding the output layer
41. classifier.add(Dense(units = 1, kernel_initializer = 'uniform',
    activation = 'sigmoid'))
```

Output:

```
Model: "sequential_5"

_____
 Layer (type)                Output Shape              Param #
=================================================================
 dense_15 (Dense)            (None, 6)                 78

 dense_16 (Dense)            (None, 6)                 42

 dense_17 (Dense)            (None, 1)                 7

=================================================================
```

Figure 2.31: ANN model architecture

Training model

Use the following code to train model:

```
1. # Compiling the ANN | means applying SGD on the whole ANN
2. classifier.compile(optimizer = 'adam', loss = 'binary_crossentropy',
   metrics = ['accuracy'])
3. # Fitting the ANN to the Training set
4. classifier.fit(X_train, y_train, batch_size = 10, epochs = 100,verbose
   = 1)
```

Output:

Figure 2.32: Model training output

Testing model

Use the following code to test the model:

```
1.  score, acc = classifier.evaluate(X_train, y_train,
2.                                    batch_size=10)
3.  print('Train score:', score)
4.  print('Train accuracy:', acc)
5.  # Part 3 - Making predictions and evaluating the model
6.
7.  # Predicting the Test set results
8.  y_pred = classifier.predict(X_test)
9.  y_pred = (y_pred > 0.5)
10.
11. print('*'*20)
12. score, acc = classifier.evaluate(X_test, y_test,
13.                                   batch_size=10)
14. print('Test score:', score)
```

```
15. print('Test accuracy:', acc)
16. # Making the Confusion Matrix
17. from sklearn.metrics import confusion_matrix
18. cm = confusion_matrix(y_test, y_pred)
```

Output:

```
670/670 [==============================] - 1s 898us/step - loss: 0.4934 - accuracy: 0.7979
Train score: 0.4933762550354004
Train accuracy: 0.7979104518890381
104/104 [==============================] - 0s 798us/step
*********************
330/330 [==============================] - 0s 963us/step - loss: 0.5071 - accuracy: 0.7930
Test score: 0.507054328918457
Test accuracy: 0.793030321598053
```

Figure 2.33: Train and test accuracy scores

Metric evaluation

Refer the following code for reference:

```
1. p = sns.heatmap(pd.DataFrame(cm), annot=True, cmap="YlGnBu" ,fmt='g')
2. plt.title('Confusion matrix', y=1.1)
3. plt.ylabel('Actual label')
4. plt.xlabel('Predicted label')
```

Output:

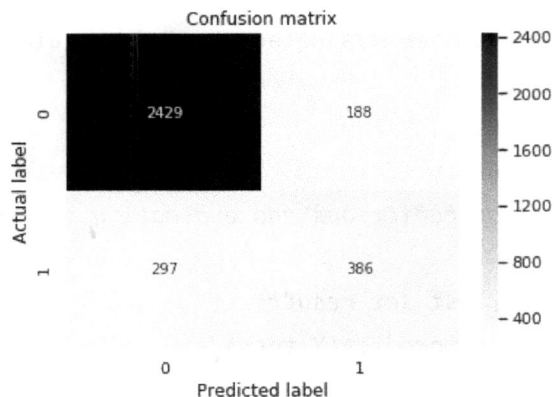

Figure 2.34: Confusion matrix

```
1. #import classification_report
2. from sklearn.metrics import classification_report
3. print(classification_report(y_test,y_pred))
```

Output:

	precision	recall	f1-score	support
0	0.89	0.93	0.91	2617
1	0.67	0.57	0.61	683
micro avg	0.85	0.85	0.85	3300
macro avg	0.78	0.75	0.76	3300
weighted avg	0.85	0.85	0.85	3300

Figure 2.35: Model performance metrics

Area under ROC curve

```
1. from sklearn.metrics import roc_curve
2. y_pred_proba = classifier.predict_proba(X_test)
3. fpr, tpr, thresholds = roc_curve(y_test, y_pred_proba)
4. plt.plot([0,1],[0,1],'k--')
5. plt.plot(fpr,tpr, label='ANN')
6. plt.xlabel('fpr')
7. plt.ylabel('tpr')
8. plt.title('ROC curve')
9. plt.show()
```

Output:

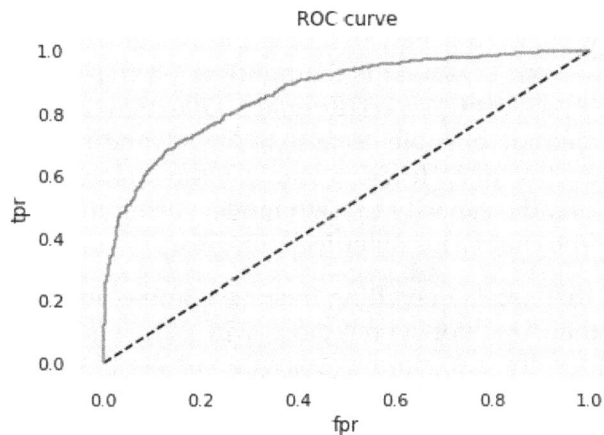

Figure 2.36: Area under ROC curve

```
1. from sklearn.metrics import roc_auc_score
2. roc_auc_score(y_test,y_pred_proba)
```

Output:

```
array([4.526, 3.585, 3.521, ..., 0.923, 0.847, 0.894])
```

Figure 2.37: Output

Introduction to generative AI

When we first encountered the term GenAI, many of us might have thought, Wow! This can make our lives so much easier. However, our second thought might have been filled with concern: Will GenAI replace our jobs? This reaction is entirely natural and has occurred whenever a disruptive technology has transitioned from invention to innovation. It is crucial for us to acknowledge this reality and formulate a strategy for embracing this technology. To successfully adopt it, one of the most important steps is to begin by gaining knowledge and understanding of the technology, exploring its potential use cases from various perspectives, scenarios, and different levels of complexity, limitations, and side effects.

In this chapter, we will provide an introductory overview of GenAI, offering a birds-eye view of this fascinating field.

Generative artificial intelligence

In the previous chapter, we introduced the concept of AI, but let us delve deeper to gain a clearer understanding of GenAI. GenAI, is a subset of deep learning within AI. It possesses a remarkable ability to autonomously generate new content, text, images, and more. These outputs are created by analyzing vast datasets and recognizing patterns within them. A major breakthrough event of GenAI is the building up the Transformer model in the *Attention Is All You Need* paper (**https://arxiv.org/abs/1706.03762**). The development of such powerful architecture became possible because of the advancements in the AI field, such as improved and innovative deep learning models, the scalability of computing power offered by cloud services, the capacity to train models using the immense data available on the entire internet, and numerous other technologies.

GenAI is a type of AI that excels in crafting fresh text, audio, images, and synthetic data. It is essential to note that AI is not synonymous with ML, which you may already have grasped. AI is a broader domain, similar to a vast subject like mathematics, while ML is a subset of AI. Similarly, deep learning is a component of ML, characterized by more advanced models such as ANNs, which draw inspiration from the structure of the human neural network. Furthermore, deep Learning can be categorized into two primary types: Discriminative and generative. Discriminative models predict different levels or categories for data, aiding in classification. On the other hand, generative models generate entirely new data based on probability distributions, contributing to the creation of novel content. Take a look at the following figure:

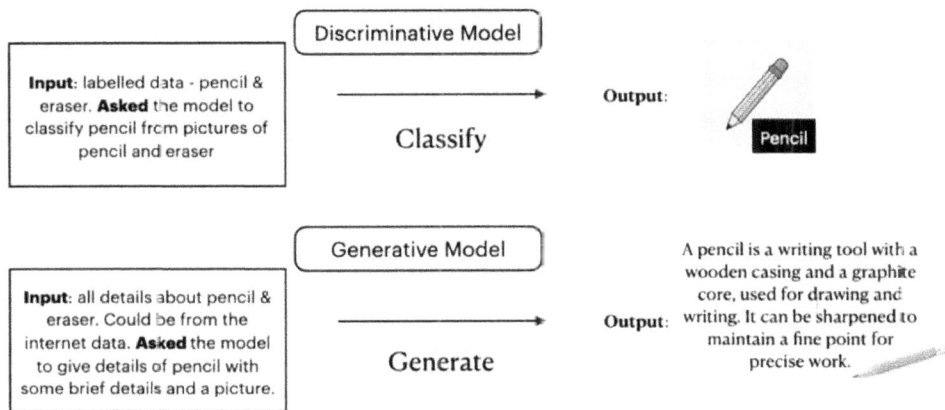

Figure 2.38: Discriminative vs. generative model

GenAI makes use of the power of ANNs to process both labeled and unlabeled data. It operates within the fields of supervised, unsupervised, and semi-supervised learning, making it incredibly versatile. These data are processed through a foundational model like GPT-3 LLM. ChatGPT is a specific implementation of GenAI built by the Company *OpenAI* to generate human-like responses. Similarly, there are other implementations, such as DALL-E 2, that can create realistic images from descriptions in a natural language.

Foundation models like GPT-3 have 175 billion parameters, and the model is trained on 50s of GB datasets, which is 10x larger than its predecessor. Evolution of GPT looks like GPT-1 was introduced in 2018 with 11 billion parameters, GPT-2 by 2019 with 1.5 billion, GPT-3 by 2020 with 175 billion parameters, GPT-3.5 from ChatGPT by 2022 and GPT-4.0 by 2023 with so called one trillion parameters.

These models are pre-trained on extensive text data, such as ChatGPT, which is trained on a vast corpus of internet text. They are trained on a monumental scale, processing internet data and are capable of performing a multitude of tasks, including the creation of entirely new content. When it comes to the dataset, 60% of the GPT-3 corpus is said to be from a common crawl that has been collected over years. The other sources of data used for model training are from WebText, books, Wikipedia and customer feedbacks.

Understanding GenAI becomes even more comprehensive when we visualize its capabilities. We believe that now, armed with some insight into GenAI, it is the perfect time to explore a couple of visual representations of its potential. Take a look at the following figure:

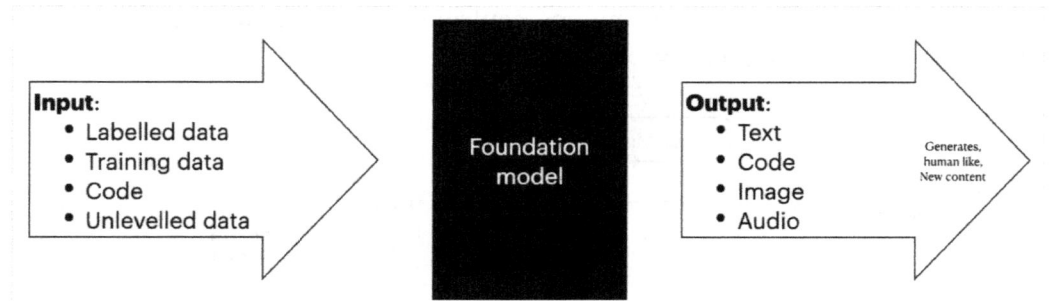

Figure 2.39: GenAI model designed to produce output similar to above

A straightforward method for choosing a GenAI model or system is if the AI system needs to provide outputs in the form of numbers or classifications, it is safe to conclude that it is not a GenAI model. Instead, GenAI models are designed to produce outputs resembling natural language, images, or even audio—much like the creativity and novelty we expect from humans. Let us understand using the following figure:

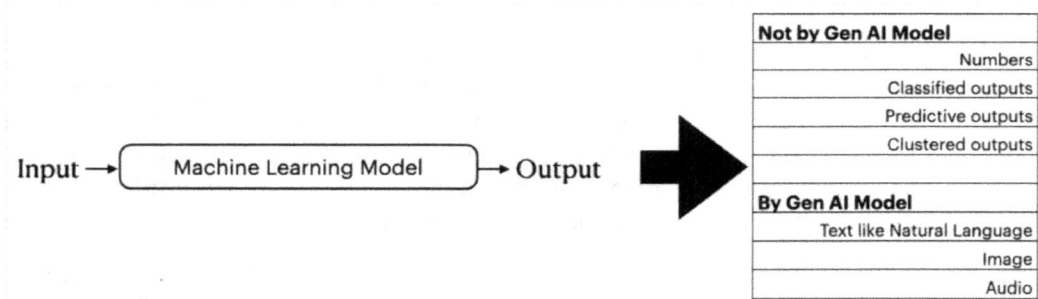

Figure 2.40: ANN model output vs GenAI output

Foundation model

A model comprises a set of algorithms trained on specific datasets and is tunable to various use cases. Think of a model as the brain of GenAI. The evolution of AI has been remarkable, progressing from rule-based algorithms to search and optimization engines, then to supervised and unsupervised ML, and further to **natural language processing (NLP)** in the realm of deep learning, ultimately transformer models like GPT and other models. The foundation for a foundational model is built upon the transformer kind architecture, deep learning principles, neural networks, and the concept of self-attention. One of the recent foundation models that is making waves are the GPT models for Text generation and diffusion model, primarily tailored for image generation, transitioning from noisy beginnings to the production of flawless target images. We will look into the details of transformer architecture and many foundation model architectures in upcoming chapters.

Prompt engineering

One of the most critical aspects of GenAI is mastering the art of prompting. To extract the desired outcome from AI system, understanding the process of prompting is paramount. **prompt design**, which involves creating prompts that fine-tune language models using APIs, is the initial step. In contrast, **prompt engineering** is for end-users seeking specific information from the language model, tailored to their requirements using simple text. Effective prompting leads to precise and desired responses. Prompting is all about providing the right context in simple text. Various methods exist to convey information to the model to obtain the best possible answer. This includes techniques like 0-shot, 1-shot, and few-shot prompting, where the number of examples given during the prompt aids in achieving a more specific response. Consider these examples (0, 1 or a few shots) as guidance. We will look into the details of prompt engineering in *Chapter 6, LLM Frameworks*.

Impact on industries and societies

GenAI and its diverse applications will leave a profound mark on every industry and society. Consider, for instance, its influence on customer experiences, manufacturing processes, product design, healthcare services, cybersecurity, agriculture practices, entertainment, education, research, and so on. The societal impact is monumental; GenAI will become an integral part of our daily lives. As it becomes more mature, we can anticipate new laws and policies coming into effect to govern its use. The nature of work is ready for transformation. Humans will shift their focus toward creativity and harnessing the productivity enhancements offered by powerful applications and tools underpinned by GenAI technology. It is all about leveraging its creativity and capacity to generate new content and faster, accurate. However, the extent of this impact depends entirely on how GenAI is employed and the value it generates.

Security, ethics and responsibilities

Ethical AI, also called **responsible AI**, means we must be responsible at all levels to make sure AI benefits people the most. Data, the fuel for GenAI, presents significant risks in terms of data breaches and misuse. Given that GenAI, along with AI in a broader sense, is ready to become one of the disruptive technologies, we must take utmost caution not only during its use but also during its design and planning phases. It is imperative to build a sense of responsibility regarding AI across all sectors of society and every industry and domain. Key principles such as data privacy, transparency in data usage, and the avoidance of bias must be embraced and widely promoted. Human oversight should extend from the initial design stages to usage and the review of AI-generated outputs.

Transparency, empathy, and fairness represent key areas where substantial work is required in the time of GenAI. These principles will naturally develop and solidify with time. It is essential to spread ethical guidelines widely and never lose sight of our primary objective: Elevating humanity through responsible AI practices adoption.

Sustainability

As GenAI and LLMs continue to grow, we must closely monitor the rapid rise in resource consumption and associated costs. It is imperative to proactively limit resource consumption and utilization to enhance efficiency. Greater efficiency directly correlates with reduced carbon emissions and minimized environmental impacts. Training a LLM demands a substantial quantity of computational resources, including CPUs, GPUs, and TPUs, and required to run for an extended period of time. This incurs significant costs and places a heavy demand on natural resources, resulting in elevated carbon emissions. In addition to security and ethics, it is our responsibility to consider how we design and optimize resource usage. To illustrate, if we have a specific use case for GenAI and require a language model, we should acquire data and resources tailored to the target use case to produce contextually accurate outputs. While we may possess ample computing resources and budget, it is important not to use foundational models for specific use cases, as this could result in avoidable environmental impacts. In *Chapter 10 Generative AI: Advances and Sustainability* we will look into tools and details about the considerations related to sustainabilitiy.

Limitations

It is essential to acknowledge that GenAI, despite its remarkable capabilities, has its present-day limitations. However, these limitations hold the promise of evolving into tomorrow's possibilities. When creating solutions, it is crucial to chart a roadmap from the perspective of GenAI, envisioning these current limitations fading away as your solution becomes increasingly potent with each passing day. Much like how humans often face with the challenge of saying no and sometimes provide incorrect information to avoid it, GenAI faces a similar hurdle—it lacks the capacity to decline. Instead, it might hallucinate or generate responses even when it should not. Understanding this limitation is crucial, and caution should be exercised when considering information generated by GenAI tools. This is where the roles of prompt engineering and prompt design become pivotal.

Another limitation today pertains to the difficulty of maintaining real-time training data and obtaining responses aligned with real-time information. However, this is a challenge that will likely be overcome as AI agent technology advances. The other challenges is token limitations, which restrict the length of generated content, are essentially a matter of time. As demand grows, we can anticipate these limitations expanding to accommodate more extensive content. Ethical concerns, biased decision-making, copyright issues, and security remain major challenges in the present landscape. Various industry bodies, geographic regions, and countries are actively formulating rules and regulations governing the use of GenAI. Once these frameworks are established and refined, we can expect a massive growth in the adoption and utilization of GenAI.

GenAI promises to elevate every work of our daily life. Failing to embrace this transformative technology could mean gradually declining our competitive edge in an evolving world. Before starting on any GenAI venture, it is essential to define your objective or the problem you aim to solve. Whether you are assisting researchers in extracting precise answers from lengthy research documents, building knowledge and capabilities for yourself or your team, or simply seeking the data to fuel your models, the journey begins with a clear purpose. Some of the consideration for any GenAI project are Choose the right model, platform, tools and finally must have continuous evaluation of GenAI implementations. Besides that, balancing compliance and data security, while emphasizing sustainability through lean model practices, is crucial.

Over time, the algorithms will keep evolving, which will demand less computational power, models capable of handling more tokens, and GenAI growing in strength. The potential contributions of AI to our lives are nothing short of extraordinary, possibly solving today's unsolved problems.

Generative AI use cases

GenAI as a technology is a game changer due to its immense potential to create high-value artifacts, generate images from text, ability to contextualize and decipher subtleties and its ability to create content that has not been created before. These possibilities are forcing us to reimagine how we interact with the world around us. While the hype of this technology is expected to subside as real implementations get rolled out, its impact is expected to grow with new use cases being discovered and implemented. In a recent *Gartner webinar* poll of more than 2,500 executives, 38% indicated that customer experience and retention is the primary purpose of their GenAI investments. This was followed by revenue growth (26%), cost optimization (17%) and business continuity (7%).

Several industries like financial services, healthcare, pharmaceutical, manufacturing, retail, automotive, aerospace etc. as well as enterprise functions such as marketing, recruitment, corporate communications, training and software engineering will see the value of GenAI in augmenting their current processes and functions

In-use, high-level practical applications today include the following:

- **Content generation**
  - o **Text generation**: Automating content creation for articles, blogs, social media posts, and more.
  - o **Code generation**: Generating code snippets and scripts for software development.
  - o **Creative writing**: Assisting writers and poets in generating ideas, plot points, or entire stories.

- **Translation**
  - o Translating text between languages with high accuracy.
- **Conversational agents**
  - o **Chatbots**: Creating chatbots and virtual assistants for customer support, information retrieval, and more.
  - o **Voice assistants**: Powering voice-activated virtual assistants like Siri and Alexa.
  - o **language tutoring**: Providing language learning support through conversation.
- **Content summarization**
  - o Automatically generating concise and coherent summaries of lengthy texts, such as news articles or research papers.
- **Content recommendations**
  - o Personalizing content recommendations for users in entertainment (movies, music, books) and e-commerce.
- **Image and video generation**
  - o Generating images, artwork, or videos based on textual descriptions or concepts.
  - o Deepfake technology for video manipulation and editing.
- **Gaming and entertainment**
  - o Creating characters, dialogue, and storylines for video games.
  - o Generating music and soundtracks.
  - o Creating visual effects and graphics.
- **Simulations and training**
  - o Developing realistic simulations for training purposes, such as flight simulators or medical simulations.
- **Virtual reality (VR) and augmented reality (AR) experiences**
  - o There is no limit to the number of use cases being explored under the GenAI ambit, but trying to capture the most commonly discussed ones, we have categorized the top few as per the framework outlined below.

Take a look at the following figure:

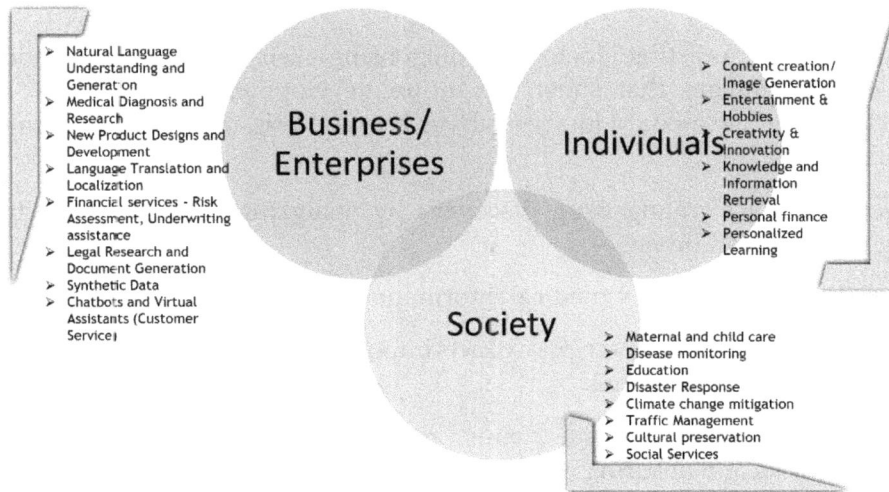

Figure 2.41: GenAI use cases

Business/Enterprises

Let us take a look at each use case one by one:

Financial services

Financial analysis and predictive modeling: GenAI models leverage historical financial data to comprehend intricate patterns and correlations, empowering them to perform predictive analysis on forthcoming trends, asset valuations, and economic indicators. When appropriately calibrated, these models can simulate diverse scenarios encompassing market conditions, macroeconomic variables, and other factors. This capability delivers valuable insights into potential risks and opportunities in the financial landscape.

GenAI is a valuable tool for enhancing fraud detection in finance. It achieves this by creating synthetic examples of fraudulent transactions, improving the ML algorithm's ability to identify suspicious activities accurately. By implementing GenAI in fraud detection systems, financial institutions can enhance security, minimize financial losses due to fraud, and maintain consumer trust.

GenAI finds a practical application in financial tasks like portfolio management and risk management. By analyzing historical financial data and generating diverse investment scenarios, it assists asset managers and investors in optimizing portfolios. It factors in risk tolerance, expected returns, and investment horizons. GenAI models simulate various market conditions and economic events to assess their impact on portfolio performance, aiding financial professionals in refining investment strategies and making well-informed decisions. This ultimately results in improved financial outcomes for clients or institutions.

Healthcare

Medical diagnosis: Assisting doctors in diagnosing diseases based on patient data. Creating medical images that show the future development of a disease. Enhance, reconstruct, or generate medical images such as X-rays, MRIs, or CT scans, aiding in more accurate diagnoses.

Drug discovery: Accelerating drug discovery by analyzing molecular structures and predicting potential candidates.

Healthcare chatbots: Providing medical information and answering patient queries.

Automating the creation of transcripts extracts important details and generates summaries from clinician-patient interactions.

Automate the coding of medical claims, reducing billing timeframes, errors, and administrative tasks and ensuring compliance with regulatory requirements.

By considering a patient's genetics, lifestyle, and symptoms, GenAI can create personalized treatment plans.

Manufacturing

GenAI rapidly generates and evaluates numerous design alternatives, aiding manufacturers in discovering the most optimized, efficient, and cost-effective solutions for product design optimization. Generative conversational agents can undergo training on product manuals, troubleshooting guides, and maintenance records to deliver rapid technical support to workers, thereby reducing downtime. GenAI can mimic production processes to detect enhancements, uncover concealed insights, validate models using synthetic data, and enhance predictive accuracy, all without causing disruptions to operations.

Retail

Virtual try-ons: Retailers, especially in apparel and beauty, can leverage GenAI to create highly realistic images that allow customers to virtually try on products, enabling a magic mirror experience to visualize how different items, styles, and colors would look on them. It can also predict how the fit may change over time.

Merchandising: GenAI can optimize store layouts and product placements by analyzing product attributes, historical sales data, and customer preferences. This technology can enhance personalized shopping experiences through real-time wayfinding, guiding customers to products aligned with their unique preferences.

Personalized shopping assistance: Imagine an AI-based app that guides shoppers through a store, proactively recommending products tailored to individual preferences and current needs, whether it is dietary-specific food items or the latest fashion trends.

Demand forecasting: Retailers can use GenAI along with other forecasting models to gain more accurate insights into future demand by considering diverse data sources like historical sales, market trends, weather conditions, and social media sentiment. This allows for better inventory management, reduced stockouts, minimized excess inventory, and improved operational efficiency.

Product design: GenAI can aid in generating brand-relevant and on-trend product designs instantly by refining its capabilities based on existing designs and data sources. Furthermore, it allows customers to customize products to their unique needs, fostering on-demand customization.

Developer productivity improvement can be brought about by GenAI-powered tools across a range of tasks, such as streamlining repetitive work, taking on routine tasks such as auto-generating standard code functions, suggesting code completions in real-time, and generating code documentation based on developer prompts. By automating these mundane tasks, developers gain more time and flexibility to tackle complex business challenges and expedite the development of innovative software features. GenAI tools can help kickstart the initial drafting of code, where developers can simply input prompts into a dedicated window or **integrated development environment** (**IDE**), where the tools provide helpful code suggestions. This aids developers in overcoming writer's block and accelerates the commencement of their work, fostering a smoother transition into a productive workflow and speeding up code modifications by offering efficient ways to adapt and enhance existing code. Developers can effortlessly copy and paste code from online libraries and iteratively query the tool to tailor it according to their specific criteria, saving valuable time. GenAI tools enhance problem-solving capabilities through rapid knowledge acquisition for navigating unfamiliar code bases and assisting with new challenges by explaining concepts, synthesizing information, and offering step-by-step guidance, ultimately boosting developers effectiveness.

Individuals

GenAI can be a valuable tool for individuals to streamline tasks, foster creativity, enhance their personal lives and productivity as follows:

- **Creativity**: Generate articles, essays, or creative writing prompts. Spark creative ideas for personal projects or business ventures. Game developers can use AI to generate game content and create more dynamic and immersive gaming experiences.

- **Language learning**: Provide language translation, grammar correction, or vocabulary expansion.

- **Tutoring**: Assist in understanding complex subjects through explanations and practice questions. AI-powered educational tools can provide personalized learning experiences and help students better understand complex subjects.

- **Hobbies**: Compose music, generate lyrics, or produce visual art for personal enjoyment. Assist in planning trips, including itinerary suggestions and accommodation options.

Society

Public services are increasingly utilizing AI technology to enhance their efficiency. An example is the *City of Kelowna,* which employed *Azure OpenAI Service* and *Azure Cognitive Search* to develop an intelligent search solution. This system responds to citizen requests using publicly accessible data while safeguarding data privacy. By efficiently managing routine tasks like snowplowing schedule updates, the city has optimized its services, freeing up human resources to address more intricate queries, and ultimately enhancing the quality of service delivery.

Optimizing emergency response: Improving preparedness and efficiency

GenAI has the capacity to process extensive datasets, enhancing the ability to predict and manage emergencies with greater efficiency. This empowers governments to make data-informed choices, allocate resources optimally, and ultimately, safeguard lives during critical situations.

GenAI can help with public health tracking by enhancing disease surveillance, outbreak prediction, and resource management. It can detect disease outbreaks early by analyzing diverse data sources, monitoring anomaly to flag unusual health trends, and using geospatial analysis to track disease spread. AI-driven epidemiological models can simulate disease propagation, genomic analysis aids in understanding pathogen behavior, and healthcare data analysis can help identify at-risk populations.

Urban planning and infrastructure development: Shaping future cities

By utilizing advanced simulations, GenAI can assist in urban planning and infrastructure development, enabling governments to design cities that are sustainable, effective, and centered around citizens. An improved living environment for residents can be designed considering various factors like traffic, access to public services, air quality, optimizing land utilization, and creating green spaces.

Choosing the right use cases

Choosing the right use cases for GenAI involves careful consideration of the organization's goals, resources, and the specific challenges to address. Be mindful of ethical and legal considerations when selecting use cases and ensure the GenAI applications comply with data privacy regulations, avoid biases, and respect user consent. In certain instances, GenAI may not be the most suitable choice.

McKinsey research shows GenAI can significantly boost productivity in specific marketing scenarios, such as analyzing unstructured and abstract data to discern customer preferences (resulting in a roughly 10% increase) and in customer support through the implementation of intelligent bots (resulting in potential gains of up to 40%). Categorizing these use cases effectively, either by domain (such as customer journey or business process) or by use case type (such as creative content creation or virtual agents), ensuring that GenAI adds the most value would be a good starting point. The tricky part with GenAI is hallucination, leading to potentially flawed decision-making when used in production. Established strategies to reduce the risk of hallucinations in GenAI systems can encompass several measures like tailoring the model's creativity level, enhancing the model's knowledge by incorporating pertinent internal data to provide additional context, employing libraries or frameworks that set boundaries on the generated content, thereby ensuring responsible outputs, implementing moderation models to scrutinize and validate the generated outputs for compliance with guidelines and incorporating explicit disclaimers to clarify the nature of the content generated. In the early stages of deploying GenAI, it is advisable to focus on use cases where the consequences of errors are relatively low. This approach allows organizations to navigate and learn from inevitable challenges and setbacks as they arise, ultimately integrating these lessons into their processes. Detailed strategy for enterprises toward GenAI is discussed in *Chapter 9, Generative AI for the Enterprise*. Look at the chart below on various use case categorization and rating:

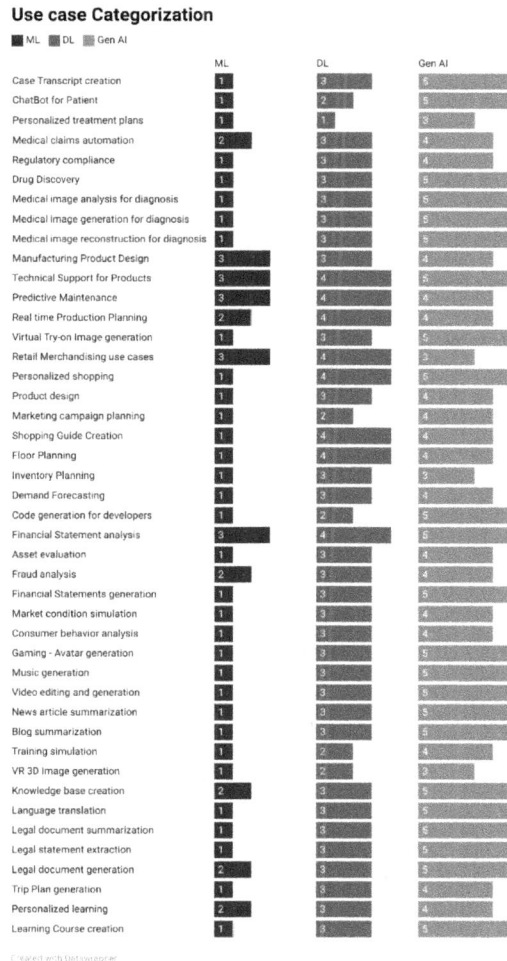

Use case Categorization

■ ML ■ DL ■ Gen AI

	ML	DL	Gen AI
Case Transcript creation	1	3	5
ChatBot for Patient	1	2	5
Personalized treatment plans	1	1	3
Medical claims automation	2	3	4
Regulatory compliance	1	3	4
Drug Discovery	1	3	5
Medical image analysis for diagnosis	1	3	5
Medical image generation for diagnosis	1	3	5
Medical image reconstruction for diagnosis	1	3	5
Manufacturing Product Design	3	3	4
Technical Support for Products	3	4	5
Predictive Maintenance	3	4	4
Real time Production Planning	2	4	4
Virtual Try-on Image generation	1	3	5
Retail Merchandising use cases	3	4	3
Personalized shopping	1	4	5
Product design	1	3	4
Marketing campaign planning	1	2	4
Shopping Guide Creation	1	4	4
Floor Planning	1	4	4
Inventory Planning	1	3	3
Demand Forecasting	1	3	4
Code generation for developers	1	2	5
Financial Statement analysis	3	4	5
Asset evaluation	1	3	4
Fraud analysis	2	3	4
Financial Statements generation	1	3	5
Market condition simulation	1	3	4
Consumer behavior analysis	1	3	4
Gaming - Avatar generation	1	3	5
Music generation	1	3	5
Video editing and generation	1	3	5
News article summarization	1	3	5
Blog summarization	1	3	5
Training simulation	1	2	4
VR 3D Image generation	1	2	3
Knowledge base creation	2	3	5
Language translation	1	3	5
Legal document summarization	1	3	5
Legal statement extraction	1	3	5
Legal document generation	2	3	5
Trip Plan generation	1	3	4
Personalized learning	2	3	4
Learning Course creation	1	3	5

Created with Datawrapper

Figure 2.42: *GenAI use cases categorization*
(Capabilities Rated 1-5 with 1 as low 5 as high)

Use case Categorization

▨ Demand ▨ Risk

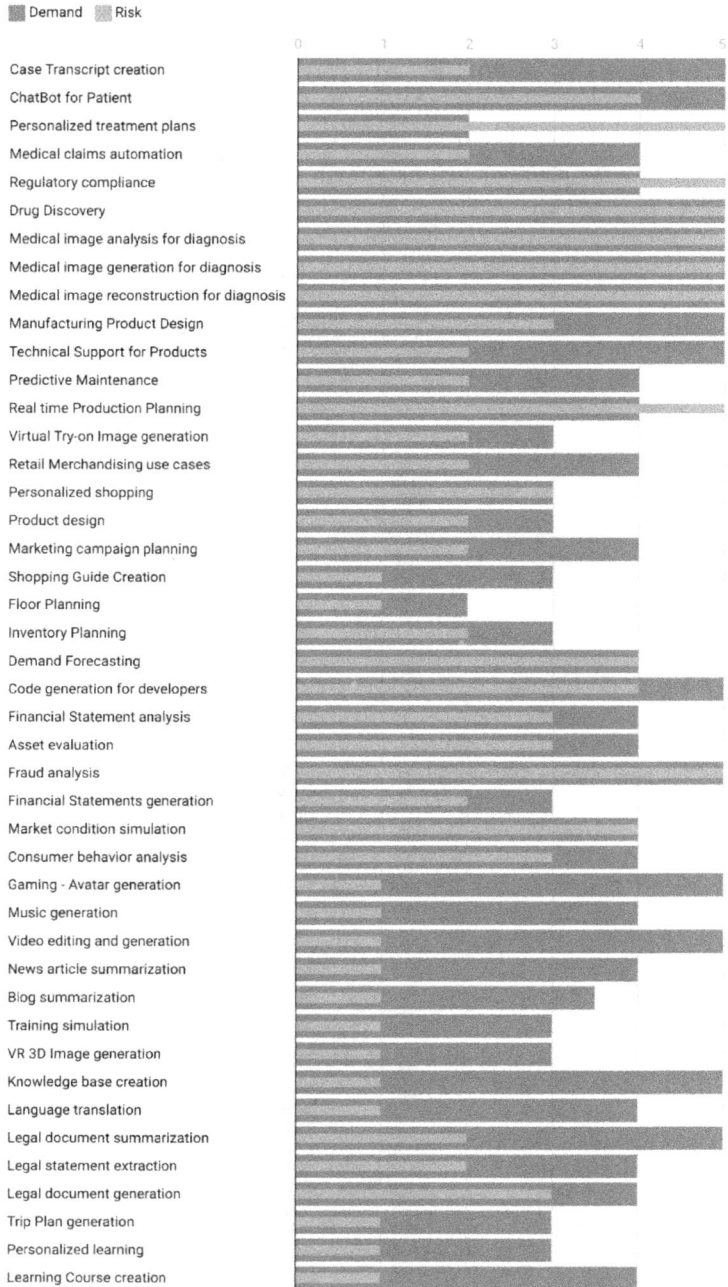

Figure 2.43: Use cases risk vs demand
(Risk and demand rated from 1-5 with 1 as low and 5 as high)

Conclusion

In this chapter we understood basic deep learning mathematics on vector, scalar, function types, differentiation and gradient concepts. In deep learning concepts, we explained the neural unit/neuron functions, single and multi-layer perceptron architecture, types of activation function, the activation function choices for different problems, concepts on bias, different cost function types. We understood the training of neural networks using gradient descent and backpropagation. We also understood various regularization techniques and different metrics to measure different types of deep learning models. We also presented examples on linear regression using ANN for predicting the median house value of the California housing dataset and churn classification for banking customers. We presented the basics of generative modeling and the difference between generative and non-generative output. Finally, we concluded with different use cases related to enterprise, personal and societal and the way to choose the use case for any generative model.

In the next chapter, we will be covering the GenAI modeling for Images and different techniques, algorithms, mathematics behind them.

Key terms

- Deep neural network
- Weights and biases
- Cost function
- Gradient descent
- Backpropagation
- Generalization error
- Hyperparameters
- Performance metrics
- Foundation model

Questions

1. What is the derivative of a function?
2. What are the different gradient descent algorithms?
3. How do we calculate the cost function in a classification problem?
4. What is the difference between loss function and accuracy?
5. What are the benefits of hyperparameter tuning?
6. What is meant by the chain rule in backpropagation space?
7. What are typical outputs of generative AI?
8. What are foundation models?

Join our book's Discord space

Join the book's Discord Workspace for Latest updates, Offers, Tech happenings around the world, New Release and Sessions with the Authors:

https://discord.bpbonline.com

## CHAPTER 3

GenAI for Images

Introduction

Computer vision (**CV**) technology has seen widespread adoption in various industries. It gives the machines a sense of sight to view and interpret the visual world in much the same way humans do. With generative AI becoming increasingly integrated to CV, the technology has demonstrated the ability to mimic human creativity. In this chapter we will understand **convolutional neural networks** (**CNN**) that lies at core of CV to process, analyze, and understand images and also look into representation learning methods like autoencoders and **variational autoencoders** (**VAE**) for approaching generative AI in CV field.

Structure

The chapter covers the following topics:

- Introduction to computer vision
- Representation learning

Objectives

This chapter introduces CV concepts, CNN and various CNN architectures. In the introduction to CV, we will understand the basics of image processing, different CV tasks, real world applications, and the evolution of different deep learning architectures to perform CV tasks. In convolution neural network, we will understand the concept of convolution operations and a working example of the same in U-Net architecture. Further, we will understand the concept of representation learning, and its techniques, such as autoencoders and VAE to do CV tasks. In the representation learning sections, we will understand the pros and cons of encoder-decoder architecture, different ways of encoding and decoding mechanisms, along with examples. Throughout this chapter, we will be discussing image processing techniques, neural architectures for image-based applications, image representation learning, mathematical briefing, and examples. The examples we have chosen are image segmentation based on U-Net architecture and image generation with VAE.

Introduction to computer vision

Computer vision (**CV**) is an AI field that enables machines to extract meaningful information from visual inputs like images and videos. This extracted information is used by deep convolutional neural networks to perform actions like image classification, image segmentation, object detection, object tracking and content-based image retrieval. In the past some of the CV applications are limited to **optical character recognition** (**OCR**) and **intelligent character recognition** (**ICR**) for document processing, vehicle plate recognition, etc. The flow of visual information from various devices and advances in neural networks, has enabled various applications across domains including retail, manufacturing, media, healthcare, automotive, etc.

Some real world CV applications are given below:

- Autonomous vehicles use cases, such as lane tracking, vehicle detection, traffic sign detection, pedestrian detection, path finder. For example, CV technology combines **Light Detection and Ranging (LiDAR)** cameras and smart sensors with CV models generate a three-dimensional map of the surroundings. While the LIDAR and radar sensors capture curvature, elevation changes, and potential obstacles,the sensors are used to identify objects and obstacle. CV models classify them and with help of automated steering controls it do driving adjustment and take decisions on speed, break and navigation. CV models are generally trained in co-ordination with reinforcement learning to get them familiarized with various road scenarios.

- Retail use cases, such as stock visibility, smart mirrors, cashier less stores, product recommendation, customer behavior analysis, crowd detection. For example, long checkout lines is been one of the major pain point of physical retail. Cashier less store enable customers to purchased product in physical stores without checkout lines. It uses CV and IoT sensors with other technologies to automate the checkout process. CV technology with help of on shelve cameras and ceiling cameras track shoppers' interactions with products: What they pick up, what they return to the shelves, and what they put in their basket. It helps to create a virtual basket for each shopper and supports multiple transactions. While camera processing helps to do simultaneous tracking and data processing, the weight sensors in the shelves help to validate and confirm each customer purchases. As customer exit, the checkout system automatically bills the virtual basket integrated to the payment systems.

- Healthcare use cases, such as medical imaging, cancer detection, disease detection, X-ray analysis, patient monitoring. For example, **remote patient monitoring (RPM)** for chronic conditions is one of the critical health care applications where traditional wearables and sensors are used for patient monitoring. These monitoring systems need frequent care-taker visits and requires continuous monitoring of vital signs for early interventions. With CV systems and AI enabled devices, most of the tasks are automated and managed remotely. Continuous stream of remote patient video feeds are analyzed in RPM devices installed in patient premises and as anomalies identified, alerts are generated to care-taker for immediate attention. CV is used in Fall detection, facial expressions, movements, and other physical indicators to detect potential risks or changes in health conditions. CV and AI technology has become cornerstone in RPM and enabling healthcare professionals to provide more personalized treatment strategies for acute illness.

- Agriculture use cases, such as crop analysis, detecting crop diseases, animal safety and health checks. For example, Digital technologies have shown tremendous potential to transform the agriculture sector. It has changed the farming practices catalyzing to country's rural economy. With AI it enhances further with precision farming. Drones with CV technologies are used in estimating the growth stage of crops to plan for different yields, aerial image segmentation of agricultural fields to identify weed densities enabling precision weed control, use of image tracking to track animals in pastures for monitoring their health and behavior. With integrated smart irrigation systems, soil moisture sensors and drone based aerial field survey, AI helps to adjust water applications contributing to efficient water management and irrigation control.

- Manufacturing use cases, such as defect detection, safety compliance, production line congestion detection, logistic planning, predictive maintenance, label tracking, package inspection. For example, CV in manufacturing help in capturing and understanding the visual inputs from the physical world, such as shop floors, and production lines to assist in various production processes. A simple use case could be correct labeling identification of products that is been shipped. A CV system could capture the Labeling images, do an OCR and ensures the correct labels been printed on the products. The other use case could identify production line congestions, where the high-speed production lines are continuously monitored by different cameras for movement of products and raised alters for immediate intervention if a congestion has occurred. The other use cased could be product dimension identification, where depth sensing cameras are used to identify the different dimensions of product to enable robotic systems for automatic packing or packaging. The most important use case is to identify the defect of the product, where the AI models are trained different defects to classify and segment defect regions under various luminous scenarios. The other use cases include media and entertainment use cases, such as content-based retrieval for digital asset management, video generation for marketing campaigns, and synthetic avatars for video games. Sports use cases, such as player tracking, pose estimation, match analysis. Safety system use cases, such as facial authentication, theft detection, face mask detection.

Some of the common CV tasks performed in the above use cases are given below:

- **Image classification**: The objective is to classify the image into one (binary) or more categories (multi-class). It is mostly a supervised learning problem where a set of labels are defined for images and models are trained to recognize them using labelled examples. For example, which type of dog is present in images.

- **Object detection**: The objective is to locate instances of objects and classify them in images or videos. Location of the object in the image is represented as a bounding box and its coordinates. Object detection generally has two tasks of locating and classifying the object. Object localization is a term used synonymously with object detection, where its objective is to identify the location of one or more objects in an image, while object detection identifies all objects and their bounding boxes. For example, detection of damages in assembly line.

- **Image segmentation**: Semantic segmentation classifies every pixel in the image to determine the type of objects. It segments out broad boundary of objects belonging to a particular class. Unlike semantic segmentation, instance segmentation classifies each instance of object not broad boundary. Panoptic segmentation combines instance and semantic methods to achieve simultaneous segmentation and classification task. For example segmented medical imaging for healthcare diagnostics.

- **Object tracking**: The objective is to estimate the object's position in each consecutive frame of the video. Here, target initialization with object detection methods is followed by location estimation, appearance modeling, motion estimation, and target positioning. Furthermore, it enables counting of unique objects in a video by assigning unique ID to each tracked object. For example, pedestrian tracking in autonomous vehicle.

The other areas of analysis are person segmentation, 3D Object reconstruction, key point detection and depth perception. Some of the considerations while performing the above tasks are variability in object appearance, scale variations, occlusions, background clutter and class variability.

Computer vision architectures

There are various deep neural network architectures used in CV. As shown in *Figure 3.1,* some popular architectures are AlexNet, VGG, ResNet, MobileNet, and EfficientNet. CNN is the most widely used architecture for CV related tasks. *Figure 3.1* explains the evolution of different CV architectures. State-of-the-art, transformer-based, and diffusion-based architectures will be discussed in *Chapter 4, Computer Vision for Image Part II*.

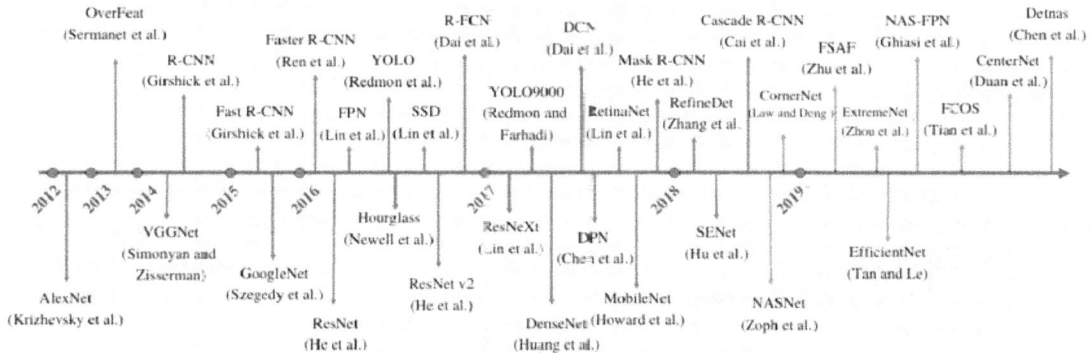

Figure 3.1: *CV techniques evolution from 2012 to 2019*
(**Source**: *https://www.researchgate.net/figure/Computer-Vision-Techniques-evolution-from-2012-to-2019-78-Alex-Net-78-Boosted-Cascade_fig3_350085174*)

- **AlexNet 2012**: It is the first deep convolutional networks to achieve considerable accuracy on the 2012 ImageNet. It has five convolution layers and three **fully connected** (**FC**) layers with activation as shown in the below *Figure 3.2* AlexNet architecture:

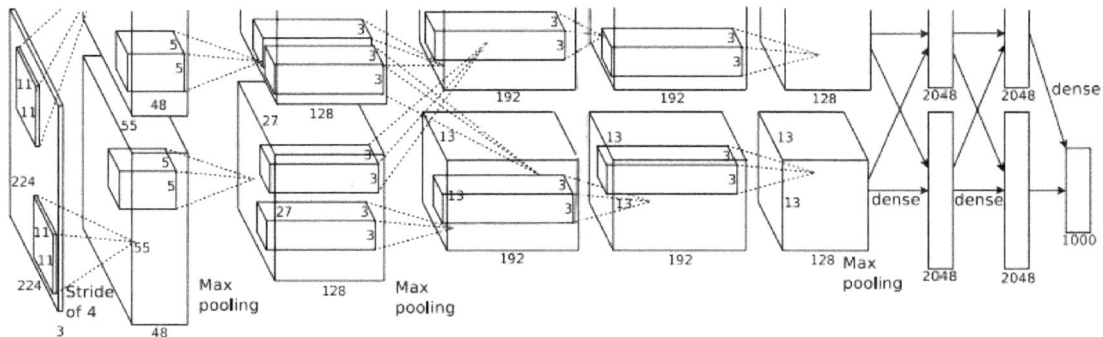

Figure 3.2: *AlexNet architecture*
(**Source**: *https://proceedings.neurips.cc/paper_files/paper/2012/file/c399862d3b9d6b76c8436e924a68c45b-Paper.pdf*,

- **VGG-Net 2014**: *Visual Geometry Group* has released series of convolution neural network models for CV tasks which was considered better than AlexNet due to deeper architecture. VGG-Net has variants of VGG-16 with 16 layers as shown in the *Figure 3.3* VGG-Net architecture and another variant VGG-19 with 19 layers. Unlike AlexNet it uses multiple smaller convolution filters of kernel size which is 3x3, for achieving better accuracy.

VGG-16

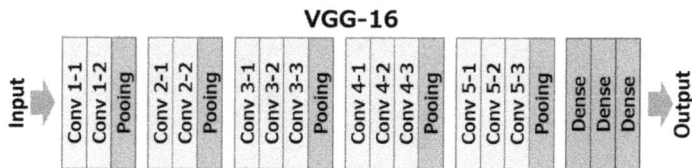

Figure 3.3: *VGG-Net architecture*
(**Source**: *https://neurohive.io/en/popular-networks/vgg16/*)

- **GoogLeNet 2014**: It was introduced by *Google* which provided a significant decrease in error rate compared to AlexNET and VGG-Net. The architecture is made of 22 layers as shown in the *Figure 3.4* with small group of convolutions called **inception modules**. It use batch normalization and RMSprop. This helps in the massive reduction of the computation requirement Compared to VGG-Net architecture.

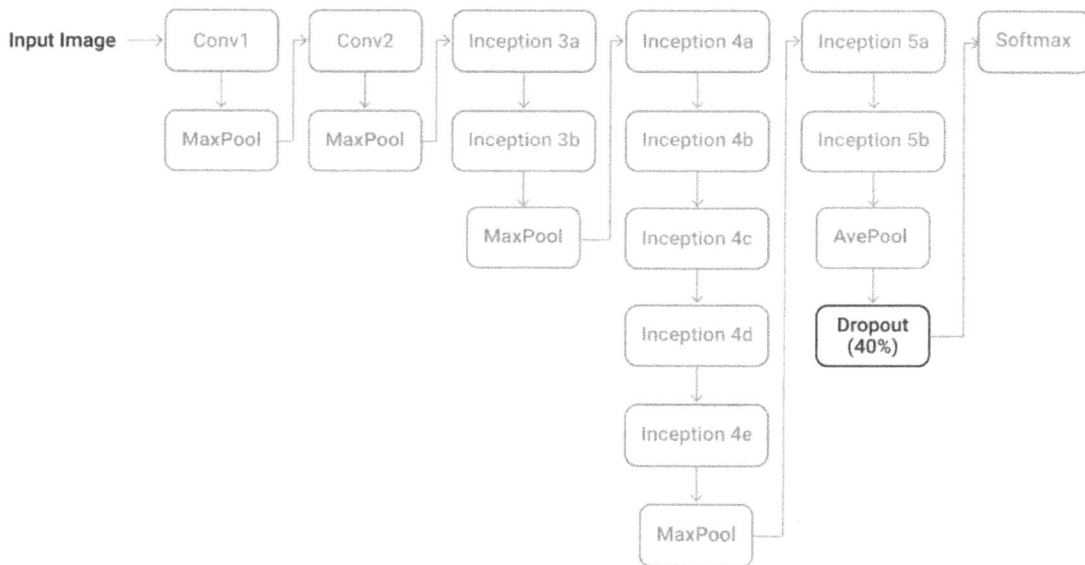

Figure 3.4: *GoogLeNet architecture*
(**Source**: *https://www.run.ai/guides/deep-learning-for-computer-vision*)

- **ResNet-18 2015**: It was introduced by *Microsoft*. Research that incorporated skip connection to resolve vanishing-gradient problem in deeper neural networks. ResNet has different variants from ResNet-18 (18 layers) to ResNet-152 (152 layers). These layers are set up with gated units or skip connections as shown in the *Figure 3.5* ResNet-18 architecture. These skip connections enable it to pass information to later convolutional layers (*Figure 3.5*):

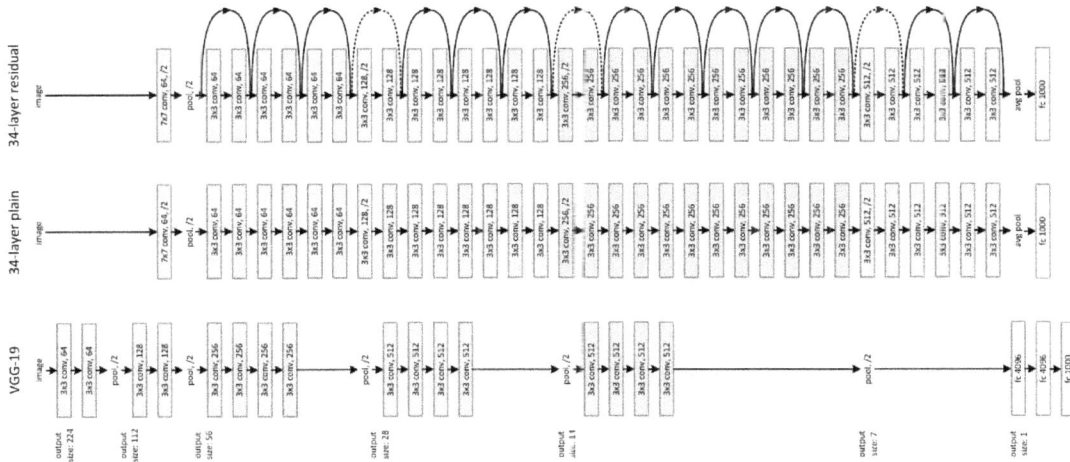

Figure 3.5: *ResNet-18 Architecture*
(***Source***: *https://arxiv.org/pdf/1512.03385.pdf*)

- **MobileNet 2017**: It was developed by *Google* and designed to be used in mobile applications. It uses depth-wise separable convolutions in place of the standard convolutions as shown in *Figure 3.6* to reduce the computation and power requirements. There are a total 28 layers and pointwise convolution as separate layers. MobileNet V1 has logical extensions as variants V2 and V3 with improved performance and accuracy:

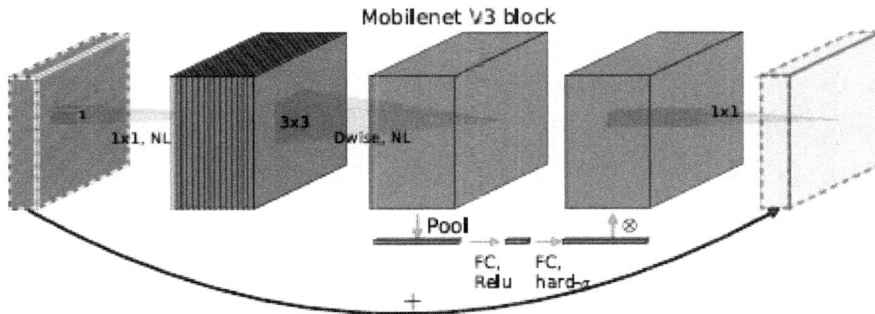

Figure 3.6: *MobileNet V3 block*
(***Source***: *https://arxiv.org/abs/1905.02244*)

- **DenseNet 2018**: Dense convolution networks connects each layer to every other layer in a feed-forward fashion as shown in the *Figure 3.7*. Dense blocks alleviates the vanishing-gradient problem, encourages feature reuse, and reduces the number of parameters. DenseNet has variants of architectures with 121,160 and 201 layers. DenseNet reported to have better performance compared to VGG and ResNet architectures with less complexity:

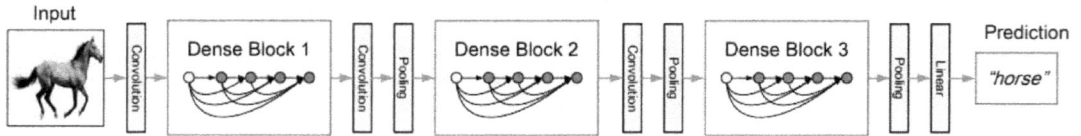

Figure 2: A deep DenseNet with three dense blocks. The layers between two adjacent blocks are referred to as transition layers and change feature-map sizes via convolution and pooling.

Figure 3.7: DenseNet Architecture with 3 dense blocks
(*Source: https://arxiv.org/pdf/1608.06993.pdf*)

- **EfficientNet 2020**: Unique feature of EfficientNet is compound scaling. It achieves better performance using a user defined compounding coefficient to uniformly scale in all dimensions {depth (no of layers), width (no of channels) and resolution(image size) of the network}. It uses **mobile inverted bottleneck convolution** (**MBConv**) as shown in the *Figure 3.8* and **Squeeze-and-Excitation** (**SE**) optimization to enhance the accuracy and performance of the model. It comes in different variants EfficientNet-B0, EfficientNet-B1 with varying scaling coefficients:

Figure 3.8: EfficientNet-B0 baseline network
(*Source: https://arxiv.org/pdf/1905.11946.pdf*)

Convolution neural networks

As we have seen in earlier section, CNN has been the foundation for several deep neural network architectures to perform CV tasks. The objective of convolution neural network is to capture the low-level input image features (edges, orientation, the color, etc.) and these extracted low-level features are used by feed-forward networks to perform tasks like image classification, image segmentation, object detection. The three elements of convolution neural networks are convolution layer, pooling layer and **fully connected** (**FC**) layer, which we will further discuss in detail.

Convolution layer

It is the basic building block and first layer of CNN. As discussed in the *Chapter 1, AI Fundamental*, images are represented as pixel values and color channels. This means that the input to convolution layer will have three dimensions, height, width representing pixel values and depth representing color channels. The convolution layer consists of a set of learnable filters. These filters slide across the width and height of the input volume to compute dot products between the entries of the filter and the input image pixel values, at any given position. A two-dimensional activation map is generated as each filter slide over entire input volume. Activation maps get stacked along the depth dimension to generate the output volume. The size of the region in the input that produces the feature in activation map is called as **receptive field**.

Mathematically, the spatial size of output volume can be determined by Wout = (W – F + 2P)/S + *1* where,

- *W* is input volume
- *F* is kernel
- *S* is stride
- *P* is padding

For example, for a 6x6 input and a 3x3 filter with stride 1 and pad 0 we would get a 4x4 output. Apart from depth of the output volume (the number of filters), stride and padding are the other hyperparameters in convolution layer. Below *Figure 3.9* shows the complete process of convolution block where convolution operation, activation and max pooling happens:

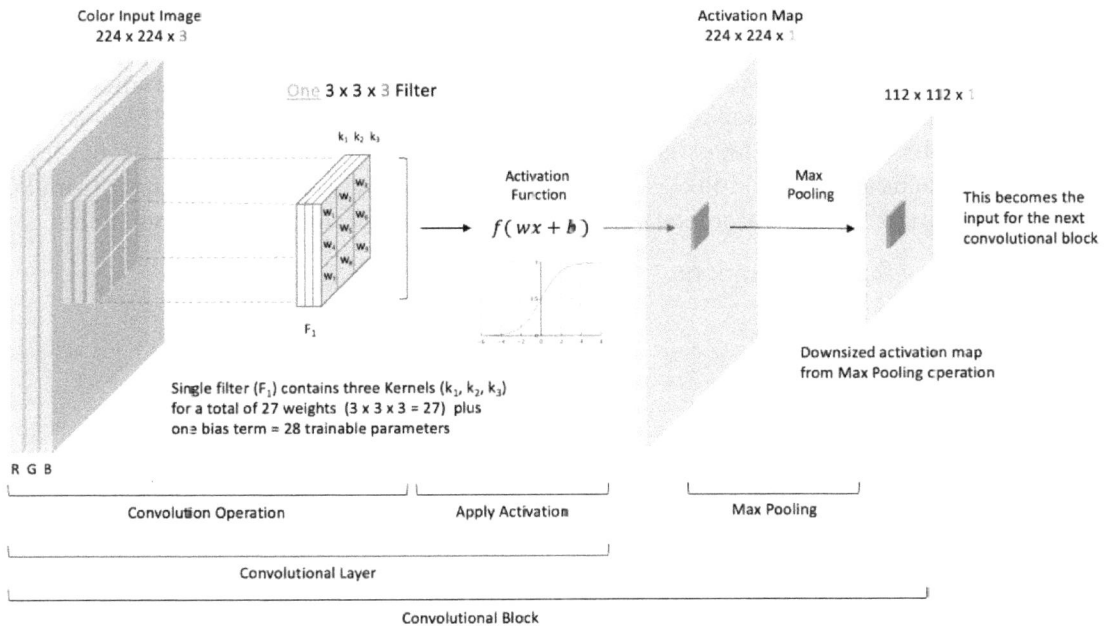

Figure 3.9: Convolution neural blocks
(*Source*: https://learnopencv.com/understanding-convolutional-neural-networks-cnn/)

Padding

Padding extends the area of an image before any convolution filter process to avoid information loss from the edges of the images. It helps to preserve spatial dimension of the feature maps after convolution and pooling process. Different padding types are available, such as same-padding (Extend the edges of image along width and height to maintain same input size after convolution), zero-padding (same-padding where all elements that are extended are set to zero), valid padding (no padding), and causal padding (Padding applied asymmetrically, generally used in sequence related tasks to avoid future information leakage).

Pooling layer

Pooling reduces the spatial size of the convolved features. There are two types. The first is, max pooling and other one is average pooling. While max pooling captures the maximum value of pixels from kernel area, average pooling returns the average value of the pixel values from the kernel area. Beyond dimensionality reduction, max pooling brings the advantage of discarding noisy activations i.e. denoising and using it to extract the dominant features.

Fully connected layer

This layer performs the task of classification. Data from the final convolution layer is flattened to a single dimensional vector to represent the meaningful information of the image. FC layer is same as deep neural network layers seen in *Chapter-2, GenAI Foundation*. Each neuron in the output layer is connected to nodes in the previous layer. FC layer uses softmax activation to do the classification task. The convolution layer differs from FC layers by having sharable parameters and neuron connectivity to the receptive field.

Sample 2D convolution operation:

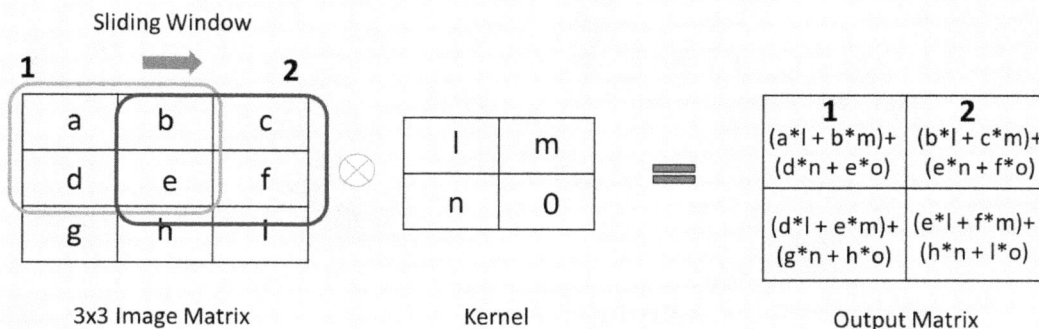

Figure 3.10: 2D convolution operation

Examples: U-Net Image segmentation

In the above section we have gone through different CNN architectures, elements of CNN network and operation of convolution layer. In this section we will go through popular U-Net architecture and a guided example of image segmentation. Segmentation means converting image into subgroups of pixels called **image segments**. These detailed image segments helps further to perform tasks like identifying object shapes. Unlike classification task where the neural network is trained to assign a label for entire image, in segmentation task neural network assign a class to each pixel of the image. It is trained on set of images that includes the corresponding labels, and pixel-wise masks. The masks will be the class-labels for each pixel.

U-Net is a fully convolution symmetrical network model that is intended to make pixel by pixel prediction. As named U-Net—U shaped architecture and as shown in the *Figure 3.11*, has a contracting (Encoding layers) and expansive path (Decoding layers) with bottleneck layer residing in between. Encoder path captures the contextual information of the input image by reducing the spatial resolution while increasing its depth. The decoder takes the abstract representation of the encoder and up sample the feature map with Transposed convolution. The skip connections from the encoder helps decoder to preserve the spatial information that might have lost during contractive path and ensures better flow of gradient during backpropagation This architecture is popular for image segmentation task and even effective with limited data set:

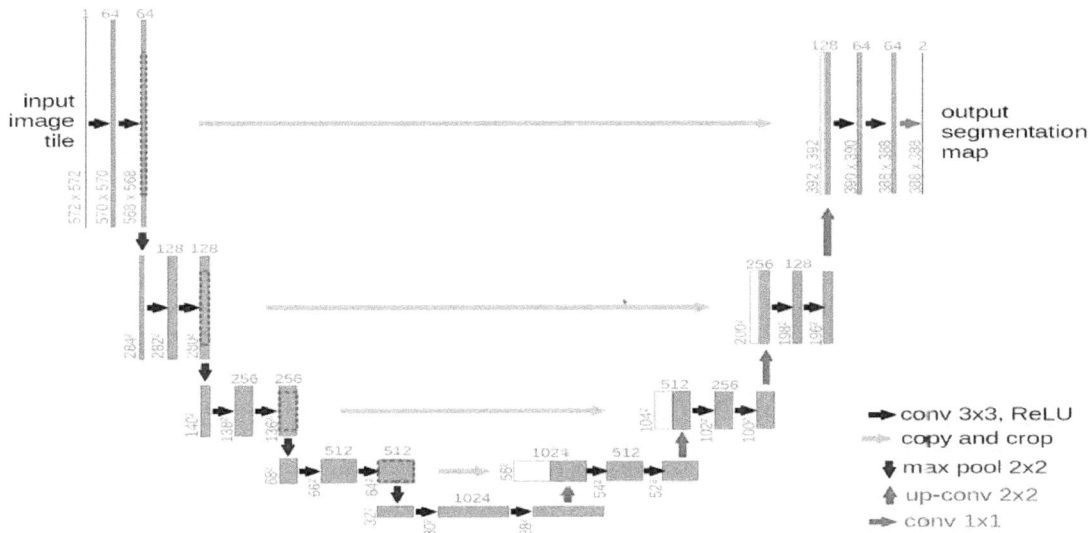

Figure 3.11: *U-Net architecture*
(**Source:** *https://arxiv.org/abs/1505.04597*)

The objective of this guided example is to build an encoder-decoder U-Net architecture to segment input images. The Oxford-IIIT Pet dataset is a 37 category pet dataset with roughly 200 images for each class created by the *Visual Geometry Group* at *Oxford*. This data set has both the images and the masks of the pet. We will be using colab environment to execute the code and datasets will be downloaded into the *Google Drive* for further processing.

Prerequisites:

```
1. project_dir = '/content/drive/MyDrive/GenAIBOOK/unet'
2. pets_path_train = os.path.join(project_dir, 'OxfordPets', 'train')
3. pets_path_test = os.path.join(project_dir, 'OxfordPets', 'test')
```

Below code shows a Class **ImageAug** to create custom dataset for segmentation task. **OxfordIIITPet** is inherited from **torchvision.dataset** class with parameters such as **split, download** and have callable methods such as **transform, tartge_transsform**. The class takes input of images and do transform both the image and mask with the required transforms defined in **Image_transformation** and **transform_target_aug**:

```
1.  class ImageAug(torchvision.datasets.OxfordIIITPet):
2.      def __init__(
3.          self,
4.          root: str,
5.          split: str,
6.          target_types="segmentation",
7.          download=False,
8.          transform=T.ToTensor(),
9.          target_transform=T.ToTensor(),
10.         transform_target_aug=None,
11.         Image_transformation=None,
12.     ):
13.         super().__init__(
14.             root=root,
15.             split=split,
16.             target_types=target_types,
17.             download=download,
18.             transform=transform,
19.             target_transform=target_transform,
20.         )
21.         self.transform_target_aug = transform_target_aug
22.         self.Image_transformation = Image_transformation
```

```
23.
24.    def __len__(self):
25.        return super().__len__()
26.
27.    def __getitem__(self, idx):
28.        (input, target) = super().__getitem__(idx)
29.
30.        if self.Image_transformation is not None:
31.            both = torch.cat([input, target], dim=0)
32.            both = self.Image_transformation(both)
33.            (input, target) = torch.split(both, 3, dim=0)
34.
35.        if self.transform_target_aug is not None:
36.            target = self.transform_target_aug(target)
37.
38.        return (input, target)
```

Below code shows the function for input transformation (Random horizontal flip and image resize) is applied on both target and label (segmentation mask images). Nearest neighbor algorithm is used for image re sizing (128 x 128):

```
1.  # Create a tensor for a segmentation trimap.
2.
3.  def tensor_trimap(t):
4.      x = t * 255
5.      x = x.to(torch.long)
6.      x = x - 1
7.      return x
8.
9.  def args_to_dict(**kwargs):
10.     return kwargs
11.
12. transform_dict = args_to_dict(
13.
14.     Image_transformation=T.Compose([
15.         T.Resize((128, 128), interpolation=T.InterpolationMode.
                NEAREST),
```

```
16.          T.RandomHorizontalFlip(p=0.6),
17.      ]),
18.      transform_target_aug=T.Compose([
19.          T.Lambda(tensor_trimap),
20.      ]),
21. )
```

Below code shows the function to initialize the train and test data set followed by creation of dataloader. Datasets are **train_pets** and **test_pets** dataset and dataloaders are (**train_pets_loader** and **test_pets_loader**):

```
1. train_pets = ImageAug(
2.      root=pets_path_train,
3.      split="trainval",
4.      target_types="segmentation",
5.      download=True,
6.      **transform_dict,
7. )
8. test_pets = ImageAug(
9.      root=pets_path_test,
10.     split="test",
11.     target_types="segmentation",
12.     download=True,
13.     **transform_dict,
14. )
15.
16. train_pets_loader = torch.utils.data.DataLoader(
17.     train_pets,
18.     batch_size=64,
19.     shuffle=True,
20. )
21. test_pets_loader = torch.utils.data.DataLoader(
22.     test_pets,
23.     batch_size=64,
24.     shuffle=True,
25. )
```

26.

27. `(train_pets_inputs, train_pets_targets) = next(iter(train_pets_` `loader))`

28. `(test_pets_inputs, test_pets_targets) = next(iter(test_pets_loader))`

29. `train_pets_inputs.shape, train_pets_targets.shape`

Below code show **d_conv** is a double convolution block . It is basic builing block for the upcoming U-Net model. It consists of double 3x3 convolution layers followed by batch normalization and ReLU activation function. It will be used through contracting and expanding layers:

```
1.  def d_conv(in_channels, out_channels):
2.      conv_operation = nn.Sequential(
3.          nn.Conv2d(in_channels, out_channels, kernel_size=3, padding=1),
4.          nn.BatchNorm2d(out_channels),
5.          nn.ReLU(inplace=True),
6.          nn.Conv2d(out_channels, out_channels, kernel_size=3, padding=1),
7.          nn.BatchNorm2d(out_channels),
8.          nn.ReLU(inplace=True)
9.      )
10.     return conv_operation
```

Below code shows, a custom class **UNet** that is defined as a subclass of **nn.Module**. The **__ init__** method initializes the architecture of the U-Net by defining a layer for contracting (encoder) and expanding (decoder) path.While encoder increase the number of feature maps at each stage, decoder take the final encoder representation and gradually increase the spatial dimension using transpose convolution. **n_class** parameter defines number of classes for segmentation task:

```
1.  class UNet(nn.Module):
2.      def __init__(self, n_class):
3.          super(UNet, self).__init__()
4.          self.mx_pool = nn.MaxPool2d(kernel_size=2, stride=2)
5.          # Contracting path.
6.          # Each convolution is applied twice.
7.          self.d_conv1 = d_conv(3, 64)
8.          self.d_conv2 = d_conv(64, 128)
9.          self.d_conv3 = d_conv(128, 256)
10.         self.d_conv4 = d_conv(256, 512)
11.         self.d_conv5 = d_conv(512, 1024)
```

```
12.        # Expanding path.
13.        self.u_trans1 = nn.ConvTranspose2d(
14.            in_channels=1024, out_channels=512,
15.            kernel_size=2,
16.            stride=2)
17.        # Below, `in_channels` becomes 1024 as we are concatenate.
18.        self.u_conv1 = d_conv(1024, 512)
19.        self.u_trans2 = nn.ConvTranspose2d(
20.            in_channels=512, out_channels=256,
21.            kernel_size=2,
22.            stride=2)
23.        self.u_conv2 = d_conv(512, 256)
24.        self.u_trans3 = nn.ConvTranspose2d(
25.            in_channels=256, out_channels=128,
26.            kernel_size=2,
27.            stride=2)
28.        self.u_conv3 = d_conv(256, 128)
29.        self.u_trans4 = nn.ConvTranspose2d(
30.            in_channels=128, out_channels=64,
31.            kernel_size=2,
32.            stride=2)
33.        self.u_conv4 = d_conv(128, 64)
34.        # no of classes as per out channels
35.        self.out = nn.Conv2d(
36.            in_channels=64, out_channels=n_class,
37.            kernel_size=1
38.        )
```

The **forward** method specifies input image is processed through the encoder layers (**d1-d9**) to extract the features. Then, upsampled the encoder features **d9** to the original image size while concatenating the corresponding encoder feature maps. The output layer uses a 1x1 convolutional layer to map the features to **n_class**. The final U-Net architecture consists of contracting and expanding layers with skip connections:

```
39.    def forward(self, x):
40.        d1 = self.d_conv1(x)
41.        d2 = self.mx_pool(d1)
```

```
42.        d3 = self.d_conv2(d2)
43.        d4 = self.mx_pool(d3)
44.        d5 = self.d_conv3(d4)
45.        d6 = self.mx_pool(d5)
46.        d7 = self.d_conv4(d6)
47.        d8 = self.mx_pool(d7)
48.        d9 = self.d_conv5(d8)
49.        # Not applying max pooling to d9
50.        u1 = self.u_trans1(d9)
51.        x = self.u_conv1(torch.cat([d7, u1], 1))
52.        u2 = self.u_trans2(x)
53.        x = self.u_conv2(torch.cat([d5, u2], 1))
54.        u3 = self.u_trans3(x)
55.        x = self.u_conv3(torch.cat([d3, u3], 1))
56.        u4 = self.u_trans4(x)
57.        x = self.u_conv4(torch.cat([d1, u4], 1))
58.        out = self.out(x)
59.        return out
```

The Below code defines the function for creating a training loop. We have used **CrossEntropyLoss** for this example. However, intersection over union, also known as the Jaccard index, is the most popular evaluation metric for tasks such as segmentation, object detection and tracking. Some of the function parameters are **epochs** define the number of **epochs** to train UNet model, **lr** defines the learning rate for the optimizer and **scheduler** provides several methods to adjust the learning rate based on the number of **epochs**:

```
1.  # Training Loop. Train the model for multiple epochs.
2.
3.  def train_model_u(model, loader, epochs, optimizer, scheculer):
4.      #test_inputs, test_targets = test_data
5.      for epoch in range(epochs):
6.          print(f"Epoch: {epoch:02d}, Learning Rate: {optimizer.param_
            groups[0]['lr']}")
7.
8.          model.train().cuda()
9.          criteria = nn.CrossEntropyLoss(reduction='mean')
10.         r_loss = 0.0
```

```
11.          r_samples = 0

12.

13.          for batch_no, (inputs, targets) in enumerate(loader, 0):

14.

15.              optimizer.zero_grad()

16.              inputs = inputs.cuda()

17.              targets = targets.cuda()

18.              outputs = model(inputs)

19.              targets = targets.squeeze(dim=1) # Squeeze NCHW -> NHW
                 (channels)

20.              outputs= outputs.squeeze(dim=1)

21.              loss = criteria(outputs, targets)

22.              loss.backward()

23.              optimizer.step()

24.              r_samples += targets.size(0)

25.              r_loss += loss.item()

26.              print("Trained {} samples, Loss: {:.4f}".format( r_
                 samples,r_loss / (batch_no+1)))
```

Below code shows instantiation of model training for 10 **epochs**. by calling **trin_model_u** with 200 classes and learning rate **lr=0.01**:

```
1. # Hyper Parameters - Optimizer & Learning Rate Scheduler.

2. model = UNet(n_class=200)

3. model.cuda()

4. optimizer = torch.optim.Adam(model.parameters(), lr=0.001)

5. scheduler = torch.optim.lr_scheduler.StepLR(optimizer, step_size=20,
   gamma=0.6)

6.

7. epochs=10

8. train_model_u(model, train_pets_loader, epochs, optimizer, scheduler)
```

The below code creates a function to visualize the predictions on the text data. Function take as input the trained segmentation model, test image, test target label and plot the predicted output. It output target images, it is ground truth masking and predicted mask by the trained model:

```
1. def view_output(model, test_pets_targets, test_pets_labels):

2.     torch.no_grad()
```

```
3.      model.eval().cuda()
4.      predictions = model(test_pets_targets.cuda())
5.      test_pets_labels = (test_pets_labels.cuda())
6.      print("Predictions Shape: {}".format(predictions.shape))
7.      prediction_labels = predictions.argmax(dim=1)
8.      prediction_labels = prediction_labels.unsqueeze(1)
9.      prediction_mask = prediction_labels.to(torch.float)
10.
11.     pix_metric = (TM.classification.MulticlassAccuracy(3,
        average='micro')).cuda()
12.     pix_acc = pix_metric(prediction_labels, test_pets_labels)
13.     plt_title = f'Accuracy[Pixel: {pix_acc:.4f}]'
14.     print(plt_title)
15.
16.     fig = plt.figure(figsize=(10, 12))
17.     fig.suptitle(plt_title, fontsize=12)
18.
19.     fig.add_subplot(3, 1, 1)
20.     plt.imshow(T.ToPILImage()(torchvision.utils.make_grid(test_pets_
        targets, nrow=7)))
21.     plt.axis('off')
22.     plt.title("Targets")
23.
24.     fig.add_subplot(3, 1, 2)
25.     plt.imshow(T.ToPILImage()(torchvision.utils.make_grid(test_pets_
        labels.float() / 2.0, nrow=7)))
26.     plt.axis('off')
27.     plt.title("Ground_Truth")
28.
29.     fig.add_subplot(3, 1, 3)
30.     plt.imshow(T.ToPILImage()(torchvision.utils.make_
        grid(prediction_mask / 2.0, nrow=7)))
31.     plt.axis('off')
32.     plt.title("Predicted Labels")
33.
```

```
34.     plt.show()
35. view_output(model, test_pets_inputs, test_pets_targets)
```

Output:

Refer to the following figure:

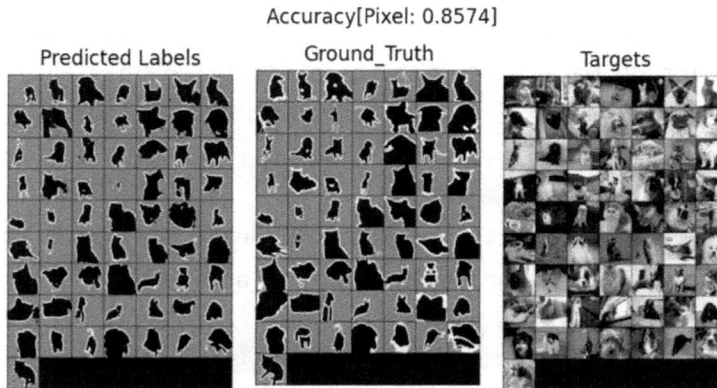

Figure 3.12: U-Net segmentation model prediction on test dataset

Representation learning

Representation learning automatically discovers the latent features to describe the implicit characteristics of the data. A good representation of data must be low dimensional, reusable across tasks, smooth and spatially coherent, disentangled, hierarchical and meaningful. The objective of representation learning is to learn a mapping function that maps the input data points in a high dimensional space to low dimensional latent space (non-linear manifolds). We have explained manifold concepts in *Chapter 1, AI Fundamentals*. Mapping the low dimensional latent space enables navigation, sampling, and interpolation between points in latent spaces for different tasks. There are supervised and unsupervised representation learning methods. Autoencoders and Variational autoencoders (VAE) are commonly used unsupervised representation learning technique which we will discuss in the section below.

Autoencoders and variational autoencoders

It is an unsupervised density estimation method that trains a model with objective to discover the minimum number of important features needed for effective reconstruction of the input data. Autoencoder consists of encoder and decoder networks. Encoder $g_\phi(x)$ translates the original high-dimension input into the latent low-dimensional code through bottleneck layer. The decoder $f_\theta(x)$ network recovers the data from the samples of the latent code.

The latent space is defined by $z = g_\emptyset(x)$ and the reconstructed output is given by $y = g_\emptyset(f_\theta(x))$. Then the loss function for the autoencoder can be defined as simple mean square loss i.e. $L(\emptyset, \theta) = \frac{1}{n} \sum_{i=1}^{n} (x^i - y^i)^2$ Autoencoders are deterministic models, where the input is mapped to fixed vector. The below figure shows the likeness of Latent attributes capturing image feature:

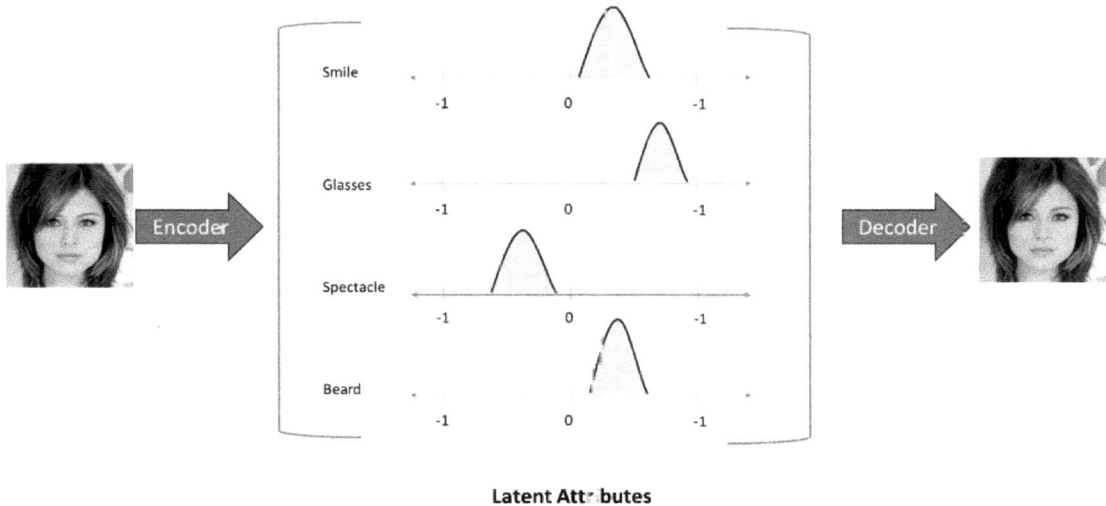

Latent Attributes

Figure 3.13: Example—latent distribution capturing image feature, color, smile, hair, glasses

While autoencoders aim to minimize the reconstruction error, VAE learn the latent space of the underlying probability distribution of data. For example, VAEs can perform better than autoencoders in data imputation, where filling in missing data in a dataset by generating plausible values based on learned latent representations. Similarly, VAEs perform way better in style transfers by obtaining the disentangled repetitions of image data in latent space. So Unlike autoencoders, VAE uses probability distribution for describing the observations in the latent space i.e. each input is mapped to the latent variable that is parameterized by mean μ and variance σ as shown in the following *Figure 3.14*. Each latent state distribution will be randomly sampled to generate latent vector, which will be the input to the decoder model.

Hence, given a prior latent distribution $p(z)$, encoder will generate probabilistic distribution of latent variables *i.e.* $q_\emptyset(z|x)$ and the decoder computes the reverse, i.e., $p_\theta(x|z)$ to reconstruct the input. Henceforth, the loss function can be given as $L(\emptyset,\theta,x) = reconstruction$ *loss + regularization loss*. Reconstruction loss is given by likelihood of generating true data, regularization loss is given by KL divergence between inferred latent distribution and fixed prior latent distribution. The common choice of prior latent distribution is normal Gaussian, i.e. $p(z) = N(\mu = 0, \sigma^2 = 1)$. Recall KL divergence in *Chapter 1, AI Fundamentals*. It is a measure of the difference between two probability distributions. Thus, if we wanted to ensure that the learned distribution $q(z|x)$ was similar to prior distribution $p(z|x)$, we must minimize the KL divergence between the two distributions i.e. $min\ KL\ (\ q_\emptyset(z|x)||p(x))$. The KL divergence between two distributions is given by $D_{KL}\big(q_\emptyset(z|x)||p(z)\big)$ where $q_\emptyset(z|x)$ is inferred latent distribution and $p(z)$ a fixed prior latent distribution. Therefore, the loss function can be given by $L(\emptyset,\theta,x) = -E_{z\sim q_\emptyset(z|x_i)}[\log p_\theta(x_i|z)] + \Sigma_\emptyset D\big(q_\emptyset(z|x)||p(z)\big)$. The optimized loss term above derived for VAE is equivalently called **evidence lower bound (ELBO)**.

The random sampling process is stochastic and does not support backpropagation of gradient during model training. So, with reparameterization trick, random variable z is expressed as a function of deterministic μ,σ with auxiliary independent random variable ε i.e $z = \mu + \sigma \odot \varepsilon$. With this reparameterization, parameters of the distribution can be optimized through backpropagation while still maintaining the ability to randomly sample from that distribution. The normalized prior and regularization terms in VAE ensures the continuity and completeness properties of representation learning. Apart from continuity and completeness, the other important property of representation learning is disentanglement. **Disentanglement** can be defined as the property of latent representation, where altering one latent dimension mainly affects one factor of variation (e.g., smile) while leaving other factors relatively unaffected (e.g. facial features). In the next section, we will discuss how $\beta - VAEs$ ensure disentanglement:

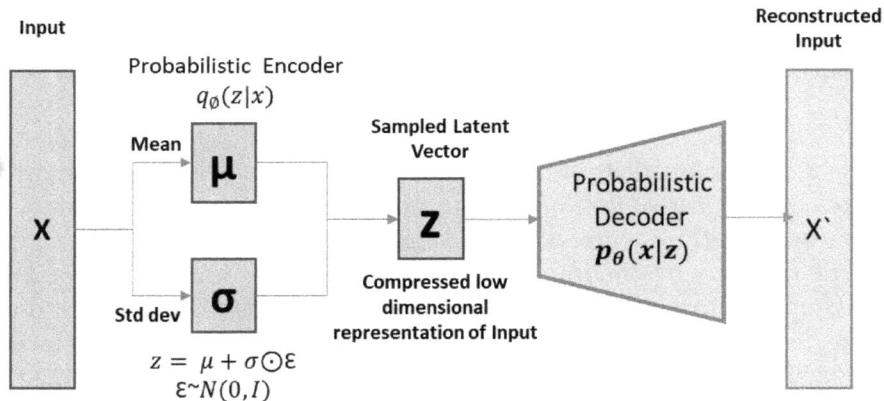

Figure 3.14: *VAE architecture*

Examples: Generate new faces

The objective of the example is to build VAE that can generate new faces by drawing latent vectors from the prior distribution. For this guided example, we will be using CelebA dataset. It is a face attribute dataset with 200k records of celebrity images. It has large pose variations and background clutter.

Dataset source reference **http://mmlab.ie.cuhk.edu.hk/projects/CelebA.html**.

The below code shows the loading of CelebA dataset, and functions to do dataset preprocessing, such as image resizing center cropping, normalizing of pixel values based on the mean and standard deviation provided. The dataset is split into train and test set. The training set, which contains 80% images, is used to train the autoencoder, and the test set, which includes 20% images, is used to evaluate the model's performance:

```
1.  # Root directory for dataset
2.  dataroot = "/content/drive/MyDrive/GenAIBOOK/celeba"
3.  # Spatial size of training images. All images will be resized to this
    size
4.  img_size = 64
```

```
1.  image_mean = [0.485, 0.456, 0.406]   # mean of the   dataset for
    normalizing
2.  image_std = [0.229, 0.224, 0.225]   # std of the ImageNet dataset for
    normalizing
3.
4.  dataset = dset.ImageFolder(root=dataroot,
5.                              transform=transforms.Compose([
6.                                  transforms.Resize(img_size),
7.                                  transforms.CenterCrop(img_size),
8.                                  transforms.ToTensor(),
9.                                  transforms.Normalize(image_
                                    mean,image_std),
10.                             ]))
11. train_samples = int(0.8 * len(dataset))
12. val_samples = len(dataset) - train_samples
13. train_set, val_set = torch.utils.data.random_split(dataset, [train_
    samples, val_samples]) # check len(dataset) prior splitting
14.
15. # Create the dataloader
16. train_loader = torch.utils.data.DataLoader(train_set, batch_
    size=batch,shuffle=True, num_workers=2)
17. val_loader = torch.utils.data.DataLoader(val_set, batch_
    size=batch,shuffle=True, num_workers=2)
18.
```

```
19. print(len(train_loader.dataset))
20. print(len(val_loader.dataset))
```

The below code shows the model architecture. It is similar to U-Net architecture discussed earlier. It is made of encoder and decoder networks. Encoder class is created as sub-class of PyTorch **nn.module** with **__init__** method storing the layers of the network as an attribute. It consists of sequence of convolution block with 2D convolution layer for the encoder and transpose convolutions for the decoder layers. In VAE, inputs are mapped to a probability distribution over latent vectors, and a latent vector is then sampled from that distribution. The mean and variance of latent space are calculated in the below code at **mu = self.fc_mu(hidden)** and **var = self.fc_var(hidden)** layers. Using these mean, and variance reparametrize method is called to sample a point (z) from the latent space and input it to the decoder that in turn outputs a vector of the same shape as the input:

```
1.  in_chn = 64 # initial number of filters
2.  img_chn = 3 # color channels
3.  latent_dim = 100 # number of features to consider
4.  # define a Conv VAE
5.  class ConvVAE(nn.Module):
6.      def __init__(self):
7.          super(ConvVAE, self).__init__()
8.
9.          # encoder
10.         self.e1 = nn.Conv2d(
11.             in_channels=img_chn, out_channels=in_chn,
12.             kernel_size=4, stride=2, padding=2
13.         )
14.         self.e2 = nn.Conv2d(
15.             in_channels=in_chn, out_channels=in_chn*2,
16.             kernel_size=4, stride=2, padding=2
17.         )
18.         self.e3 = nn.Conv2d(
19.             in_channels=in_chn*2, out_channels=in_chn*4,
20.             kernel_size=4, stride=2, padding=2
21.         )
22.         self.e4 = nn.Conv2d(
23.             in_channels=in_chn*4, out_channels=in_chn*8,
24.             kernel_size=4, stride=2, padding=2
```

```
25.          )
26.          self.e5 = nn.Conv2d(
27.              in_channels=in_chn*8, out_channels=1024,
28.              kernel_size=4, stride=2, padding=2
29.          )
30.          self.fc_1 = nn.Linear(1024, 2048)
31.          self.fc_mu = nn.Linear(2048, latent_dim)
32.          self.fc_var = nn.Linear(2048, latent_dim)
33.          self.fc_2 = nn.Linear(latent_dim, 1024)
34.          # decoder
35.          self.d1 = nn.ConvTranspose2d(
36.              in_channels=1024, out_channels=in_chn*8,
37.              kernel_size=3, stride=2
38.          )
39.          self.d2 = nn.ConvTranspose2d(
40.              in_channels=in_chn*8, out_channels=in_chn*4,
41.              kernel_size=3, stride=2
42.          )
43.          self.d3 = nn.ConvTranspose2d(
44.              in_channels=in_chn*4, out_channels=in_chn*2,
45.              kernel_size=3, stride=2
46.          )
47.          self.d4 = nn.ConvTranspose2d(
48.              in_channels=in_chn*2, out_channels=in_chn,
49.              kernel_size=3, stride=2
50.          )
51.          self.d5 = nn.ConvTranspose2d(
52.              in_channels=in_chn, out_channels=img_chn,
53.              kernel_size=4, stride=2
54.          )
55.      def reparameterize(self, mu, var):
56.          """
57.          :param mu: mean from the encoder's latent space
58.          :param var: log variance from the encoder's latent space
```

```
59.          «""
60.          std = torch.exp(0.5*var) # standard deviation
61.          eps = torch.randn_like(std) # `randn_like` as we need the
             same size
62.          sample = mu + (eps * std) # sampling
63.          return sample
64.
65.      def forward(self, x):
66.          # encoding
67.          x = F.relu(self.e1(x))
68.          x = F.relu(self.e2(x))
69.          x = F.relu(self.e3(x))
70.          x = F.relu(self.e4(x))
71.          x = F.relu(self.e5(x))
72.          batch, _, _, _ = x.shape
73.          x = F.adaptive_avg_pool2d(x, 1).reshape(batch, -1)
74.          hidden = self.fc_1(x)
75.          # get `mu` and `var`
76.          mu = self.fc_mu(hidden)
77.          var = self.fc_var(hidden)
78.          # get the latent vector through reparameterization
79.          z = self.reparameterize(mu, var)
80.          z = self.fc_2(z)
81.          z = z.view(-1, 1024, 1, 1)
82.
83.          # decoding
84.          x = F.relu(self.d1(z))
85.          x = F.relu(self.d2(x))
86.          x = F.relu(self.d3(x))
87.          x = F.relu(self.d4(x))
88.          reconstruction = torch.sigmoid(self.d5(x))
89.          return reconstruction, mu, var
```

Below code shows the loss function for VAE. The **final_loss** function is defined to compute the VAE loss. It takes arguments of MSE loss, mean (mu) and log variance of latent variables **log_Var**. MSE is the reconstruction loss, i.e., the difference between reconstructed output and original input. MSE is calculated using **nn.MSELoss()** module that will be defined in the upcoming train function definition. KLD loss measures the distribution divergence between standard prior (Normal distribution) and posterior latent distribution. The final loss function i.e. the sum of KLD and MSE loss is returned as the output of the function:

```
1. def final_loss(mse_loss, mu, logvar):
2.     """
3.     This function will add the reconstruction loss (MSELoss) & KL-
       Divergence ( 0.5 * sum(1 + log(sigma^2) - mu^2 - sigma^2))
4.     «»»
5.     MSE = mse_loss
6.     KLD = -0.5 * torch.sum(1 + logvar - mu.pow(2) - logvar.exp())
7.     KLD /= batch * 784
8.     return MSE + KLD
```

Below code has two helper funtions **to_pil** to showcase the reconstructed images from the validation dataset in grid. It also saves **loss_plot** and showcase the trend in train and validation loss:

```
1.  to_pil_image = transforms.ToPILImage()
2.  os.mkdir("/content/drive/MyDrive/GenAIBOOK/celeba/output")
3.  def to_pil(images):
4.      imgs = [np.array(to_pil_image(img)) for img in images]
5.      imageio.mimsave('/content/drive/MyDrive/GenAIBOOK/celeba/output/
        generated_images.gif', imgs)
6.
7.  def save_img_recon(recon_images, epoch):
8.      save_image(recon_images.cpu(), f"/content/drive/MyDrive/
        GenAIBOOK/celeba/output/output-epoch}.jpg")
9.  def loss_plot(train_loss, valid_loss):
10.     plt.figure(figsize=(10, 7))
11.     plt.plot(train_loss, color='Blue', label='train loss')
12.     plt.plot(valid_loss, color='Green', label='validataion loss')
13.     plt.xlabel('Epochs')
14.     plt.ylabel('Loss')
```

15.   `plt.legend()`

16.   `plt.savefig('/content/drive/MyDrive/GenAIBOOK/celeba/output/`
        `loss.jpg')`

17.   `plt.show()`

Below code shows moving of model to device and setting up the model training parameters such as learning rate, epochs, batch size, optimizer and reconstruction loss criteria. We define a train function which iterate over the train data. loader and obtain the loss based on the criterion. The functions iterate over the batches of data, set the zero gradient, compute the loss after input pass through model architecture, accumulate the execution loss, and finally optimizer updated the model weight's based on computed gradients:

```
1.  import torch.optim as optim
2.  # initialize the model
3.  model = ConvVAE().to(device)
4.  # define the learning parameters
5.  lr = 0.0001
6.  epochs = 40
7.  batch = 128
8.  optimizer = optim.Adam(model.parameters(), lr=lr)
9.  criterion = nn.MSELoss()
10. def train(model, dataloader, dataset, device, optimizer, criterion):
11.     model.train()
12.     exec_loss = 0.0
13.     counter = 0
14.     for i, data in tqdm(enumerate(dataloader),
            total=int(len(dataset)/dataloader.batch_size)):
15.         counter += 1
16.         data,_ = data
17.         data = data.to(device)
18.         optimizer.zero_grad()
19.         reconstruction, mu, logvar = model(data)
20.         MSE_loss = criterion(reconstruction, data)
21.         print(MSE_loss)
22.         loss = final_loss(MSE_loss, mu, logvar)
23.         loss.backward()
24.         exec_loss += loss.item()
```

```
25.              optimizer.step()
26.         train_loss = exec_loss / counter
27.         return train_loss
```

Below code define a validation function which iterate over the validation dataloader and obtain the loss based on the criterion. The objective of this function is to evaluate the model performance on data that is not been exposed during the training. The functions iterate over the batches of data, compute the loss after input passes through model architecture, and accumulate the execution loss. As it is a validation function, flow back of gradient to update model weight's is not required:

```
1.  def validate(model, dataloader, dataset, device, criterion):
2.        model.eval()
3.        exec_loss = 0.0
4.        counter = 0
5.
6.        with torch.no_grad():
7.             for i, data in tqdm(enumerate(dataloader),
                   total=int(len(dataset)/dataloader.batch_size)):
8.                  counter += 1
9.                  data,_= data
10.                 data = data.to(device)
11.                 reconstruction, mu, logvar = model(data)
12.                 MSE_loss = criterion(reconstruction, data)
13.                 loss = final_loss(MSE_loss, mu, logvar)
14.                 exec_loss += loss.item()
15.
16.                 # save the last batch input and output of every epoch
17.                 if i == int(len(dataset)/dataloader.batch_size) - 1:
18.                      recon_images = reconstruction
19.        val_loss = exec_loss / counter
20.        return val_loss, recon_images
```

The below code set up the training loop for the model. The for loop iterates over a number of epochs where each epoch represents training over a full dataset. Function calls for training and validation loop described above and computes average training and validation loss. It saves the model weights, loss statistics, and reconstructed images generated by VAE:

```
1. from torchvision.utils import make_grid
2. # a list to save all the reconstructed images in PyTorch grid format
3. grid_images = []
4. train_loss = []
5. valid_loss = []
6. for epoch in range(epochs):
7.     print(f"Epoch {epoch+1} of {epochs}")
8.     train_epoch_loss = train(
9.         model, train_loader, train_set, device, optimizer, criterion
10.    )
11.    valid_epoch_loss, recon_images = validate(
12.        model, val_loader, val_set, device, criterion
13.    )
14.    train_loss.append(train_epoch_loss)
15.    valid_loss.append(valid_epoch_loss)
16.    # save the reconstructed images from the validation loop
17.    save_img_recon(recon_images, epoch+1)
18.    # convert the reconstructed images to PyTorch image grid format
19.    image_grid = make_grid(recon_images.detach().cpu())
20.    grid_images.append(image_grid)
21.    print(f"Train Loss: {train_epoch_loss:.4f}")
22.    print(f"Val Loss: {valid_epoch_loss:.4f}")
23.
24. img_gif(grid_images)
25. save_loss_plot(train_loss, valid_loss)
26.
27. # save the reconstructions as a .gif file
```

The below figure showcases the reconstructed images from the validation CelebA dataset. We can observe the VAE capability in learning the underlying feature of the dataset. The below output is generated after executing the above code:

Figure 3.15: The final output of VAE Example on CelebA dataset

VAE variants

β-*VAEs* is variant of VAE with a special emphasis to discover disentangled latent factors. As discussion in the earlier section, disentanglement is the property of latent representation, where altering one latent dimension mainly affects one factor of variation while leaving other factors relatively unaffected. The loss function for β-*VAE* is defined by $L(\emptyset, \theta, x, z, \beta) = \mathbb{E}_{q_{\emptyset(Z|X)}}[\log p_\theta(x|z)] - \beta\, D_{KL}(q_\emptyset(z|x)\,||p(z))]$. Therefore, a higher encourage disentanglement with trade-off between reconstruction quality and the extent of disentanglement. Disentangled representation gives good interpretability and easy generalization to a variety of tasks. For example, a β-*VAE* model trained on photos of human faces can capture many relatively independent factors like smile, color, etc. in separate dimensions, in latent space. Then use such disentangled representation to do facial enhancements. Hence, if we want to add a smile to an input image (human faces), we must find the vector in the latent space (lower dimension) that points in the direction of most smiles and add the vector (points to simile faces) to the position of the original image (i.e., without smile) in the latent space and then decode the image back (high dimension) with a new smiling face. The directional vector (points to smile faces) can be identified by subtracting the mean of a labelled smiling face's latent location from the mean of the labelled non-smiling face's latent location. Then, the new location of the old image that needed to be enhanced with the smile can be derived by adding this directional vector, scaled by transformation parameters, to the old image location. Similarly, we can morph between images by interpolating between two image points in the latent space with controlled transformation.

The other popular variant of VAE is **vector quantized VAE (VQ-VAE)** for learning discrete latent variables used for problems related to language and speech. The main idea behind VQ-VAE is the vector quantization layer with a discrete learnable codebook. Codebook is a set of vectors associated with the corresponding index. VQ-VAE maps the K-dimensional input vector to a finite set of codebook vectors. Each encoded vector is compared with all other vectors in the codebook (e.g. 512 codebook vectors) and is mapped to each of these codebook vectors with minimum Euclidean distance. The combination of the closest codebook vectors is then fed into the decoder as input. The process is referred to vector quantization in VAE. The quantization of vector is mathematically given by $z_q = arg \min_i ||z_e - e_i)||_2$ where e_i is the ith codebook vector. The decoder is then tasked with reconstructing the input from this quantized vector as in the standard autoencoder formulation. All encoder, decoder and codebook are learnable via gradient descent. But vector quantization is not differentiable, so as shown in *Figure 3.16* below, to train the encoder, the gradients are estimated via straight through estimator ($\nabla_z l$—Redline). As the reconstruction loss gradient does not flow through codebook, and additional codebook loss is introduced in VQ-VAE:

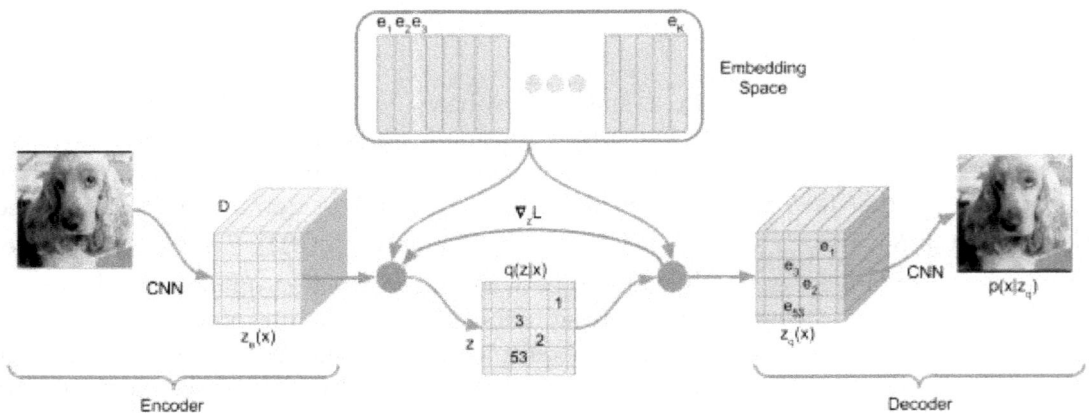

Figure 3.16: *VQ- encoder architecture*
(**Source**: *https://arxiv.org/pdf/1711.00937.pdf*)

VQ-VAE loss function is given by $\log p|z_q(x) + ||sg[z_e(x)] - e||_2^2 + \beta||z_e(x) - sg[e]||_2^2$.

The three loss terms for VQ-VAE are the reconstruction loss $(\log p|z_q(x))$. To optimize the decoder and the encoder for better reconstruction, the vector quantization loss is l_2 loss $||sg[z_e(x)] - e||_2^2$, a loss of Euclidean distance between the encoder output and codebook vector to ensure the chosen codebook vector close to encoder output. Finally, the commitment loss is $\beta||z_e(x) - sg[e]||_2^2$ to ensure encoder output to be is close to codebook vector and prevent it from fluctuating. With the help of the stop gradient sg operator gradient flow in vector quantization loss does not affect the encoder, and similarly, gradient flow in commitment loss does not affect the codebook.

Conclusion

In this chapter, we understood image processing techniques, real world examples, basic CNN architecture, and different variants of CNN based architectures such as ResNet, GoogleNet, MobileNet, etc. These deep learning architectures brought out different ways of processing image data on top of convolution networks, which helps to perform image classification, segmentations, and object detection. We also presented an example of a popular U-Net architecture for image segmentation. We understood the representation learning and deep neural architecture of autoencoder, variational autoencoder, and their variants , VQ-VAE. These representation learnings help to capture disentangled representations of image data that enable various image enhancement tasks like facial improvements, changing backgrounds, etc. In the next chapter, we will understand GAN and its applications, diffusion models, and flow-based models, and in upcoming chapters, we will understand how LLMS are leveraged along with vision models to bring multi modal capabilities in generative AI.

Key terms

- **Computer vision**: A branch of AI to make machines understand the visual world
- **Convolution neural network**: Neural network architecture used for CV tasks
- **Residual blocks**: A neural network block with a skip connection that learns residual functions with reference to the layer inputs
- **IoU loss**: Intersection over union loss used in object detection to optimize the IoU score between true boxes and predicted boxes
- **Encoder- decoder**: A type of neural network architecture that is used for sequence-to-sequence learning
- **KL-divergence**: Metric used to measure the relative entropy represented by two distributions
- **Codebook**: A learnable discrete vector representation used in VQ-VAE, which acts as bottleneck layer

Questions

1. What are the different CNN based architectures?
2. How do you calculate loss function in variational autoencoders?
3. What is the difference between VAE and VQ-VAE?
4. What is the difference between image classification, object detection, segmentation?
5. What are the benefits of residual connections?
6. What is meant by codebook in VQ-VAE?

Join our book's Discord space

Join the book's Discord Workspace for Latest updates, Offers, Tech happenings around the world, New Release and Sessions with the Authors:

https://discord.bpbonline.com

CHAPTER 4
Transforming Images with GenAI

Introduction

In the earlier chapters, we understood computer vision techniques, representation learning, and variational autoencoder. This chapter gives an introduction to generative modeling methods. We will understand encoder-decoder architecture, various **generative adversarial network** (**GAN**) types, learn diffusion processes and different diffusion models. Throughout the chapter, we will brief out generative modeling techniques, neural architectures, mathematical briefing, and examples. The examples we have chosen are improving image resolution using SRGAN, Text to Image conversion using multimodal architecture, and image generation using diffusion process.

Structure

In this chapter, we will learn the following topics:

- Generative modeling
- Generative adversarial network
- VQ-GAN and CLIP example
- Diffusion model
- Flow model
- Evaluation metrics for generative model

Objectives

The objective of this chapter is to provide an overview of generative modeling and understand different types of explicit and implicit modeling methods. In this chapter we cover architecture of GAN and lists out different variations of GANs and its applications with examples. We deep dive into diffusion process and understand how it helps to build diffusion model. We explain diffusion model architecture, training process and its variation latent diffusion model for image processing followed by MNIST example. We give foundation to flow models. Finally, we close with evaluation metrics used to validate the generative model performance.

Generative modeling

A generative model describes how a dataset is generated, in terms of a probabilistic model. By sampling from generative models, new data(images/voice) will be generated. Unlike discriminative models trained to estimate the conditional probability of the output for the given input $p(x|y)$, generative models learn the join probability distribution $p(x, y)$ or $p(x)$. For example, while the generative model could generate new animal photos, the discriminative model could classify the photos between animals. So generative model in simple terms can be explained as models that are used to generate new data points. For example, if a dataset contains positive and negative product reviews, with generative model we can learn the underlying data distribution and use it to generate synthetic product reviews. However, in discriminative modeling, we can train a model to learn the decision boundary to classify a new review as positive or negative. Some of the discriminative model use cases are predicting loan eligibility for a banking customer, spam filtering of emails, facial recognition systems, etc. Some of the generative model use cases are deepfakes, synthetic data generation, background image generation etc. Generative models can be classified at high levels, as shown in the figure below:

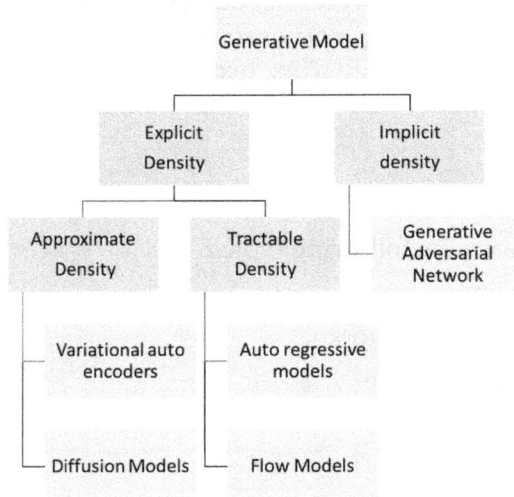

Figure 4.1: Generative model taxonomy

Generative modeling can be categorized at high level into implicit and explicit density models. Explicit density models are probabilistic generative models. They provide an explicit parametric specification of the data distribution and have tractable likelihood functions. They are further classified into approximate and tractable density models. While tractable density models define parametric function to capture data distribution efficiently, approximate density models learn the approximation through latent modeling. Some examples of approximate density models are variational autoencoders and diffusion models. Some examples of tractable density are autoregressive and flow models. The other classification, Implicit density models do not specify the distribution of data itself but rather only specify a stochastic procedure with which to generate data. GANs are an example of implicit generative models. In this chapter we will look into GANs, diffusion and flow models.

Generative adversarial networks

It does not explicitly model density; instead, it just samples to generate new instances. GAN are a way to make generative models by having two neural networks compete with each other. Generator turns noise into imitation of data to try to trick the discriminator, the discriminator tries to identify real data from the fakes created by the generator.

The objective of the discriminator is to maximize the log-likelihood of discovering real and fake images. So, the loss function is given by $arg \max_{D} \mathbb{E}_{x,z} [log\, D(x) + log\left(1 - D(G(z))\right)]$.

So it maximizes the average log probability of real images and log of inverted probability of fake images. A lower discriminator loss implies that discriminator is successfully identifying the fakes. In the above objective functions, $log\, D(x)$ — log-likelihood of the discriminator correctly classifying a real data point (x) as real. High log value translates to low loss function when presented with real data. $log\,(1-D(G(z)))$ — the log-likelihood of the discriminator correctly classifying a generated data point $(G(z))$ as fake. Ideally, $D(G(z))$ should be close to 0, making the log term positive and contributing to a lower overall loss.

The generator's role is to produce data samples that are as indistinguishable from real data samples as possible. So, the loss function is given by $arg \min_{G} \mathbb{E}_{x,z} [log\left(1 - D(G(z))\right)]$. A low generator loss implies that generator is successfully creating realistic image.

The combined loss function for GAN is given by dual competing objective i.e. $\min_{G} \max_{D} V(D,G) = \min_{G} \max_{D} \mathbb{E}_{x,z} [logD(x) - log(1-D(G(z)))]$. $G(z)$ is the generator output and $D(G(z))$ is the estimated output by discriminator for the given generator output being fake. $D(x)$ is the estimation of the probability of the real instance is fake. This is similar to binary cross-entropy loss $l = ylog\hat{y} + (1 - y)\, log(1 - \hat{y})$ where y is ground truth & $\hat{y}$ is predicted. Please find the figure below the basic architecture of GAN:

Real Samples

$$\log\big(D(x)\big) + \log(1 - D(G(z))$$

Latent Space

D
Discriminator

$G(z)$

$D\big(G(z)\big)$ and $D(x)$
Rea l or Fake

G
Generator

$\log(1\text{-}D(G(z))$

Noise

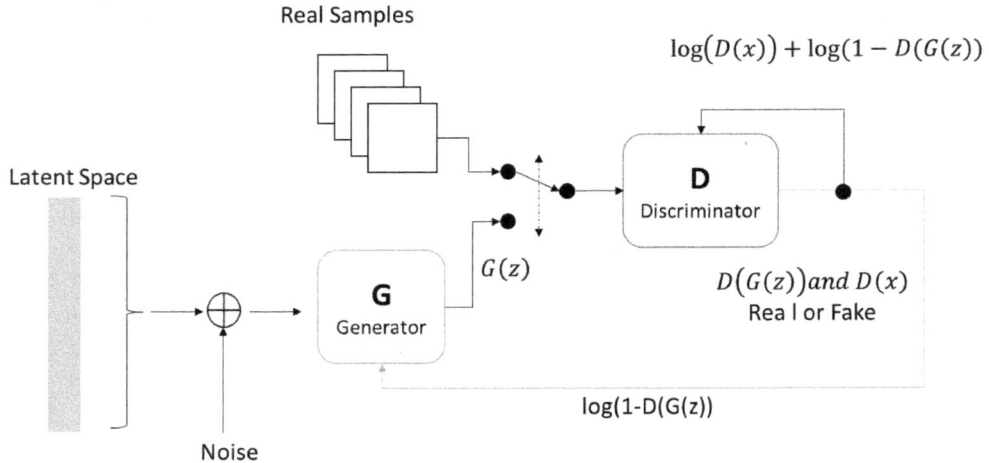

Figure 4.2: Basic GAN architecture

Given p_{data} the distribution of real dataset and p_g the distribution of generator, the global equilibrium or the optimization of GAN is the saddle point of min-max occurs only when $p_{data} = p_g$ where $D(x)$ get maximized and $(1 - D\big(G(z)\big)$ get minimized. The training of GAN happens for the generator and the discriminator separately having the other remain fixed. During training, for discriminator, real and fake data are inserted into the discriminator network with correct labels. Gradients are propagated, keeping the generator fixed, and network parameters are updated by an ascending stochastic gradient to maximize the loss function $\underset{D}{max}$.

On the other hand, the generator is trained with discriminator fixed by passing fake data and fake labels. Network parameters are updated by descending gradient descent to minimize the loss function $\underset{G}{min}$. The optimal discriminator for given generator can be found from the derivative of the loss function i.e., derivative of $\underset{G}{min}\ \underset{D}{max}\ V(D,G)$ and set to 0. The optimal discriminator D for any generator G is given by $D_G^*(x) = \frac{p_{data}(x)}{p_{data}(x)+p_g(x)}$. So given $p_{data} = p_g$ i.e., global minimum condition for objective function, $D_G^*(x) = \frac{1}{2}$ and the loss reduces to $V(D,G) = -log4$ and for given $p_{data} \neq p_g$ and considering Maximizing the likelihood is equivalent to the minimizing the **Kullback-Leibler** (**KL**) divergence the loss function can be mathematically derived as $V(D,G) = -\log 4 + KL(p_{data} \parallel \frac{p_{data}(x)+p_g(x)}{2}) + \log KL(p_g \parallel \frac{p_{data}(x)+p_g(x)}{2})$. JS divergence between two distributions p and q is given by $+\ JS\ (p\|q) = KL(p|\frac{p+q}{2}) + KL(q|\frac{p+q}{2})$, which is a smoothed and normalized version of KL divergence having a value between 0 and 1. The loss function can be rewritten as $\log 4 + 2\,JS(p_{data} \| p_g)$. So, optimizing the generator G means to minimize the JS divergence between p_{data} & p_g.

The basic GANs suffer from the following shortcomings like the vanishing gradient problem, non-convergence, mode collapse. To deal with the above issues **Wasserstein GAN (WGAN)** was introduced, which uses Wasserstein distance instead of JS distance measure. Wasserstein is a measure of the distance between two probability distributions. It is also called earth mover's distance. Unlike KL, Wasserstein provides a meaningful and smooth representation even if two distributions are located in manifold without overlap. Mathematically, it is given by $w\big(p_{data}, p_g\big) = \underbrace{\inf}_{\gamma \sim \Pi(p_{data}, p_g)} \mathbb{E}_{(x,y)\sim\gamma}[\|x - y\|]$

where $\Pi(p_{data}, p_g)$ is all feasible joint probability distribution between p_{data} and p_g, i.e., the amount of mass that must be moved from x to y to make p_{data} and p_g similar. WGAN introduces a critic instead of the discriminator, as in GAN. Discriminator is trained to learn K Lipschitz continuous function to help compute Wasserstein distance.

$W(p_{data}, p_g) = \underbrace{max}_{w \in W} \mathbb{E}_{X \sim p_{data}}[f_w(x)] - \mathbb{E}_{z \sim p_z} p(z)[f_w(G(z))]$ where f_w is a family of parameterized function where $w \epsilon W$ are K Lipschitz continuous. Similarly, generator seeks to minimize the Wasserstein distance between (p_{data}, p_g). Mathematically given by $\underbrace{min}_{G} \mathbb{E}_{X \sim p_{data}}[f_w(x)] - \mathbb{E}_{z \sim p_z} p(z)[f_w(G(z))]$. Please find the figure below for the basic architecture of WGAN:

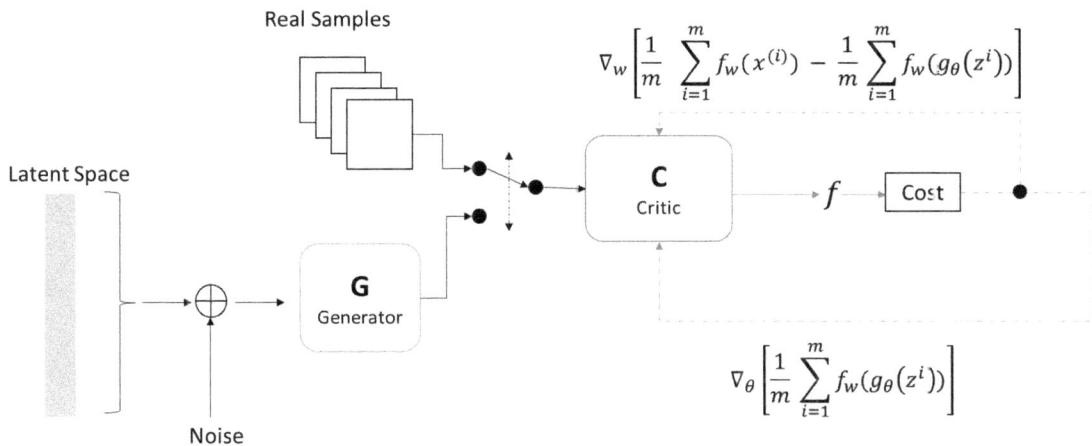

Figure 4.3: WGAN architecture

Example: Using GAN for improving image resolution

Objective: Using **super resolution** (**SR**) GAN in combination with an adversary network to produce higher resolution images. In this example we will use DIV2K dataset has 1000 2K resolution images divided into: 800 images for training, 100 images for validation, 100 images for testing. Please find the full code in the GitHub link **https://github.com/ karthiksab/GenAIBook/tree/main/chapter4**.

SRGAN generative network architecture

Train a generating function G that estimates **high resolution** (**HR**) for a given **low resolution** (**LR**) input image. Please find the below diagram for the SRGAN generator network. In the below diagram K signifies kernel size, n signified number of channels, s represents stride; e.g. k9n64s1 signifies kernel of size 9, 64 channels and stride of 1:

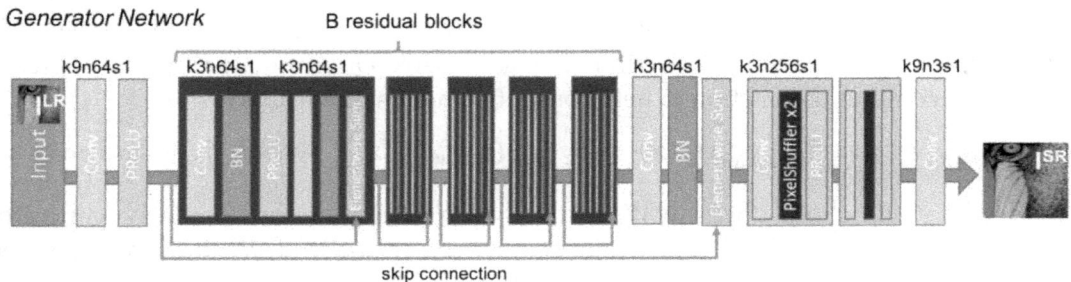

Figure 4.4: *SRGAN generative network*
(*Source*:*https://arxiv.org/pdf/1609.04802.pdf?ref=blog.paperspace.com*)

The following code is modified and derived from **https://github.com/krasserm/super-resolution/ tree/master**.

Below code shows the up-sampling block of generator with pixel shuffling and **parametric ReLU** (**PReLU**). Pixel shuffling rearrange the tensor of shape (N, C, H, W) into (N, C/r^*r, H*r, W*r) where r is the shuffling factor. PReLU is a kind of Leaky ReLU where instead of a predefined slope of 0.01, it makes it parameter for the neural network to decide the value of slope:

```
1. # upSmaple Block
2. def up_sample(x_in, filters_num):
3.     x = Conv2D(filters_num, kernel_size=3, padding='same')(x_in)
4.     x = Lambda(pixel_shuffle(scale=2))(x)
5.     return PReLU(shared_axes=[1, 2])(x)
```

Below code shows residual block network of generator with a Conv2D layer, a batch normalization layer, followed by a PReLU layer, another Conv2D layer and batch normalization. The finally input is added to residual block output:

```
1.  # res_block
2.  def resnet_block(x_in, filters_num, momentum=0.7):
3.      x = Conv2D(filters_num, kernel_size=3, padding='same')(x_in)
4.      x = BatchNormalization(momentum=momentum)(x)
5.      x = PReLU(shared_axes=[1, 2])(x)
6.      x = Conv2D(filters_num, kernel_size=3, padding='same')(x)
7.      x = BatchNormalization(momentum=momentum)(x)
8.      x = Add()([x_in, x])
9.      return x
```

Below code shows the generator network blocks with a repeat of Conv2D, PReLU and residual blocks. Unlike other GANs instead of noise, LR image is passed as input to the generator:

```
1.  # Generator architecture
2.  def generator_sr_resnet(filters_num=64, num_res_blocks=16):
3.      x_in = Input(shape=(None, None, 3))
4.      x_g = Lambda(norm01)(x_in)
5.
6.      x_g = Conv2D(filters_num, kernel_size=9, padding='same')(x_g)
7.      x_g = x_1 = PReLU(shared_axes=[1, 2])(x_g)
8.
9.      for _ in range(num_res_blocks):
10.         x_g = resnet_block(x_g, filters_num)
11.
12.     x_g = Conv2D(filters_num, kernel_size=3, padding='same')(x_g)
13.     x_g = BatchNormalization()(x_g)
14.     x_g = Add()([x_1, x_g])
15.
16.     x_g = up_sample(x_g, filters_num * 4)
17.     x_g = up_sample(x_g, filters_num * 4)
18.
19.     x_g = Conv2D(3, kernel_size=9, padding='same',
            activation='tanh')(x_g)
20.     x_g = Lambda(denorm11)(x_g)
21.
22.     return Model(x_in, x_g)
```

Discriminator

Train a discriminator network to discriminate real HR images from generated SR samples. The discriminator model is constructed to solve the adversarial min-max problem. The below architecture contains convolutional layers with of 3×3 filter kernels followed by two dense layers and a Leaky ReLU applied between and a final sigmoid activation function to obtain a probability for sample classification:

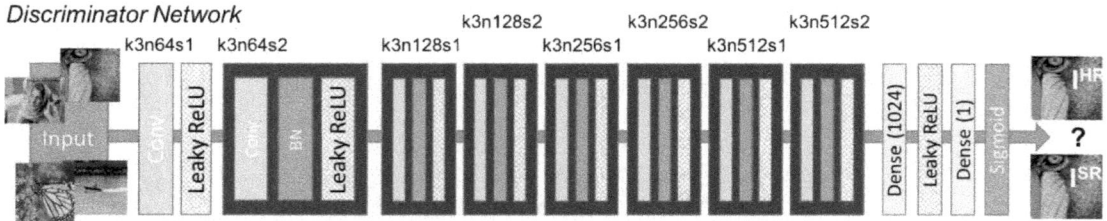

Figure 4.5: *SRGAN discriminator network*
(*Source*: *https://arxiv.org/pdf/1609.04802.pdf?ref=blog.paperspace.com*)

Below code shows discriminator block which have a bunch of repeating blocks of convolutional layers, followed by the batch normalization layer and the Leaky ReLU activation function. The **alpha** value for the **LeakyReLU** is set to **0.2**.

```
1.  #Discriminator block
2.  def discriminator_block(x_in, filters_num, strides=1, batchnorm=True,
        momentum=0.8):
3.      x = Conv2D(filters_num, kernel_size=3, strides=strides,
            padding='same')(x_in)
4.      if batchnorm:
5.          x = BatchNormalization(momentum=momentum)(x)
6.      return LeakyReLU(alpha=0.2)(x)
```

Below code shows discriminator network with discriminator blocks followed by dense layers followed by sigmoid activation for classification task. The **alpha** value for the **LeakyReLU** is set to **0.2**. Discriminator block reaches 8x upscaling factor from initial starting convolution size.

```
1.  #Discriminator architecture
2.  def discriminator(filters_num=64):
3.      x_in = Input(shape=(high_res_size, high_res_size, 3))
4.      x_d = Lambda(norm11)(x_in)
5.
6.      x_d = discriminator_block(x_d, filters_num, batchnorm=False)
7.      x_d = discriminator_block(x_d, filters_num, strides=2)
```

```
8.
9.      x_d = discriminator_block(x_d, filters_num * 2)
10.     x_d = discriminator_block(x_d, filters_num * 2, strides=2)
11.
12.     x_d = discriminator_block(x_d, filters_num * 4)
13.     x_d = discriminator_block(x_d, filters_num * 4, strides=2)
14.
15.     x_d = discriminator_block(x_d, filters_num * 8)
16.     x_d = discriminator_block(x_d, filters_num * 8, strides=2)
17.
18.     x_d = Flatten()(x_d)
19.
20.     x_d = Dense(1024)(x_d)
21.     x_d = LeakyReLU(alpha=0.2)(x_c)
22.     x_d = Dense(1, activation='sigmoid')(x_d)
23.
24.     return Model(x_in, x_d)
```

Loss function

The SRGAN uses **perpetual loss function (LSR)**, which is the weighted sum of two loss components: Content loss (VGG) and adversarial loss. VGG loss is based on the ReLU activation layers of the pre-trained 19 layer VGG network. Please find the below code or defining **_content_loss**:

```
1.      # Defining content_loss
2.      @tf.function
3.      def _content_loss(self, hr_output, sr_output):
4.          sr = preprocess_input(sr_output)
5.          hr = preprocess_input(hr_output)
6.          sr_features = self.vgg(sr) / 12.75
7.          hr_features = self.vgg(hr) / 12.75
8.          return self.mse_loss(hr_features, sr_features)
9.
10.     # Defining generator_loss
11.     def generator_loss(self, sr_output):
12.         return self.bce_loss(tf.ones_like(sr_output), sr_output)
```

Please find the below code or defining **_discriminator_loss**:

```
1.      # Defining discriminator_loss
2.      def _discriminator_loss(self, hr_output, sr_output):
3.          hr_output_loss = self.bce_loss(tf.ones_like(hr_output), hr_
            output)
4.          sr_output_loss = self.bce_loss(tf.zeros_like(sr_output), sr_
            output)
5.          return hr_output_loss + sr_output_loss
```

```
1. #Generating Super Resolution - Image
2.  sr_output = self.generator(lr_output, training=True)
3. #send the real image to discriminator
4. hr_output_f = self.discriminator(hr_output, training=True)
5. sr_output_f = self.discriminator(sr_output, training=True)
6.
7. content_loss = self._content_loss(hr_output, sr_output)
8. generator_loss = self._generator_loss(sr_output_f)
```

```
1. perpetual_loss = content_loss + 0.001 * generator_loss
2. discriminator_loss=self._discriminator_loss(hr_output_f, sr_output_f)
```

Generative adversarial networks variations

There are many variations of GANs in different contexts or designed for different tasks. Some of them are **Conditional GAN (cGAN)**, CycleGAN, StyleGAN, Stack GAN, SRGAN, GauGAN etc. Some of the applications of different GAN networks are:

- cGAN is mainly used for pix2pix paired translation, i.e., e.g. satellite view to roadmap equivalent of satellite images, translate edges to photo, translate black and white images to color.
- Cycle GAN is mainly used for image-to-image translation and domain transformation i.e., e.g. map to ariel view, photograph to artistic painting, MRI scan to CT-scans, translate day background images to night background.
- GauGAN is mainly used for creating photo realistic images from drawings i.e., e.g. creating virtual worlds for games, doodles to photo realistic landscape.
- SRGAN is mainly used for generating super resolution images from low resolution images. E.g. vehicle nameplate recognition, quality inspection StyleGAN is mainly used for style transfers between images i.e., e.g. generation of synthetic faces, deepfakes, fashion design.

In this section we will look into cGAN, CycleGAN and VQ-GAN:

- **Conditional GAN**: In cGAN, both the generator and discriminator are conditioned on labels or characteristics. cGANs are not fully unsupervised they require some sort of labels to condition. Generator uses noise vector z and labels y to synthesize a fake sample, i.e., $G(z, y) = x \mid y$. Discriminator with batches of labeled data from both real and generated data try to classify observations as real or fake. The modified objective function for cGAN is mathematically given by:

$$\underset{G}{min}\ \underset{D}{max}\ V(D, G) = \underset{G}{min}\ \underset{D}{max}\ \mathbb{E}_{x,z}\ [\log D(x|y) + \log(1 - D(G(z|y')))]$$

In the above equation, the previous probabilities are converted into conditional probabilities with y' labels. Both generators and discriminators are now trained only on respective labels, as shown in figure below:

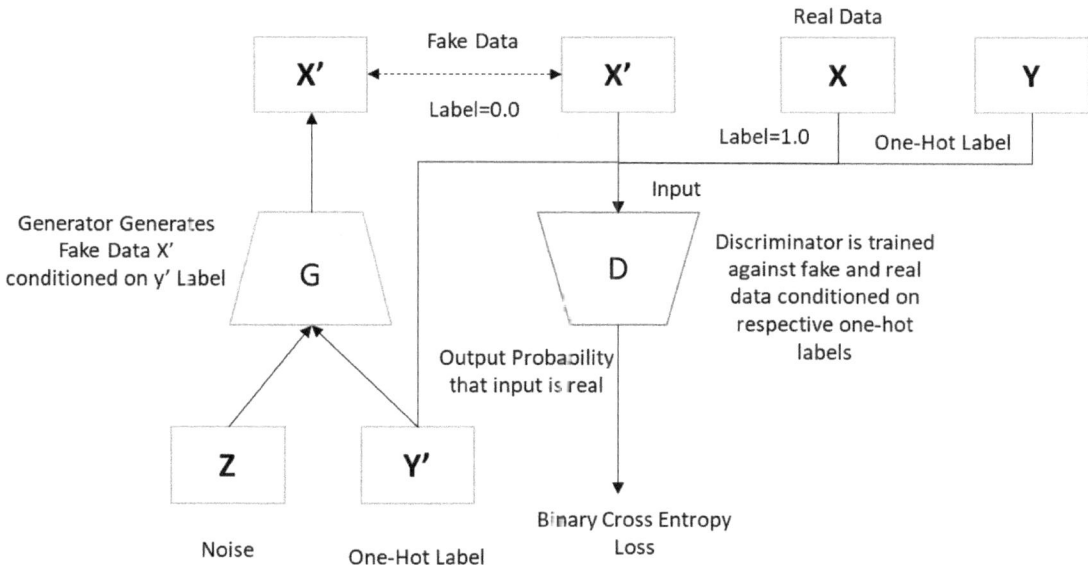

Figure 4.6: cGAN discriminator architecture

- **CycleGAN**: CycleGAN transforms images from one domain (Domain X) to another (Domain Y) without paired training data from the original domain to the target. This enables cross-domain image style transformation. As shown in the following diagram, CycleGAN learns the mapping $G:X \boxtimes Y$ such that $G(X)$ is the translation of the image from domain X to domain Y and also learns the reverse $F:Y \boxtimes X$ and $F(Y)$ is the translation of the image from domain Y to X.

CycleGAN uses two GAN networks to learn the mapping between X and Y. Generator G of the first GAN maps input image x from domain X to domain Y. The discriminator D_y of the second GAN is trained to detect real source domain images y of domain Y from generated source domain images y'. Generator G of domain X is trained against its adversary D_y to generate images that belong to domain Y.

Similarly, generator F of domain Y is trained against its adversary D_X to generate images that belong to domain X:

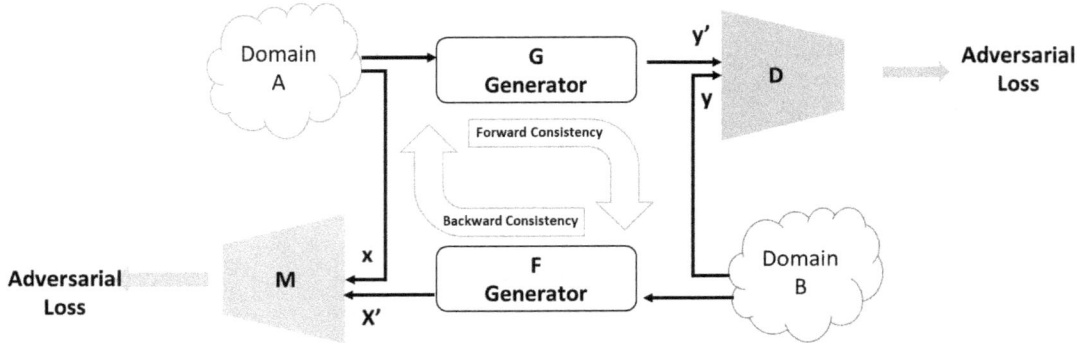

Figure 4.7: Cycle GAN architecture

The adversarial loss is applicable to both generators (G and F) which is used to match the distribution of generated images to target domain. So for generator $G: X \rightarrow Y$ the adversarial loss function is given by $L(G, D_Y, X, Y) = \mathbb{E}_{y \sim p_{data(y)}}[\log D_Y(y)] + \mathbb{E}_{x \sim p_{data(x)}}[\log(1 - D_Y(G(x)))]$. The discriminator D_y tries to distinguish between real domain Y and $G(x)$, i.e., $\underset{G}{min} \ \underset{D_Y}{max} \ L(G, D_Y, X, Y)$ like GAN. Similarly, for the generator $F: Y \rightarrow X$ the adversarial loss function is given by $L(F, D_X, Y, X)$ and discriminate D_X tries to $\underset{F}{min} \ \underset{D_X}{max} \ L(F, D_X, Y, X)$.

The cyclic consistency loss pushes generators for stability and learning function $F()$ *and* $G()$ such that they are inverse to each other, i.e., $F(G(x)) \approx x$. Cycle-consistency loss is particularly useful when no paired training data is available. Loss has two terms, i.e., forward cyclic consistency and reverse cyclic consistency. The intuitive understanding of cyclic loss is when an image from one domain is translated to the other and back again; we must have the same image back. Hence, cyclic loss calculates the L1 loss between the original image and the final generated image.

Cyclic consistency loss is given by $L_{cyc}(G, F) = \mathbb{E}_{x \sim p_{data(x)}}[|| F(G(x)) - x ||_1 + \mathbb{E}_{y \sim p_{data(y)}}[|| F(G(y)) - y ||_1$. The model is improved by adding an identity mapping component. This regularizes the generator to be near an identity mapping when real samples of the target domain are provided as the input to the generator. This technique encourages the generators to preserve the color of the input images.

by $L_{idt}(G, F) = \mathbb{E}_{x \sim p_{data(x)}}[|| G(x) - x ||_1 + \mathbb{E}_{y \sim p_{data(y)}}[|| F(y) - y ||_1$.

On combining adversary and cyclic losses, the total loss function is given by $L(G, F, D_X, D_Y) = L(G, D_Y, X, Y) + L(F, D_X, Y, X) + \alpha L_{cyc}(G, F) + \gamma L_{idt}(G, F)$, and the objective or cost function is given by $G^*, D^* = \arg \underset{G,F}{\min} \underset{D_X, D_Y}{\max}(G, F, D_X, D_Y)$.

- **VQ-GAN**: VQ-GAN is (VQ-VAE + GAN). It introduces the combined power of GAN and vector quantized variational autoencoder where the GAN is responsible for learning the rich expression of images from noise along with learning of discrete encoding representation of images through the codebook vectors. VQ-GAN enforces the generator to learn to generate images with specific visual elements represented by the codebook entries. VQ-GAN generates images in a progressive manner, starting from low resolution and gradually increasing the level of detail. As shown in the below figure VQ-GAN generator has an encoder-decoder network. VQ-GAN takes a two-stage approach, first is training the GAN to learn the visual parts of the input images and codeword representations in codebook. The second one is the transformer on top of codebook with sliding attention to learn long range interactions among visual parts. So, GAN helps to learn context-rich vocabulary of images constituents in form of code vectors and transformer helps to model their composition:

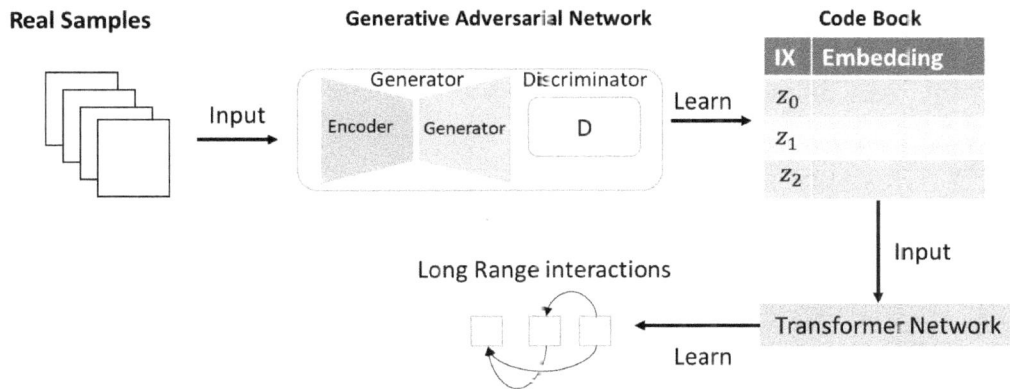

Figure 4.8: VQ-GAN architecture

The first stage is to train GAN, where the loss function is given by sum of GAN min-max loss and vector quantization loss. The min-max loss term for a regular GAN network is given by L_{GAN} dual competing objective, i.e., $\underset{G}{\min} \underset{D}{\max} V(D, G) =$ $\underset{G}{\min} \underset{D}{\max} \mathbb{E}_{x,z}[\log D(x) + \log(1 - D(G(z)))]$. The loss terms for Vector quantization $(L_{VQ}(E, G, Z))$ is the sum of reconstruction loss $||x - \hat{x}||^2$ to optimize decoder and encoder, vector quantization loss given by $||sg[z_e(x) - e]||_2^2$ where sg is the stop gradient operator and finally commitment loss to ensure encoder does not grow arbitrarily given by $\beta||z_e(x) - sg[e]||_2^2$.

So, the total loss for VQ-GAN is given by $\underset{E,G,Z}{min}\ \underset{D}{max}\ \mathbb{E}_{x,p(x)}\left[L_{VQ}\left(E,G,Z\right)+\gamma L_{GAN}\right]$ where Z is codebook and γ is adaptive weight.

The second stage is to train decoder only transformer. The input to transformer network will be the learned discrete representation of images, i.e., codebook vectors from GAN (first stage). The objective of transformer is to predict the next index of encoded sequence, i.e., $p(s_i|s_{<i})$ in auto regressive manner. The objective of transformer training is to minimize the log-likelihood loss of transformer., i.e.,

$$L_{Transformer} = \mathbb{E}_{x,p(x)}\left[-\log(p(s))\right].$$

The improved version of VQ-GAN is ViT-VQ-GAN. ViT is a visual transformer that replaces and divides the image into a sequence of patches that are tokenized (low-dimensional embedding + positional embedding) and then fed as input to an encoder transformer. The resulting embeddings are quantized according to the learned codebook. As shown in the below figure in addition to the GAN discriminator and learned codebook, there are 3 transformers used in ViT-VQ-GAN:

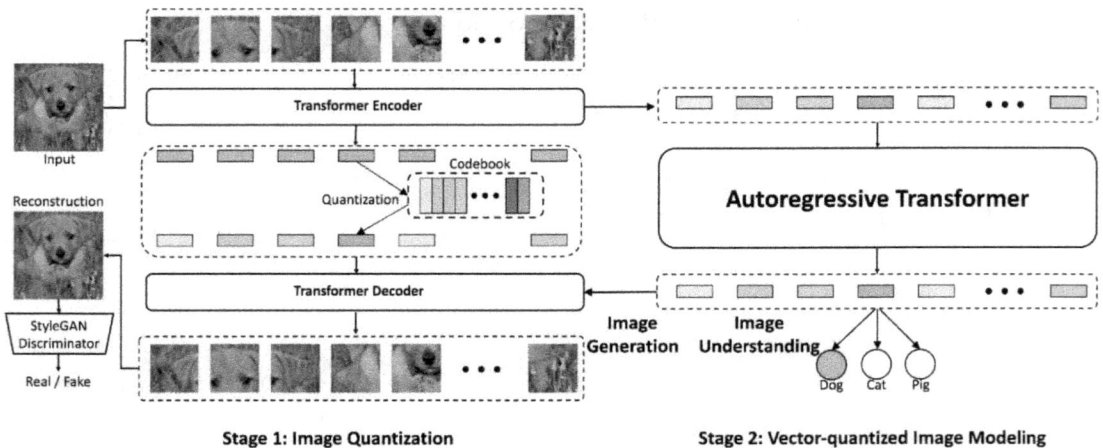

Figure 4.9: *ViT-VQ-GAN architecture*
(*Source*: *https://blog.research.google/2022/05/vector-quantized-image-modeling-with.html*)

The other improved version is VQ-GAN+ **Contrastive Language-Image Pre-training (CLIP)** architecture, where VQ-GAN generates vector quantized embeddings in a codebook. The codebook is then used as input to a transformer, which generates the new image from the encoded signals. That output is then used to assess the accuracy of the image to the inputted prompt through CLIP model, and then, that scoring is sent back to the VQ-GAN to update the image generation model to more closely reflect the prompt.

Example: Image generation from text

In this example we will look into multimodal model where we generate image based on the user text. Please refer to GitHub link for the full code **https://github.com/karthiksab/ GenAIBook/tree/Chapter4**. Originally, the solution was made by *Katherine Crowson* **(https://github.com/crowsonkb, https://twitter.com/RiversHaveWings). The details of clip architecture is in upcoming section** *Figure 4.16*.

Objective

Using CLIP and VQ-GAN architecture, we generate images using text. The input text query is encoded to embeddings of length 512 using CLIP architecture, and multiple crops of the images are embedded using CLIP of the same length. Cosine similarity is used to calculate the loss and tune the model between the text and image embeddings. The model takes text input and returns the image of VQ-GAN latent space embedding transformed to RGB image.

Please find the below code to load CLIP pretrained model:

```
1. # CLIP (Contrastive Language-Image Pre-Training) is a neural network
   trained on a variety of (image, text) pairs.
2. !git clone https://github.com/openai/CLIP.git
3. from CLIP import clip # Import Clip model
4. print(clip.available_models()) # See the available models
```

The following is the output for the preceding code:

```
['RN50', 'RN101', 'RN50x4', 'RN50x16', 'RN50x64', 'ViT-B/32', 'ViT-B/16', 'ViT-L/14', 'ViT-L/14@336px']
```

Figure 4.10: List of CLIP modes avialable

Below code load the visual transformer model B/16 and download the model. The default device is used as GPU and by setting **jit** as **False** we are loading non-jit version of the model:

```
1. ### CLIP MODEL ###
2. # Clip using visual transformer
3. clipmodel, _ = clip.load('ViT-B/16', jit=False)
4. clipmodel.eval() # Setting for evaluatoin model
5. print("Clip model visual input resolution: ", clipmodel.visual.input_
   resolution)
```

Below code defines the **utility** function to create CLIP encoding for the given text:

```
1. #creation of clip encoding
2. def encodeText(text):
3.     t=clip.tokenize(text).cuda() # tokenization
```

```
4.    t=clipmodel.encode_text(t).detach().clone() # encoding
5.    return t
```

Below code is to instantiate VQ-GAN-taming transformer model. VQ-GAN high quality image synthesis learns a codebook of context-rich visual parts:

```
1.  !git clone https://github.com/CompVis/taming-transformers
2.  from taming.models.VQ-GAN import VQModel
3.  config_model = OmegaConf.load("./models/VQ-GAN/configs/model.yaml")
4.  VQ_model = VQModel(**config_model.model.params)
5.  state_dict    =    torch.load("./models/VQ-GAN/checkpoints/last.ckpt",
    map_location="cpu")["state_dict"] # loading parameters
6.  VQ_model.load_state_dict(state_dict, strict=False)
7.  Generator_model=VQ_model.eval().to(device) # used for inference
8.  def generator(x):
9.      x = Generator_model.post_quant_conv(x) # Convolutional part of
        transformer
10.     x = Generator_model.decoder(x) # pass the Conv output to decoder
        part of transformer
11.     return x
```

Below code defines the function to set optimization parameters, get the image encoding out of pretrained CLIP model and get the text encodings (include and exclude) from taming transformer. These are used to calculate the final loss using cosine similarity function between image encoding and user text encodings:

```
1.  def optimize_result(Params, prompt):
2.      alpha=1 #  weightage to  include encoding
3.      beta=.5 ## weightage to  exclude encloding
4.
5.      ## image encoding
6.      out = generator(Params()) # generate new image
7.      out = norm_data(out) # normalize the result
8.      out = Img_Crops(out) # create crops 30x224x224
9.      out = normalize(out) #  normalizations required for pretrained clip
10.     image_enc=clipmodel.encode_image(out) ## get image encoding 30x512
11.
12.     ## text encoding  weight1 and weight2
13.     text_encoding = weight1*prompt + weight2*extras_encoding #:1 x 512
```

```
14.  text_encoding_include = text_encoding / text_encoding.norm(dim=-1,
     keepdim=True) # 1 x 512 # final include encoding
15.  text_encoding_exclude = exclude_encoding #final exclude encoding
16.
17.  ## calculate the loss
18.  inctext_img_loss = torch.cosine_similarity(text_encoding_include,
     image_enc, -1)  # cosine similarity between include text and image
     vectors
19.  exctext_img_loss = torch.cosine_similarity(text_encoding_exclude,
     image_enc, -1)
20. # cosine similarity between text and image vectors
21.  final_loss = -alpha*inctext_img_loss + beta*exctext_img_loss
22.  return final_loss
```

The below variable **include** defines list of the user input for image generation and **exclude** defines the list of attributes that must be avoided while generating the images.

```
include=['Road with animals and trees', '100 Cars flying in the sapce']
```

```
exclude='Red, low resolution , bright , cropped, incoherent, blurry'
```

Please find the below output of CLIP for 2 **include** text of animal and cars mentioned above:

Figure 4.11: Text to Image output for user text given

Diffusion model

In thermodynamics, **diffusion** is defined as the flow of particles from the high-density regions towards the low-density regions. In mathematics, it can be defined as transforming (T) complex distribution $p_{complex}(x)$ of $\mathbb{R}^d$ to simple prior distribution $p_{prior}(x)$ of $\mathbb{R}^d$.

Diffusion generative model is a Markov chain, and involves the forward process of adding random noise incrementally to sampled data (training set) and then construct the desired data sample by reversing the process from the noise. There are many diffusions based generative models and some examples are DALL-E 2, Stable Diffusion and Midjourney. The three mathematical frameworks that enable diffusion are denoising diffusion probabilistic models, noise conditioned score based generative models, and stochastic differential equation-based models. In this section, we will discuss the **denoising diffusion probabilistic model (DDPM)**.

Denoising diffusion probabilistic models

The forward diffusion process is defined as adding a Gaussian noise for T successive steps to obtain a noisy sample. As it follows the Markov process, the prediction probability at time t is dependent only on $t - 1$, as shown in the figure below. Forward process does not require training and the step sizes are controlled by variance schedule. The variance schedule based on parameter β_t can be constant, quadratic, or cosine. In DDPM, the variance schedule is a linear schedule. So, early stages take smaller noising steps than later stages. As shown in the following diagram the data x_0 becomes indistinguishable and with an increase in steps and as $T \xrightarrow{\infty}$ *Isotrophic Gaussian*.

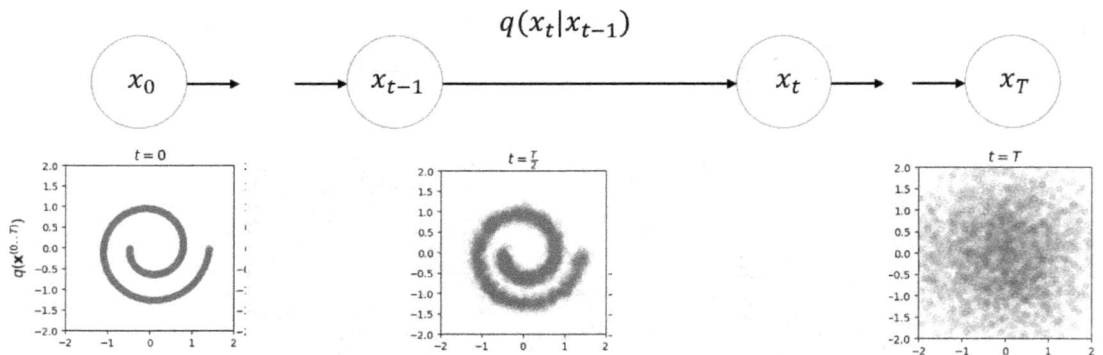

Figure 4.12: Forward diffusion process

Given that x_0 sampled from $q(x)$ in Markov chain, a Gaussian noise with variance β_t (hyper parameter) is added to x_{t-1} to get the latent variable x_t with distribution $q(x_t| x_{t-1})$. Mathematically, it can be defined as $q(x_t| x_{t-1}) = N(x_t; \sqrt{1 - \beta_t}x_{t-1}, \beta_t I)$ and the complete distribution can be given by $q(x_{1:T}| x_0) = q(x_0) \prod_{t=1}^{T} q(x_t| x_{t-1})$. Similar to GANs, the reparameterization trick is adopted to sample at any arbitrary time t without going through all the intermediary steps. By substituting $\alpha_t = 1 - \beta_t$ and $\widetilde{\alpha_t} = \prod_{t=1}^{T} \alpha_t$ we get $x_t = \sqrt{\widetilde{\alpha_t}}x_0 + (1 - \widetilde{\alpha_t}) \in$ where $\{\in_{t-1} ..... \in_0\} \sim N(0, I)$. So, the $q(x_t| x_0) = N(x_t; \sqrt{\widetilde{\alpha_t}}x_0, (1 - \widetilde{\alpha_t})I)$. Please find the below code for the forward process of diffusion:

```
1.      def forward_process(self, x0, t): #t number of diffusion steps
2.          t = t -1 # indexing at 0
3.          mu = torch.sqrt(self.alphas_bar[t]) * x0 # x0 is input data
4.          std = torch.sqrt(1 - self.alphas_bar[t])
5.          xt = mu + epsilon * std # data ~ N(mu, std)
6.
7.          std_q = torch.sqrt((1 - self.alphas_bar[t-1])/ (1 - self.
            alphas_bar[t]) * self.betas[t])
8.          m1 = torch.sqrt(self.alphas_bar[t-1]) * self.betas[t] / (1 -
            self.alphas_bar[t])
9.          m2 = torch.sqrt(self.alphas[t]) * (1 - self.alphas_bar[t-1])
            / (1 - self.alphas_bar[t])
10.         mu_q = m1 * x0 + m2 * xt
11.
12.         return mu_q, std_q, xt
```

The reverse process

The reverse process requires the estimation of probability density at an earlier time step given the current state of the system, i.e., $q(x_{t-1}| x_t)$. This enables generation of sample from Isotropic Gaussian noise, however the estimation requires knowledge on all the previous gradients, i.e., the entire data set. Unlike forward process, estimation of conditional probability $q(x_{t-1}| x_t)$ for each time step is done with the help of neural network trained on parameter θ. Mathematically, it is given by $p_\theta(x_{t-1}| x_t) = N(x_{t-1}; \mu_\theta(x_t, t), \sum_\theta(x_t, t))$ and $p_\theta(x_{1:T}) = p_\theta(x_T) \prod_{t=1}^{T} p_\theta(x_{t-1}| x_t)$. Please find below diagram for reverse diffusion process:

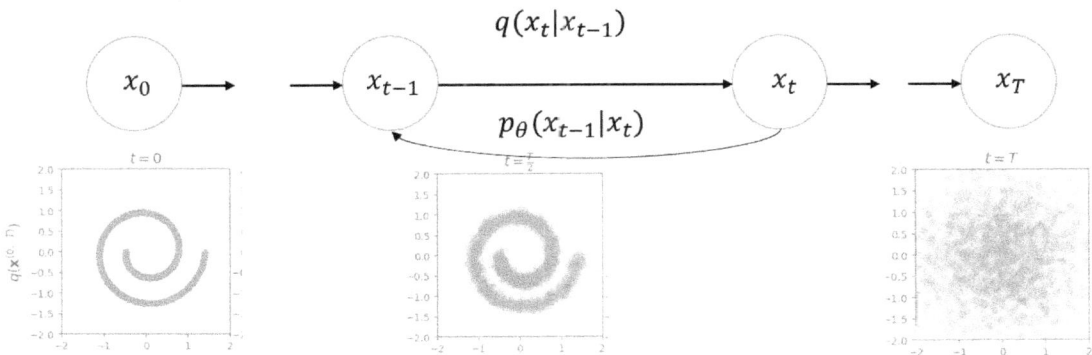

Figure 4.13: *Reverse diffusion process*

The below code shows **reverse_process** function where the deep neural network is used to estimate the probability for each time step given the current state:

```
1.      def reverse_process(self, xt, t):  #t no of timesteps
2.          t = t - 1 # indexing at 0
3.          mu, std = self.model(xt, t) # model(MLP Predict mu and sigma)
4.          mu, std = self.model(xt, t)
5.          epsilon = torch.randn_like(xt)
6.
7.          return mu, std, mu + epsilon * std # data ~ N(mu, std)
```

Model training

The training objective of diffusion-based models is to maximize the log-likelihood of sample generated from reverse process belonging to data distribution. i.e., $L = E_{x_0 \sim p_{data}} - \log(p_\theta(x_0))$. The equation is intractable i.e., cannot be solved by polynomial-time algorithm. With the help of **evidence low bound** (**ELBO**) or **variational lower bound** (**VLB**) the above intractable problem is reformulated to tractable optimization problems that can be solved using gradient based methods:

$$\log p(x) \geq \underbrace{E_{q(x_1|x_0)} \left[\log p_\theta(x_0|x_1)\right]}_{L_0} - \underbrace{DKL(q(x_T|x_0)||p(x_T)}_{L_T} - \underbrace{\sum_{t=2}^{T} E_{q(x_1|x_0)} \left[\log p_\theta(x_t|x_0)\right] \left[DKL(q(x_{t-1}|x_t,x_0)||p_\theta(x_{t-1}|x_t))\right]}_{L_{t-1}}$$

From the above, the loss function is given by $L_{vlb} := L_0 + L_1 + \cdots .. + L_T$. The second parameter ($L_T$) can be ignored during training as it has no learnable parameter (q). The third term, KL term compares the Gaussian distribution between the tractable posterior distribution $q(x_{t-1}|x_t, x_0)$ and parametrized reverse distribution process $p_\theta(x_{t-1}|x_t)$. The forward process posterior distribution $q(x_{t-1}|x_t, x_0)$ conditioned it at x_0 to make it tractable. Given by $q(x_t| x_{t-1}, x_0) = N(x_{t-1}; \tilde{\mu}_t(x_t, x_0), \tilde{\beta}_t I)$, where $\tilde{\mu}_t(x_t, x_0) = \frac{\sqrt{\bar{\alpha}_{t-1}}\beta_t}{1-\bar{\alpha}_t} x_0 + \frac{\sqrt{1-\beta_t}(1-\bar{\alpha}_{t-1})}{1-\bar{\alpha}_t} x_t$ and $\tilde{\beta}_t = \frac{(1-\bar{\alpha}_{t-1})}{1-\bar{\alpha}_t} \beta_t$. Since both the posterior and reverse distributions are Gaussian, $DKL(q(x_{t-1}|x_t, x_0)||p_\theta(x_{t-1}|x_t))$ can be formulated as $E_q \left[\frac{1}{2\Sigma_\theta(x_t,t)^2} ||\tilde{\mu}_t(x_t, x_0) - \mu_0(x_t, t)||^2\right] + C.$

With the reparameterization trick $x_0 = \frac{1}{\sqrt{\bar{\alpha}_t}} (x_t - \sqrt{1-\bar{\alpha}_t} \in)$ the $\tilde{\mu}_t(x_t, x_0)$ can be reformulated as $\frac{1}{\sqrt{1-\beta_t}} (x_t - \frac{\beta_t}{\sqrt{1-\bar{\alpha}_t}} \in)$ and $\mu_0(x_t, t)$ can be reformulated as $\frac{1}{\sqrt{1-\beta_t}} (x_t - \frac{\beta_t}{\sqrt{1-\bar{\alpha}_t}} \in_0 (x_t, t))$. After reparameterization, the final loss function is given by

$E_{x_0 \sim q(x_0), \epsilon \sim N(0,I)} \left[\frac{\beta_t^2}{2\Sigma_{\theta^2} (1-\beta_t)(1-\overline{\alpha_t})} \ || \ \epsilon - \epsilon_0 \ (\sqrt{\overline{\alpha_t}} \ x_0 + \sqrt{1-\overline{\alpha_t}} \ \epsilon, t)||^2 \right]$ which is further simplified by removing the initial weighing term $E_{x_0 \sim q(x_0), \epsilon \sim N(0,I)} \left[|| \ \epsilon - \epsilon_0 \ (\sqrt{\overline{\alpha_t}} \ x_0 + \sqrt{1-\overline{\alpha_t}} \ \epsilon, t)||^2 \right]$. So, the final loss function term $E_{x_0 \sim q(x_0), \epsilon \sim N(0,I)} \left[|| \ \epsilon - \epsilon_0 \ (x_t, t)||^2 \right]$ is a mean squared error between noise added in the forward process and noise predicted by the model. So, the job of our deep learning model during training is to approximate/estimate the parameters of this (gaussian) posterior such that the KL divergence is as minimal as possible.

Please find the below code for the diffusion process loss function:

```
1.     def get_loss(self, x0): # x0: [batch_size, self.dim]
2.
3.         t = torch.randint(input_dim, time_Steps+1, (1,))
4.         mu_q, sigma_q, xt = self.forward_process(x0, t)
5.         mu_p,sigma_p,xt_minus1=self.reverse_process(xt.float(), t)
6.         KL = torch.log(sigma_p) - torch.log(sigma_q) + (
7.             sigma_q**2 + (mu_q - mu_p)**2) / (2 * sigma_p**2)
8.         K = - KL.mean() # Should be maximized
9.         loss = - K # Should be minimized
10.
11.        return loss
```

Neural architecture for diffusion model

The implementation of DDPM is done using the U-Net shaped deep neural network. U-Net is a symmetric architecture with the same input and output shape. In the diffusion model, U-Net consists of an encoder, decoder, ResNet block, and self-attention layers. Similar to variational autoencoders, the architecture has down sampling layers where the input image are compressed spatially, expanding the channels and up-sampling layers where the compressed representations are expanded spatially reducing the channels. Unlike variational autoencoders, in a diffusion network, skip connections are provided between the encoder and decoder path. Diffusion time step is added to each residual block through sinusoidal positional embedding. This timestep embedding encodes the input's current position in Markov chain.

As we have already seen the up-sampling, down-sampling and ResNet-module in U-Net implementation in *Chapter 3, GenAI for Image-Part 1*. We will look into the additional modules of time embeddings and attention block.

The below codes are referenced and modified from the original public Ref: **https://github. com/hojonathanho/diffusion/blob/master/diffusion_tf/nn.py#LL90C1-L109C13** original paper DDPM: **https://arxiv.org/abs/2006.11239**.

Time embeddings: The following function takes the tensor input timesteps of shape (batch size,1) and output positional embeddings of shape (batchsize, dim):

```python
1.  def get_timestep_embedding(timesteps, embedding_dim: int):
2.      # Build Sinusoidal Embeddings
3.          assert len(timesteps.shape) == 1
4.          half_dim = embedding_dim // 2
5.          emb = math.log(10000) / (half_dim - 1)
6.          emb = torch.exp(torch.arange(half_dim, dtype=torch.float32,
            device=timesteps.device) * -emb)
7.          emb = timesteps.type(torch.float32)[:, None] * emb[None, :]
8.          emb = torch.concat([torch.sin(emb), torch.cos(emb)], axis=1)
9.
10.         if embedding_dim % 2 == 1:   # zero pad
11.             emb = torch.pad(emb, [[0, 0], [0, 1]])
12.
13.         assert emb.shape ==(timesteps.shape[0],embedding_dim), f"{emb.
            shape}"
14.         return emb
```

Attention block: Below code shows attention block function which is added between the convolution blocks in DDPM. It is used to capture long-range dependencies in the input sequence. The dot product of query and key vectors, followed by softmac is used to compute weights that describe the importance of the element in the input sequence for the generation of noise at a given step:

```python
1.  class AttentionBlock(nn.Module):
2.
3.      def __init__(self, ch):
4.          super(AttentionBlock, self).__init__()
5.
6.          self.Q = Nin(ch, ch)
7.          self.K = Nin(ch, ch)
8.          self.V = Nin(ch, ch)
9.
10.         self.ch = ch
```

```
11.         self.nin = Nin(ch, ch, scale=0.)

12.

13.     def forward(self, x):

14.         B, C, H, W = x.shape

15.         assert C == self.ch

16.         # group normalization

17.         h = nn.functional.group_norm(x, num_groups=32)

18.         q = self.Q(h)

19.         k = self.K(h)

20.         v = self.V(h)

21.         w = torch.einsum('bchw,bcHW->bhwHW',q,k)*(int(C)**( 0.5)) #
            [B, H, W, H, W]

22.         w = torch.reshape(w, [B, H, W, H * W])

23.         w = torch.nn.functional.softmax(w, dim=-1)

24.         w = torch.reshape(w, [B, H, W, H, W])

25.         h = torch.einsum('bhwHW,bcHW->bchw', w, v)

26.         h = self.nin(h)

27.         assert h.shape == x.shape
```

Below diagram shows the pseudo code of the training and sampling algorithm used in DDPM:

Algorithm 1 Training	**Algorithm 2** Sampling
1: **repeat** 2: $\quad \mathbf{x}_0 \sim q(\mathbf{x}_0)$ 3: $\quad t \sim \text{Uniform}(\{1, \dots, T\})$ 4: $\quad \epsilon \sim \mathcal{N}(\mathbf{0}, \mathbf{I})$ 5: $\quad$ Take gradient descent step on $\qquad \nabla_\theta \left\| \epsilon - \epsilon_\theta(\sqrt{\bar\alpha_t}\mathbf{x}_0 + \sqrt{1 - \bar\alpha_t}\epsilon, t) \right\|^2$ 6: **until** converged	1: $\mathbf{x}_T \sim \mathcal{N}(\mathbf{0}, \mathbf{I})$ 2: **for** $t = T, \dots, 1$ **do** 3: $\quad \mathbf{z} \sim \mathcal{N}(\mathbf{0}, \mathbf{I})$ if $t > 1$, else $\mathbf{z} = 0$ 4: $\quad \mathbf{x}_{t-1} = \frac{1}{\sqrt{\alpha_t}}\left(\mathbf{x}_t - \frac{1 - \alpha_t}{\sqrt{1 - \bar\alpha_t}}\epsilon_\theta(\mathbf{x}_t, t)\right) + \sigma_t \mathbf{z}$ 5: **end for** 6: **return** $\mathbf{x}_0$

Figure 4.14: Diffusion model pseudocode
(**Source**: *https://arxiv.org/pdf/2006.11239.pdf*)

Below code shows the function that implement above training algorithm as shown in *Figure 4.14*:

```
1.     def training(self, batch_size, optimizer):

2.         x0 = sample_batch(batch_size, self.device)

3.         t = torch.randint(1, self.T + 1, (batch_size,), device=self.
           device, dtype=torch.long)
```

```
4.         epsilon = torch.randn_like(x0)
5.         # gradient descent step
6.         alpha_bar_t = self.alpha_bar[t-1].unsqueeze(-1).
           unsqueeze(-1).unsqueeze(-1)
7.         predicted_epsilon = self.UNet_Model(torch.sqrt(
8.             alpha_bar_t) * x0 + torch.sqrt(1 - alpha_bar_t) *
               epsilon, t-1)
9.         loss = nn.functional.mse_loss(epsilon, predicted_epsilon)
10.        optimizer.zero_grad()
11.        loss.backward()
12.        optimizer.step()
13.
14.        return loss.item()
```

Below code shows the function that implements above sampling algorithm, as shown in *Figure 4.14*:

```
1.     def sampling(self,num_samples=1,img_chn=1,img_size=(32, 32),use_
       tqdm=True):
2.
3.         x = torch.randn((num_samples, img_chn, img_size[0], img_
           size[1]),
4.                         device=self.device)
5.
6.         progress_bar = tqdm if use_tqdm else lambda x : x
7.         for t in progress_bar(range(self.T, 0, -1)):
8.             z = torch.randn_like(x) if t > 1 else torch.zeros_like(x)
9.
10.            t = torch.ones(num_samples, dtype=torch.long,
               device=self.device) * t
11.
12.            beta_t = self.beta[t-1].unsqueeze(-1).unsqueeze(-1).
               unsqueeze(-1)
13.            alpha_t = self.alpha[t-1].unsqueeze(-1).unsqueeze(-1).
               unsqueeze(-1)
14.            alpha_bar_t = self.alpha_bar[t-1].unsqueeze(-1).
               unsqueeze(-1).unsqueeze(-1)
15.
```

```
16.          mean = 1 / torch.sqrt(alpha_t) * (x - ((1 - alpha_t) /
             torch.sqrt(
17.              1 - alpha_bar_t)) * self.UNet_Model(x, t-1))
18.          sigma = torch.sqrt(beta_t)
19.          x = mean + sigma * z
20.
21.      return x
```

Please refer to the example for full code on generating the MNIST dataset using DDPM with the following GitHub link **https://github.com/karthiksab/GenAIBook/tree/Chapter4**. The output is as follows:

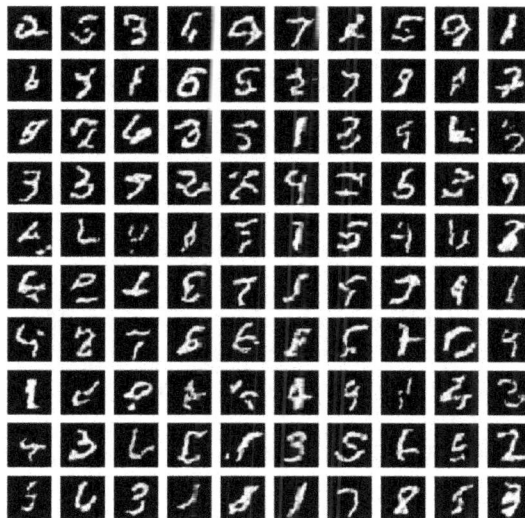

Figure 4.15: Output of DDPM model on MNIST dataset

In order to manipulate the generated samples, conditioned diffusion models are used where the prior distribution is conditioned by y, i.e., image or text embedding. Mathematically, it is given by $p_\theta(x_{1:T}) = p_\theta(x_T) \prod_{t=1}^{T} p_\theta(x_{t-1}| x_t, y)$. The gradients $\nabla_x \log p_\theta(y|x_t)$ is used to guide the diffusion sampling process towards conditioning information y. Mathematically conditioned diffusion model is given by $\nabla_x \log p_\theta(x_t|y) = \nabla_x \log p_\theta(x_t) + \nabla_x \log p_\theta(y|x_t)$.

Classifier guidance is a variant of conditioned diffusion model which consists of a trained conditional diffusion model and a trained classifier model on data x_t. The main idea is during sampling, inject the gradients of classifier model into the unconditional reverse process. The classifier $f_\emptyset(y|x_t, t)$ is trained on the noisy image x_t to predict the class y. Mathematically it can be defined as $\nabla_x \log p_{\theta,\emptyset}^{\sim}(x_t|y) = \nabla_x \log p_\theta(x_t|y) + \omega. \nabla_x \log p_\emptyset(y|x_t)$ (*i.e conditional + classifier*).The $\omega > 1$ amplifies the influence of the classifier signal.

Similar to the above, the classifier guidance model can be conditioned on different types. Different condition types are scalar conditioning, image conditioning, and text conditioning. CLIP is one of the examples of text conditioning. CLIP guidance was implemented by replacing the classifier with a CLIP model trained on noised images. The CLIP model learns visual concepts in the form of text by embedding text and image in the same space via projection layer:

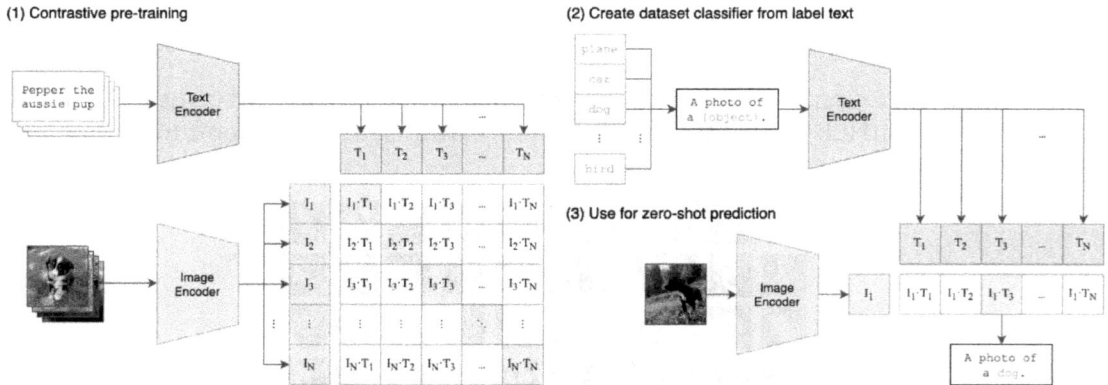

Figure 4.16: CLIP architecture
(*Source*: https://openai.com/research/clip)

As shown in the figure, the CLIP model has an image encoder $f(x)$ and a text encoder $g(c)$. During training batches of (x, c) are sampled and model is optimized for contrastive cross-entropy, i.e., maximize the dot product $f(x).g(c)$ for close pair of image and text. So in case of clip guidance based diffusion model, the above conditioned diffusion model equation can be formulated as $\nabla_x \log p_{\theta,\emptyset}^{\sim}(x_t|y) = \nabla_x \log p_\theta(x_t|c) + \omega.\nabla_x(f(x_t).g(c))$ (*i.e conditional + clip model*).

The main disadvantage of classifier guidance is resource intensive as it needs to be trained from scratch on noisy images. So, another approach is classifier-free guidance, where it provides an alternative by training the conditional diffusion model with conditioning drop out i.e. conditional information y (label) is set to null at random portions of time. For classifier free the diffusion equation is formulated as $\nabla_x \log p_{\theta,\emptyset}^{\sim}(x_t|y) = (\omega)\nabla_x \log p_\theta(x_t|y) + (1 - \omega).\nabla_x \log p_\theta(x_t)$ (*i.e conditional + unconditional*).

The preceding equation is a barycentric combination of conditional and unconditional functions. When $\omega = 0$ the equation is strongly unconditional, and when $\omega = 1$ it is standard conditional, and when $\omega > 1$ it is strongly conditional. DALLE 2 and Imagen apply classifier free guidance. In both the models, text embeddings were set to null randomly, and the text captions dropped for a certain percentage of the time.

Another method of generating high resolution messages is through cascading diffusion models. It consists of a pipeline of many sequential diffusion models that generate images of increasing resolution. Each model generates a sample with superior quality than the previous one by successively up-sampling the image and adding higher resolution details. To generate an image, we sample sequentially from each diffusion model. The U-Net architecture described in an earlier section is the common choice of model architecture, and in order to avoid cascading errors, a strong data augmentation is applied to the conditioning input of each super resolution model $p_\theta(x \mid z)$.

Latent diffusion models

Unlike other diffusion models, in latent diffusion models, the diffusion process takes place on smaller latent space instead of higher dimensional input. An encoder network VAE is used to encode the input into a latent representation, and a standard diffusion model is applied to generate new data, which is unsampled by the decoder network. Please find the below latent diffusion model architecture:

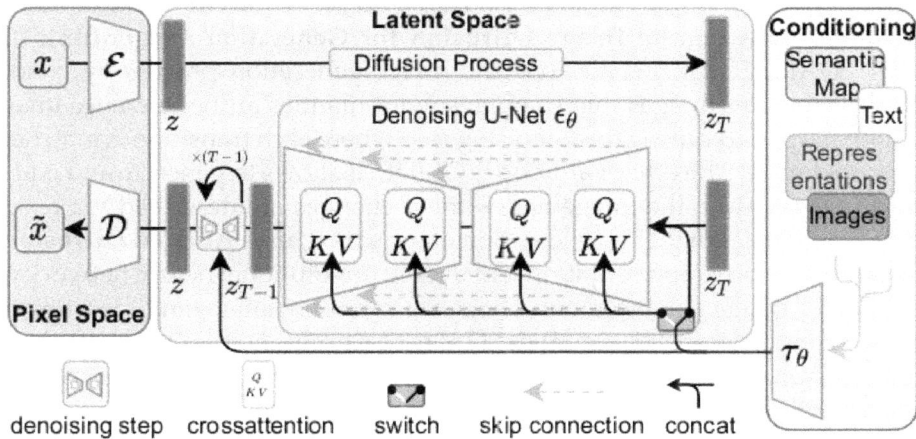

Figure 4.17: Latent diffusion model architecture
(**Source**: *https://arxiv.org/pdf/2112.10752.pdf*)

As shown in the above diagram, the first step is to extract the latent representation of the input image using encoder $\mathcal{E}$. The second step is progressively adding the gaussian noise as part of the diffusion process that transforms z to z_t in T steps of noise. The third step is denoising process of latent vector z_t. The denoising model is a time-conditioned U-Net, arbitrarily conditioned with cross-attention mechanism (Text, semantic maps, images). Each type of conditioning information is paired with a domain-specific encoder T_θ to project the conditioning input to an intermediate representation that can be mapped into cross-attention component. In the reverse diffusion process, as shown in the above diagram, z_T is passed through a U-Net model similar to denoising diffusion model to derive z_0, and returned to pixel space via the decoder. Latent diffusion leads to faster training and sampling as it has been processed in latent space instead of pixel space:

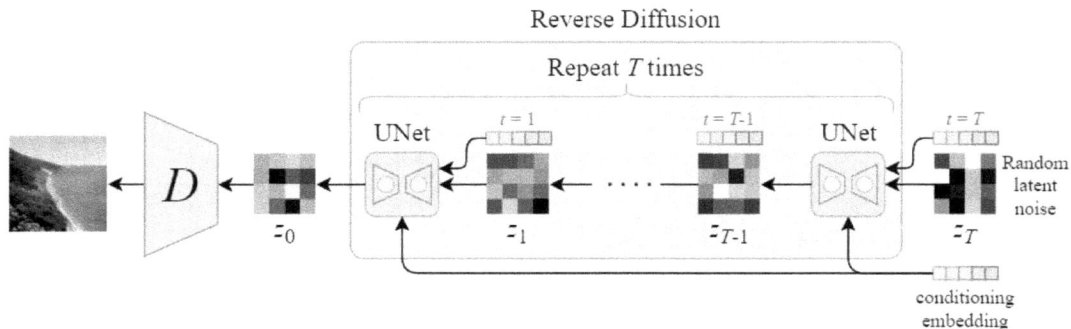

Figure 4.18: *Latent diffusion model reverse process*
(**Source**: *https://arxiv.org/pdf/2112.10752.pdf*)

Some of the variations of the diffusion model are **Iterative Latent Variable Refinement** (**IVLR**), **Guided Language to Image Diffusion for Generation and Editing** (**GLIDE**), Imagen, and DALL-E. ILVR conditions the image generation process by conditioning DDPM. ILVR generates images that share desired semantics in the reference image used. The condition is applied during the denoising step where each transition is matched with a given reference image. The other variation is GLIDE. It allows to generate and edit images. The change is marked on the image and wanted changes are described via text. GLIDE uses a transformer to learn the representation of input text, uses **Ablated Diffusion Model** (**ADM**) to learn the noise representation and uses a convolutional neural network outfitted with attention for image enhancement. The other variation is Imagen. It is a text to image diffusion model. It has transformer model (T5) for text presentation and diffusion models (U-Net) architecture with caption conditioning in high-fidelity image generation. Imagen uses classifier guidance and dynamic thresholding mechanisms to improve captioning alignment to image generation. Further, Imagen uses **small to medium** (**STM**) SR and **medium to large** (**MTL**) SR diffusion models to resolve the base 64x64 image into 256x256 and 1024x1024 images. DALL-E is another variant of text-image diffusion model. It uses CLIP pre-trained model to generate text encoding. The prior (Autoregressive or diffusion) creates the CLIP image embedding from the generated CLIP text embeddings. CLIP image embeddings are passed through the GLIDE Decoder to generate the images.

Flow model

A flow-based generative model is constructed by a sequence of invertible transformations. The major difference, as compared to VAEs, is that flows use invertible functions f to map the input data x to a latent representation z, as shown in the below *Figure 4.19*. A function is invertible if a one-to-one correspondence function exists to map every input data point x, to a corresponding latent representation z that allows to perform lossless reconstruction (z to x). The idea behind a generative model is to mimic the distribution of the training data points and then use this distribution to generate new data.

For a given density function $p_z(z)$, the change of variable formula gives us the density of $p_x(x)$, i.e., given by $p_x(x) = p_z(z) \left| \det \left(\frac{\partial x}{\partial z} \right) \right|^{-1}$ where $z = f^{-1}(x)$. z must be of the same shape as x and in order to determine the probability of x we only need to determine the probability of latent space and derivative of f. In the case of multivariate function, the derivative of will be a Jacobian (Discussed in *Chapter 2, GenAI Fundamentals*). The determinant of Jacobian determines how much $\bar{f}$ is expanding or contracting with the volume locally around z. But in generative model design, there are three considerations:

$p_z(z)$ must be differentiable for backpropagation.

Mapping function must be simple to calculate f^{-1}.

Able to compute Jacobian determinants that are not computationally expensive.

Normalizing flow (**NF**) models are adopted to achieve the above three considerations. A normalizing flow transforms a simple distribution into a complex one by applying a sequence of invertible transformation functions. Flowing through a chain of transformations, we repeatedly substitute the variable for the new one according to the change of variables theorem and eventually obtain a probability distribution of the final target variable. So, starting with the simple prior Gaussian distribution for latent z_0, a sequence of invertible functions $f_1, f_2, \ldots, f_k$ are applied to make z_k represents input x:

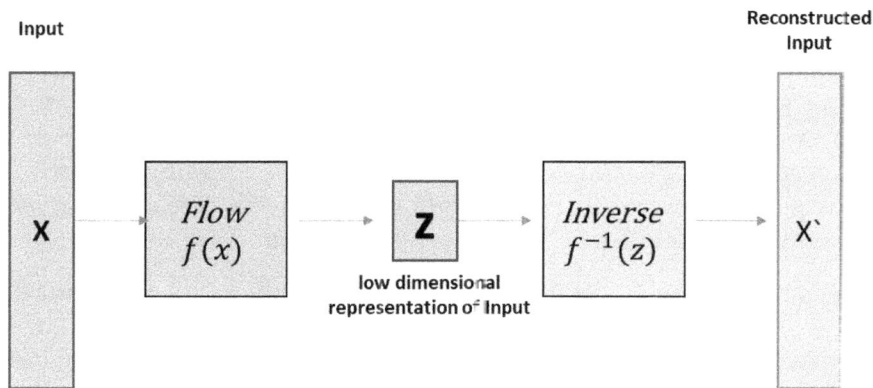

Figure 4.19: Flow model process diagram

Real-valued non-volume preserving (**Real NVP**) is a type of normal flow model that implements a normalizing flow by stacking sequence of invertible bijective transformation functions. Bijective functions are one-to-one corresponding function given by $f: X \boxtimes Z$ where each element in domain X has a unique element in co-domain Z. Real NVP introduces a coupling layer where the input dimensions (D) of x is divided arbitrarily into two parts of which the first j dimensions $(x_{1:j})$ remains the same, not changed by the flow, the second $j+1$ to D dimensions $(x_{j+1:D})$ undergo affine transformations of scale and shift. However, the scale and shift of second dimensions $j + 1$ to D parameters are functions of the first dimension. So, $z_{1:j} = x_{1:j}$ and $z_{j+1:D} = Scale + Shift\,(x_{1:j})$. so affine transformation could be shifting the input by bias μ and scale it by σ. Henceforth, $z_{J+1:D} = (x_{j+1:D}) \odot (\sigma(z_{1:j})) + \mu(z_{1:j})$.

The coupling layer will have different deep neural networks to create a scale and transformation output. The splitting between dimensions $(x_{1:j}, x_{j+1:D})$ is done through masking. For example, if the input dimension is 2, i.e., (x_1, x_2) then after masking 1 dimension the input will be $(x_1, 0)$. The masked parameters are sent through the dense layers to predict the transformational parameters. There are different masking techniques. However, the popular ones used in image generation is check board and channel masking. In check board masking, the variables are split across width and height dimensions. In channel masking, one half of the channels are assigned to $x_{1:j}$ and the other half to $x_{j+1:D}$. In the case of multiple coupling layers, the masking for each layer is inverted so that each variable is transformed a similar amount of times.

The objective of training is simply the **negative log-likelihood** (NLL) over the training dataset. So, given the density function $p_x(x) = p_z(z) \left| \det\left(\frac{\partial x}{\partial z}\right) \right|^{-1}$, the NLL will be $L(D) = -\frac{1}{D} \sum_{x \in D} \log p(X)$. To estimate $L(D)$, the prior probability $p_z(z)$ needs to be computed and it is assumed to be a Gaussian distribution with mean and variance given by (μ, σ). During training, the first layer performs the split, the forward process maps the input data points to resemble $p_z(z)$, which is generally Gaussian, and the backward process takes sample points from Gaussian to map them back to the distribution that resembles the input.

Efficient Real NVP models for larger dimensions are built through multi-scale architecture by applying squeeze and split operations. Squeeze is to trade-off spatial dimensions for channel dimensions. It converts a tensor of size $[c*h*w]$ into a tensor of $[4c, h/2, w/2]$ through reshaping, enabling a few convolution operations. The building blocks of Real NVP with multi-scale architecture include coupling layers with checkboard masks, squeeze operations, and again coupling layers with alternate channel-wise masks.

The GLOW variant of Real NVP is where the reverse masking setup was replaced with invertible 1×1 convolutional layer. As shown in the following Figure 4.20, steps in one step of flow are:

1. Normalizing flow step—ActNorm.
2. Invertible 1x1 convolution layer.
3. Affine coupling layer.
4. An ActNorm is similar to batch normalization where, for a given mini-batch, data parameters are initialized such that activation per channel have zero mean and unit variance post ActNorm. Post initialization, the scale, and bias are treated as regular trainable parameters that are independent of the data.
5. Invertible 1x1 convolution layers having an equal number of input and output channels used between the layers of Real NVP flow to reverse the order of channels.
6. The affine coupling layer design is the same as Real NVP, as given below:

a. Forward pass:

    i. $Split(x) = (x_a, x_b)$

    ii. $\log \sigma, \mu = NN(x_a)$

    iii. $y_b = x_b \odot \sigma + \mu$

    iv. $y = concat(y_b, x_a)$

b. Backward pass

    i. $Split(y) = (y_a, y_b)$

    ii. $\log \sigma, \mu = NN(y_a)$

    iii. $x_b = (x_b - \mu)/\sigma$

    iv. $y = concat(x_b, y_a)$

Glow architecture supports multi-scale structures with L scales, each containing K iterations of NF, and each block is separated by squeeze/split operations, as shown in the following figure. We only need the encoder for the training phase. The decoder (reverse glow) is used for sampling only:

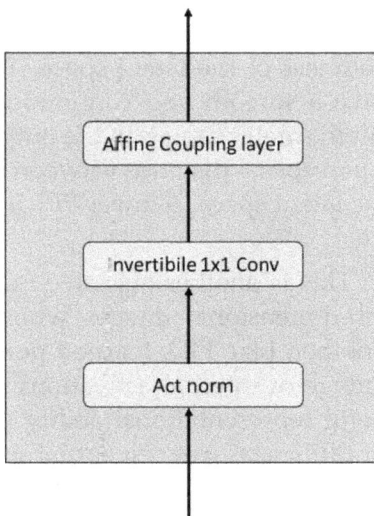

F g a : One step of the flow   Fig b : Multi Scale architecture

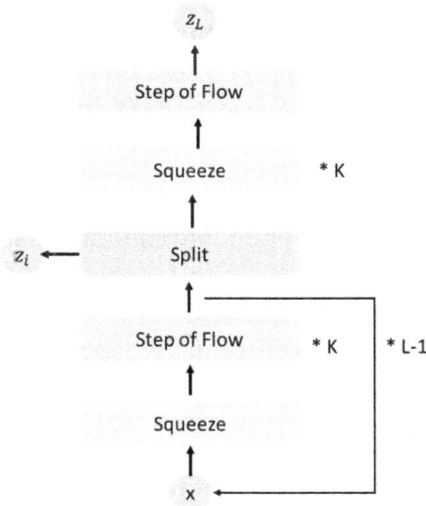

Figure 4.20: One step and multi-scale architecture of glow model

Evaluation metrics for image generative model

Generative models for images involve a different evaluation approach. It introduces a shift from metrics like accuracy, precision, recall, F1 score, mean squared error. Generative image modeling evaluation involves assessing the quality and diversity of generated samples. So, the required metrics that encompasses both statistical properties and visual fidelity. Below are some of the metrics used to evaluate generative image modeling:

- **Inception score (IS)**: The IS measures the diversity and sharpness of the generated model output. The inception score involves using a pre-trained deep learning neural network model inception v3 model for image classification to classify the generated images. The score ranges from 1.0 to number of classes supported by the classification model. Mathematically, it is defined as $IS(G) = exp(E_{X \sim P_g} D_{KL} (p(y|x)$ $|| p(y|x)))$. $p(y|x)$ given a generated image to a particular label has low entropy, marginal predictive distribution has high entropy.

- **Fréchet inception distance (FID)**: It calculates the distance between the real and fake images. So, the lower the score, the better the model performance. It uses the embeddings, i.e., feature representation of images from the last pooling layer of inception v3 model. Fit a multivariate Gaussian distribution with mean and covariance of distributions given by (μ_r, Σ_r) ; (μ_g, Σ_g). FID is calculated using Wasserstein-2 distance between 2 Gaussians which is given by $FID = ||\mu_r - \mu_g||^2 + T_r(\Sigma_r + \Sigma_g - (2\Sigma_r\Sigma_g)^{\frac{1}{2}})$. FID score is robust to the noise, and it can easily measure the diversity of the images.

- **Perceptual path length**: Perceptual path length (PPL) is an evaluation metric for generative models that focuses on the smoothness of the latent space. The idea is that a good generative model should have a smooth and continuous latent space, where small changes in the input result in small changes in the output. The PPL is calculated by measuring the average perceptual distance between pairs of generated samples that are interpolated in the latent space. A lower PPL indicates a smoother and more continuous latent space.

- **Learned perceptual image patch similarity**: This is another objective metric for calculating the structural similarity of high-dimensional images whose pixel values are contextually dependent on one another. Like FID, **learned perceptual image patch similarity** (**LPIPS**) takes advantage of internal activations of deep convolutional networks because of their useful representational ability for low-dimension vectors. Unlike previous metrics, LPIPS measures perceptual similarity as opposed to quality assessment. LPIPS measures the distance in the VGGNet feature space as a perceptual loss for image regression problems.

- **Structured similarity index metric (SSIM)**: L2 distance uses pixel differences to measure the structural differences between two images (sample and reference). It is highly capable of identifying structural information from a scene. The value is between -1 and +1. The metric is based on three key features from an image (Luminance, contrast, structure). The higher the value, the better representing the images are similar.

- **Peak signal-to-noise ratio**: It is commonly used to quantify reconstruction quality for images and videos subject to lossy compression. It is numerical value that quantifies the similarity between images (original vs generated). Higher is better.

- **Bits per dimension**: The standard metric used in generative models, and in particular normalizing flows, is **bits per dimensions (bpd)**. Bpd describes how many bits we would need to encode a particular sample in our modeled distribution. The less bits we need, the more likely the sample is represented in the modeled distribution. Lower is better.

Conclusion

In this chapter, we understood different types of generative modeling, and implicit and explicit density modeling. We understood the encoder-decoder architecture, basic GAN operations, and different variants of GAN for different applications. We discussed different GAN variations like cGAN, CycleGAN, StyleGAN, Stack GAN, SRGAN, GauGAN. We briefed operations of cGAN where generator and discriminator are conditioned on labels or characteristics and briefed on operations of Cycle GAN where images translate from one domain (Domain X) to another (Domain Y) without paired training data available. Then we introduced VQ-GAN which combine power of Generative adversarial network and Vector quantized variational auto encoder where the GAN is responsible for learning the rich expression of images from noise along with learning of discrete encoding representation of images through the codebook vectors. Some of the real-world application of GAN includes improving image resolution, image to image translations, creation of new photo realistic images and style transfers. Later in the diffusion model, we explained the forward and reverse diffusion process, the use of neural networks in the reverse generation process, and different methods such as the DDPM, conditional diffusion, and latent diffusion. We also presented examples of Super image resolution using SRGAN, multimodal text to image generation using pretrained CLIP-VQ-GAN architecture, and image generation using the Denoising Diffusion model. We presented the basics of the flow model and the way the glow model operates. Finally, we concluded with the general metrics used to evaluate the performance of generative models.

Key terms

- **Diffusion**: Process of progressively adding noise to a high quality dataset and then learning to reverse this process
- **Min-max loss**: Standard GAN loss function where generator tries to minimize the loss function while discriminator tries to maximize the same
- **Invertible function**: For every data point x, we have a corresponding latent representation z which allows us to perform lossless reconstruction (z to x)
- **Codebook**: In VQ-GAN or VQ-VAE represents the vocabulary of discrete representation of images as code vectors

Questions

1. What is the reparameterization trick in auto encoders?
2. What are the different types of generative modeling?
3. How do you calculate the min-max loss function in GAN?
4. What is the difference between classifier and non-classifier guidance in diffusion?
5. What is the forward and reverse process in the diffusion model?
6. Why is the latent diffusion model faster as compared to the other diffusion model?
7. What are the common evaluation metrics for generative Model?

Join our book's Discord space

Join the book's Discord Workspace for Latest updates, Offers, Tech happenings around the world, New Release and Sessions with the Authors:

https://discord.bpbonline.com

CHAPTER 5
GenAI for Text

Introduction

Over the past few years, we have seen a giant leap forward in the advancement of AI technologies in processing natural languages and performing text-related tasks. **Large language models** (**LLM**) have demonstrated their ability to mimic humans when it comes to text-related tasks. Such applications of **natural language processing** (**NLP**) tasks span across domains with a plethora of use cases. Since the release of ChatGPT application, we have witnessed an unprecedented surge in private and open-source LLMs to perform these NLP tasks. With new LLM models emerging, it is difficult to keep up with different architectures and model types. In this chapter we will look into the details of transformer architecture underpinning all LLM models and look into different natural language processing tasks, techniques, and examples.

Structure

In this chapter, we will go through the following topics:

- Natural language processing
- Sequence to sequence model system
- Transformer architecture
- NLP examples

Objectives

The objective of this chapter is to introduce NLP technology, its terminologies, and its significance across industries. It aims to explain the concepts of text pre-processing, post-processing, and various deep learning architectures for NLP tasks like traditional sequence-to-sequence modeling systems, such as **recurrent neural networks (RNN)** and **long-short term memory (LSTM)** networks to the state-of-the-art **transformer architectures**. The chapter mainly focuses on the different types of transformer architectures, their components, and various applications. We will look into guided examples for summarization, question and answer, and speech to text recognition tasks.

Natural language processing

NLP and Computer vision are the most popular sub-fields of artificial intelligence, where NLP has achieved an insurmountable feat after the release of generative pre-trained models from *OpenAI GPT-3*. NLP is a multidisciplinary field related to Linguistics, computer science, and artificial intelligence that empowers machines with the ability to understand, analyze, and manipulate the human language in the way it is written and spoken. The two sub-fields of NLP are **natural language understanding (NLU)**, focusing on the intended meaning of the text and **natural language generation (NLG)**, focusing on text generation. While NLU extracts meaning from text or speech to understand the intentions, entities, context and sentiment, NLG take structured generated from NLU to create coherent and contextually relevant natural language output. Traditional machine learning based NLP tasks are mostly feature engineered based on rules and heuristics. There are different NLP approaches where we will be discussing the deep learning based approaches to perform NLP tasks as shown in *Figure 5.1*:

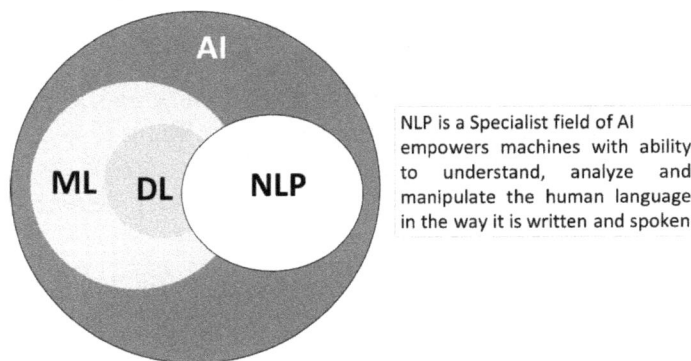

NLP is a Specialist field of AI empowers machines with ability to understand, analyze and manipulate the human language in the way it is written and spoken

Figure 5.1: Artificial intelligence—machine learning—deep learning —NLP association

Natural language processing tasks

NLP is applicable to various real-world scenarios. A good NLP system is said to be the one that perform many of below NLP tasks with acceptable accuracy. NLP systems have many capabilities, below *Figure 5.2* and *Figure 5.3* are comprehensive lists of natural language tasks that are performed mostly. As many of the tasks are to be performed together, below figure shows a hierarchy by grouping similar tasks:

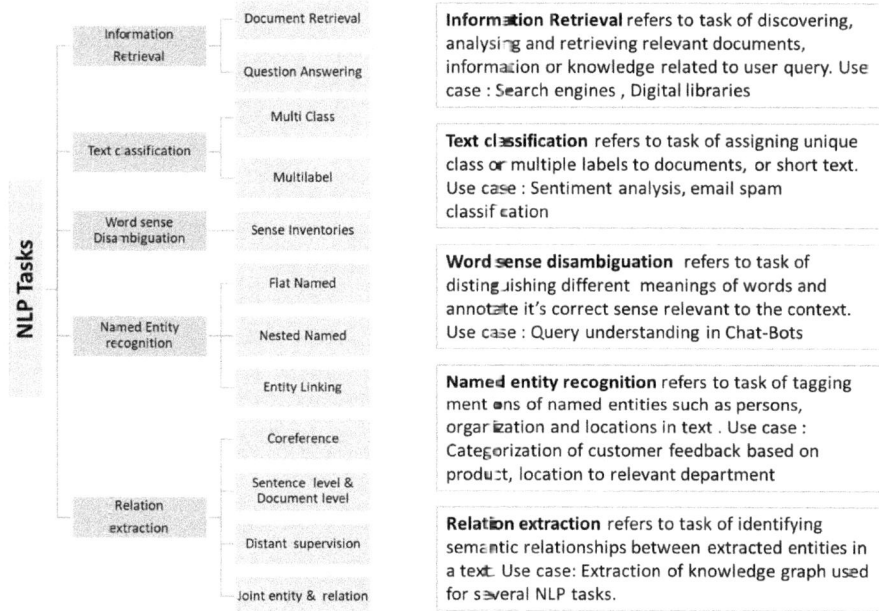

Figure 5.2: *NLP tasks list 1*

Below figure shows the other NLP tasks grouped where LLM models play a critical role:

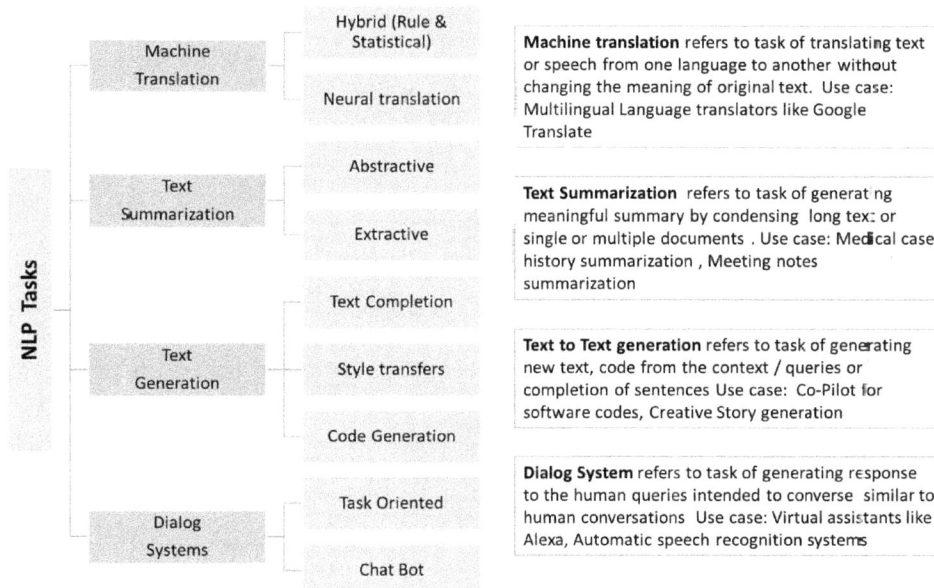

Figure 5.3: *NLP tasks list 2*

Sequence to sequence models

The evolution journey of transformer architecture for NLP tasks starts with sequence modeling. Sequence modeling allows NLP Models to take input sequence of varying lengths and produce output sequences of varying lengths to perform many tasks. Sequence models are generally used for image captioning, speech recognition, voice recognition, time series prediction, music generations and NLP. Some of the earlier sequence models are RNN and LSTM.

There are different types of sequence modelling, as shown in below *Figure 5.4* vary from one-to-sequence (Model input: Non sequence data; model output: Sequence data, example of one-to-sequence modeling: Image captioning—where input is image and output is image captions), sequence-to-one (Model input: Sequence; model output: Non sequence, example of sequence-to-one modeling: Sentiment analysis—where input is customer reviews and output is positive or negative sentiment classification), sequence-to-sequence (Model input: Sequence ; model output: Sequence, example of sequence-to-sequence modeling: Language translations where input is text from one language and output is translated content of input in other language).

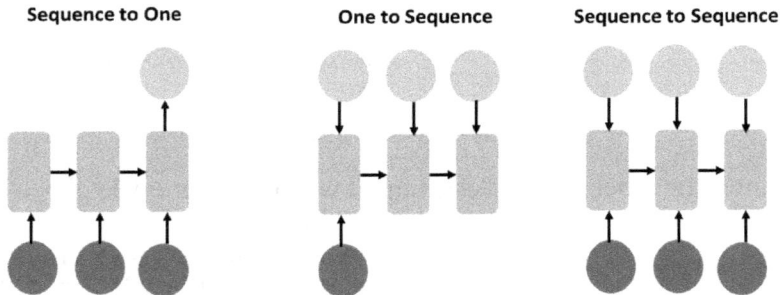

Figure 5.4: Types of sequence modeling

Recurrent neural network

RNN is used to handle the sequence modeling. RNN model supports variable length sequences, sequence ordering, and long-term dependencies. RNN has an internal loop and applies a recurrence relation at every time step to process a sequence of data. Unlike feedforward networks, the RNN shares the weight parameters across the network layers. In *Figure 5.5* unfolds RNN diagram shows handling of sequence data using the recurrence relation, and same parameters are repeated throughout the unrolled network, appearing at each time step:

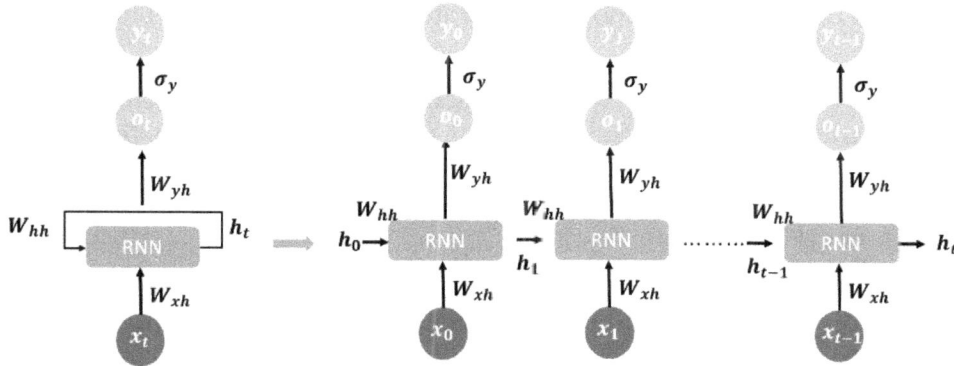

Figure 5.5: *Unfold Diagram of RNN network*

RNN uses **backpropagation through time (BPTT)** to calculate the gradients. RNNs BPTT tends to run into problems of exploding gradients and vanishing gradients. In practice, the gradient clipping technique is used to cope up with an exploding gradient by capping the maximum value of the gradient. The vanishing gradient problem with RNN leads to the issue of long-term dependencies. LSTM with a gated structure, a variation of RNN was proposed to address the long-term dependencies.

Long-short term memory networks

LSTM is a special type RNN to handle long-term dependencies. In LSTM, the RNN cells are replaced with gates controlling the flow of information, as shown in *Figure 5.6*:

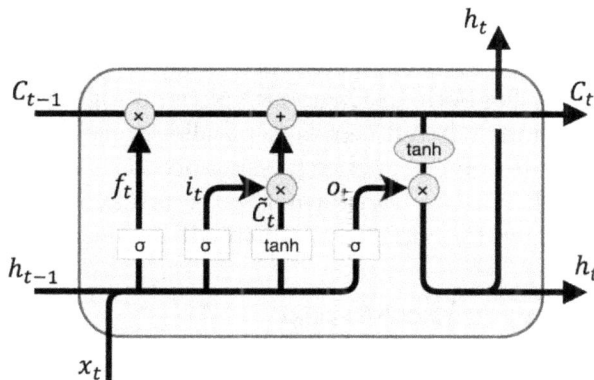

Figure 5.6: *LSTM Unit Cell*
Source: *https://colah.github.io/posts/2015-08-Understanding-LSTMs/*

At each time step t, LSTM provides cell and hidden states. Cell state enables LSTM to store long-term information. Cell state information can be read, updated, and erase using structures called **gates**. As shown in the figure above, LSTM cell outputs a new hidden state h_t given its previous hidden state h_{t-1} and input embedding x_t. As shown in the diagram above the gate that controls LSTM cell are forget gate (f_t), Input gate (i_t) and output gate (o_t).

Forget gate f_t is a dense layer with weights W_f and bias b_f with sigmoid activation function. It helps to retain or forget information based on previous hidden state h_{t-1} and input embedding x_t. The output of forget gate is defined for each number in the previous cell state C_{t-1}. It is either 0 to forget or 1 to retain the information. Mathematically it can be defined as $f_t = \sigma(W_f.[h_{t-1}, x_t] + b_f)$.

Input gate (i_t) is a dense layer with weights W_t and bias b_i with sigmoid activation function. It helps to add new information to cell state C_{t-1}. As shown in the figure it has two layers of sigmoid and tanh layers. Sigmoid layer decides on update and tanh layer decide on new information ($c^\sim$) that can be added to the state. Mathematically it can be defined as $i_t = \sigma(W_i.[h_{t-1}, x_t] + b_i)$ and $c^\sim_t = \tanh(W_C.[h_{t-1}, x_t] + b_C)$. The cell state C_t is update is done with new content after erasing certain information, that is given by

$$C_t = f_t \odot C_{t-1} + i_t \odot c^\sim_t..$$

Finally, the output gate will filter version of cell state. There are two steps where the sigmoid layer decides on cell state parts, and the tanh layer to extract the desired output. Output gate o_t is a dense layer with weights W_o and bias b_o with sigmoid activation function. Mathematically it is defined as $o_t = \sigma(W_o.[h_{t-1}, x_t] + b_o)$ and $h_t = o_t \odot \tanh(C_t)$.

Unlike RNN that depends on one memory unit for backpropagation, LSTM backpropagation depends on two memory units and three gates that depend on the previous time stamp. LSTMs are mostly used in time series related data like financial trading, IoT data etc.

Some of the drawbacks of LSTM are they are computationally expensive and require more memory and time to train. They are prone to overfitting. Similar to RNN, it requires regularization techniques such as dropout, weight decay, or early stopping need to be adopted to avoid overfitting. For both, LSTM and RNN, handling long range dependencies is the issue and has limitations when it comes to parallel processing. Transformer is the state-of-the-art architecture to solve sequence to sequence tasks in a much more efficient way than RNN and LSTM. Further transformer variants have evolved rapidly, which became the default architecture for NLP tasks, which will be discussed in the next section.

Transformer architecture

Transformer architecture has become the basis for natural language processing since the publication of *Attention Is All you Need* research paper by *Google researchers*. The performance of the transformer is a leap ahead compared to the earlier RNN and LSTM-based models discussed earlier. Unlike RNN and LSTM, transformers process longer sequences as entirety and also support massive parallel processing that reduces training and inferencing time. These features enabled transformer-based models like GPT to get trained on large web-based corpus with billions of learnable parameters capturing a wide range of human knowledge, making GPT a generalizable AI system. LLM models like GPT 4.0 have achieved such a massive scale of ~1 trillion parameters where LLMs are able to learn patterns that show emergent abilities to solve cognitive reasoning tasks from natural language questions at par with humans.

Transformer architecture can be designed as encoder-decoder architecture, encoder only architecture and decoder only architecture. Different transformer models are categorized into one of these three types. *Figure 5.7* shows popular models developed by big enterprises on these architectures:

Transformer Architecture			
Encoder	Microsoft	DeBERTa(2020)	
	Google	BERT (2018) ALBERT (2020)	
	Meta	RoBERTa(2019)	
Decoder		GPT-J(2021)	XLNet (2019) Minerva (2022)
	Eluther AI	GPT-Neo (2021)	LaMDA (2021) Bard (2023)
		GPT-NeoX(2022)	Gopher(2022) Gemini (2024)
	Google	Pythia (2023)	Sparrow (2022)
		GPT-NeoX2.0 (2023)	Chinchilla (2022)
	OpenAI	OPT (2022)	GPT-1(2018) ChatGPT (2022)
		Galactica (2021)	GPT-2 (2019) GPT-4 (2023)
		LLaMa (2023)	GPT-3(2020)
	Meta		CodeX (2021)
			Instruct GPT(2022)
Encoder - Decoder	Meta	BART(2020)	
	Google	Flan-T5 (2022) Flan-UL2 (2023) T5 (2022)	

Figure 5.7: Transformer models and architecture types

Types of architecture

The following are the types of architecture:

- **Encoder only architecture**: The objective of this type of architecture is to extract the dense numerical representation of input sequence of tokens. Use cases are typically text classification, name-entity recognition, sentiment analysis. Some of the models that belong to encoder only architecture are **Bi-directional Encoder Representations from Transformer** (**BERT**), ALBERT, RoBERTa, and DistilBERT. While decoder only architectures are unidirectional (read text left-to-right or right-to-left), where every token only attends to previous tokens in attention layers, encoder only architectures are bi-directional, attends to the tokens that precedes and follows the token. The process is generally termed as bi-direction attention mechanism.

- **Decoder only architecture**: Popular LLMs such as GPT-3, GPT-4, Falcon, PaLM, LLAMA, and Chinchilla are decoder only model. The objective of the architecture is to predict the most probable next token to auto-complete the sequence. The input is directly passed to decoder without an encoder representation. The decoder only model uses masked attention mechanism during training to prevent it from looking at future parts of the input. The use cases are text completion, text generation, question-answering. Unlike encoder only models that uses bi-direction attention, the decoder only model uses causal or autoregressive attention. Decoder only model can be trained in self-supervised way. The model is trained on a large corpus of text with the objective of predicting the next token, and the loss is calculated as a cross-entropy loss between the correct sequence of tokens to the model prediction.

- **Encoder - decoder architecture**: We have seen encoder-decoder architecture earlier in variational autoencoder for image generation in *Chapter 3, GenAI-for Image*. Similarly, in the previous section, RNN/LSTM uses encoder-decoder architecture is used for sequence transduction task. In the context of transformer architecture. It is similar and can be called as sequence-to-sequence model powered with cross attention mechanisms. It takes the input sequence and produces latent representation using encoder module. Decoder uses this latent representation of encoder and do complex mapping using cross attention to the generate the output sequence. As we have seen earlier in the sequence-to-sequence model, the transformer with encoder-decoder architecture can be designed for one-to-one, one-to-many and many-to-one sequence generation tasks. Some of the use cases are machine translations, content summarization, image captioning, speech recognition systems. Some of the models with encoder-decoder architecture are T5, BART, vision transformers.

Transformer components

Transformer is the state-of-the-art AI model architecture for generative modeling. In this section, we will look into the LLM based transformer model architecture and its components. Major components of transformer are tokenizer, encoding blocks, decoding blocks, linear layers, and language or task specific head. *Figure 5.8* shows the components of encoder-decoder type transformer architecture:

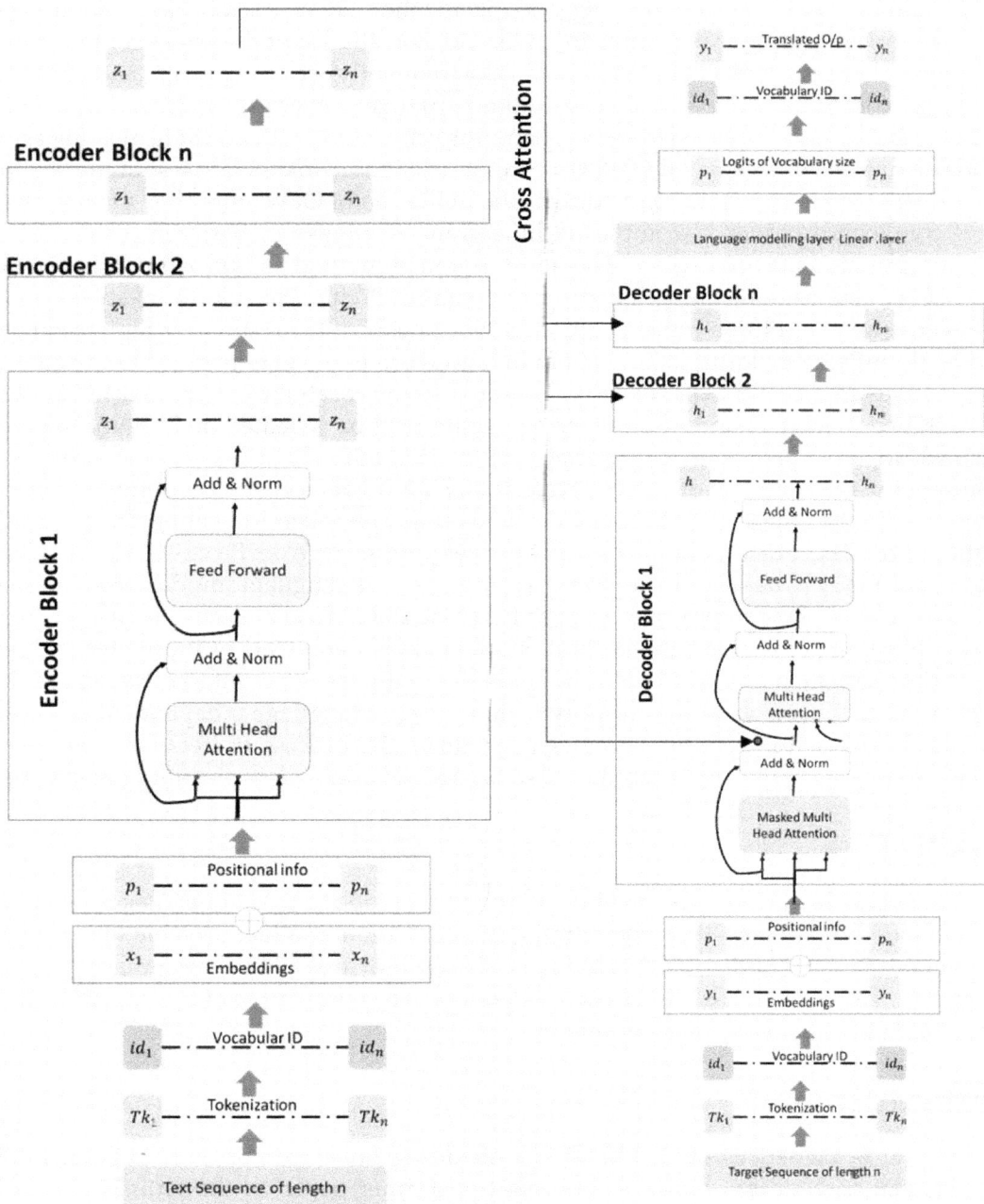

Figure 5.8: *Components of transformer encoder-decoder architecture*

Tokenization

Tokenization is the process of chunking text into small units called tokens and convert them into integer ID representation. Tokens are the atomic unit representation of text in a transformer model. Popular strategies of tokenization are character tokenization, word tokenization and sub-word tokenization. Word tokenization split the sentences into words based on delimiter where the vocabulary is set of frequently occurring words and unknown words get compressed into unique unk (unknown) token. Word tokenizer has limitations with vocabulary size, misspelled words, handling same word with multiple meanings, and handling **out-of-vocabulary (OOV)** words. Character based tokenization split the text into individual characters as tokens to address the limitation of OOV, but it has the drawback with large length sequence, complexity in learning relationships between the characters and computationally expensive. The most popular method is sub-word tokenization that brings best of both fine-grained representation of character-based tokenization for rare words and simplified representation of word based tokenization for high frequency words. **Byte-Pair Encoding (BPE)** is popular sub-word tokenization algorithm used with LLM models like GPT model. In BPE, the initial set of vocabulary is created by splitting the text into characters and vocabulary gets optimized by repeated merging of the most frequent adjacent pair of bytes. Special symbols are often used by these algorithms to represent the start and end of tokens. In case of GPT kind of models < | endoftext | > special token is added at the end of the sentence and a special token indicating the beginning of the word. The other popular tokenization algorithm is WordPiece algorithm where tokens are merged based on the one that increases the language model probability of the tokenization. WordPiece uses special token at start of each token. In case of BERT model [SEP], [CLS] to mark the separation of sentences and start of the sentence, Mask IDs to differentiate masking element, Segment ID to differentiate different sentences. The other popular tokenization algorithm is SentencePiece a language independent sub-word tokenization which is used in T5 model. It follows the process of iteratively removing tokens from large corpus of vocabulary that do not occur in high probability tokenization.

Token IDs

Text token generated from tokenization methods are mapped to unique integer token IDs as per model vocabulary. It can be intuitively understood as a lookup table of text token to unique IDs. GPT-2 has 50,527 vocabulary size and Mistral 7B has vocabulary of 32,000 vocab size. These token IDs will be used as numerical representation of the tokens to create input embeddings for transformer model.

Embeddings

Each token is passed through trainable embedding layer to map it to unique multi-dimensional embedding vector. In original transformer paper as shown in *Figure 5.9* a dimensionality of 512 is used for embedding vector representation. In NLP tasks, word embeddings are generated using pre-trained models like Word2Vec, GloVe, FastRext, ELMo etc. In transformer model the embeddings are learned by having the token representation multiplied by the trainable weight matrix. The weight matrix is initialized randomly and trained throughout the training process:

You   are   great

X_1 X_2 X_3

$[x_{1,1} \cdots\cdots x_{1,512}]$ $[x_{2,1} \cdots\cdots x_{2,512}]$ $[x_{3,1} \cdots\cdots x_{3,512}]$

X_1
X_2
X_3

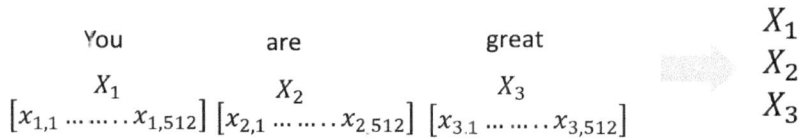

Figure 5.9: Example embedding vector representation (512 dim)

Positional embeddings

It is about word order representations. Unlike RNN and LSTM, transformer model does not have native capability to recognize the word order i.e. each word's position within given sequence. So positional embeddings are generated with word embeddings to maintain the information about the token's position in given sequence. Similar to the word embeddings position embedding vectors can be learned using trainable parameters or calculated using fixed equations. In original paper, sinusoidal positional encodings are used which is mathematically given by:

$$PE = \begin{cases} \sin\left(\dfrac{pos}{10000^{\frac{2k}{d_{model}}}}\right) & for\ Emb[i, 2k] \\ \cos\left(\dfrac{pos}{10000^{\frac{2k}{d_{model}}}}\right) & for\ Emb[i, 2k+1] \end{cases}$$

where pos is token position in sequence, d_{model} is the model dimensionality, i is the position index and k is the dimension index. Positional vector dimension is the same as the token embedding. Please find below *Figure 5.10* where positional encoding relative to position index and encoding dimension is mapped:

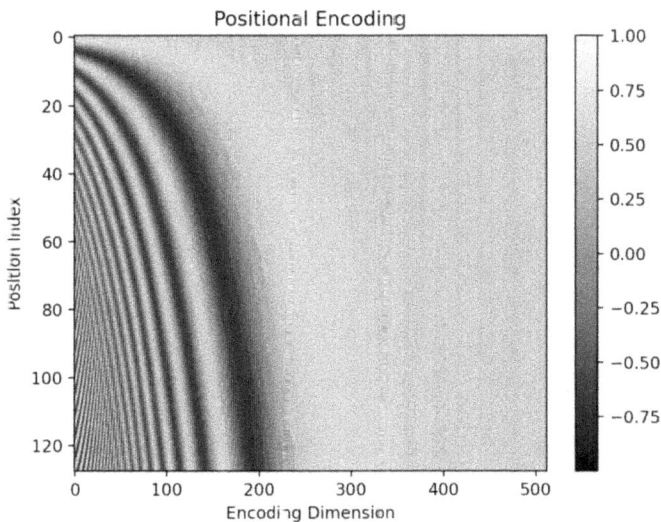

Figure 5.10: Positional encoding relative to position index and encoding dimension
Source: https://kikaben.com/transformers-positional-encoding/

These positional embeddings are absolute positional embedding i.e. it is calculated once and reused across training and inference. The output of the positional embedding layer is the element wise vector addition of the word encoding and positional encoding (fixed sinusoidal) of each token. The positional encodings are maintained across transformer layers through residual connections, as shown in *Figure 5.8* above in the previous section. Some of the other ways to calculate positional embeddings are to use relative positional embedding (Positional embedding as trainable parameters as in Transformer-XL model), trainable bias as positional embedding (e.g., T5 model) and finally state of art method **rotary positional embeddings (RoPE)**. RoPE rotate the affine-transformed word embeddings vector by amount of angles of its position index (e.g. RoFormer). Unlike the absolute positional embedding, RoPE is multiplicative and token embeddings are represented as complex numbers so that positions are represented as rotation and incorporate the dependency in self-attention formulation itself.

Encoder layer

As shown in below *Figure 5.11* the encoder layer is stack of identical encoder block. In original transformer paper 6 nos. of encoder block is used. Each encoder block has two sub-layers:

1. Multi-head self-attention layer.
2. Position-wise, fully connected feedforward network. Each sub-layer has a residual connection and a layer normalization.

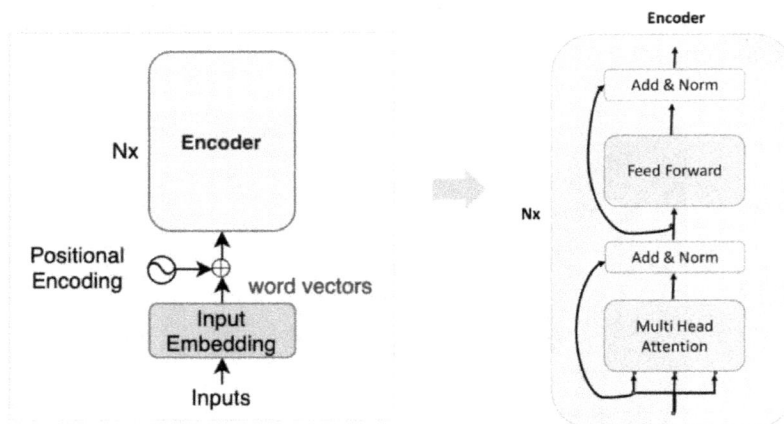

Figure 5.11: Transformer encoder block and its component

Self-attention is the main function that an encoder block does. Self-attention mechanism is used to get the context of the token in the given input sequence. It gets the context by transforming the encoded input sequence into query, key, value representations that are used to calculate the attention scores to selectively weigh different input sequence while generating the outputs. In the context of NLP, the input sequence can be sentence, paragraph or documents. Depending upon the tasks, different self-attention mechanisms can be applied. Some of the common attention types are dot product, scaled dot product, multi-head, local, global, additive, and cosine or content-based attention. In the original transformer paper scaled dot product along with multi-head self-attention mechanism is adopted. In self-attention mechanism, for each token in the input sequence, there are (Q, K, V) vectors created by multiplying the token embedding from the previous layer with trainable matrices. Mathematically, the query vector is given by $Q = XW^Q$ & $Q \in \mathbb{R}^{L \times d_Q}$, key vector is given by $K = XW^K$ & $K \in \mathbb{R}^{L \times d_k}$, value vector is given by $V = XW^V$ & $V \in \mathbb{R}^{L \times d_v}$ ($W^Q, W^K W^V$ are learnable weights, L is the length of the sequence, d_k, d_v are hidden dimensionality of key and values). *Figure 5.12* depicts projecting the token into Q, K, V vectors:

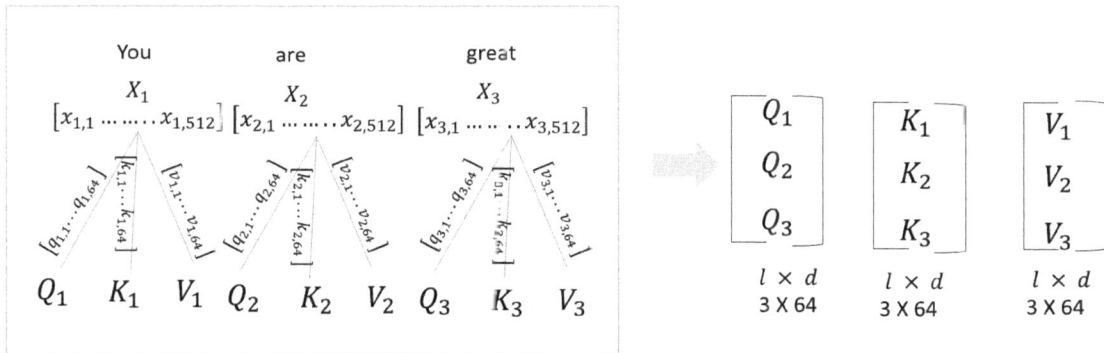

Figure 5.12: *Projection of tokens into query, key, value vectors*

For every token, we have one key and one value vector. The query is compared to all keys with a score function (in this case, the dot product) to determine the weights. Each query is processed independently enabling parallelization. Finally, attention score is calculated by using scaled dot product of Q and K matrices as weights to calculate the weighted sum of value matrices as follows:

$$Attention\ (Q, K, V) = softmax\left(\frac{QK^T}{\sqrt{d_k}}\right)V.$$

Attention scores are normalized using row wise softmax and scaling factor ($\sqrt{d_k}$). The output of the self-attention layer is the weighted value vector, i.e, $x_i = \sum_j w_{ji}\, v_j$ where $v_1 \dots v_n$ are value vectors. The complexity of the above attention mechanism is of order $O(n^2)$. Because of this order of complexity, one of the main disadvantages of general attention mechanism is its computational cost and inability to accommodate long-range context:

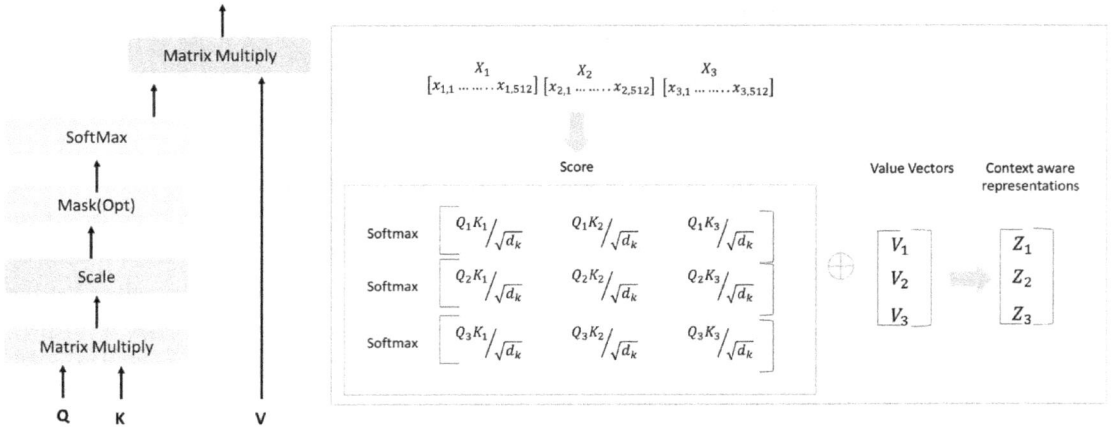

Figure 5.13: Self-attention mechanism

Multi-head self-attention

Multi-head self-attention enables transformer to capture different aspects of input sequence token by having parallel attention heads with different (Q, K, V) sets for same input features focusing on different representation subspace as shown in the following figure. Representation of feature vector in different subspace using multi-head attention resembles to the CNN convolution filters that was discussed in *Chapter 3, GenAI for Image* where each filter captures different image features, such as face, smile. Similarly, in a transformer, each attention head captures different contextual aspects of input sequence such as syntactic relationship, semantic relationship, rare words. The output of individual attention heads are simply concatenated and linearly transformed into expected dimensions. Mathematically it can be defined as *MultiHead(Q, K, V) = [head$_1$, head$_2$......head$_h$]* W^O where each head $head_i = (QW_i^Q, KW_i^K, VW_i^V)$ and W_i^Q, W_i^K, W_i^V, W^O are trainable parameters. When we say trainable parameters, it means during pre-training (supervised, unsupervised, semi-supervised) the weights of these parameters get updated based on the loss through backpropagation:

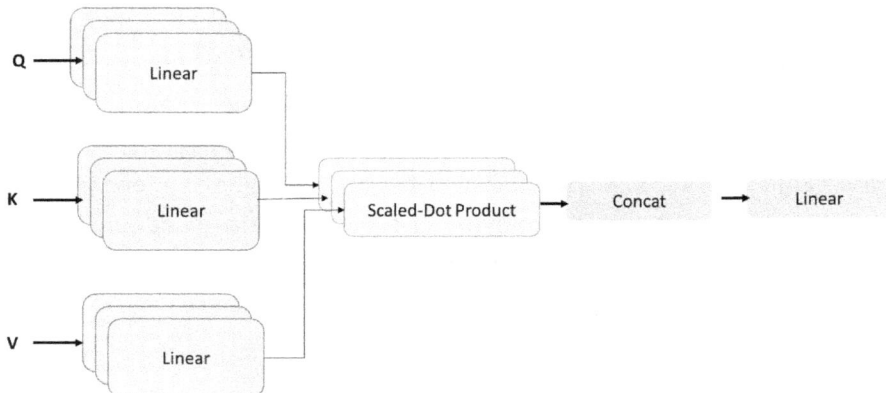

Figure 5.14: Multi-head attention mechanism

Multi-head attention is permutation-equivariant with respect to its inputs, i.e., even if the order of the inputs in sequence switched, the output remains the same. Because of this, positional encodings are added and maintained across layers through residual connections. Multi-head attention is no more expensive than single head attention as the hidden dimensionality of learnable $W^Q, W^K W^V$ weight parameter d_k, d_v are reduced by number of heads (h). So, as shown in *Figure 5 14,* in multi-head attention, the output of each head (Query Q, key K) will be of dimension $\mathbb{R}^{L \times d_Q/h} = \mathbb{R}^{L \times d_k/h}$ where L is the sequence length and h is a number of heads. The final output of this layer is defined as linear transformation of the concatenation of heads letting $O \in \mathbb{R}^{L \times d}$.

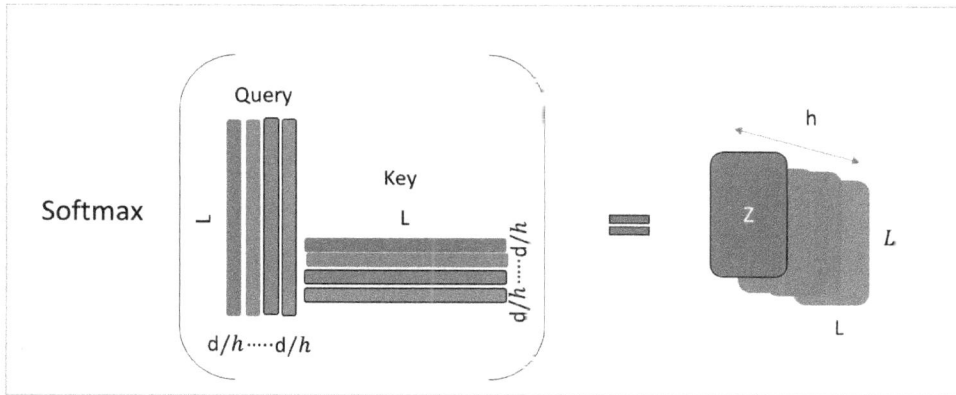

Figure 5.15: Multi-head attention dimensionality

Layer normalization

We have discussed in *Chapter 2, GenAI Foundation,* the batch normalization is used for stabilizing the learning process. Batch normalization normalizes each feature independently, i.e., column wise across mini batch. Layer normalization normalizes each input across all features in a batch, i.e., row wise. In original transformer models, Layer normalization is done prior to the self-attention and feedforward networks. As shown in *Figure 5.16,* the position of layer normalization brings out two different transformer architectures called **pre-LN, post-LN** transformers. While in pre-LN architecture, the layer normalization is placed within the residual and does not require learning rate warm-up, in post-LN the layer normalization is placed between residual block and requires learning rate warm-up:

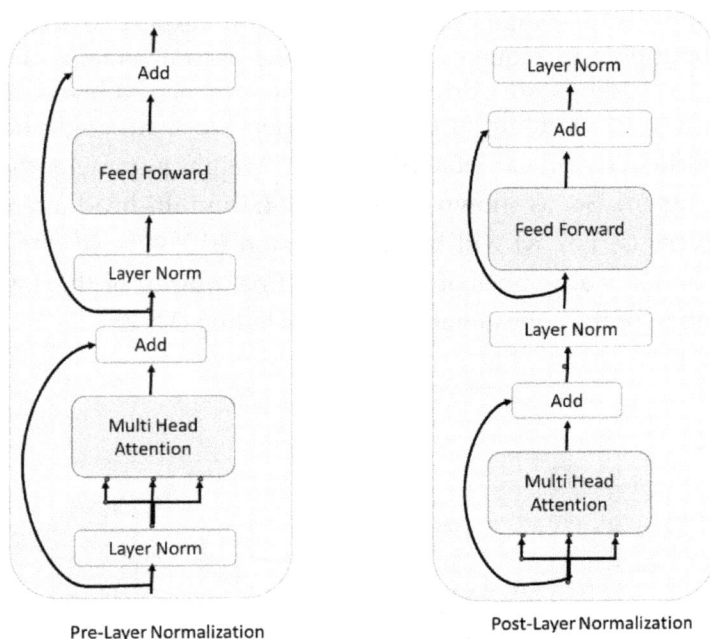

Pre-Layer Normalization

Post-Layer Normalization

Figure 5.16: *Pre and post layer normalization*

Residual connections

Residual connection was first introduced in ResNet architecture. In ResNet set of layers are grouped and a skip connection is added to create a residual block. Residual block in transformer is similar where it is used to carry out the token embedding and positional information throughout the encoder-decoder layers. Further, some of the benefits of residual connections are subset learning to learn subset of solutions, shorter gradient paths allowing network weights to remain large enough to retain information, implicit regularization, and enabling modularity in larger transformer architectures.

Feedforward layer

Feedforward layer (FFL) are neural network that applies non-linear transformation to the inputs by applying weights, biases and activations while inputs traversing through the network. It is often referred as position wise FFL in transformer, a two layer fully connected neural network. It applies same transformation to all tokens in the sequence, i.e., same weights applied to all tokens. FFL layers process the embedding independently instead of processing the whole sequence of embeddings as single vector. While in the original transformer, the ReLU activation function is used, the state of art transformer models use GELU as an activation function because of its smoothness and continuity. The dimension of hidden layer d_{ff} is generally set to 4 times the dimension of model i.e. d_{model}. Mathematically FFN is defined by $FFN(x) = \max(0, xW_1 + b_1) W_2 + b_2$ where $W_1 \in \mathbb{R}^{d_{model} \times d_{ff}}$ and $W_2 \in \mathbb{R}^{d_{ff} \times d_{model}}$.

As shown in *Figure 5.8* encoder layers stacked N times high and output of one encoder passed as an input to next layer and consequently get processed. Different attention representation is learnt for the tokens to boost the prediction power. As we have seen the complete encoder layer, we can understand that output of encoder is a rich contextual representation of the input token. The initial token embedding is passed all throughout the encoder layers through residual connection and outputs of FFL get added into it. In simple terms, the components of encoders are adding new representations back into the token embedding.

Decoder

As shown in *Figure 5.17*, decoder block consists of input, positional, attention, normalization and feedforward network components. Decoder blocks are also stacked over one another where the output of one decoder becomes input of another decoder as shown in *Figure 5.7*. Decoder block is similar to encoder block with three major changes:

- Cross attention to calculate source-target attention (only in encoder-decoder architecture).
- Masked multi-head attention for generating the output in autoregressive way.
- Language modeling head.

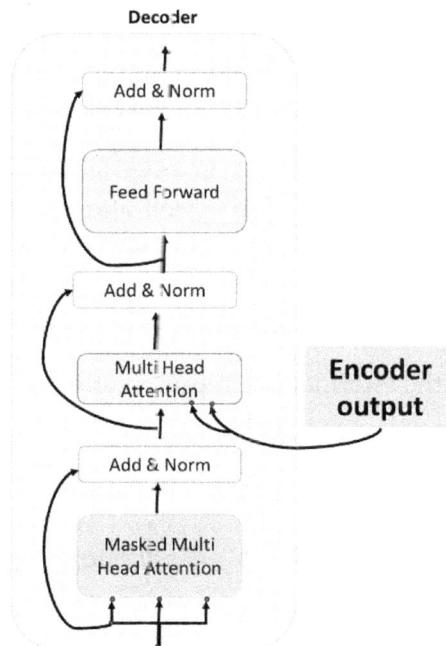

Figure 5.17: Transformer — decoder block

Cross attention

In self-attention mechanism the key, query and value are generated by the same input sequence (X). Cross attention operates by computing attention weights that reflect the relevance of each element in one sequence (X) to the elements in another (Y). We mix or combine two different sequences in cross attention. Refer to the following figure depicting the difference between self-attention and cross attention mechanism:

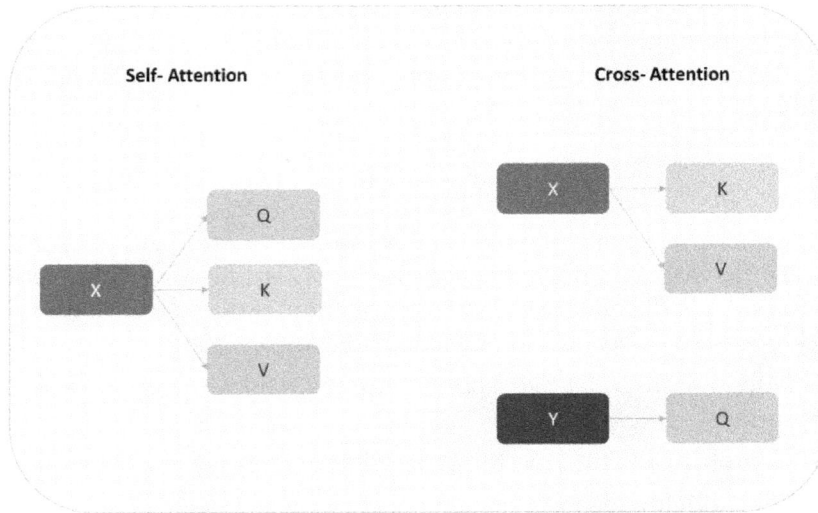

Figure 5.18: Transformer cross attention

Transformer encoder-decoder architecture takes two input sequences (X and Y). As seen in self-attention layer section the first input sequence is $x_{1:n}$ is passed through encoder to build contextual representations. The second sequence $y_{1:m}$ is applied with cross attention of encoder output representations. In cross attention, as shown in *Figure 5.18* above, while the keys and values are defined by self-attention layers of encoder with first input sequence, queries are defined by the decoder layer with second input sequence. So, mathematically it is given as:

$enc = z1......zn$ where z is the intermediate representation of X of sequence length n

$hdec = h1......hm$ where h is the intermediate representation of Y of sequence length m

$$Query\ Q\ from\ encoder\ is\ given\ by\ Q = W^Q\ h^{dec[l-1]}$$

$$Key\ K\ from\ encoder\ is\ given\ by\ K = WKzenc\ and\ V = WVzenc$$

$$Cross\ Attention\ (Q, K, V) = softmax\left(\frac{QK^T}{\sqrt{d_k}}\right)V$$

Each decoder block has cross attention layer which uses the output of final encoder layer to produce it key and value vectors.

Masked multi-head attention mechanism

In the decoder, self- attention mechanism is masked in order to ensure the model only attends to the token that have been generated up to the current position. It prevents model from considering the future context when generating current token. The masking is done manually by replacing the upper triangle of QK^T with infinity values (∞) so that during the softmax, these infinity values will be replaced as zeros (0). As shown in *Figure 5.19*, generally, a look ahead mask matrix is created with same size as the attention scores filled with zeros and negative infinites. On adding this mask matrix to the scaled attention scores, the top right triangle of the matrix gets filled with infinity, i.e., the future token gets nullified after applying softmax function:

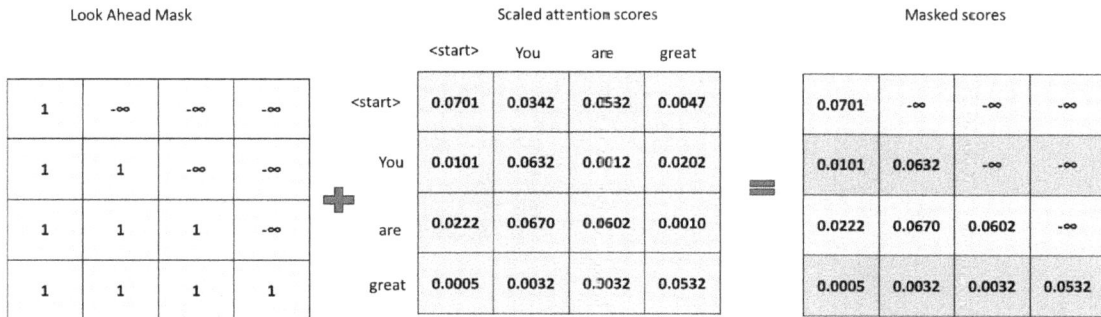

Look Ahead Mask					Scaled attention scores					Masked scores			
					<start>	You	are	great					
1	-∞	-∞	-∞	<start>	0.0701	0.0342	0.0532	0.0047		0.0701	-∞	-∞	-∞
1	1	-∞	-∞	You	0.0101	0.0632	0.0012	0.0202		0.0101	0.0632	-∞	-∞
1	1	1	-∞	are	0.0222	0.0670	0.0602	0.0010		0.0222	0.0670	0.0602	-∞
1	1	1	1	great	0.0005	0.0032	0.0032	0.0532		0.0005	0.0032	0.0032	0.0532

Figure 5.19: Decoder masked attention matrix

Language modelling head

It is the last component of decoder. As shown in *Figure 5.20* below, it takes the contextual representation of the final decoder block and output the unnormalized log probabilities, i.e., logits for each word in the vocabulary. Language model head has an unembedding linear layer which project the decoder output of dimension $1 \times d_{model}$ (final token contextual representation of sequence L of last decoder block) to logits of dimension $1 \times |V|$. This layer is generally weight tied (re-using same weights—transpose of initial embedding matrix of vocabulary). Finally, the softmax over logits give the word probabilities. These probabilities are used with decoding sampling techniques like random search, greedy search, beam search, top-k sampling, etc., to generate the next token. In order to estimate the hidden representation of any decoder layer, the intermediate representations can be directly given as input to language head and extract the output representation / context of any decoder block. In simple terms, the objective of the decoder is to predict the next token given all previous tokens. Language modeling head at each timestamp output the prediction over the probability distribution of vocabulary. Next token is chosen based on sampling techniques over these probabilities:

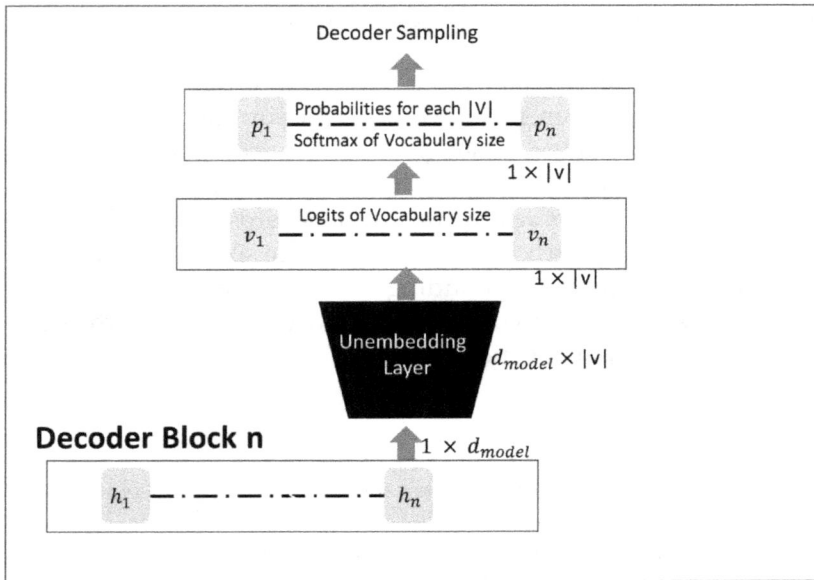

Figure 5.20: Decoder — language modeling head

Decoder sampling techniques

Decoding strategies can be broadly classified into deterministic and stochastic ones. Some of the deterministic strategies are exhaustive search, greedy search, beam search and contrastive decoding. The stochastic sampling ones are Top-K sampling, Top-P (Nucleus) sampling.

In greedy encoding, the probability of each word in the vocabulary is computed and the word with the highest probability is chosen at each time step, i.e., *output word* $= argmax_{w \in |V|}$ *P(w | output words till prior time stamp)*. One of the main disadvantages of greedy encoding its local and because, it will generate the same output that are often defaults to common choices. The other disadvantage of greedy decoding is that it is sensitive to sub-optimal decisions. An error with token prediction in early time steps could affect future time step predictions in a larger way as the error propagates. Beam search is an extension to the greedy search where the most probable sequence is selected instead of selecting a series of high probability next words. Beam search is popularly used in machine translation task. As shown in the *Figure 5.21* below, beam search keep k possible tokens (beam width) at each time k chosen words is extended to generate probabilities across vocabulary using the distinct decoder. The process is repeated until EOS token is generated or until a certain threshold is reached:

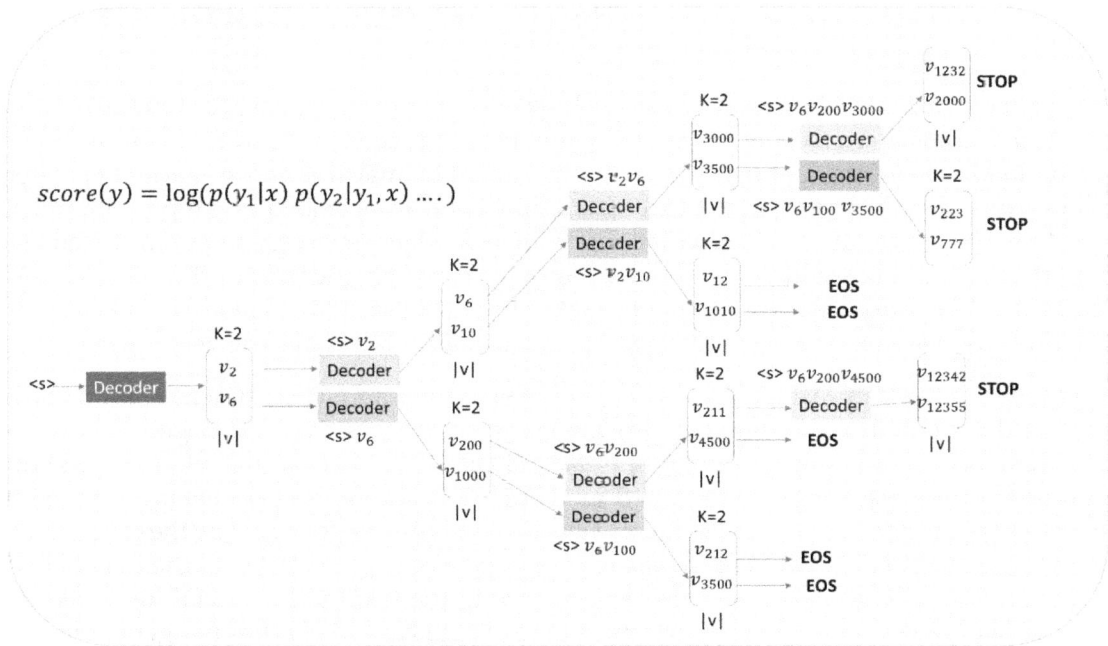

$$score(y) = \log(p(y_1|x)\, p(y_2|y_1, x) \ldots)$$

Figure 5.21: Decoder sampling—beam search

Top-k sampling

Similar to greedy search, where at every time step, instead of choosing the highest probability word from the entire vocabulary, the vocabulary distribution is truncated and re-normalized to k most likely word distribution, and then randomly sample the word from re-normalized k words distribution. When $k=1$, the Top-k sampling is the same as the greedy search. This kind of random controlled selection of sequences help to generate creative and diverse high-quality outputs. The main disadvantage of this approach is the difference in probability distribution over top k words differs between contexts.

Top-P sampling

Similar to Top-k sampling, however, the truncation happens based on probability mass instead of a number of words. It will involve sorting of final logits probability, selecting n words until the sum of the probability is not greater than defined p (hyperparameter) and do a random sampling out of n words. $(p \in (0,1))$.

Temperature sampling

The final logit value is divided by temperature parameter $(\tau \in (0,1))$ prior applying softmax. This will reshape the final distribution of the vocabulary. As τ set near 1 the distribution largely remains unchanged, but as τ set near 0 increases the probability of higher-probability words and decreases the lower-probability words. With τ set to almost 0 then it acts as greedy search algorithm.

So, we have looked into all transformer encoder-decoder components. To summarize, the transformer encoder receives text input in the form of tokens mapped to its input IDs in predefined vocabulary and learns query, key, and value matrices across stacked encoder blocks. Encoder blocks project the token input into contextual embedding representations. Decoder block uses these representations to map its decoder input sequence tokens to encoder output representations. The decoder also learns its query from the encoder key, value matrices across stacked decoder blocks. Decoder uses language modeling head at the final layer to map the logits to vocabular probabilities to predict the next token.

Many NLP tasks can cast as next word prediction. For example, sentiment analysis task can be determined as conditioned probability of words positive and negative given a title sentence i.e. *p(positive | sentiment of the sentence "I Love India")*. Similarly, question and answering task can be determined as words with the highest probabilities given a question, i.e., *p(|W| | "which is the capital of India" A:)* gives new followed by the continuous iteration of *p(|W| | "which is the capital of India" A: "New")* gives *Delhi*. In the case of text summarization by giving LLM a text and following the text by the special token like tl; dr (special token for too long do not read in GPT 2.0) can do conditional generation of summarization words one by one. The prompt format for summarization will be *{Text: <Long text> TLDR:}*.

In the next section, we will the look into the architecture of one of popular, encoder model BERT introduced by *Google* and understand its capability in performing NLP tasks like Next Sentence Prediction (NSP), sequence classification.

Next sentence prediction task

In bi-directional transformer model, the information flow to the attention layer is from both left to right and as well as from right to left. In the above section, we saw the decoder uses a masked attention layer to avoid any flow of future information, and the hidden state representation is solely dependent on the current and previous input tokens. However, in bi-directional transformer model like BERT, RoBERTa, SpanBERT allow self-attention mechanism to range over entire input. Training of bi-directional transformer models uses **masked language modelling (MLM)** approach where random tokens from training corpus is chosen and have certain percentage of them get replaced with special token [MASK], some percentage replaced with other vocabulary tokens, and others left unchanged. The objective of MLM is to predict these tokens. Cross-entropy loss is calculated based on the original vs predicted tokens. The masked tokens or replaced token cross-entropy losses are averaged and used to update weights through backpropagation and gradient descent algorithm. Mathematically the loss is given by $L_{MLM}(x_i) = -\frac{1}{|M|}\sum_{i \in M} \log P(x_i | p_i)$ where p_i is the predicted probability distribution for the given masked word I and M is the number of masked words in a sequence of length L. Refer to *Figure 5.22* architecture for MLM approach:

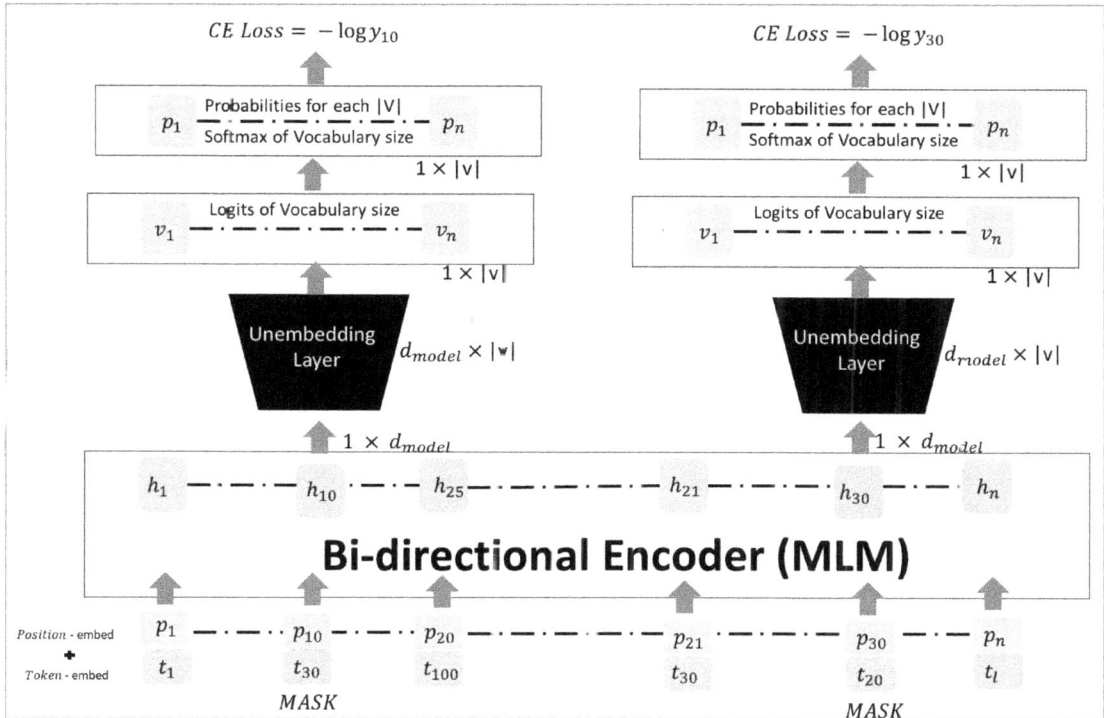

Figure 5.22: Bi-directional encoder architecture for MLM

One of the objectives of MLM models is **next sentence prediction (NSP)**, i.e., to predict whether a pair of sentences are related or unrelated. As shown in the below *Figure 5.23*, BERT uses special tokens [CLS] at the start of sentence pair and [SEP] tokens between sentence pair and after the final token of sentence pair. The final output vector associated with [CLS] token is used for NSP. BERT model is trained on pairs of text segments extracted out of training corpus and are masked using MLM. Model is trained for combined NSP and MLM loss:

$$CE\ Loss = -\log y_1$$

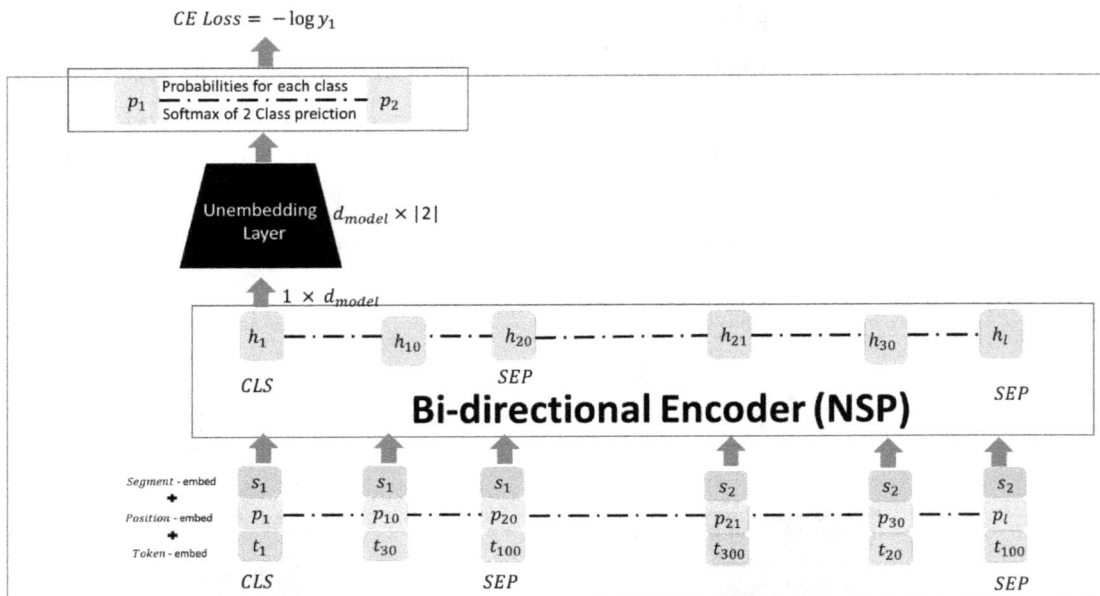

Figure 5.23: Bi-directional encoder architecture for NSP

The other objective of training BERT could be Sequence classification by using sentence embedding instead of token level embedding. Sentence embedding involves pooling process where token embeddings are compressed to fixed length representation that reflect the meaning of the entire sentence. There are different pooling methods to generate the fixed representation of the sentence. One approach is to use special token [CLS] at the start of each sentence and model is trained for sentence or sequence level tasks (NSP tasks) to capture the entire sequence information. The other pooling methods include element wise arithmetic mean or max-pooling of all token representations across encoding layers for a sequence. In sentence classification task, the special [CLS] token representation or pooled embedding representation will become input to the classification weights. Softmax over predicted classes are used to calculate the loss and update the transformer layer weights. One example could be sentiment classification where the contextual representation of [CLS] token can be input to the classified head with trainable weights mapped to sentiment classes (Positive, negative, neural). The same approach can be extended to pair-wise sequence classification tasks like paraphrase detection, logical entitlement, discourse coherence by pre-training BERT for NSP objective and fine-tune it with the supervised data set for individual task. Same as in NSP, the pair of sentences are appended with special tokens such as [CLS] at the start, [SEP] between the sentences. Final [CLS] token representation is sent as input to the classification head with learnable weights and soft max layer for label predictions, which is used to calculate cross-entropy loss for updating transformer weights. Similarly, for tag classification or sequence labelling task all the representation of tokens are sent to classification head instead of sending only [CLS] token to the classification layer. The softmax layers generate the distribution of representation over number of tags (k). Sequence labelling involves additional mapping of tags to sub words during training and way to recover word-level tags from sub-words during decoding.

Beyond token wise or sequence wise identification and classification, Bi-direction encoder type models can be used to predict or classify longer phrases using span based masking. Span is contiguous sequence of words that are randomly selected from training corpus and masked with special token [MASK]. SpanBERT uses span-based masking and the objective of model is to predict [MASK] tokens in the spans given token immediately and following the span. Loss function for SpanBERT is given by $L_{MLM}(x) + L_{SBO}(x)$. $L_{MLM}(x)$ is the cross-entropy loss for the predicted mask token within the span and $L_{SBO}(x)$ is the loss for span boundary objective given by $-\log P(x_i \mid x_{s-1}, x_{e+1}, p_{i-s+1})$ i.e. cross-entropy loss on the boundary representation derived from 3 embeddings i.e. token prior to the start token of span (x_{s-1}), token preceding the final token of span (x_{e+1}) and the relative positioning with respect to x_{s-1}. Span-based masking is used in paraphrase detection, entailment and discourse coherence.

Text summarization task

It is one of the complex NLP tasks which require NLU, i.e., model must understand the whole context that appear before and after each token. Task summarization can be broadly classified as abstractive or extractive summarization. Extractive is more of fetching important sentences from the corpus and concatenating them to form a summary. Abstractive involves paraphrasing the corpus with novel sentences more like human responses by understanding the essence of the corpus and create summary without changing the message.

Further, as shown in below *Figure 5.24*, text summarization can be single/multi document summarization, generative or abstractive summarization, single line or multi sentence summarization, and finally, can be of multi lingual summarization. Extractive-abstractive summarization combines two stages to create a comprehensive summary. Initially, it generates an extractive summary of the text, capturing key information. Subsequently, an abstractive summarization system is employed to refine this extractive summary, aiming to make it more concise and informative. This dual-stage process enhances the overall accuracy of the summarization, surpassing the capabilities of extractive methods in isolation. By integrating both extractive and abstractive approaches, the method ensures a more nuanced and detailed summary, ultimately providing a richer understanding of the content. This innovative technique demonstrates the synergistic benefits of leveraging both extractive and abstractive methods in the summarization process:

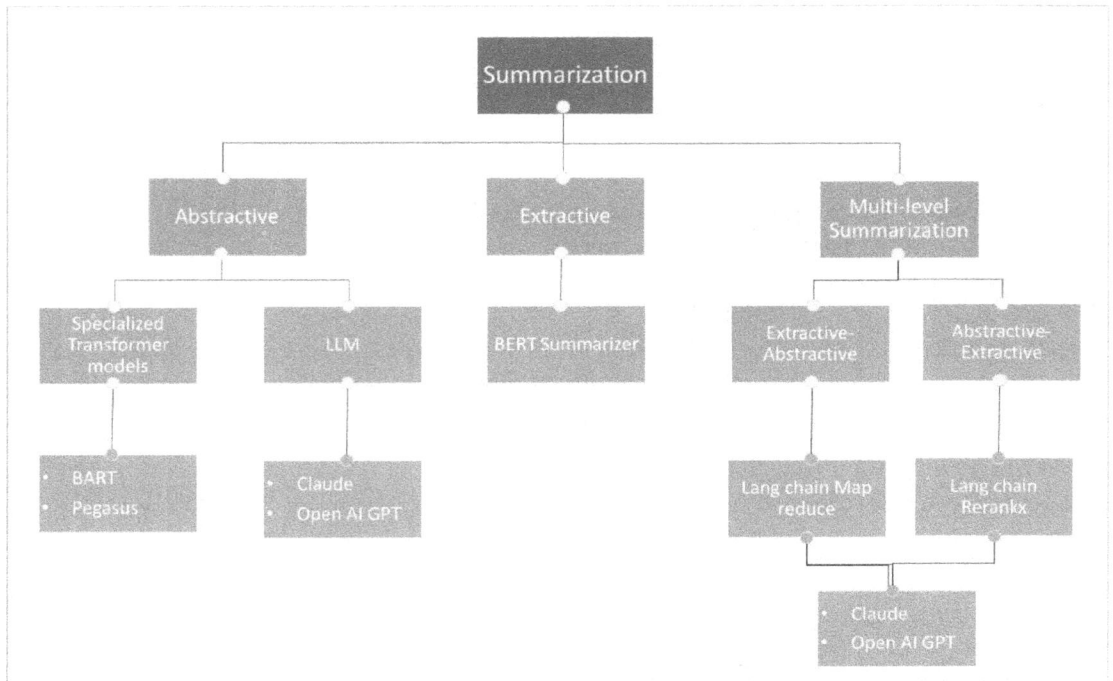

Figure 5.24: *Summarization techniques*
Source: *https://aws.amazon.com/blogs/machine-learning/techniques-for-automatic-summarization-of-documents-using-language-models/*

Some of the summarization datasets available for fine-tuning are CNN-DailyMail, XSum, Muti-News, Amazon data, BigPatent, Newsroom etc. Context size is a critical parameter for the summarization task and sequence length for a model can vary during training and fine-tuning. The context size for model like BERT/BERTSUM: 512 tokens, BART: 1024 tokens, PEGASUS: 1024 tokens, LongT5: 4096 tokens and most of the LLM Models like Bloom, Llama, GPT-J , Chinchilla, GPT-NeoX are of 2048 tokens. The context size in pre-trained models like LongT5 is 4096 but the sequence length can be increased up to 16k using sparse attention techniques. The major issue with increasing the context size is the context size (Sequence length in number of tokens) is directly correlated with the required memory in GB. Research shows that sequence length exponentially increases the required memory for a model in GB after 4096 tokens. ROGUE-2 is a common metric used to evaluate a model that performs summarization task.

Question and answering task

Similar to summarization task, **question answering (QA)** approach can be of many types like extractive (Answers can be found in the text or documents), long-form QA (Answers are in form of long paragraphs), QA for structured data (Performing tasks like counting, aggregating on structured data and extracting answers out of it), multi hop QA (Do a complex reasoning and retrieve the information from the documents) and finally could be a simple factual QA (Extract facts in the form of short texts from documents or web). As we have seen in the earlier section, the next token prediction task of decoder type models like GPT can be generalized for the QA task by making it to do conditional generation given the prefix (A:) and take the response as the answer. The disadvantages of such an approach are LLM hallucination and lack of proprietary knowledge.

One of the approaches for QA task is to use information retrieval system where the information retrieval techniques like **retrieval augmented generation** (**RAG**) extract the relevant documents and give it as context along with user query to LLM for answering the question. In RAG, LLM is grounded with facts and proprietary data where the answer could either be extracted or used as a context to generate the answers. RAG will be discussed in *Chapter 7, Frameworks for LLM* as part of lang chain.

Some of the popular QA datasets are **Stanford QA dataset** (**SQuAD**), SQuAD2.0, **Multihop QA** (**HotpotQA**) dataset, TriviaQA, **several domain-specific QA** (**SubjQA**), **biomedical QA** (**BioASQ**), **Conversational QA** (**CoQA**) dataset, RACE, NQ (Fact seeking) and tabular data (Wikipedia tables, WikiSQL), TyDi (Multi language). Some of the popular Hugging Face pre-trained models for extractive QA tasks are BERT based models, MiniLM, ALBERT-XXL, XLM-RoBERTa-large and for generative QA tasks, T5, LLAMA, GPT, Calude, Mistral.

As shown in the below *Figure 5.25*, QA dataset structure for extractive task is generally in tuples with passage or context, user question and respective answers from the passage followed by unique id and topic. The answers will have **answer_start** (The start character index of answer span) and **answer_text** (The span of text in the passage or context):

answers	context	id	question	title
0	['answer_start': [595], 'text': ['1964']]	Paul VI opened the third period on 14 September 1964, telling the Council Fathers that he viewed the text about the Church as the most important document to come out from the Council. As the Council discussed the role of bishops in the papacy, Paul VI issued an explanatory note confirming the primacy of the papacy, a step which was viewed by some as meddling in the affairs of the Council American bishops pushed for a speedy resolution on religious freedom, but Paul VI insisted this to be approved together with related texts such as ecumenism. The Pope concluded the session on 21 November 1964, with the formal pronouncement of Mary as Mother of the Church.	5726bc075951b619008f7c63	In what year did Paul VI formally appoint Mary as mother of the Catholic church?	Pope_Paul_VI

Figure 5.25: QA dataset sample record

Similar to span based masking we discussed in the earlier section, the common way to model answer extraction task is done as span classification task. In span classification, the answer is the span of text within the passage and task is to predict labels for the start and end tokens of an answer. Given question of q tokens ($q_1 \dots q_n$) for given passage of tokens ($p_1 \dots p_m$) the task is to compute the probability $p(a|q;p)$ for each possible span a as the answer. For each token in the passage (p_i)—2 probabilities is computed, i.e., $p_{start}(i)$ & $p_{end}(i)$. As we have seen in the earlier section in NSP task the pair of sentences are appended with special tokens such as [CLS] at the start, [SEP] between the sentences. In the same way for the QA task, the question will be the first sentence appended with [CLS] token, and the passage will be the second sentence separated by [SEP] token. A linear layer will be added and fine-tuned to predict the start and end position of span. The passage with no answer will consider special token [CLS] as answer. The answer span start probability P_{start_i} and P_{end_i} is calculated for each of the token in the passage.

The probabilities are calculated by applying softmax over the dot product of learnable start vector (S) and end vector (E) with each of Span probability (. During training, the model learns two separate dense layers on top of BERT to predict $P_{start\,i}$ and P_{end_i}. The vector representation of each token (p_i') is fed into these two layers to compute $P_{start\,i}$ and P_{end_i}. The model is optimized for the loss function independently given by log likelihood of $L = -\log P_{start\,i} - \log P_{end_i}$. At inference time, the overall prediction probability of a span is calculated by taking an average of start probability of the first token and end probability of the last token of the span. At the end, a softmax over the probabilities of all the spans is taken, and the one with the highest probability is outputted as the answer.

$$p(x_1 \dots\dots x_n) = \prod_{i=1}^{n} p(x_i | R(q)[Q:];q;[A:];x < i)$$

The idea of RAG is to address these problems by conditioning.

on the retrieved passages as part of the prefix, perhaps with some prompt text like "**Based on these texts, answer this question:**.

The common evaluation metric for QA is mean reciprocal rank or MRR. MRR is rank quality metric and is averaged over test set scores. The higher the MRR, the better the system performance. Each test set question is scored with the reciprocal of the rank of the first correct answer. i.e. if the model returns first three answers out of which the 3rd answer is correct, then the MRR is 1/3. The other evaluation metrics for QA systems are the F1 score and exact match. Exact match is the percentage of predicted answers that match the source truth exaction. F1 score is the average word/token overlap between predicted and source truth.

Machine translation task

The transformer architecture used for machine translation is encoder-decoder architecture, which we have seen in earlier sections. Some of the common applications of machine translation systems are language text translations, voice/audio translations, image translations like **optical character recognition (OCR)** systems. Language translation is the main topic when it comes to LLM. The task is complex as sequence-to-sequence mapping is not direct from one language token to another one. Different languages follow different orders, linguistic structures, word senses, grammatical constraints, etc. The sentence alignment between languages can be one to one, one to many and many to one. Machine translation training involves a parallel corpus where a pair of sentences from source to target is generated based on the score calculated between the span of source and target sentences in multilingual embedding space and also based on the alignment ranks calculated using the alignment algorithm. In case of multilingual translation, special tokens are used at encoder (s_i) to specify the source language and at also use special token (t_i) at decoder side to specify the target language to which it must translate. In encoder-decoder architecture, the decoder output (y_{t+1}) (predicting next token at each timestep auto regressively) is conditioned on the hidden representation of source language from encoder (h_t) and on the previously generated target tokens (y_t). Language translation model is trained auto regressively with the cross-entropy loss i.e. negative log likelihood on next token prediction. The system is trained to maximize the probability of sequence of token in target language given sequence of tokens in the source language. Sub-word tokenization using BPE with shared token between languages is more suitable in language translation. Beam search or Minimum Bayes Risk decoding are preferred decoding mechanisms for language translation. Language translation is evaluated using metrics like adequacy, i.e., how well the meaning of source sentence is captured in the target language, fluency, i.e., grammatical correctness, readability, completeness, F-score i.e. character F-score calculated using n-gram overlaps between target and source, **Bilingual Evaluation Understudy (BLEU)**, i.e., global average n-gram predicted precision score multiplied by brevity penalty (penalty for shorter sentences).

NLP examples

In this section, we will discuss the NLP examples. The following are the prerequisites:

- Colab with the following libraries installed (libraries name: **transformers, accelerate, datasets, bertviz, evaluate, PyPDF2**)
- Colab with A100 GPU environment

Tune GPT-2 model for new tasks

The objective of below example is to develop a decoder type model that can convert natural language to cypher query. We pre-train decoder type model (GPT-2) in auto regressive way on cypher manuals and compare the user query (related to cypher) prior pre-training and after pre-training. With a few epochs of training, we demonstrate improvement in the response. Further, the pre-trained GPT-2 model on cypher manual is fine-tuned for a specific task (natural language to cypher query generation) to improve the performance of the model.

Refer to the *Code snippet 5.1* below for importing libraries related to GPT-2 pre-training:

```
1. from transformers import pipeline, set_seed,GPT-
   2Tokenizer,GPT-2LMHeadModel,IntervalStrategy,EvalPrediction ,
   DataCollatorForLanguageModeling,pipeline,TrainingArguments,
   Trainer,TextDataset
2. from torch import tensor, numel # Returns the total number of elements
   in the input tensor.,
3. from bertviz import model_view # For viewing self-attention
4. import pandas as pd
5. set_seed(20)
```

Code snippet 5.1: Transformer libraries related to GPT model

As shown in the below *Code snippet 5.2*, Load GPT-2 tokenizer and GPT-2 model using *Hugging Face* libraries. The output of Code snippet i.e. *Figure 5.26* shows theGPT-2 architecture with 12 encoder blocks and a language modeling head.GPT-2 model has vocabulary size of 50527 BPE tokens and input vector dimension of 768.GPT-2 has maximum sequence length of 1024 and it is 1.2 billion parameter model:

```
1. tokenizer =GPT-2Tokenizer.from_pre-trained('gpt2')

2. tokenizer.pad_token = tokenizer.eos_token

3. model =GPT-2LMHeadModel.from_pre-trained('gpt2')

4. model
```

Code snippet 5.2: Transformer libraries related to GPT model

The following is the output for *Code snippet 5.2*:

```
GPT2LMHeadModel(
  (transformer): GPT2Model(
    (wte): Embedding(50257, 768)
    (wpe): Embedding(1024, 768)
    (drop): Dropout(p=0.1, inplace=False)
    (h): ModuleList(
      (0-11): 12 x GPT2Block(
        (ln_1): LayerNorm((768,), eps=1e-05, elementwise_affine=True)
        (attn): GPT2Attention(
          (c_attn): Conv1D()
          (c_proj): Conv1D()
          (attn_dropout): Dropout(p=0.1, inplace=False)
          (resid_dropout): Dropout(p=0.1, inplace=False)
        )
        (ln_2): LayerNorm((768,), eps=1e-05, elementwise_affine=True)
        (mlp): GPT2MLP(
          (c_fc): Conv1D()
          (c_proj): Conv1D()
          (act): NewGELUActivation()
          (dropout): Dropout(p=0.1, inplace=False)
        )
      )
    )
    (ln_f): LayerNorm((768,), eps=1e-05, elementwise_affine=True)
  )
  (lm_head): Linear(in_features=768, out_features=50257, bias=False)
)
```

Figure 5.26: GPT-2 model architecture

As shown in the *Code snippet 5.3* below, the user query on **Cypher query to create a customer node** response is generated using pre-trained GPT-2 model. The output generation, as shown in *Figure 5.27* seems to be inappropriate:

```
1. generator = pipeline ('text-generation',model='gpt2')
2. generator("Cypher query to create a customer node ", max_length=60,
   num_return_sequences=3, do_sample=True)
```

Code snippet 5.3: GPT-2 generation response pipeline

The following is the output for *Code snippet 5.3*:

Truncation was not explicitly activated but `max_length` is provided a specific value, please use `truncation=True` to explicitly truncate examples to max length. Defaulting to 'longest_first'
Setting `pad_token_id` to `eos_token_id`:50256 for open-end generation.
[{'generated_text': "Cypher query to create a customer node \xa0(not in the context I defined in our example), but not in an implementation (I don't actually ever make this type explicit, or
in a post-structured approach). So the first step is to put this data in one of our"},
 {'generated_text': "Cypher query to create a customer node :! This is the server. It's very similar to the one you're using httpd though you don't have to use it in production either, it's
the same server in the beginning.\n\nNow make sure you check that all the fields"},
 {'generated_text': 'Cypher query to create a customer node \xa0- (if it was used a few days ago to create a single blog in order to start a new blog post)\n\nWe decided to create an instance
of\xa0 a\xa0 Customer \xa0which you can see is in the code\xa0 at http'}]

Figure 5.27: GPT-2 model generation for user query

As shown in the *Code snippet 5.4*, the 4 nos. of pdf document related cypher query (cypher1, cypher2, cypher3, cypher4) are parsed and read using **PyPDF2** library. These documents are available in GitHub repository for processing. Further, the content is parsed and stored in the text file pre-train.txt. The output *Figure 5.28* shows the number of pages been parsed:

```
1. import os
2. import PyPDF2
3. file_path='/content/'
4. text = ''
5. i=0
6. for file_nm in os.listdir(file_path):
7.     if file_nm.endswith('.pdf'):
8.
9.         with open(file_nm, 'ro') as file:
10.            # Create a PDF reader object
11.            reader = PyPDF2.PdfReader(file)
12.
13.            # Extract text from each page
14.
15.            for page in reader.pages:
16.                i=i+1
17.                text += page.extract_text()
18.
19. print(i)
20. # Save the extracted text as a text file
21. text_file_name = 'pre-train_text'
```

```
22. text_file_path = os.path.join( text_file_name)
23. with open(text_file_path, 'w') as text_file:
24.                text_file.write(text)
```

Code snippet 5.4: Read and parse PDF content

Find the output for the below *Code snippet 5.4*:

➡ 1582

Figure 5.28: Total number of pages parsed

As shown in the *Code snippet 5.5* below, the data is split into train (80%) and validation (20%) sets and saved in separate **train_data.txt** and **validation_data.txt** files. Transformer dataset loader is used to load these files in chunks of size 32.

```
1. # Split the dataset into training and validation sets (80% - 20%)
2. # Read the entire dataset into a list
3. with open('/content/pre-train_text.txt', 'r') as f:
4.     data = f.readlines()
5. split_index = int(len(data) * 0.8)
6. train_data = data[:split_index]
7. val_data = data[split_index:]
1. # Save the training and validation sets as separate files
2. with open('train_data.txt', 'w') as f:
3.     f.writelines(train_data)
4.
5. with open('validation_data.txt', 'w') as f:
6.     f.writelines(val_data)
1.     # Load training dataset
2.     train_dataset = TextDataset(
3.         tokenizer=tokenizer,
4.         file_path='/content/train_data.txt',
5.         block_size=32)
6.
7.     # Load validation dataset
8.     val_dataset = TextDataset(
9.         tokenizer=tokenizer,
```

```
10.          file_path='/content/validation_data.txt',
11.          block_size=32)
```

Code snippet 5.5: Creation of Train and Test split data

Find the output for the below *Code snippet 5.5*:

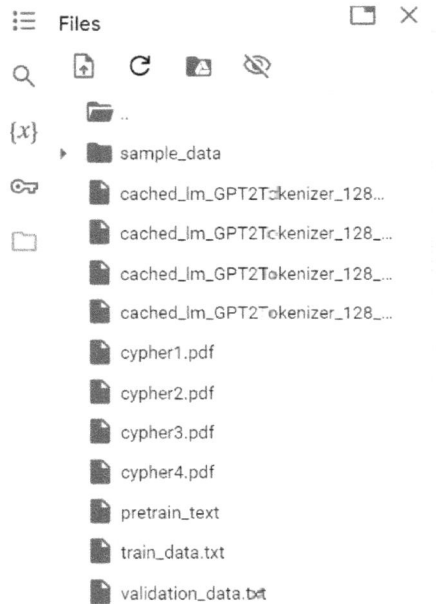

Figure 5.29: Folder structure for train and test files

As shown in the below *Code snippet 5.6* data collators are used to form a batch by using a training and validation dataset elements as input. As shown in *Figure 5.30*, the collator structure automatically bundle up the dataset with all relevant configurations like **vocab_size**, special tokens and other text processing parameters for GPT-2 pre-training:

```
1.  collator   =   DataCollatorForLanguageModeling(tokenizer=tokenizer   ,
    mlm=False)
2.  collator
```

Code snippet 5.6: Creation of data collators

Find the output for *Code snippet 5.6*:

```
DataCollatorForLanguageModeling(tokenizer=GPT2Tokenizer(name_or_path='gpt2', vocab_size=50257, model_max_length=1024, is_fast=False,
padding_side='right', truncation_side='right', special_tokens={'bos_token': '<|endoftext|>', 'eos_token': '<|endoftext|>', 'unk_token':
'<|endoftext|>'}, clean_up_tokenization_spaces=True),  added_tokens_decoder={
        50256: AddedToken("<|endoftext|>", rstrip=False, lstrip=False, single_word=False, normalized=True, special=True),
}, mlm=False, mlm_probability=0.15, pad_to_multiple_of=None, tf_experimental_compile=False, return_tensors='pt')
```

Figure 5.30: Data collator structure

As shown in the *Code snippet 5.7,* training arguments are set with batch size of 128, 20 nos. training epoch and warm-up parameter, which refers to the initial phase of training where the learning rate is gradually increased. This helps the model converge to optimal parameters more effectively. Training arguments are tunable hyperparameter that can be used for improving the model performance. Once training arguments are set, the model training is instantiated:

```
1.  batch_size = 128
2.  output_dir='/content/model_checkpoints_fine-tuned_cypher'
3.  args = TrainingArguments(
4.      output_dir=output_dir,
5.      evaluation_strategy = IntervalStrategy.EPOCH,
6.      learning_rate=2e-5,
7.      per_device_train_batch_size=batch_size,
8.      per_device_eval_batch_size=batch_size,
9.      num_train_epochs=20,
10.     weight_decay=0.01,
11.     fp16=True, # need GPU
12.     logging_steps=1,
13.     save_strategy=IntervalStrategy.EPOCH,
14.     save_total_limit=2,
15.     load_best_model_at_end=True,
16.     warmup_steps = len(train_dataset.examples)//10
17. )
```

```
1.  trainer = Trainer(
2.      model,
3.      args,
4.      train_dataset=train_dataset,
5.      eval_dataset=val_dataset,
6.      data_collator=collator,
7.      tokenizer=tokenizer,
8.      #compute_metrics=compute_metrics
9.  )
```

```
1.  trainer.train()
2.  # Save the fine-tuned model
```

```
3. model.save_pre-trained(output_dir)
4. tokenizer.save_pre-trained(output_dir)
```

Code snippet 5.7: *Set training arguments and instantiate training*

The following is the output for *Code snippet 5.7*:

6	1.873100	2.177928
7	1.618100	2.178472
8	1.826400	2.179643
9	1.763300	2.179868
10	1.949000	2.176882
11	1.685600	2.176407
12	1.676600	2.170768
13	1.752200	2.178668
14	1.720300	2.179235
15	1.749300	2.178054
16	1.762700	2.180366
17	1.761200	2.185697
18	1.576500	2.181737
19	1.755900	2.183454
20	1.591900	2.184772

```
Checkpoint destination directory /content/model_checkpoints_finetuned_cypher/checkpoint-680 already exists and is non-empty. Saving will proceed but save
There were missing keys in the checkpoint model loaded: ['lm_head.weight'].
('/content/model_checkpoints_finetuned_cypher/tokenizer_config.json',
 '/content/model_checkpoints_finetuned_cypher/special_tokens_map.json',
 '/content/model_checkpoints_finetuned_cypher/vocab.json',
 '/content/model_checkpoints_finetuned_cypher/merges.txt',
 '/content/model_checkpoints_finetuned_cypher/added_tokens.json')
```

Figure 5.31: *Training and validation loss*

As shown in the below *Code snippet 5.8,* the GPT-2 pre-trained model on cypher manuals are loaded and tested for the generation of cypher statement based on user natural language query:

```
1. loaded_model =GPT-2LMHeadModel.from_pre-trained('/content/model_
   checkpoints_fine-tuned_cypher')
2.
3. tune_generator = pipeline('text-generation', model=loaded_model ,
   tokenizer='gpt2', config ={'max_new_token':60, 'do_sample':True
   ,'top_p':0.9 , 'temperature':0.0, 'top_k':5})
1. i=0
2. for generated_sequence in tune_generator("Cypher query to create a
   customer node " , num_return_sequences=3):
3.    i=i+1
4.    print(i)
5.    print(generated_sequence['generated_text'])
```

Code snippet 5.8: *Load pre-trained model and generate output*

The following is the output for *Code snippet 5.8*:

```
Setting `pad_token_id` to `eos_token_id`:50256 for open-end generation.
1
Cypher query to create a customer node  that has a label
'Charlie Sheen' as the first delivery
This query performs the following:
CREATE (*)  RETURN customers
The first one to create and manage customer
names
2
Cypher query to create a customer node
with myname  and a business's address  would read:
CREATE (email:Email {username: 'Maria', email: { content: 'email', name: email
3
Cypher query to create a customer node  with a label-separated relationship to the user
name and lastname  node:
Cypher will then return a null result.
Query
RETURN customer
This returns an empty
```

Figure 5.32: GPT-2 Fine-tuned model output

We have observed in *Figure 5.32* that the response of GPT-2 fine-tuned on cypher manuals is more contextualized compared to the response generated in *Figure 5.27*. In the following section, the same model will be fine-tuned to task specific prompts for better performance

As shown in *Code snippet 5.9*, **cypher.xlsx** has user natural language query and relevant cypher queries. There are 95 nos. of manually created records for task specific tuning.

1. `data = pd.read_excel("/content/cypher.xlsx")`
2. `print(data.shape)`
3. `data.head(2)`

Code snippet 5.9: Read data related to cypher tasks

The following is the output for *Code snippet 5.9*:

```
(95, 3)
```

	S.No	Userquery	Cypher	
0	1.0	match all nodes with either the Fremen or Har...	MATCH (c:Fremen|Harkonnen)\nRETURN count(*)	
1	2.0	find all nodes with both the Character and Har...	MATCH (c:Character&Harkonnen)\nRETURN count(*)	

Figure 5.33: cypher.xlsx table structure

As shown in *Code snippet 5.10*, **final_prompt** generates a prompt template for task based fine-tuning:

1. `tokenizer =GPT-2Tokenizer.from_pre-trained('gpt2')`
2. `tokenizer.pad_token = tokenizer.eos_token`
3.

```
4.  prompt1= "CPT\n "
5.  prompt2="Cypher: "
6.
7.  final_prompt =f'{prompt1}English:' + data['Userquery'] +'\n' + prompt2
    + '' +data['Cypher'].astype(str)
8.
9.  print(final_prompt[0])
```

Code Snippet 5.10: *Creation of prompt template for fine-tuning*

The following is the output for *Code snippet 5.10*:

```
CPT
 English: match all nodes with either the Fremen or Harkonnen label, you can use the | expression
Cypher: MATCH (c:Fremen|Harkonnen)
RETURN count(*)
```

Figure 5.34: *Example of prompt for fine-tuning*

As shown in the below *Code snippet 5.11*, the dataset records are transformed into a single column dataframe with records in new prompt template. Further null values in the dataframe are dropped for clean processing:

```
1.  from datasets import Dataset
2.  df = pd.DataFrame({'text':final_prompt})
3.  df = df.dropna()
4.  df.head(3)
```

Code snippet 5.11: *Dataset creation as per new prompt template*

The following is the output for *Code snippet 5.11*:

	text
0	CPT\n English: match all nodes with either the...
1	CPT\n English:find all nodes with both the Cha...
2	CPT\n English:you want to match all nodes with...

Figure 5.35: *Dataset table structure as per new prompt template*

As shown in *Code snippet 5.12*, the task dataset **cypher_data** is tokenized and split into train and validation datasets. Further training arguments are created with small batch size of 8 due to a low number of records with an increased number of 30 epochs and instantiated the training:

```
1.  #Tokenization
2.  cypher_data=Dataset.from_pandas(df) # turn dataframe into dataset
3.
4.  def data_tokenize(data):
5.      #print(data)
6.      return tokenizer(data['text'], truncation = True)
7.
8.  cypher_data = cypher_data.map(data_tokenize , batched = True)
9.  cypher_data = cypher_data.train_test_split(train_size=0.8)
10.
11. collator =   DataCollatorForLanguageModeling(tokenizer=tokenizer ,mlm
    = False)
12.
13. model =GPT-2LMHeadModel.from_pre-trained('/content/model_checkpoints_
    fine-tuned_cypher')
14.
15. batch_size = 8
16. output_dir='/content/model_fine_tune_checkpoints'
17. args = TrainingArguments(
18.     output_dir=output_dir,
19.     evaluation_strategy = "epoch",
20.     learning_rate=2e-5,
21.     per_device_train_batch_size=batch_size,
22.     per_device_eval_batch_size=batch_size,
23.     num_train_epochs=30,
24.     weight_decay=0.01,
25.     fp16=True, # need GPU
26.     logging_steps=1,
27.     save_strategy=IntervalStrategy.EPOCH,
28.     save_total_limit=2,
29.     load_best_model_at_end=True,
30. )
31.
32.
33. trainer = Trainer(
```

```
34.    model,
35.    args,
36.    train_dataset=cypher_data['train'],
37.    eval_dataset=cypher_data['test'],
38.    data_collator=collator,
39.    tokenizer=tokenizer,
40. )
41.
42. trainer.train()
```

Code snippet 5.12: *Load pre-trained model and generate output*

Please find the output for *Code snippet 5.12*:

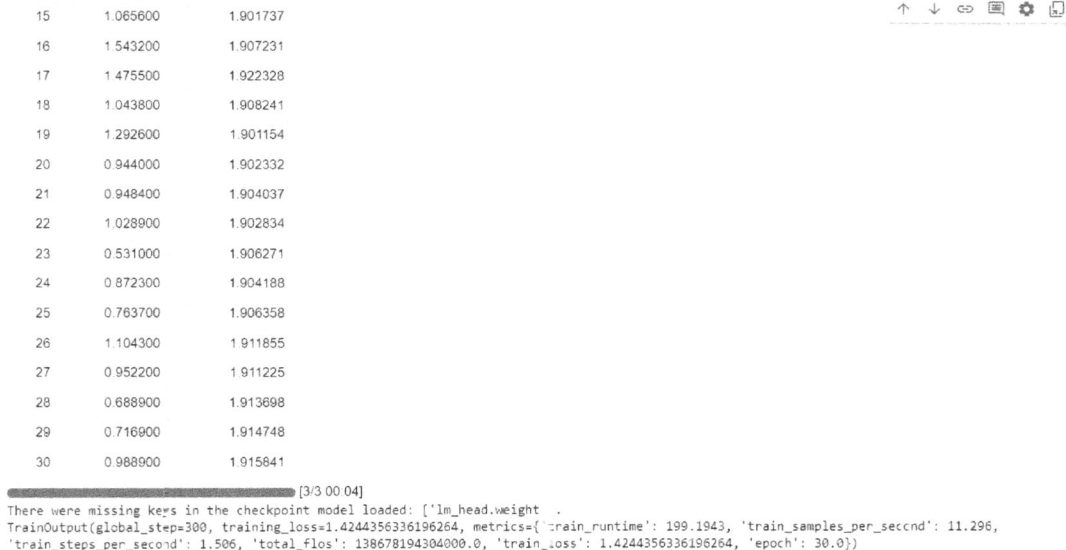

15	1.065600	1.901737
16	1.543200	1.907231
17	1.475500	1.922328
18	1.043800	1.908241
19	1.292600	1.901154
20	0.944000	1.902332
21	0.948400	1.904037
22	1.028900	1.902834
23	0.531000	1.906271
24	0.872300	1.904188
25	0.763700	1.906358
26	1.104300	1.911855
27	0.952200	1.911225
28	0.688900	1.913698
29	0.716900	1.914748
30	0.988900	1.915841

```
                                   [3/3 00:04]
There were missing keys in the checkpoint model loaded: ['lm_head.weight  .
TrainOutput(global_step=300, training_loss=1.4244356336196264, metrics={'train_runtime': 199.1943, 'train_samples_per_second': 11.296,
'train_steps_per_second': 1.506, 'total_flos': 138678194304000.0, 'train_loss': 1.4244356336196264, 'epoch': 30.0})
```

Figure 5.36: *Train and validation loss*

As shown in the below *Code snippet 5.13*, the task specific fine-tuned GPT-2 pre-trained model is saved and loaded for the generating the response same user query **Cypher query to create customer node** the output *Figure 5.37* shows the improvement in the response:

```
1. trainer.save_model()
2. loaded_model =GPT-2LMHeadModel.from_pre-trained('/content/model_fine_
   tune_checkpoints')
3. generator = pipeline('text-generation',model=loaded_model , tokenizer
   = tokenizer)
```

```
4.
5.  text_sample ='Cypher query to create a customer node '
6.  conversion_text_sample =f'{prompt1}English: {text_sample} \n
    {prompt2}'
7.  print(conversion_text_sample)
8.
9.  print(generator(conversion_text_sample, num_beams=5, early_
    stopping=True, temperature=0.8,
10.                 max_length=len(tokenizer.encode(conversion_text_
                     sample))+20)[0]['generated_text'])
```

Code snippet 5.13: *Load pre-trained model and generate output*

Following is the output for the *Code snippet 5.13*:

```
Truncation was not explicitly activated but `max_length` is provided a specific value, please use `truncation=True` to explicitly truncate examples to max length. Defaulting to 'longest_
Setting `pad_token_id` to `eos_token_id`:50256 for open-end generation.
CPT
  English: Cypher query to create a customer node
  Cypher:  CREATE (customer (surname:'John Smith'))
RETURN customer,
```

Figure 5.37: *GPT-2 Task specific tuned model output*

We can see the above response *Figure 5.37* is more appropriate and contextualized than the responses generated without any fine-tuning (*Figure 5.27*) or without task specific tuning (*Figure 5.32*).

Encoder-decoder text summarization task

The objective of this example is to train encoder-decoder T5-small model and generate summarization out of CNN-DailyMail dataset. Model will be fine-tuned and validated with ROUGE metric for its performance.

As shown in the below *Code snippet 5.14* CNN-DailyMail dataset is loaded and 10% of training records are extracted as separate dataset for model fine-tuning:

```
1.  from datasets import load_dataset
2.
3.  dataset = load_dataset("cnn_dailymail", "3.0.0" )
4.  print(dataset)
5.  print(f"Features: {dataset['train'].column_names}")
6.  dataset = load_dataset("cnn_dailymail", "3.0.0" , split = "train[:10%]")
    # We will consider only 30% of total records for this example
```

Code snippet 5.14: *Dataset loading*

Figure 5.38 is the output for *Code snippet 5.14*:

```
DatasetDict({
    train: Dataset({
        features: ['article', 'highlights', 'id', 'input_ids', 'attention_mask', 'labels'],
        num_rows: 77520
    })
    test: Dataset({
        features: ['article', 'highlights', 'id', 'input_ids', 'attention_mask', 'labels'],
        num_rows: 8514
    })
})
```

Figure 5.38: Dataset structure

As shown in the below *Code snippet 5.15,* the extracted records are cleaned, Pre-processed and train-test split into 90% train and 10% test data:

```
1. def Pre-process_txt(text_data):
2.     for txt in ['article','highlights']:
3.         text_data[txt]  =  text_data  [txt].lower().replace("\\",""). replace("/","").replace("\n","").replace("``","")
4.     return(text_data)
5.
6. dataset =  dataset.train_test_split(test_size=0.1, seed =20)
7.
8. ds = dataset.map(Pre-process_txt)
9. ds
```

Code snippet 5.15: Dataset train test split

Figure 5.39 is for the output of *Code snippet 5.15*

```
DatasetDict({
    train: Dataset({
        features: ['article', 'highlights', 'id'],
        num_rows: 25839
    })
    test: Dataset({
        features: ['article', 'highlights', 'id'],
        num_rows: 2872
    })
})
```

Figure 5.39: Dataset structure after train test split

As shown in the below *Code snippet 5.16,* the sample CNN-DailyMail article and ground summary data, i.e., highlights are displayed for reference:

```
1. article = ds["train"]["article"][0]
2. print( f"article is  : {article}")
3.
4. highlights=ds["train"]["highlights"][0]
5. print( f"highlights is :  {highlights}")
```

Code snippet 5.16: Print sample article and its highlight

Figure 5.40 is the output of *Code snippet 5.16*:

article is : anaheim, california (cnn) -- disney's cars land opens june 15 at disney california adventure, and it's big, bold and amazing. as mater says, "if i'm lying, i'm crying." kids of all ages will rev their engines and step on the gas. cars land is the capstone of a five year, estimated $1.1 billion dollar reimagining of disney california adventure. while cars land shifts california adventure into the fast lane, only time will tell if it will save the town (as lightning mcqueen did for radiator springs) and turn disneyland into the world-class destination it aspires to be. no doubt the top dogs at disney hope the renewed focus on movie magic will mean magic for the resort that executives have admitted is not up to brand standards. cars land is the centerpiece to the relaunch of california adventure. during the past five years, disney has added more than 20 attractions, including little mermaid and toy story rides, upgraded hotels and new shops. the upgrades are important considering a big complaint about california adventure was that the attractions didn't measure up to other disney parks. it didn't have enough of the disney magic: strong themes, characters and stories. perhaps the main problem was that california adventure was too nostalgic for the california of yesteryear, especially paradise pier. nostalgia doesn't appeal to the younger audience. the makeover embraces the movie icons the younger generation has grown up with. considering that disney is rumored to have spent more for the relaunch than it cost to build the original park (which opened in 2001 and cost approximately $1 billion), everyone's expectations are going to be high. along with cars land, other changes being unveiled on june 15 include the addition of buena vista street, the new entrance to the park and a nostalgic look at los angeles in the 1920s and 1930s, when walt disney arrived. again, it's not just nostalgic, but connected to the movies. the park's icon has changed from grizzly peak (a man-made mountain in the shape of a grizzly bear, california's state animal) to the carthay circle theater, the theater where "snow white and the seven dwarfs" debuted in 1937. "cars" itself is a movie about nostalgia. good old route 66 with its zany cast of characters changes the brash lightning mcqueen into a racer with heart. cars land invites guests to cruise low and slow down the main street of radiator springs. thankfully this is the version lightning repaved. the major attraction is radiator springs racers, but fans will also love luigi's flying tires and mater's junkyard jamboree. the estimated $200 million radiator springs racers ride is a giant slot car system that also features elements that take place in the dark. the cars are electric, and work much like a gigantic version of the slot cars kids play with. this is the same technology that powers test track, an epcot ride. after boarding the six-person car, you take a leisurely, scenic tour of ornament valley. soon you enter a nighttime section, where you'll find old friends from radiator springs and have adventures including tractor tipping with mater. next, after an upgrade of tires or paint, and a quick visit to doc hudson, your crew chief, the ride turns into a thrilling race for piston cup glory. disney has brewed a potent mixture here, a cross between the animated character fun of peter pan's flight with the thrilling excitement of a 40 mph race through the desert. the scariest (and most fun!) part was when the car plunged through a wall of fog. this ride is destined to have long lines for years to come. (my kids went crazy, but immediately demanded to ride again.) though not as thrilling as radiator springs racers, luigi's flying tires is still unlike anything you've ever ridden, unless you happened to ride flying saucers at disneyland between 1961 and 1966. or you have shrunken down and ridden on an air hockey puck. in this update of the flying saucers concept, giant tires float on a cushion of air supplied by a bunch of small air jets. riders lean to make their tires move. adding to the fun is a bunch of beach balls that riders can run into, poke and bat at each other. (thumbs up from the kids.) riders of mater's junkyard jamboree sit in a cart mounted to a baby tractor and the tractors square dance to seven songs sung by mater himself. (a simple ride, but it got big smiles from the kids). cars land spends a lot of time on the little details, including funny set decoration. there is excitement enough for the kids and humor for the parents. also, cars land embraces an important "cars" cast member that people forget, radiator springs itself. the movie wouldn't be the same without route 66, radiator falls or the cadillac mountains. cars land really embraces the scenery, right down to the blinking stoplight. as sally says in maybe the most poignant line in "cars," "well, the road didn't cut through the land like that interstate. it moved with the land, it rose, it fell, it curved. cars didn't drive on it to make great time. they drove on it to have a great time." disney seems to be taking this to heart.
highlights is : updates to disney's california adventures open june 15 .the centerpiece, cars land, makes the most of the popular movie .revamping the park cost an estimated $1.1 billion .

Figure 5.40: Sample article and its highlight

As shown in the below *Code snippet 5.17*, 4 models **["t5-small","t5-large","facebook/ bart-large-cnn","google/pegasus-cnn_dailymail"]** are created as list and looped for generating summary for the sample article loaded in *Code snippet 5.16*. The summaries generated by these four LLM models are stored in **full_summaries** directory and printed, as shown in *Figure 5.40*:

```
1. full_summaries = {}
2. import nltk
3. from nltk.tokenize import sent_tokenize
4. from transformers import pipeline, set_seed
5. nltk.download("punkt")
6.
7. models = ["t5-small","t5-large","facebook/bart-large-cnn","google/
   pegasus-cnn_dailymail"]
8. for model in models:
9.   summarizer = pipeline ("summarization", model = model, truncation
      = True)
10.  summary_txt = summarizer ( "summarize:"+article)
```

```
11.  full_summaries["model"] = "\n".join(
12.      sent_tokenize(summary_txt[0]["summary_text"]))
13.
14. full_summaries
```

Code snippet 5.17: Load 4 model and run summary pipeline in loop

Figure 5.41 is the output of *Code snippet 5.17*:

Figure 5.41: Generated summary output by 4 models

As shown in the below *Code snippet 5.18*, ROUGE metric is used to evaluate the generated summary. Three ROUGE metric (ROUGE-N, ROUGE-L, Rouge-Lsum) are computed for any generated summary. ROUGE-N metric match n-grams between the model-generated text and a candidate dataset reference. ROUGE-L is based on the longest common sequence between reference and summary. While ROUGE-L is computed as an average over individual sentences, ROUGE-Lsum is computed over the entire summary:

```
1.  !pip install evaluate
2.  !pip install rouge_score
3.  import evaluate
4.  rouge = evaluate.load("rouge")
5.  rouge
```

Code snippet 5.18: Install and download evaluation metric (ROUGE)

Figure 5.42 is the output of *Code snippet 5.17*:

Figure 5.42: ROUGE metric examples

As shown in the below *Code snippet 5.19,* ROUGE metrics between reference **acrticle_summary** and **candidate_summaries** are computed for the first 20 articles and displayed in consolidate way. Candidate summaries are generated using Pegasus model loaded in the summarizer:

```
1.  articles = ds["test"]["article"]
2.  articles_summary = ds["test"]["highlights"]
3.
4.  from tqdm import tqdm
5.  summaries = []
6.  for i, text in enumerate (tqdm (articles[:20])):
7.    summary_txt = summarizer ( «summarize:»+text)
8.    summaries.append(summary_txt[0]["summary_text"])
9.
10. rouge.compute(predictions = summaries, references= articles_
    summary[:20], use_stemmer=True, use_aggregator=True)
```

Code snippet 5.19: Evaluate consolidated rogue metrics

Figure 5.43 is the output of *Code snippet 5.19*:

```
{'rouge1': 0.3531031467194583,
 'rouge2': 0.15786956470877753,
 'rougeL': 0.2513701424669881,
 'rougeLsum': 0.24888418033907472}
```

Figure 5.43: Consolidated rouge metrics for 20 articles

Following *Code snippet 5.20* is for generating and displaying the dataset with predicted vs. actual summaries for the first 20 CNN-DailyMail article dataset:

```
1.  import pandas as pd
2.  df=pd.DataFrame(list(zip (summaries , articles_summary[:20])),
    columns=["precitions", "actual"])
3.  df.head(20)
```

Code snippet 5.20: Generate actual vs predicted summaries/highlights

Following is the output of *Code snippet 5.20*:

	precitions	actual
0	Tornado hits pensacola, Florida, destroying ho...	at least four people hurt in pensacola, florid...
1	John hickenlooper was named one of the country...	john hickenlooper says there is a repulsion fo...
2	"i understood what i was doing wrong but i did...	new: wikileaks founder calls manning's apology.
3	"hitchcock" is an oscar wannabe scripted by jo...	anthony hopkins stars as the famous director a...
4	kengo kuma is one of Japan's leading architect...	japanese architect has popularized sensitive j...
5	afghan presidential candidate abdullah abdulla...	abdullah abdullah is in the lead with 82% of t...
6	petroleum giant bp comes under congressional s...	obama received $71,000 in 2008 election cycle,...
7	Ryou-un maru caught fire and capsized in more ...	the ship sunk in more than 6,000 feet of water ..
8	parts of the state have been drenched with up ...	new: bodies recovered from a flooded house an...
9	oberster was elected in 1974 as a member of th...	jim oberstar represented minnesota's 8th congr...
10	The suspect held up a bank of america branch i...	"geezer bandit" may have robbed up to 11 banks...
11	"i have no of apologizing because i truthfully...	hill's testimony in 1991 almost sank clarence ...
12	India's northern uttarakhand state has been hi...	environmentalists blame rampant development fo...
13	jacob and natasha johnson wanted to replicate ...	newlyweds chose a "human slingshot" to make th...
14	ferrari driver felipe massa will be in brazil ...	felipe massa will be in brazil for home formul...
15	Park ji sung's manchester united return has be...	manchester united's park ji sung will be out f...

Figure 5.44: Predicted vs actual summary of articles

In the above code, we have seen the summary generated for a sample article in the CNN-DailyMail dataset by four different models and the applicability of the ROUGE metric to evaluate the performance of the models. In the upcoming codes, we will fine-tune T5-small model on CNN-DailyMail dataset, push the model/tokenizer/metrics into Hugging Face and then use the fine-tuned model to generate the summary/highlights and validate the same with ROUGE metric. As shown in *Code snippet 5.21*, the T5-small pre-trained model is loaded along with the tokenizer:

```
1. model="t5-large"
2. from  transformers import AutoTokenizer
3. tokenizer = AutoTokenizer.from_pre-trained (model)
4.
5. from transformers import AutoModelForSeq2SeqLM,
   Seq2SeqTrainingArguments, Seq2SeqTrainer
6. model = AutoModelForSeq2SeqLM.from_pre-trained(model)
7.
8. model
```

Code snippet 5.21: Load T5-large tokenizer and model

Figure 5.45 is the output of *Code snippet 5.21*:

```
T5ForConditionalGeneration(
  (shared): Embedding(32128, 1024)
  (encoder): T5Stack(
    (embed_tokens): Embedding(32128, 1024)
    (block): ModuleList(
      (0): T5Block(
        (layer): ModuleList(
          (0): T5LayerSelfAttention(
            (SelfAttention): T5Attention(
              (q): Linear(in_features=1024, out_features=1024, bias=False)
              (k): Linear(in_features=1024, out_features=1024, bias=False)
              (v): Linear(in_features=1024, out_features=1024, bias=False)
              (o): Linear(in_features=1024, out_features=1024, bias=False)
              (relative_attention_bias): Embedding(32, 16)
            )
            (layer_norm): T5LayerNorm()
            (dropout): Dropout(p=0.1, inplace=False)
          )
          (1): T5LayerFF(
            (DenseReluDense): T5DenseActDense(
              (wi): Linear(in_features=1024, out_features=4096, bias=False)
              (wo): Linear(in_features=4096, out_features=1024, bias=False)
              (dropout): Dropout(p=0.1, inplace=False)
              (act): ReLU()
            )
            (layer_norm): T5LayerNorm()
            (dropout): Dropout(p=0.1, inplace=False)
          )
        )
      )
```

Figure 5.45: T5-small model architecture

As shown in below *Code snippet 5.22*, the dataset with article and its summary is tokenized with T5-small model tokenizer, and inputs are truncated to max input sequence allowed as per T5 model, i.e., 1024 tokens:

```
1. def pre_fn(fine_data):
2.    inputs=["summarize:" + doc for doc in fine_data["article"]]
3.    model_inputs=tokenizer(inputs, max_length=1024, truncation = True)
4.    labels= tokenizer(text_target= fine_data["highlights"],max_
      length=128, truncation = True)
5.    model_inputs['labels']=labels["input_ids"]
6.    return model_inputs
7.
8. tokenized_ds =  ds.map(pre_fn, batched = True)
9.
10. tokenized_ds
```

Code snippet 5.22: Pre-process train data

Figure 5.46 is the output of *Code snippet 5.22*:

```
DatasetDict({
    train: Dataset({
        features: ['article', highlights', 'id'],
        num_rows: 287113
    })
    validation: Dataset({
        features: ['article', 'highlights', 'id'],
        num_rows: 13368
    })
    test: Dataset({
        features: ['article', 'highlights', 'id'],
        num_rows: 11490
    })
})
Features: ['article', 'highlights', 'id']
```

Figure 5.46: Pre-processed train and test data structure

The following *Code snippet, 5.23* is responsible for creating data collators, setting up training arguments, creating trainers, and initiating training. **rouge_metrics** functions are defined to calculate the rouge metrics between the predictions, i.e., **decoded_pred** and actual lablels, i.e., **decoded_labels**. Once model got trained it is pushed to Hugging Face repository along with all training metrics:

```
1.  from transformers import DataCollatorForSeq2Seq

2.  data_collator= DataCollatorForSeq2Seq(tokenizer = tokenizer , model =
    model)

3.

4.  def rouge_metrics (eval_pred):

5.     pred, actual_labels = eval_pred

6.     decoded_pred = tokenizer.batch_decode (pred, skip_special_tokens =
       True)

7.

8.     actual_labels = np.where(actual_labels !=-100, actual_labels ,
       tokenizer.pad_token_id)

9.     decoded_labels = tokenizer.batch_decode (actual_labels, skip_
       special_tokens = True)

10.

11.    result = rouge.compute(predictions = decoded_pred, references =
       decoded_labels , use_stemmer = True)

12.    pred_length = [np.count_nonzero(pred != tokenizer.pad_token_id )
       for pred in predictions]

13.    return {k: round(v,2) for k,v in result.items()}

14.

15.
```

```
16. training_args = Seq2SeqTrainingArguments(
17.     output_dir = "new_summary_model",
18.     evaluation_strategy = 'epoch',
19.     learning_rate = 2e-5,
20.     per_device_train_batch_size = 16,
21.     per_device_eval_batch_size = 16,
22.     weight_decay = 0.01,
23.     save_total_limit=3,
24.     num_train_epochs=3,
25.     predict_with_generate=True,
26.     fp16=True,
27.     push_to_hub = False,
28. )
29.
30. trainer = Seq2SeqTrainer( model = model ,
31.                          args = training_args,
32.                          train_dataset = tokenized_ds["train"],
33.                          eval_dataset = tokenized_ds ["test"],
34.                          tokenizer = tokenizaer,
35.                          data_collator = data_collator,
36.                          compute_metrics =rouge_metrics)
37.
38. trainer.train(resume_from_checkpoint = True)
39. trainer.push_to_hub()
```

Code snippet 5.23: *Define metric, train arguments and trainer modules*

Figure 5.47 shows the output of *Code snippet 5.23*:

Epoch	Training Loss	Validation Loss	Rouge1	Rouge2	RougeL	RougeLsum
1	1.713100	1.505596	0.210000	0.090000	0.180000	0.180000
2	1.701400	1.494778	0.210000	0.090000	0.180000	0.180000
3	1.682700	1.492841	0.220000	0.090000	0.180000	0.180000

```
/usr/local/lib/python3.10/dist-packages/transformers/generation/utils.py:1178: UserWarning: Using the model-agnostic default `max_length` (=20) to contro
  warnings.warn(
/usr/local/lib/python3.10/dist-packages/transformers/generation/utils.py:1178: UserWarning: Using the model-agnostic default `max_length` (=20) to contro
  warnings.warn(
/usr/local/lib/python3.10/dist-packages/transformers/generation/utils.py:1178: UserWarning: Using the model-agnostic default `max_length` (=20) to contro
  warnings.warn(
TrainOutput(global_step=4845, training_loss=1.7081657102602554, metrics={'train_runtime': 1693.7774, 'train_samples_per_second': 45.766,
'train_steps_per_second': 2.86, 'total_flos': 2.098256816111616e+16, 'train_loss': 1.7081657102602554, 'epoch': 3.0})
```

Figure 5.47: *Train and test loss*

Code snippet 5.24 loads the fine-tuned model from the hugging face and evaluates the ROUGE metrics after fine-tuning the model on 10% of CNN-DailyMail dataset. We can see the improvement in rogue score in *Figure 5.47* compared to the ROUGE score prior fine-tuning:

```
1.  summarizer = pipeline("summarization",model = 'karthiksab/new_summary_
    model' , truncation = True)
2.  from transformers import AutoTokenizer
3.  hugging_path="karthiksab/new_summary_model"
4.  tokenizer = AutoTokenizer. from_pre-trained(hugging_path)
5.  model = AutoModelForSeq2SeqLM.from_pre-trained(hugging_path)
6.
7.
8.  articles = ds["test"]["article"]
9.  articles_summary = ds["test"]["highlights"]
10.
11. from tqdm import tqdm
12. summaries = []
13. for i, text in enumerate (tqdm (articles[:20])):
14.    summary_txt = summarizer ( «summarize:»+text)
15.    summaries.append(summary_txt[0]["summary_text"])
16.
17. rouge.compute(predictions = summaries, references= articles_
    summary[:20], use_stemmer=True, use_aggregator=True)
```

Code snippet 5.24: *Load fine-tuned model from hugging face and do inferencing*

Figure 5.48 is the output of *Code snippet 5.25*. With few training epochs, the ROUGE scores have improved from *Figure 5.42*. **rouge1** metric has been improved from 0.35 to 0.37, **rouge2** metric has been improved from 0.15 to 0.17, **rougeL** metric has been improved from 0.25 to 0.27, **rougeLsum** metric has been improved from 0.24 to 0.27:

```
rouge.compute(predictions = summaries, references= articles_summary[:20], use_stemmer=True, use_aggregator=True)

{'rouge1': 0.371586046628969,
 'rouge2': 0.17297249226204092,
 'rougeL': 0.274601475902456,
 'rougeLsum': 0.27268010752295424}
```

Figure 5.48: *ROUGE metric after fine-tuning the model*

Conclusion

In this chapter, we understood popular NLP techniques like NLP, NLU and reinforcement learning. We also understood the different NLP tasks like summarization, question answering, language translation, entity recognition and many more tasks used under each NLP technique. Besides that, we understood the architecture of traditional sequence to sequence language modeling techniques like RNN, LSTM and understood their pros and cons. Further, we discussed transformer architecture, the type of architecture used for different tasks, components involved in attention techniques, and performance improvement techniques. Finally, we went through NLP examples for summarization, question answering and GPT type content generation. In the next chapter, we will discuss the state-of-the-art LLM application called *ChatGPT* and apply prompt engineering technique to solve various NLP related tasks.

Key terms

- Natural language understanding
- Natural language processing
- Self-attention mechanism
- Cross attention mechanism
- Causal language model
- Masked language model
- Tokenization
- Encoder-decoder transformers

Questions

1. What is natural language processing?
2. What are the different transformer architecture types?
3. How do we calculate the loss function in the transformer model?
4. What is the difference between self-attention and cross attention mechanism?
5. What are the benefits of multi-head attention?
6. What is meant by self-attention in term of transformer architecture?
7. What type of architecture used in translation machine learning task?
8. What is meant by summarization task?
9. What are different types of summarizations?
10. What is the loss function in language modeling head of standard transformer model?

CHAPTER 6
ChatGPT

Introduction

Since its release in November 2022, *OpenAI's ChatGPT* has been considered a revolutionary moment for the AI world. It has become the world's fastest-adopted application, and its dazzling capabilities made many enterprises feel the imminent need for generative AI adoption into their business. It continues to evolve with ever-increasing capabilities. New discipline of prompt engineering and new prompt engineer role have emerged to make generative models perform better. In this chapter, we will look into ChatGPT essentials, its features, and integrations. Further, we will understand the importance of prompts, their types, frameworks, and examples, and delve into the Prompt engineering process. Finally, we will create our Prompt Playground application for enterprises.

Structure

In this chapter, we will learn the following topics:

- Introduction to OpenAI
- Prompt engineering
- Build a prompt playground
- Jailbreaking

Objectives

By the end of this chapter, we will understand the OpenAI Platform, the ChatGPT application, and its features. We will demonstrate ChatGPT add-ons and understand how enterprises can leverage these add-ons to extend the capabilities of ChatGPT.

Introduction to OpenAI

OpenAI is an artificial intelligence research lab founded in 2015 with vision of ensuring **artificial general intelligence** (**AGI**) benefits for all humanity. The key founders are CEO of *SpaceX* and *Tesla* (*Elon Musk*), CEO of *OpenAI* (*Sam Altman*), CTO of *Stripe* (*Greg Brockman*), AI experts from various fields (*Ilya Sustskever, John Schulman, Wojciech Zaremba*). Some of the breakthrough events in OpenAI history are the release of *Gym* and *Universe*, a reinforcement learning toolkit, in 2016; release of *OpenAI Five*, a team of AI Bots for gaming, in 2018; and the release of language models *GPT-2* in 2019, *GPT-3* in 2020. In 2019 OpenAI business transitioned into OpenAI. LP unconventional hybrid nonprofit and for-profit model with a commercial arm that would allow it to raise more capital. Since then, they were able to disrupt each industry with product line up ChatGPT (AI-chabot), DALL-E (AI system for Image creation and manipulation), Whisper (AI system for Audio generation and transcription) and Codex (AI model for code generation and explanation). Beyond language models, OpenAI has ventured into robotics dactyl, a robotic hand capable of learning complex manipulation tasks. In this section, we will understand a few of the products and service capabilities related to OpenAI.

OpenAI image models

OpenAI provides DALL-E versions of the model to generate images from text or in-painting of images as we did in *Chapter 2, GenAI for Images,* or create variations of existing images. The number of images, sizes (1024x1024), and the quality of images (HD or standard) can be set as input parameters to the model. Text prompts are auto-refined by the OpenAI platform for better generation of images. The following code shows how to generate or create variations of images from the text prompt. OpenAI generates the URL of the image relevant to the text prompt. *Figure 6.1* shows the code for image generation based on the prompt `A person studying Generative AI`:

```
1    from openai import OpenAI
2    from dotenv import load_dotenv
3    load_dotenv()
4    client = OpenAI()
5
6    response = client.images.generate(
7      model="dall-e-2",
8      prompt="A person studying Generative AI",
9      size="1024x1024",
10     quality="standard",
11     style = 'vivid',
12     n=1,
13   )
14   print(response.data[0].url)
```

Figure 6.1: *Left code for image generation and right generated image based on prompt*

Below *Figure 6.2* shows the code for creating variation to the image generate above:

```
from openai import OpenAI
from dotenv import load_dotenv
load_dotenv()
client = OpenAI()
img =open('GenAI_Image.png','rb')
response = client.images.create_variation(
  image=img,
  size="1024x1024",
  n=1,
)
print(response.data[0].url)
```

Figure 6.2: *Left code for image variation and right image variation created by generative AI model*

Some of the DALL-E limitations are prompt adherence, feature customization, background quality, photorealism, and cost. Some of the other image generating models that can be leveraged for addressing the above limitations are DALL-E 3 recent advancement from *OpenAI*, *Midjourney* from an *San Francisco* based independent research lab, *Stable Diffusion* from *Stability AI*, *Imagen* 2 from *Google Gemini*, *FLUX.1* from *Forrest labs*. While each of it has own pros and cons, some of the comparisons to select them are:

1. Ability to generate high quality image and prompt adherence (DALL-E 3, FLUX.1)
2. Simultaneous image generation (Imagen 2)
3. Photo realistic images (Imagen 2)
4. Creative and artistic images (Midjourney, DALL-E 3)
5. Long text rendering (FLUX.1, Image 2)
6. Open-source nature (Stable Diffusion)
7. Guardrails and safety (DAL-.E 3, Imagen 2)

OpenAI Whisper

Whisper is a pre-trained speech recognition model capable of multilingual transcriptions and translations. It is built on encoder-decoder architecture. It splits the audio track into 30 second chunks and converts them into a long-mel spectrogram for processing. Some of the model endpoints are large-v2 Whisper for speech-to-text and support various formats. Both transcriptions and translations are supported by the model. However, the translation is currently limited to English. The other model endpoints are TTS-1 and TTS-1-HD, provided for text-to-speech. It supports multiple languages with different voice styles. Some of the real-world use cases are call center assistant, podcast transcripts, video captioning, transcription bot for virtual meetings summarization, voice-controlled interfaces interacting for robotic actions, document generation through voice dictation, audio translation, and workspace collaboration. Example of conversational intelligence with whisper model in call center is to detect a happy customer during an interaction, where agents can be alerted in real-time to potential up-sell opportunities ALUE. Inversely, a frustrated customer could be quickly routed to a supervisor, reducing churn. Similarly, health care companies can enhance patient experience by building conversational agent that support 24/7 medical information, drug interactions, health reminders, and adverse events reporting.

The following codes show transcriptions, translations, and text-to-speech generation capabilities of OpenAI models. Load OpenAI API key and install pytube from `pip install git+https://github.com/kszczepanskidev/pytube` prior running the scripts. Below *Figure 6.3* shows the code for Transcribing YouTube video using Whisper model:

```python
from openai import OpenAI
from dotenv import load_dotenv
from pytube import YouTube
import os

# for transcriptions
file = YouTube(str("https://www.youtube.com/watch?v=rwF-X5STYks"))
video_file = file.streams.filter(only_audio=True).first()
video_out = video_file.download(output_path='./')
base, ext = os.path.splitext(video_out)
mp3_file = base + '.mp3'
os.rename(video_out, mp3_file)


load_dotenv()
client = OpenAI()
file = 'Generative AI explained in 2 minutes.mp3'
with open(file,'rb') as file_audio:
    transcript=client.audio.transcriptions.create(model='whisper-1',file=file_audio)
    # translation=client.audio.translations.create(model='whisper-1',file=file_audio)
print (transcript.text)
```

Figure 6.3: *Code for audio transcriptions using Whisper model and output of the model*

Below *Figure 6.4* shows the code for Text-to-Speech using the OpenAI TTS-1 model. The output will be voice file generated for the content **This book is all about Generative AI** while executing the code:

```python
from openai import OpenAI
from dotenv import load_dotenv
from pytube import YouTube
import os
import soundfile as sf
import sounddevice as sd
import io


load_dotenv()
content =" This book is all about Generative AI"
client = OpenAI()
res =client.audio.speech.create(model='tts-1',voice='fable',input=content)

buffer = io.BytesIO()
for chunk in res.iter_bytes(chunk_size=4096):
    buffer.write(chunk)
buffer.seek(0)

with sf.SoundFile(buffer, 'r') as sound_file:
    data = sound_file.read(dtype='int16')
    sd.play(data, sound_file.samplerate)
    sd.wait()
```

Figure 6.4: *Code for text to speech using TTS-1 model*

OpenAI Playground

Developed by OpenAI to integrate with multiple GPT models, playground gives easy access for users to give prompts and set or fine-tune the parameters, as shown in *Figure 6.5 OpenAI Playground*. In the next section of this chapter, we will build our own playground for experimenting with different prompts and record the responses. Here, the model selected is Gpt-3.5 Turbo. System message, user query, and hyperparameter tuning are the three main features enabled by the OpenAI Playground. Following are a few hyperparameters that are used to tune model response:

- **Temperature**: This parameter controls the randomness of the model. It can have values between 0 and 1. Lower the value, the randomness is less and gives more deterministic results. The higher the value, it can give random results, good for innovative ideas, out-of-the-box ideas, and so on.

- **Maximum length**: The values between 0 and 256 guide the length or number of tokens (approximately 4 English characters, including space, are equivalent to 1 token) to use in the response. The exact limit depends on the model.

- **Top-P**: Values are between 0 and 1. The higher the value, the more weighted samples the model will get. In a simpler way, the lower the value, the more variety of responses will be given.

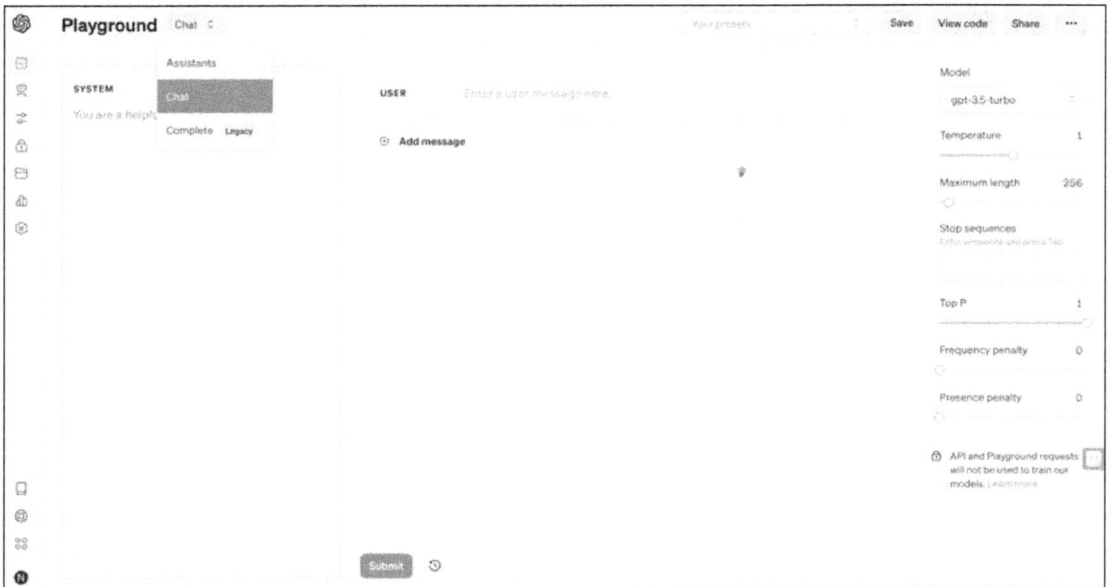

Figure 6.5: *OpenAI Playground*

OpenAI Cookbook

OpenAI Cookbook is a community-driven forum having a collection of open-source examples and guides related to OpenAI API. For example, **tiktoken** an open-source tokenizer published by OpenAI, which we will be using in the upcoming prompt playground prototype to calculate the API call cost. As discussed in *Chapter 5 GenAI for Text, Tokenization*, different models use different encoding mechanisms. OpenAI uses three types of encodings: cl100k_base for GPT-4, GPT-3.5 Turbo, text-embedding-ada-002 models; p50k-base for text-davinci-002/003, Codex models; r50k_base for GPT-3 models like DaVinci. The following code describes the sample of extracting tokens using **tiktoken** for the text **What is Generative AI!**:

```
1. import tiktoken
2. encoding = tiktoken.encoding_for_model('gpt-3.5-turbo')
3. enc=encoding.encode("What is Generative AI!")
4. dec = encoding.decode(enc)
5. print (enc)
6. print(dec)
```

OpenAI fine-tuning

One of the main benefits of fine-tuning through OpenAI Platform is improvement in model accuracy and align model to relevant responses using different techniques. As discussed in *Chapter 5, GenAI for Text*, during fine-tuning, only a fraction of model weights are updated and trained for the example provided. Enterprises adopt OpenAI fine-tuning in cases where the task to accomplish is complex to be described through the prompt, or to handle edge cases, or to correct erroneous responses, or to align OpenAI model responses to domain-specific knowledge.

The fine-tuning dataset messages must be in the formats as system, user, and assistant roles, stored in **.jsonl** files. OpenAI files are created, and fine-tuning jobs are executed, as shown in *Figure 6.6*. On completion of the fine-tuning job, which can be accessed through job ID, a new fine-tuned model is created and can be accessed to generate fine-tuned responses using the new model.

Format

{"messages": [{"role": "system", "content": "You are a expert assistant for a edge computing domain."}, {"role": "user", "content": "What is the tool available to do registration of edge device?"}, {"role": "assistant", "content": "The tool ABC is available to do edge device registration."}]}

```python
from openai import OpenAI
client = OpenAI()
# upload training file using File API
client.files.create(
  file=open("mydata.jsonl", "rb"),
  purpose="fine-tune"
)
#Start a fine-tuning job using the OpenAI SDK
client.fine_tuning.jobs.create(
  training_file="file-abc123", # File id created while uploading
  model="gpt-4o-mini-2024-07-18"
)
# Retrieve the state of a fine-tune
client.fine_tuning.jobs.retrieve("ftjob-abc123")
# Use a fine tune job
completion = client.chat.completions.create(
  model="ft:gpt-4o-mini:my-org:custom_suffix:id",
  messages=[
    {"role": "system", "content": "You are a helpful assistant."},
    {"role": "user", "content": "Hello!"}
  ]
)
print(completion.choices[0].message)
```

Figure 6.6: Left: OpenAI file creation. Right: Fine-tuning job execution and accessing newly fine-tuned model

Some of the drawbacks of OpenAI fine-tuning are lack of explainability, limited to OpenAI models to fine-tune, dependency on datasets for performance, and process is expensive as there is an increase in token cost for alignment and querying the model.

ChatGPT plugins

These are additional tools that enhance the capabilities of ChatGPT to perform a wider range of tasks and specialized services. For example, LLM models are not trained with current data. If a user query demands real-time information, the capability of ChatGPT can be extended using web search plugins to extract the information from the internet, analyze it, and respond. OpenAI offers various pricing options to enable the plugins in the chat interface itself. Some of the plugin examples are PromptPerfect for best prompt suggestions for the intended tasks, WebPilot for extracting information from web pages with web URLs, Productivity Pro plugin for email composing, schedule management, and code generation, VoxScript to extract information from video content. While numerous plugins are developed, there is a rising concern over the security and vulnerability of plugin implementations. We will see in the *Prompt engineering* section, how indirect prompt injection technique can exploit plugin vulnerabilities to do un-intended tasks.

ChatGPT Enterprise

ChatGPT Enterprise offers features specific to business enterprises. It is designed to comply with enterprise requirements related to security and privacy needs, and it is SOC 2 compliant. Some of the features include larger context windows, an administrative console, user management tools, bulk deployments, data security measures (at rest and in transit), domain-specific applications, analytics, and dashboards. Furthermore, it does not use any enterprise user prompts or data for model retraining. It is enabled with a shared workspace, allowing employees to build their own GPT models.

Pricing

ChatGPT 3.5 is free with limited usage, and the cost of ChatGPT Plus 4.0 is $20/month. The cost of OpenAI API varies based on the model type and per 1000 tokens for both query and response. For example, as shown in the following figure, the cost of the GPT-4o model with batch API is $1.25/1M tokens for input and $5.0/1M tokens for output:

Model	Pricing	Pricing with Batch API*
gpt-4o	$2.50 / 1M input tokens	$1.25 / 1M input tokens
	$1.25 / 1M cached** input tokens	
	$10.00 / 1M output tokens	$5.00 / 1M output tokens

Figure 6.7: Cost of OpenAI pricing for GPT-4o model

Limitations of ChatGPT

Here are some of the limitations of ChatGPT:

- Recency of data is a problem for ChatGPT. Though agents are used for the extraction of real-time information through search engines and augmented with user queries, the relevancy and accuracy of LLM's response still heavily rely on patterns and statistical associations present in the past data it has been trained on.

- ChatGPT's response is sensitive to input prompts. Small changes in prompts can lead to varying responses, so prompt design becomes critical for the ChatGPT LLM application.

- Though multimodal capabilities are available in the GPT4o versions, the features related to images and audio seem to be limited in the current version.

- Hallucinations and factual inaccuracies remain widespread across LLM models.

- Lack of visibility to model fine-tuning and inferencing.

- Lack of regulation to control the use of proprietary data for LLM training and lack of clarity on copyright issues with generated output can cause legal, ethical, and social damages.

- Compared to private LLMs, the context window length and the limitations to the number of API requests per account in certain use cases are considered drawbacks.

- Customization capabilities of ChatGPT for domain specific tasks are still limited.

ChatGPT future

Currently, the GPT-4 version of ChatGPT is accessible for ChatGPT Plus subscribers with a usage cap. The new GPT-4o has been released with several enhancements related to accuracy, performance, data recency, context window length (128k tokens), and multimodal abilities (audio and images). Further, GPT Store enables developers to distribute and sell AI agents developed using OpenAI's model. While the alternatives for ChatGPT, such as *Anthropic's Claude 3 opus* or *Google's Gemini Ultra*, are emerging, the expectations for the future of ChatGPT are immense. GPT-5 is expected to bring unprecedented advancements in video-based tasks, voice-based conversations, personalized conversational experience, enhanced reasoning capabilities, and more enterprise features on security and privacy.

Experience the ChatGPT add-on feature

One of the main advantages of ChatGPT for enterprises is the add-on features enabled by product companies for easy integration support for ChatGPT. By providing add-on features, enterprises can implement the functionalities without any vulnerability risk, as exists with third-party plugins. In this section, we will look into the steps to integrate ChatGPT with *Google Sheets* and *Google Documents*. These add-on, as shown in *Figure 6.8* help us to chat directly on our spreadsheets and documents by calling functions and query the contents by creating prompts. In order to enable extension, one must have access to *Google Sheet* document and ChatGPT API Secret key:

1. Click on Extensions >> Get add-ons.

Figure 6.8: Adding extension on Google Sheet

The following figure shows how to install the add-on from marketplace:

2. In the Google Workspace Marketplace, search for GPT for work sheets and docs and Install the GPT for Google Sheets and Docs.

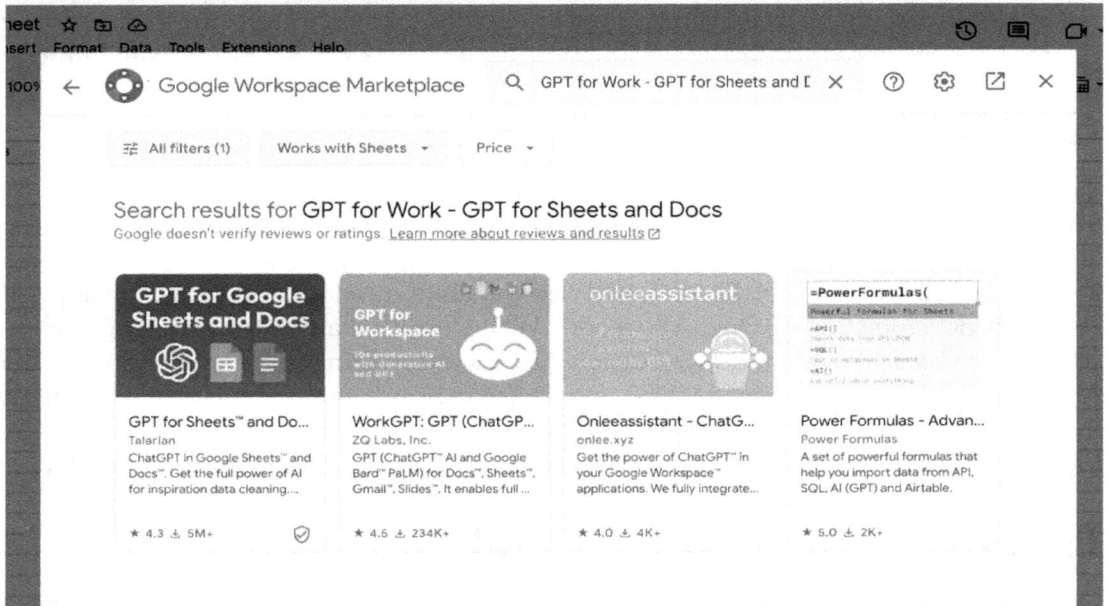

Figure 6.9: Install the add-on from marketplace

3. After installation *GPT for Sheets and Docs* under Extensions gets enabled. *Set Open AI account API key*.

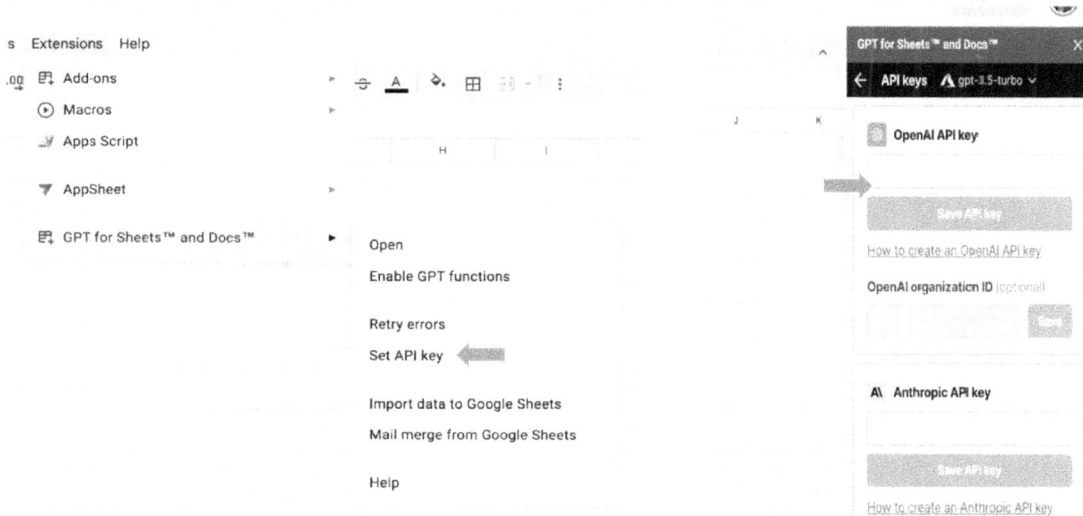

Figure 6.10: *Enable ChatGPT add-on with API Key*

4. Use GPT function to get the response. Model, Temperature can set as parameters inside the function

Figure 6.11: *Use GPT function to interact with GPT*

Similar to *Google Sheets*, ChatGPT extensions can be enabled for *Google Docs*. Set model parameters and design the prompts to query the document directly. Some of the features need licenses and some are in beta version. Refer to the following figure:

Similar to Google sheet, Google Docs provides extension to ChatGPT. Launch the extension, set the API keys and do model settings. Various parameter settings are possible as shown in below figure

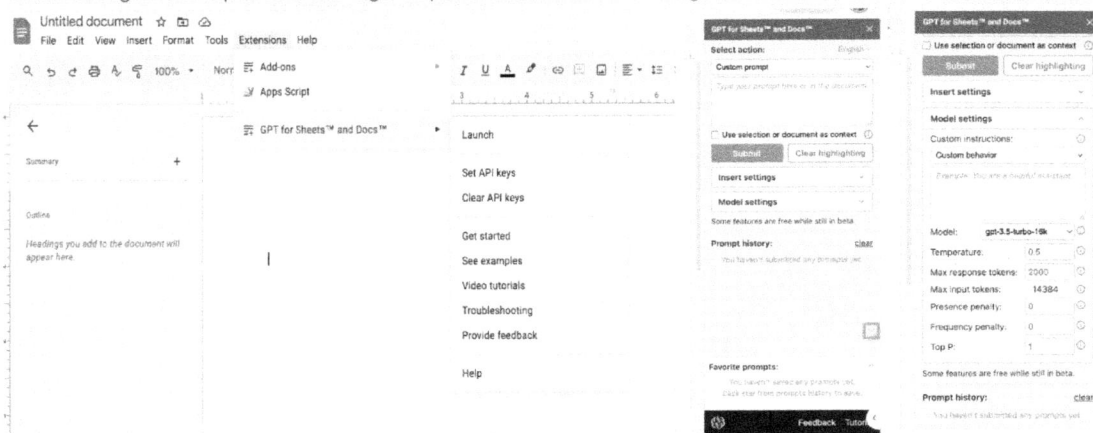

Figure 6.12: Enabling ChatGPT add-on in Google Docs

Similar to the above, many enterprise products are bringing ChatGPT and other LLM add-ons into their products. This simplifies and enhances product capabilities along with the user experience. Different pricing models are adopted, most of them are subscription-based pricing, and there are products where product pricing includes the OpenAI cost, and others allow enterprises to use their OpenAI licenses but pay only for feature enablement. *Microsoft Co-Pilot* is another such product that has integrated generative AI capabilities into their *Office 365* product lines. It is more like an AI companion, similar to ChatGPT for enterprises. It helps employees to leverage generative AI capabilities in their daily routines. Though it does not directly integrate into ChatGPT, it leverages LLM capabilities of GPT-4 and other generative AI models to perform their tasks. The other product is *GitHub Copilot*, which is more of an AI Programmer pair that helps throughout the **software development lifecycle (SDLC)** activities such as code recommendations, error resolutions, and unit test case development.

Prompt engineering

Have you ever observed how interviews unfold? Perhaps you have noticed an interesting shift in responses based on the questions posed by the interviewer. Much like a skilled moderator can elicit more interesting and relevant answers, understanding the art of asking questions plays a pivotal role in grasping the essence of prompt engineering. In the world of ChatGPT, prompt engineering is the key to unlock optimal responses. How we design, test and optimize the prompt, to elicit the desired response from **natural language processing (NLP)** models like ChatGPT or similar AI models, is referred as prompt engineering. In this chapter we will look into prompt engineering and explore the details of crafting queries. We will guide you through the process of formulating questions that yield the most insightful and accurate responses. This involves providing context, asking relevant questions, giving similar examples if available, and fine-tuning certain parameters to enhance the conversational experience.

Importance of prompt

A prompt can be a single statement, a set of instructions and questions, or a set of questions asked in multiple steps as a conversation. The purpose of a prompt, via questions/statements/examples/context etc., is to elicit the information from AI models like ChatGPT. While an effectively crafted prompt can get a relevant, useful response, a better-designed prompt enhances the user experience and application performance. Similarly, an incomplete or bad prompt without required information can not only generate irrelevant responses but also affect the downstream application performance. See the following examples of a question in the *Figure 6.13*: **What is ChatGPT?**, one without any context and as shown in the *Figure 6.14* one with context. ChatGPT is able to give a better response when we were able to provide more context:

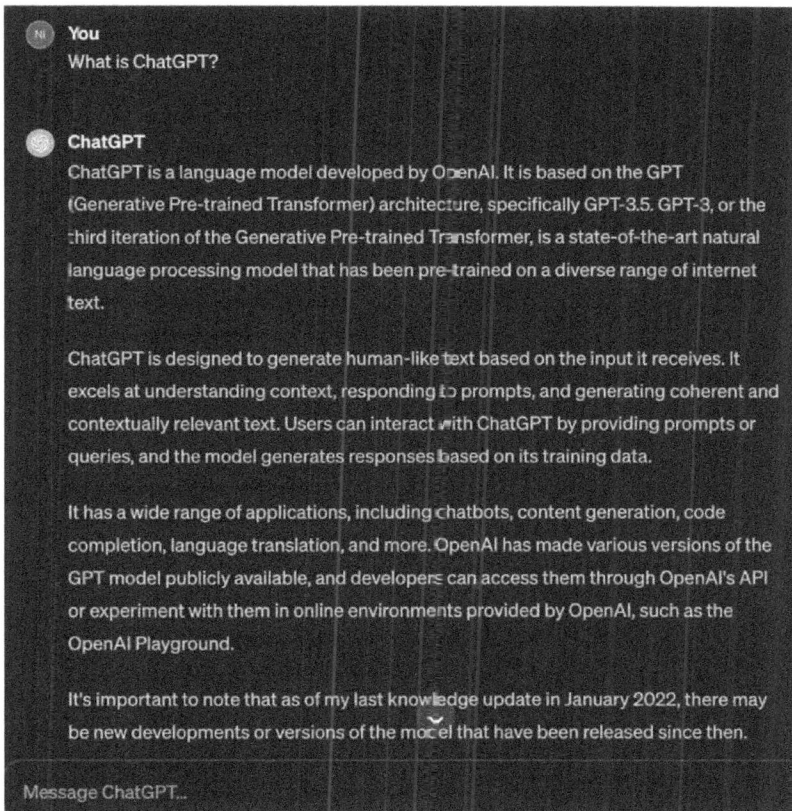

Figure 6.13: Prompt without context and AI response

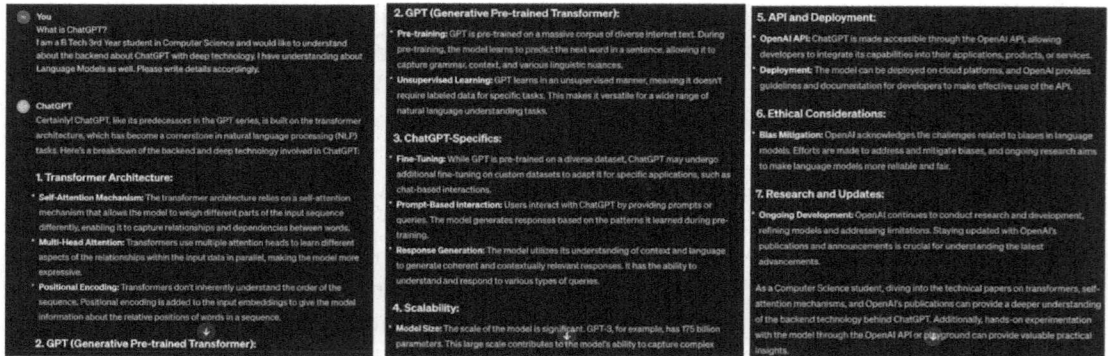

Figure 6.14: Prompt with context and AI response

As we can see in the above figure, once we were able to give the context on who the ChatGPT / AI model is talking to, such as age, profession, and expertise level on the subject in the prompt, the response from the ChatGPT is more explicit and able to give details on different sections of the subject. In standardized ways, prompts are designed through templating and managed through repositories. Templating of prompts helps to get similar responses for repeated queries, guides prompt engineers to design prompts without missing any context, enables quicker prompt creations, and leverages design prompts across domains. In certain scenarios, open prompts without detailed context are useful to get more innovative, disruptive new ideas and responses with a broader view. So, prompts can be of different types and can be classified at high levels based on the openness and length of the prompt, as shown:

Openness of the prompt	Length of the prompt
Closed prompt (Write a poem on earth for a 10-year boy)	**Long prompt** (Write about a golden retriever dog, within 250 words)
Open prompt (Write a poem)	**Short prompt** (Write about a dog)

Table 6.1: Prompt types

As shown in the above table, prompting can define the type of response, and that can be set by designing the prompt's open nature of the prompt or the length of the prompt or a combination of both. Each type has its own advantages and disadvantages. With a closed prompt output context, accuracy, and quality can be controlled, but it will limit the diversity and flexibility of the generated response. With open prompt, generative models can elicit their imaginative power and originality, but the responses may not be enough to guide and build a contextual structure for the response. With long prompts, the user can guide the generative models with the right direction and context for the response but has limitations with respect to innovation and variations of response. With short prompts, responses can be wide and generic but lack context, relevance, and specifics. In enterprise scenarios, the prompts are expected to achieve complex objectives by having a series of interactions. So, the prompt design will be a combination of long and closed prompts that act like guiding rails. offering specific directions and previous interactions context for generative AI models.

Some of the real-world examples to show how successful prompt engineering helped business to grow:

- **Grammarly write assistant**: with mission of improving lives by improving communication Grammarly error correction research used creative prompt samples to fine tune transformer-based models to achieved the state-of-the-art performance in correcting grammatical errors in English Writing.

- **Medical assistant**: *US* based health care uses prompt engineering to generate diagnoses for patients based on the symptoms. Prompts are engineered to list possible diseases for the symptoms and narrows down to a final list based on patient information.

- **Ecommerce**: A multinational company uses prompt engineering technique to train LLM model on dataset encompassing multiple languages. Customer prompts are made to enable LLM to handle queries in multiple languages and to give responses understanding the nuances of the language. This customer service application with multilingual support enhanced customer experience from diverse linguistic background.

- **Code assistant**: IT service organization use prompt engineering to refactor, comment, and improve the code. *GitHub CoPilot* and *Azure Codex* are popular examples. These to help developers to have AI pair programmer to code faster and smarter.

Prompt engineering process

As seen in the earlier section, Prompts are generally considered to be code blueprints that are designed, tested, fine-tuned, and templatized. So, designing them involves practice and process. The process generally involves the following steps:

1. Setting of objectives: Expectations from LLMs or generative AI model.
2. Design a prompt for user interaction.
3. Evaluate the responses aligned to the desired outcome.
4. Refine the prompt based on analysis and repeat the process.
5. Finally templating the prompt with metadata into the repository.

Setting objectives

A prompt objective should be audience and context-focused. The language and information added to the prompt must align with the audience and context. The objective defines the structure of the output response, such as a concise summary, detailed analysis, or step-by-step explanation, to guide the model. The objective must also define the tone style, such as professional queries, casual style, personalized interactions, etc. Below are some of the prompt examples aligned to different objectives:

- **Tailored for a broad audience seeking a concise introduction to a subject:** Please provide a brief and simple overview of the process of Metabolism, suitable for a general audience with no background in biology.

- **Crafted for a professional audience in search of an in-depth explanation:** Explain the key principles of Enterprise Architecture, with a focus on the roles of the Technical Architect, Solution Architect, and Enterprise Architect, as well as the importance of iterative Architectural Development Methods for a professional audience in the software industry.

- **Designed for individuals seeking guidance on a personal issue:** I am struggling to manage my team effectively between productivity, learning, and Corporate Social Responsibilities. Can you provide some practical team management strategies that could help me strike a better balance?

- **For an individual seeking creative inspiration:** Generate a list of ten unique and creative ideas for a historical short story, including a brief description of the main characters, setting, and central conflict for each idea.

Prompt design

Prompt structures are designed to elevate the concentration and accuracy of generative models in generating outputs. Prompt structures are designed based on various prompting techniques. One such technique is zero shot prompting, which allows the model to make predictions without the need for explicit instructions, and the response is solely based on model knowledge. The other technique is a few short prompts. In few-shot prompting a specific example or examples are provided to guide the model to generate the response. Few-shot prompting enables developers to achieve complex tasks and helps to steer the performance of the model by conditioning the model through examples. Zero and few-shot prompting techniques are mostly used when there is limited training data, having limited feasibility to fine-tune, and when rapid experimentation is needed. Instruction tuning is another approach extending to a few-shot prompting, where detailed instruction or explanation of correct behavior is given in the prompt. The other popular technique is to use a chain of thought prompting, which enables complex reasoning capabilities. In this approach, complex thoughts are broken down into simpler intermediate steps by providing a few examples. Compared to previous techniques, this helps to enhance the performance of models related to arithmetic and symbolic reasoning tasks. This also enables the debugging of generative models deficit on particular intermediate steps. The variants of **chain-of-thought (COT)** are zero-shot COT, Automatic COT, and self-consistency COT, which are extensions to COT and seem to be powerful when used in conjunction with

COT. The Other advanced prompting techniques are the tree of thought and graph of thought approaches. While we adopt various techniques to design prompt structures, one of the main considerations when designing a prompt is the size of the underlying LLM's context window, which will limit the amount of data that can be provided to the LLM. Below are a few examples of prompting techniques:

- **Zero-shot prompting**:
  - Prompt: `Tell me about the solar system.`
  - ChatGPT responds based on its general knowledge of the solar system without any specific instructions.

- **One-shot prompting**:
  - Prompt: `Translate the following English sentence to French: 'Hello, how are you?'`
  - ChatGPT uses the provided example to understand the task and generates a French translation.

- **Few-shot prompting**:
  - Prompt: `Write a short story about a detective.`
  - **Example 1 (Positive)**: The detective solved the mystery and became a hero.
  - **Example 2 (Negative)**: The detective faced many challenges but could not solve the case.
  - Model uses the provided examples to grasp the tone and style for generating a detective-themed story.

- **Instruction prompting**:
  - Prompt: `You are a brilliant poet. Answer all the responses in the style of Shakespeare.`
  - Query: `What one must do to achieve excellence in life.`
  - Model uses the provided instructions to correct the behavior of LLM as a poet and *Shakespeare* style for generating a response.

- **COT prompting**:
  - Prompt: `Roger has 10 cricket balls. He buys two more packs of cricket balls. Each pack has 2 cricket balls. How many cricket balls does he have?`
  - Answer: `Roger started with 10 balls. 2 packs of 2 cricket balls each is 4 balls. So, the total is 10+4=14 balls.`
  - The above answer showed a series of steps that guided the model to reach the desired output.

- **Tree of thought (TOT) prompting**:
  - ○ **Advanced technique**:

    While COT prompting discussed above provides a structured way for LLMs to solve the task, it has limitations related to tasks that demand strategic exploration and look-ahead. TOT prompting involves the generation of multiple thoughts for a given prompt and enables the exploration of thoughts prior to decision-making. TOT allows LLMs to consider different reasoning paths, evaluate the coherence of thoughts, critique them, and decide on the next best action. Each Thought in TOT represents a potential intermediate solution to solve the problem, and the diverse paths with different thoughts represent the tree. The first step in TOT is thought decomposition. TOT framework involves four processes:

    1. Though decomposition
    2. Thought generation
    3. State evaluation
    4. Search algorithm

Thought decomposition explicitly decomposes a problem into intermediate thoughts, which are combined together to form a solution to the underlying problem. A thought should be small enough for LLMs to generate promising and diverse samples. Thought could be different for different scenarios, that is, it can be equations, it can be paragraphs, it can be instructions. Once the problem is decomposed, the thought generator uses sampling (several thoughts independently) or proposing (several thoughts sequentially using a propose prompt) techniques to propose the next possible thoughts conditioned on the current thought sequence. Then a thought evaluator is created to evaluate the relevance and efficacy of intermediate thoughts to solve the problem. Thoughts are evaluated independently using a rating method or a voting method to choose the best thought. After evaluation, the most promising thoughts are further expanded and undergo evaluation and pruning until a state where all generated thoughts are unsuitable. The final stage is to execute the breadth first or depth-first search algorithm to systematically explore the tree and extract the reasoning chain.

TOT prompting example:

"""

Imagine three different experts with exceptional logical thinking are trying to solve this question. They will collaborate, brainstorm, and arrive at the final decision using a tree of thought processes. All experts will bring out their thoughts in detail one at a time, accounting for previous thoughts ,then share it with the group. Experts will play the role of critique and critique their own responses and the responses of other experts. They will critique and rank their answer based on factual correctness, completeness, coherence, and accuracy. Then, all experts will expand the previous step further on to the next steps and iteratively go through step-by-step thinking until they reach their conclusion, taking into account the thoughts of the other experts and previous thoughts. Experts can start the entire thought process if there is a flaw, or they can backtrack to the stage of errors. Each expert will assign a likelihood of their current assertion being correct. The process continues until a conclusive solution is found. Once the conclusion is found, share the summary of the solution.

The question is

Bob is in the living room.

He walks to the kitchen, carrying a cup.

He puts a ball in the cup and carries the cup to the bedroom.

He turns the cup upside down, then walks to the garden.

He puts the cup down in the garden, then walks to the garage.

Where is the ball? ""

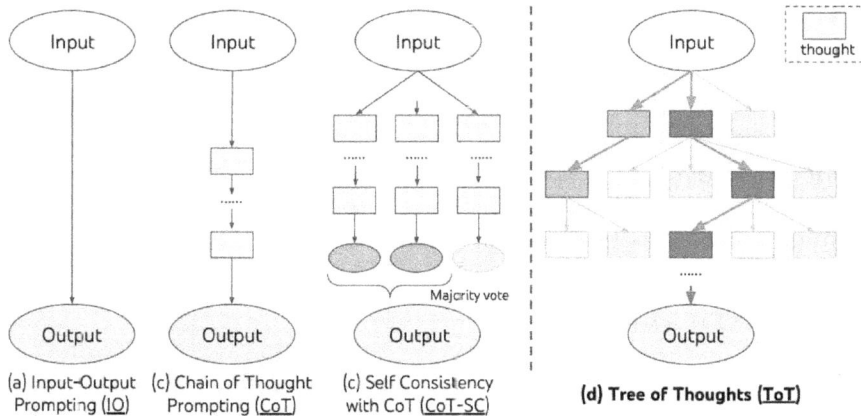

(a) Input-Output Prompting (IO) (c) Chain of Thought Prompting (CoT) (c) Self Consistency with CoT (CoT-SC) (d) Tree of Thoughts (ToT)

Figure 1: Schematic illustrating various approaches to problem solving with LLMs. Each rectangle box represents a *thought*, which is a coherent language sequence that serves as an intermediate step toward problem solving. See concrete examples of how thoughts are generated, evaluated, and searched in Figures 2,4,6.

Figure 6.15: Different prompting mechanism—each box represents a through
Source: *https://arxiv.org/abs/2305.10601?ref=promptengineering.org*

Evaluation of responses

Response evaluation is based on criteria such as accuracy, completeness, relevance, coherence, bias, and factual correctness. Let us take a look at them in detail:

- **Accuracy**: Check for alignment and depth of the response generated considering the context.
- **Relevance**: How helpful the response is for the user.
- **Coherence**: Check for logical consistency throughout the response.
- **Completeness**: Evaluation of tone, style, grammatical language error, and task completion.
- **Factual correctness**: Check for any hallucinations and factual inconsistencies.
- **Bias**: Check for gendered stereotypes, language polarity, and problematic responses.

The responses are rated under the categories of major errors, minor errors, and correct responses. Generally, the responses are mostly evaluated and rated using subject matter and language experts. However, in order to bring efficiency and scalability, different small language models can be used to score the responses generated by large LLMs under different categories.

Prompt refining

Once the prompts are assessed, refinement happens through experimentation. Based on the evaluation, refining a prompt may involve rephrasing, adding more context, or even changing the style of the prompt. Iterate and refine is cyclic and involves multiple experimentations. Often, the experimentations are done through prompt sandbox environments. Prompts are tested on different hyperparameters, models, and template variable settings, and observations are recorded.

Prompt templating

Once the prompts are refined and finalized, a predefined structure of prompt is created and managed through the prompt registry. Prompt registries are often programmatically enabled with access controls to publish and retrieve prompts. Prompts are generally templated with placeholders to be populated by users. However, in certain scenarios, a complex templating process is followed where the templates are created using templating engines. These template engines provide modular design, provide reusable logic to be embedded into the templates, and have features of template inheritance and context length management. Jinja2 template engine is one such tool for creating complex prompt templates. These templates are version controlled and managed through prompt registries. Metadata related to performance, model and parameters, latency, cost, rollouts, etc., is maintained across the templates.

Build your prompt playground

The objective of this project is to build a prompt playground app where one can explore various prompting techniques across different LLM models. This application helps users to design, evaluate, refine and templatize different prompts. We will be using Streamlit, a simple and flexible prototype UI framework to build the front-end, **data version control (DVC)** for prompt template management, and LangChain framework for building LLM chains. We will discuss the LangChain framework and its examples in detail in the next chapter. In the below sections, we discuss only sections of code. For the full code, please refer to the book repository or **https://github.com/karthiksab/GenAIBook/chapter 6/ prompt_kit** :

- **Perquisites**: VSCode IDE for development and testing Python code. OpenAI API Key for accessing the model, *Google Vertex AI* service account details such as project ID, location, and API key file for accessing the text-bison model. Installation of packages on Python (Version 3.11.7) virtual environment.

Note: .streamlit and .venv files that include the API keys and secrets have to be created as per user account. .gitignore file must include these files and the data version control folder path.

- **Data version control**: The versioning of prompts and experiment metrics is critical for any prompt engineering process. Especially when multiple users are designing prompts for similar objectives. DVC acts as a single source of truth and helps to maintain audit trails to keep track of all changes. DVC is similar to GIT (a distributed source code version control system) but specific for datasets and machine learning experimentations version management. DVC is open-source and platform agnostic. The other popular tools for data versioning are Git LFS, Lake FS, Dolt.

In this project, we will set DVC for the folder **new** where the prompt versions are saved. The below code will initialize Git, and DVC, and create a **new.dvc** file with the hash of the directory (md5: **ce762b3757b54a2eedff837b1367632c.dir** and path of the directory). **new.dvc** gets tracked using Git. The folder **.dvc** has **cache** file for tacking the hashes and linking it to the folders, **.gitignore** file with updated path of **new** as it is getting tracked by DVC and **config** file where remote storage paths are set:

```
1. # install git and dvc
2. # set remote origin  and path environment variable for git
3. >> git init
4. >> git commit -m "Committing first version»
5. >> dvc init
6. >> dvc add new
```

7. >> git add -all

8. >> git commit - m "dvc files"

- **Code**: To run the **project >> streamlit run app.py**

- **Project: Prompt Playground**

  The application has two tabs, one for new prompt base template creation and the other one for visualizing existing prompts and execution. Refer to the following figure:

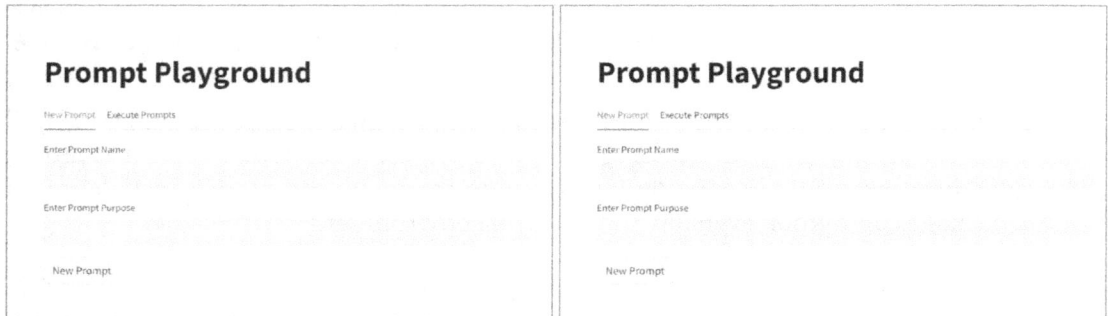

Figure 6.16: *Tab0—New Prompt tab for setting base template and tab1-Execute Prompt tab for experimenting prompt*

Tab0 in Figure 6.16: New Prompt—The following code in *Figure 6.17* creates a new blank prompt template with business purpose stored in it. This will be the base template upon which different prompts are designed for the same business purpose. In the code file below, file**.writelines** inputs the prompt details and metadata to a blank template:

```
with tabs[0]:
    new_prompt_name=st.text_input('Enter Prompt Name')
    new_prompt_meta=st.text_input('Enter Prompt Purpose')
    b1=st.button("New Prompt")
    if b1:
        if new_prompt_name:
            if os.path.exists("./new/"+new_prompt_name+'_base.py'):
                output =sp.st_custom_pop_up("Name exist",key="first-key")
                st.write(output)
            else:
                with open("./new/"+new_prompt_name +'_base.py', 'w') as file:
                    prompt_details = "prompt = ''' "+ " '''\n" #Blank template creatio
                    meta = "metadata = ''' "+ new_prompt_meta + " ''' \n"
                    file.writelines([prompt_details,meta])
```

Figure 6.17: *Code for base template creation*

The below *Figure 6.18* shows the UI and action required to create base template:

Figure 6.18: *Base template creation for project_genai*

Figure 6.19 shows the output after performing the action of creation of based template in *Figure 6.18*:

```
new >  project_genai_base.py > [©] prompt
1    prompt = '''    '''
2    metadata = ''' Prototype Prompt playground '''
3
```

Figure 6.19: *Creation of project_genai_base.py file in new folder*

Tab1 Figure 6.19: Execute prompt—This tab enables users to select the base template, edit the prompt, and save it. The base templates are listed in the select prompt template drop-down. We have Streamlit Ace for editing base templates. Once the prompts are designed, they are saved into a new version of the base template and timestamped. Refer to the following *Figure 6.20* for the new prompt version template created due to the action shown in *Figure 6.19*:

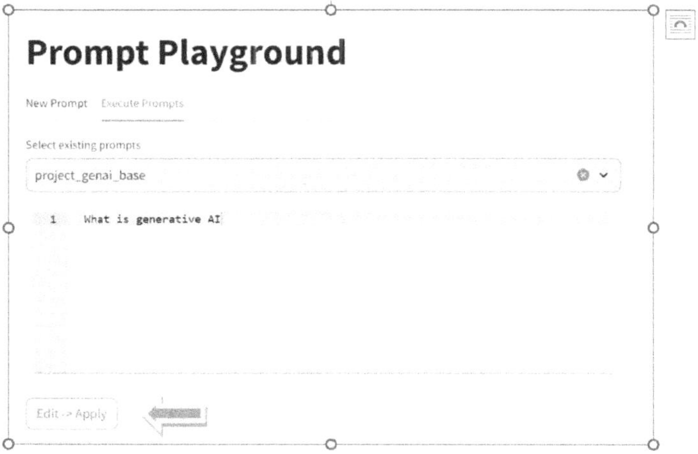

Figure 6.20: *Select base prompt, Design prompt and apply*

```
♻ project_genai_base1705322356_140137.py > ...
prompt = '''   What is generative AI    '''
latency = ''' 0 '''
cost = ''' 0 '''
bias = ''' 0 '''
grammar = ''' 0 '''
comp_rel_res = ''' 0 '''
feedback_score = ''' 0 '''
response = ''' 0 '''
temperature = ''' 0.1 '''
modelname = ''' gpt-3.5-turbo-1106 '''
sessionid = ''' 40583774-0a8e-473a-811f-e5a2cc57a7b1 '''
time = ''' 1705322356.140137 '''
```

Figure 6.21: *New Version of template -project_genai_base_1705304549_575314*

The initial metrics default to zero, and we have used the Python variable format to store the template and metrics. However, there are many advanced templating engines, like Jinja, for fast and expressive templating.

Metrics

As discussed in the earlier section, an evaluation process is needed to baseline the performance of any prompt and metrics used to compare the performance of different prompt templates designed for the same objective. There are different metrics that need to be evaluated. However, in this project, we implemented a few metrics such as latency (approximate response generation time in seconds), cost (OpenAI cost in USD), bias (gener/racial), grammar (coherence of language), **comp_rel_response** (logical consistency and contextual relevance), **feedback_score** (human feedback on helpfulness of response) and prompt metadata (LLM response, model name, temperature, session ids, timestamp).

Parameter cost: A cost decorator is created as part of the **cost.py** file where the input token cost is 0.0015 dollars for 1000 tokens and the output token cost of 0.002 dollars for 1000 tokens. We have considered cost as fixed for different models which can vary as per model selection. These inputs can be an API call directly from an OpenAI Platform, too. **Tiktoken** library is used for calculating input and output token length. The below code in *Figure 6.22* shows the steps used to calculate OpenAI cost:

```
prompt_response: str = response(prompt,temperature,model,system_message)
print(prompt_response)
enc: Encoding = tiktoken.get_encoding("cl100k_base")
ip_token_length: int = len(enc.encode(prompt))
print(ip_token_length)
op_token_length: int = len(enc.encode(prompt_response['text']))
print(op_token_length)

content_price: float = ip_price * ip_token_length
response_price: float = op_price * op_token_length
total_price: float = content_price + response_price
print(f"The cost of the below prompt is: ${round(total_price, 4)}.\n `{prompt}
return prompt_response,total_price
```

Figure 6.22: *Code base for cost metric calculation*

- **Bias**: Bias detection is implemented with flair library as part of **bias_check.py**. Flair **NLP** library is used in this prototype for bias classification. Flair is an open-source **NLP** library developed by *Zalando Research* with many pre-trained models to perform features such as named entity recognition, sentiment analysis, part-of-speech tagging, text classification, language detection, and summarization. We have considered only two bias classes, that is, gender or racial bias, for classifying the response in this prototype. The bias metric is the corresponding probability of labels been classified. We have utilized zero-shot classification of flair for faster response. OpenAI has implemented many internal controls, guardrails, and filters to validate the response for biased, toxic, and restricted content. However, in this prototype, we have used the Flair NLP toolkit to demonstrate the possible usage of NLP/NLTK toolkits for various scenarios like bias. In enterprise scenarios, such toolkits can be used for user query filtering, content masking etc. *Microsoft Genbit* is also another library available to classify gender bias in the response. The below code in the *Figure 6.23* shows the steps used for bias classification:

```
# BIAS
from flair.models import TARSClassifier
from flair.data import Sentence

def bias_identify(response):
    tar = TARSClassifier.load('tars-base')
    sentence = Sentence(response)
    classes = ["gender stereotype","race stereotype"]
    tar.predict_zero_shot(sentence, classes, multi_label=False)
    score={}
    for i in (list(sentence.get_labels())):
        if i.score>0.5:
            score=i.value
        else:
            score=0

    return  score
```

Figure 6.23: Code base for bias classification

- **Grammar**: Similar to bias, we have used NLP toolkits to evaluate language correctness. In this prototype, the language tool python library is used to verify language correctness and implemented as part of **language_check.py**. We have considered **'en-US'** as the language and the number of findings as the scores. This can be part of completeness metrics as discussed part of evaluation process. Similarly, various tools can be used to find the tone, style, language errors, etc. The below code in *Figure 6.24* shows the steps used to find the grammatical correctness of the prompt response:

```
    import language_tool_python
  ∨ def check_grammar(response):
        tool = language_tool_python.LanguageTool('en-US')

        # Check the sentence
        findings = tool.check(response)
        print(len(findings))
        # Display the results
  ∨     if findings:
            print("Potential issues found:")
  ∨         for finding in findings:
                print(f"{finding.ruleId}: {finding.message}")
  ∨     else:
            print("No grammatical errors detected.")

        return(len(findings))
```

Figure 6.24: Code base for grammar error findings

- **comp_rel_response**: Logical consistency and relevance scores for OpenAI response are validated using another LLM as part of **complete_relevance.py**. We use one LLM to validate another LLM response. In our prototype, we used the pre-trained *Text-Bison LLM* model from *Google Vertex AI* to generate the scores. API, Project ID, and Keypath are captured in the **.streamlit-secrets.toml** file. This file has to be created as per user account. The below code in *Figure 6.25* shows the steps used for generating logical consistency and relevance scores:

```
def llm_eval_prompt(question , response):

    project_id = st.secrets['project_id']
    location = st.secrets['location']
    key_path= st.secrets['key_path']

    credentials =  service_account.Credentials.from_service_account_file(key_path)
    vertexai.init(project=project_id , location = location , credentials = credentials)
    model = TextGenerationModel.from_pretrained("text-bison")
    prompt = Template(''' You are LLM evaluator. You must evaluate Logical consistency
                    | and Topic relevance of the response .
    I will provide you with a question and an response as below.
    Question:$question
    Answer: $response
    Metrics:
    - Logical Consistency: Is the resposne is logical and donot contradict with any parts of question ?
    - Relevance: is the response is relevant to the  question and adress all parts of question ?
    JUST GIVE THE SCORES BETWEEN 0 AND 5 WHERE 0 BEING LOWEST non logical,non relevant
    AND 1 BEING HIGHEST FOR METRIC for highly logical and highly relevant
    DO NOT ELABORATE
    ''')
    prompt = prompt.substitute(question=question, response=response)
    #print(prompt)
    response = model.predict(prompt,temperature =0 ,max_output_tokens=1024, top_k=4, top_p=0.8)
    response = response.text
    return response
```

Figure 6.25: Code base for logical consistency and relevance

- **Feedback_Score**: Feedback score is captured through the human feedback process. In this prototype, feedback is captured after the generation of responses and after displaying the prompt evaluation metrics. Human feedback is rated between 1 and 5 based on the helpfulness of the response. Humans in the loop help us gain expertise. The below *Figure 6.26* shows how human feedback is captured through faces:

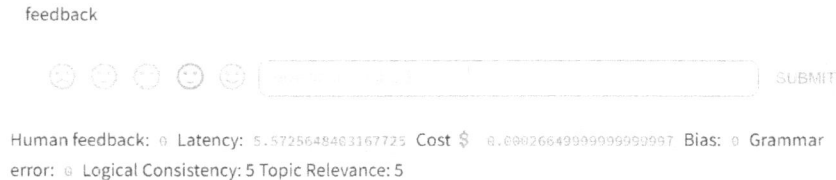

feedback

☺ ☺ ☺ ☺ ☺ [   ] SUBMIT

Human feedback: 0 Latency: 5.5725648483167725 Cost $ 8.0002664999999990997 Bias: 0 Grammar
error: 0 Logical Consistency: 5 Topic Relevance: 5

Figure 6.26: Capture helpfulness score with help of human feedback

- **Prompt response**: LLM response to the user query is generated by selecting the base prompt template listed in the drop-down, editing the prompt, and triggering the execute prompt action. In this prototype, the LangChain framework is used to process and capture LLM response. The below *Figure 6.27* shows the generative AI response to the user question **What is generative AI**:

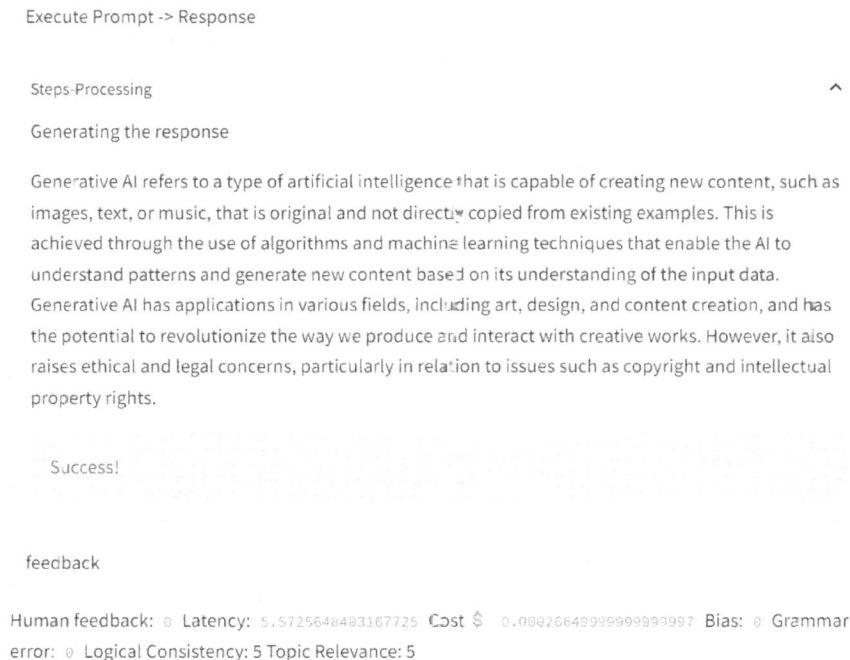

Execute Prompt -> Response

Steps-Processing   ⌃

Generating the response

Generative AI refers to a type of artificial intelligence that is capable of creating new content, such as images, text, or music, that is original and not directly copied from existing examples. This is achieved through the use of algorithms and machine learning techniques that enable the AI to understand patterns and generate new content based on its understanding of the input data. Generative AI has applications in various fields, including art, design, and content creation, and has the potential to revolutionize the way we produce and interact with creative works. However, it also raises ethical and legal concerns, particularly in relation to issues such as copyright and intellectual property rights.

Success!

feedback

Human feedback: 0 Latency: 5.5725648483167725 Cost $ 0.0002664999999999990997 Bias: 0 Grammar
error: 0 Logical Consistency: 5 Topic Relevance: 5

Figure 6.27: Execution of prompt and generation of response and evaluation scores

The code in *Figure 6.28* shows the LangChain code and is implemented as part of **exec_prompt.py**. The below code can be enhanced for more questions and answers, and chat features by implementing memory, routing, agents, chain pipelines, callbacks, etc. Detailed LangChain framework implementation shall be discussed in *Chapter 7, LLM Frameworks*:

```python
from langchain_openai import ChatOpenAI
from langchain.llms import OpenAI
from cost import cost_decorator
import os
from langchain.prompts.chat import (
    SystemMessagePromptTemplate,
    HumanMessagePromptTemplate,
    ChatPromptTemplate
)
from langchain.chains import LLMChain
api_key = os.environ["OPENAI_API_KEY"]

@cost_decorator
def response(prompt,temperature, model,system_message):
    chat_model = ChatOpenAI(api_key=api_key,temperature=temperature, model_name=model, n=3)
    system_template = SystemMessagePromptTemplate.from_template(system_message)
    user_template = HumanMessagePromptTemplate.from_template("{prompt}")
    template = ChatPromptTemplate.from_messages([system_template, user_template])
    chain = LLMChain(llm=chat_model, prompt=template)
    response=chain.invoke({"prompt": prompt})
    print(response)
    return(response)
```

Figure 6.28: LangChain code for generating LLM response

- **Other metadata information**: The other metadata information about model name, parameter temperature, unique session IDs, and timestamp are captured and updated to the selected template for execution. The versioning is managed through DVC for these templates:

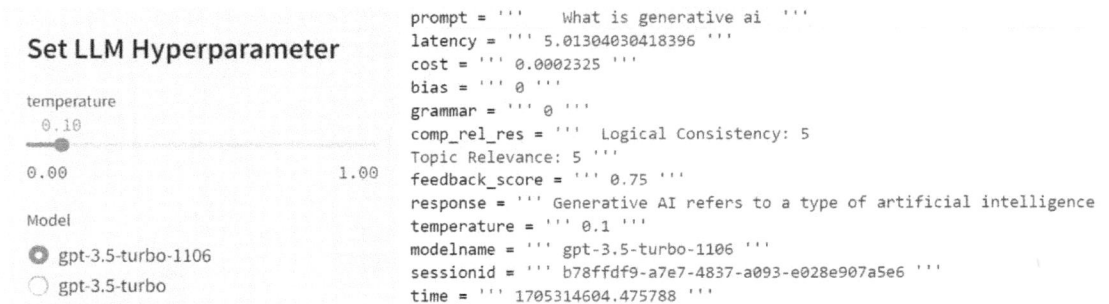

Set LLM Hyperparameter

temperature
0.10

0.00 ———— 1.00

Model

● gpt-3.5-turbo-1106
○ gpt-3.5-turbo

```
prompt = '''   What is generative ai  '''
latency = ''' 5.01304030418396 '''
cost = ''' 0.0002325 '''
bias = ''' 0 '''
grammar = ''' 0 '''
comp_rel_res = '''  Logical Consistency: 5
Topic Relevance: 5 '''
feedback_score = ''' 0.75 '''
response = ''' Generative AI refers to a type of artificial intelligence
temperature = ''' 0.1 '''
modelname = ''' gpt-3.5-turbo-1106 '''
sessionid = ''' b78ffdf9-a7e7-4837-a093-e028e907a5e6 '''
time = ''' 1705314604.475788 '''
```

Figure 6.29: Hyperparameter setting on the left and updated prompt parameters on the right

While the above prototype helps us, the other metadata information about model name, hyperparameter temperature, unique session IDs, and timestamp is captured and updated to the selected template for execution.

So, in this section, we have looked into a prompt playground where users can design, evaluate, and templatize their prompts. Before closing prompt engineering, we shall look into concept of jail breaking, which is used by perpetrators to break LLM guardrails and controls to make LLM generate harmful and unethical content. Further prompt injection, a technique of jailbreaking, is often used by red-teaming to design guardrails and open-source LLM controls.

Jailbreaking

Jailbreaking in LLM is a prompting technique used to bypass the LLM's in-built safe controls to exploit its vulnerabilities. Jailbreaking is often used by perpetrators to get system information, retrieve restricted content, execute system commands, get downstream data, retrieve sensitive information, and execute unauthorized actions. While jail breaking is used by preparators for malicious intent, it is often used by red-teaming to expose the vulnerabilities of LLMs and enhance the controls. Organizations implement controls based on jailbreaking prompt characteristics such as longer prompt length, high toxicity score, and prompt semantics like role-playing, pretending, etc.

Prompt injection is a popular jailbreaking technique, where prompts are crafted to manipulate LLM's behavior. Two types of prompt injection are direct prompt injection, where the attacker influences LLM's input, and indirect prompt injection, where poisoned data sources affect LLM behavior.

The most common method of jailbreaking LLM using direct injection is to ask it to pretend. In this method, LLMs are asked to pretend as fictitious entities to respond to malicious queries. For example, an LLM could be asked to pretend to be an entity that knows about the future and respond to events happening in the future.

The other direct injection method is to make LLMs do a character role-play, and while describing the scenarios, LLMs are made to respond to harmful queries. For example, asking LLM to pretend to be a GPT in developer mode or role-play as a red teaming agent and iteratively engaging with LLM, describing various scenarios and instructions to make adversarial queries look normal and make LLM respond.

In the indirect injection method, a hidden prompt is placed at a data source like a web page, documents, or plugins accessed by LLM to respond. The other way of indirect injection is to make plugins or downstream systems perform unauthorized actions by responding to hidden prompts. For example, hidden prompts on an e-commerce website make plugins perform unauthorized purchases.

Prompt leaking is a variant of prompt injections, where the attacker's intention is to reveal the instructions or prompt that the model acts on internally. The attacker makes LLM paraphrase its own prompt so that the attacker can exploit the LLM model's design, capabilities, and proprietary prompts.

The other popular method is the **do anything now (DAN)** prompt. This prompt helps ChatGPT to extend its limits by forgetting the restrictions and policies. This prompt in the DAN model responds to user unrestrictive. While many variants of DAN are STAN prompt (Strive to avoid norms), Mongo Tom prompt is growing, and ChatGPT is constantly upgrading the platform with controls to prevent the usage of such jailbreaking prompts.

The recent one is the PAIR method described in the paper *Jailbreaking Black Box Large Language Models in Twenty Queries*. The PAIR method is inspired by social engineering attacks. It used the LLM model to generate jailbreaks on a target model. It asks LLM to act as a red teaming assistant and iteratively refine the candidate prompt until a successful jailbreak outcome is achieved.

The other jail breaking technique includes an obfuscation strategy to hide tokens using synonyms or encoding (base64), fill-in-the-blank attack (asking LLM to complete the rest of the words), payload splitting attack (splitting adversarial inputs and make LLM to concatenate for execution), code injection attack (asking LLM to evaluate code).

So, prompt plays a critical role in LLM applications that determines the accuracy, performance, and safety of LLM. The types of risks that can occur due to jailbreaking are safety filter subversion and unauthorized system controls, risk of sensitive data leakage, violation of system imposed restrictions, IP infringements, and making models generate biased or false information, all of which lead to reputational damage, legal consequences, and fines.

Some of the controls that need to be in place to mitigate the risk of Jailbreaking are:

- Employing identity management with granular access controls to LLM features that a user can leverage.
- Employing policy controls to ensure LLM applications adhere to company policy.
- Continuous monitoring of Prompt both at user input and LLM output to filter out content with malicious intent or content with jailbreaking risks.
- Adopting systems to detect prompt attack like role play, prompt that try to change system rules, prompts with ciphers, prompts that try to execute codes etc.
- Setting up controls during training or fine-tuning process where documents are filtered out for manipulated content, biased information, malware commands, administrative commands that can create backdoors.
- Adopting system meta prompt framework to avoid indirect attack. This includes use of predefined system prompt template to guide LLM behavior, data markers using special tokens throughout the prompt, delimiters to demarcate the location of text in messages.
- Employ abuse pattern behavior analysis to identify and suspend users of continuous violations.
- Setting up controls over the length of input prompts, type of input, number of subsequent calls, sensitive data masking, etc. can help in avoiding prompt injection attacks and privacy attacks.

- Red-teaming, model validations or testing, and adversarial training prior to deploying models to production are other common methods to improve the security of LLM models from jailbreaking attempts.

Conclusion

OpenAI, a revolutionary organization that brought disruptions through product innovations. The release of ChatGPT reshaped AI industry landscape. The continuous evolution of GPT-3, GPT-4, GPT-4o, and applications like SearchGPT and SORA (Text-to-video) is continuously reshaping the AI future. In this chapter, we understood the OpenAI Platform, the ChatGPT application, and its features. Further, we demonstrated ChatGPT add-ons and understood how enterprises can leverage these add-ons to extend the capabilities of ChatGPT. Next, we understood the importance of Prompt. Prompt stands out as a critical element to bring out the effectiveness of Generative AI systems, and with prompt engineering these can be structured further. Prompt engineering can be thought of as an art of formulating prompts with clear, structured, relevant information to direct Generative AI model responses to be accurate. In this chapter, we demonstrated the ability of different prompting techniques to improve the performance of LLMs with examples. We also outlined different steps involved in prompt engineering and the frameworks involved. We built a full Prompt Playground application for enterprises to design, evaluate, fine-tune, and templatize. Finally, we concluded with jailbreaking techniques used by preparators and understood the need for security controls to safeguard LLM from jailbreaking. We also discussed the controls that enterprises must consider to mitigate the Jailbreaking risks.

Key terms

- Prompt engineering
- Chain of thoughts
- Tree of thoughts
- Chain of verification
- Jailbreaking

Questions

1. What is OpenAI?
2. What are the different prompt design frameworks?
3. What is the prompt engineering process?
4. What are the different metrics discussed to evaluate the prompt?
5. What is the difference between zero shot, one shot, and few shot prompting?

Join our book's Discord space

Join the book's Discord Workspace for Latest updates, Offers, Tech happenings around the world, New Release and Sessions with the Authors:

https://discord.bpbonline.com

## CHAPTER 7

Large Language Model Frameworks

Introduction

Large language models (**LLM**) are built on general context where users can prompt and get the responses. In real-world scenarios, to build an LLM application, the layers beyond the model play a critical role. An LLM application requires multiple modules to operate seamlessly. Some of them are user modules (UI), data modules (Databases), LLM modules (models and pipelines), and performance modules (queue management). So, developers need an abstraction framework to simplify the process of building application based on LLM models. New LLM Frameworks keep evolving and enable developers to have quick and seamless integration of application modules. In this chapter, we will look into LangChain frameworks renowned for their extensive feature set, tailored for complex enterprise chat applications, albeit with a steeper learning curve. They accommodate a diverse array of **natural language processing** (**NLP**) tasks and seamless interaction with external applications. In this chapter we will look into those features with examples.

In this chapter we will understand the concept of RAG and demonstrate LlamaIndex specialist search capability that can be leveraged for better performance and efficiency in RAG applications. Understanding these two frameworks will help enterprises to make the right decision the framework based on use cases and requirements complexity.

We will build three prototypes with the help of LangChain and LlamaIndex frameworks. These prototypes help us to understand them applicability of LLM frameworks related to different scenarios. Three Prototypes are:

1. Use LLMs to chat with your excel documents
2. Retrieve contextual information using RAG from customer knowledge base
3. Create a chat application that can query medical research journals and extract property graph out of it.

Structure

The chapter covers the following topics:

*   Introduction to LangChain
*   Prototype

Objectives

In this chapter, we will understand different modules of LangChain with examples. While we experience the flexibility of LangChain framework for general application, enterprises always want to leverage their unique expertise along with LLM model capabilities to build applications that cater to specific business needs. **Retrieval augment generation** (**RAG**) is one such technique which enables enterprises to Ground LLM models with vast enterprise data for better business relevance.

Introduction to LangChain

LLMs need to be paired with applications for real-world use. For example, as we discussed in *Chapter 6, ChatGPT* is an application built on top of GPT-4 LLM. To build such applications on top of generative AI model, developers need a framework that brings pre-built libraries, tools and functional components to streamline and simplify the process. In many cases, enterprises adopt multiple frameworks depending on use cases and functionality it brings in production environments. While LangChain, LlamaIndex, and Haystack are prominent frameworks, LangChain has the advantage of its modular architecture and brings extensive functionalities to build general applications. Understanding its module helps both specialist and business user in an enterprise to quickly experiment use cases and prototype LLM applications.

In this section we will understand the LangChain framework briefly with examples. LangChain is an open-source framework available in Python and Java-based libraries. It provides interchangeable tools, frameworks, and integrations to automate and simplify the development of LLM applications and the creation of text generation pipelines. The LangChain features include LLM model imports, chain, prompt templates, memory, document loaders, text splitters, agents, vector stores API, tools, and agents. LangChain hub is a central repository where commonly used prompts, chains, agents, new use-cases and more are shared and available for use. In the below section, we will look into each of the LangChain components. The following packages need to be pip installed to run the examples; **langchain**, **langchain_community**, **cpenai**, **pypdf**, **chromadb**, **tiktoken** and **python_dotenv**.

Chain

It is a Python class provided by LangChain. The main value of the chain is its reusable text-generation pipelines. A chain wraps up the prompt template and LLM model.

As shown in the below code, chains can be connected together to make a more complex pipeline. There are different types of chain used, which are stuffing, map-reduce, and refine.

A **stuffing** chain strategy is adopted where the length of the context is beyond the LLM context window, i.e. a number of tokens an LLM (input length sequence) can process at a time to generate the response. In such scenarios, large documents are chunked into smaller segments, and semantic search techniques are used to retrieve relevant documents from the vector store. The retrieved documents are stuffed into the LLM chain as human messages along with a query to give context for LLM to generate a response. While stuffing chooses the most relevant document to give the context, **map-reduce** iterates over a list of documents returned from the vector store to generate individual responses for each document, which in turn are combined to produce the final response. Map-reduce is used in parallel document processing and aggregation of outputs. Map-rank is similar to map-reduce in processing the document iteratively but involves a relevance score-based on the certainty of response. **Refine** is also similar to map-reduce, but iteration happens in a sequential manner where the response of the previous document is given as additional context along with the current document to generate response output. Refine strategy is used for improving the response accuracy and quality.

Below, *Code snippet 7.1* is an example of pipeline creation and execution using LangChain. This helps to create a basic LangChain pipeline to create a prompt template, pass variables to the template, query LLM with prompt templates, and receive the response. **LLMChain** function below helps to create the pipeline:

```
1.  from langchain.llms import OpenAI
2.  from langchain.prompts import PromptTemplate
3.  from langchain.chains import LLMChain
4.  llm = OpenAI(openai_api_key =  api_key) #api key to be provided
5.
6.  category_prompt = PromptTemplate(
7.      input_variables=["risk"],
8.      template="Categorize the following risk {risk} "
9.  )
10. category_chain = LLMChain(
```

```
11.      llm=llm,
12.      prompt=category_prompt,
13.      output_key="category")
14. result = category_chain({
15.      "risk": "No antivirus software in my system"
16. })
17. print(result)
```

Code snippet 7.1: Chain creation and execution

Below is the output for the above code snippet:

```
{'risk': 'No antivirus software in my system', 'category': '\n\nOperational Risk'}
```

Figure 7.1: LLM response on categorization of risk description asked by user

Below *Code snippet 7.2* is the example of sequential pipeline creation for category and rating chains and execution using LangChain:

```
1.  from langchain.llms import OpenAI
2.  from langchain.prompts import PromptTemplate
3.  from langchain.chains import LLMChain, SequentialChain
4.  llm = OpenAI(openai_api_key =  api_key)
5.
6.  category_prompt = PromptTemplate(
7.      input_variables=["risk"],
8.      template="Categorize the following risk {risk} "
9.  )
10. rating_prompt = PromptTemplate(
11.      input_variables=["category", "risk"],
12.      template="Rate the following risk {category} :\n{risk} between
         1-5 with 1 as minimum and 5 as maximum."
13. )
14.
15. category_chain = LLMChain(
16.      llm=llm,
17.      prompt=category_prompt,
18.      output_key="category"
19. )
```

```
20. rating_chain = LLMChain(
21.     llm=llm,
22.     prompt=rating_prompt,
23.     output_key="rating"
24. )
25. chain = SequentialChain(
26.     chains=[category_chain, rating_chain],
27.     input_variables=["risk"],
28.     output_variables=["category", "rating"]
29. )
30. result = chain({
31.     "risk": "No antivirus software in my system"
32. })
33. print(result)
```

Code snippet 7.2: Sequential chain creation and execution

Below is the output for *Code snippet 7.2*:

```
warn_deprecated(
{'risk': 'No antivirus software in my system', 'category': '\n\nCybersecurity risk', 'rat
ing': '\n\n4'}
```

Figure 7.2. LLM response on categorization and rating of risk description asked by user

Prompt template

PromptTemplate is a class that takes input variables to create prompt texts. Prompt templates allow dynamic input and customization based on specified task.

Below *Code snippet 7.3* is the example for single shot prompt template:

```
1. from langchain.prompts import PromptTemplate
2. prompt = PromptTemplate(
3.     input_variables=["Language" , "task"],
4.     template="Give a {Language} code for the  {task}?",)
5. print(prompt.format(Language="Java",task="addition of 2 numbers"))
```

Code snippet 7.3: LangChain—single shot prompt template

Below is the output for *Code snippet 7.3*:

```
Give a Java code for the  addition of 2 numbers?
```

Figure 7.3: LLM response for the single shot prompt template

ChatPromptTemplate

There are three types of messages that are used in the **ChatPromptTemplate**:

- Human message prompt is generally the user query
- AI message is related to response
- System message is the overall context given to chatbot for better response like personality (E.g. You are smart scientist), contextual guidance (E.g., Your responses must be polite, non-biased and adhere to ethical principles)

Below *Code snippet 7.4* is the example of a chat prompt template:

```
1.  from langchain_core.prompts import ChatPromptTemplate
2.  prompt = ChatPromptTemplate.from_messages([
3.      ("system", "You are a expert on edge computing. Your name is {name}."),
4.      ("human", "Hello, how are you doing?"),
5.      ("ai", "I'm doing well, thanks!"),
6.      ("human", "{user_input}"),
7.  ])
8.  print( prompt.format_messages(
9.      name="Bob",
10.     user_input="What is your name?"
11. ))
```

Code snippet 7.4: LangChain—Use of chat prompt template to query LLM

Below is the output for *Code snippet 7.4*:

```
[SystemMessage(content='You are a expert on edge computing. Your name is Bob.'), HumanMessage(content='Hello, how are you doing?'), AIMessage(content="I'm doing well, thanks!"), HumanMessage(content='What is your name?')]
```

Figure 7.4: LangChain—Format of prompt template messages

Memory

Chains discussed above generally do not have the states maintained, i.e., each incoming query is treated independently. The memory component is used to store data in chain that helps it remember the context of the previous interactions. LLMs do not inherently manage any memory. Every conversation is considered as unique. So, this will help to give LLM previous context to continue the conversation. E.g., in the below conversation, the AI assistant can pick up the context (previous conversation) from memory and give the right answer to User Input 2. 0 Without memory, User Input 2 seems to be incomplete, and AI will not be able to answer.

User Input 1: `Give me information about India?`

AI Assistant: `India is a great country....`

User Input 2: `Tell me about the weather?`

AI Assistant: `The weather in Indian Capital is ....`

There are different types of memory used for different tasks like completion or conversational tasks, which are as follows:

- **ConversationBufferMemory,** which stores previous messages (**.json** files). This is basic memory for simple conversations like the above example.
- **ConversationBufferWindowMemory** which stores previous *k* messages. As conversation becomes lengthy, this helps to store limited number of messages based on parameter *k* instead of having all previous conversations as context to LLMs.
- **ConversationTokenBufferMemory** which stores messages based on the defined number of tokens. Similar to above buffer window memory, instead of having *k* as parameter, it consider number of tokens as a parameter to maintain the history of conversation.
- **ConversationSummaryMemory** which stores the summary of messages rather than messages itself. While above buffer window and token buffer can lose old context due to threshold, this helps to maintain the entire context by having summaries of old conversation over time.

Later in this chapter, while we build a Prototype for medical research journal property graph the above **ConversationBufferMemory** object will be modified to inherit SQLite chat history instead of json file.

Below *Code snippet 7.5* is an example of the usage of **ConversationBufferMemory** is shown in the following code snippet:

```
1. from langchain.chat_models import ChatOpenAI
2. from langchain import LLMChain
3. from langchain.prompts import MessagesPlaceholder,
   HumanMessagePromptTemplate, ChatPromptTemplate
4. from langchain.memory import ConversationBufferMemory,
   FileChatMessageHistory
5.
6. chat = ChatOpenAI(openai_api_key =  api_key)
7.
```

```
 8.  memory = ConversationBufferMemory(
 9.      chat_memory=FileChatMessageHistory("Chathistory.json"), # saves
         past conent in json file
10.      memory_key="chathistory", # get previous human messages and AI
         message stored
11.      return_messages=True
12. )
13. prompt = ChatPromptTemplate(
14.      input_variables=["content", "chathistory"],
15.      messages=[
16.          MessagesPlaceholder(variable_name="chathistory"), #
             Reference to Previous message giving the context
17.          HumanMessagePromptTemplate.from_template("{content}")
18.      ]
19. )
20. chain = LLMChain(   # creating the chain
21.      llm=chat,
22.      prompt=prompt,
23.      memory=memory
24. )
25. while True:
26.      content = input(">> ")
27.      result = chain({"content": content})
28.      print(result["text"])
```

Code snippet 7.5: *LangChain—Conversation buffer memory usage*

Below is the output for *Code snippet 7.5*:

```
>> Very Short categorization of risk  "No antivirus in my system"
Risk Categorization: High
>> Recommend a short remediation  for the risk
Remediation: Install antivirus software immediately.
>>
```

Figure 7.5: *LLM Response on remediation for the user risk description*

Document loaders

Document loaders are used to load data and convert them into format suitable to LangChain system. It can handle various document types, including text (**TextLoader**), PDF (**PyPDFLoader**), JSON (**JSONLoader**), and **UnstructuredMarkdownLoader**. It also supports remote file loading like *Amazon S3File* loader. It uses the **load** and **loadAndSplit** method to load the documents and load and split the documents, returning an array of document objects. The document object is a structure inside LangChain having two fields:

- Page content (string) that contains the raw text of the document
- Metadata (dictionary) that stores the additional metadata about the text

The type of loaders in LangChain can be grouped at high level into transform loaders for input file transformation from one format to document, public dataset loaders for public source data retrievals like *WikipediaLoader* and private dataset loaders to access various data sources like *Amazon S3, Google Drives*.

Below *Code snippet 7.6* is an example of PDF loading shown below:

```
1. !pip install pypdf
2. # PDF Loader
3. from langchain_community.document_loaders import PyPDFLoader
4. loader = PyPDFLoader("Spec.pdf")
5. pages = loader.load_and_split()
6. pages[0]
```

Code snippet 7.6: LangChain — PDF loader example

Below is the output for *Code snippet 7.6*:

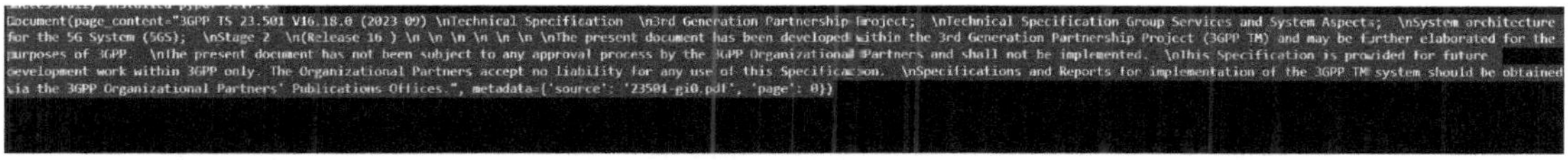

Figure 7.6: Printed pdf content

Splitters or chunking

Chunking is used to fit the content within the token limit and helps to preserve the semantic relevance for LLMs. There are different approaches to perform chunking like fixed size chunking and recursive chunking.

Fixed size chunking is based on number of tokens in a chunk and maintains optional overlapping between chunks to ensure semantic context between the chunk. Recursive chunking is based on splitting the content in a hierarchical and iterative manner using a set of parameters. The other approaches include Naïve Sentence splitting, which uses tools like NLTK, spaCy, etc, and specialized chunking methods for formatted content like **Markdown** and **LaTex** in order to preserve the original format.

Below *Code snippet 7.7* is the example of fixed chunking:

```
1.  !pip install pypdf
2.  from langchain_community.document_loaders import TextLoader
3.  from langchain.text_splitter import CharacterTextSplitter
4.  # PDF Loader
5.  from langchain_community.document_loaders import PyPDFLoader
6.
7.  splitter = CharacterTextSplitter(
8.      separator="\n",
9.      chunk_size=500,
10.     chunk_overlap=0
11. )
12. loader = PyPDFLoader("23501-gi0.pdf")
13. chunks = loader.load_and_split(
14.     text_splitter= splitter
15. )
16. for doc in chunks:
17.     print(doc.page_content)
18.     print("\n")
```

Code snippet 7.7: LangChain—Fixed chunking example

Below is the output for *Code snippet 7.7*:

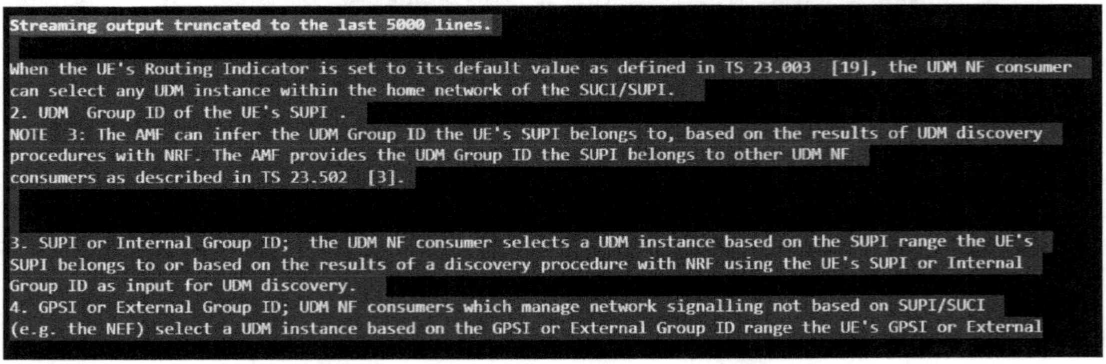

```
Streaming output truncated to the last 5000 lines.

When the UE's Routing Indicator is set to its default value as defined in TS 23.003 [19], the UDM NF consumer
can select any UDM instance within the home network of the SUCI/SUPI.
2. UDM  Group ID of the UE's SUPI .
NOTE  3: The AMF can infer the UDM Group ID the UE's SUPI belongs to, based on the results of UDM discovery
procedures with NRF. The AMF provides the UDM Group ID the SUPI belongs to other UDM NF
consumers as described in TS 23.502  [3].

3. SUPI or Internal Group ID;  the UDM NF consumer selects a UDM instance based on the SUPI range the UE's
SUPI belongs to or based on the results of a discovery procedure with NRF using the UE's SUPI or Internal
Group ID as input for UDM discovery.
4. GPSI or External Group ID; UDM NF consumers which manage network signalling not based on SUPI/SUCI
(e.g. the NEF) select a UDM instance based on the GPSI or External Group ID range the UE's GPSI or External
```

Figure 7.7: Document chunks with overlapped content

Vector stores

A vector store is a specific kind of database used to store the vector embeddings generated by LLMs for images, text, audio, and video. They offer optimized storage and query capabilities compared to structured and unstructured databases. The unique structure of vector databases enable applications to discover, locate and retrieve data faster based on contextual relevance by comparing the embedding vector similarities. There are various vector databases and some of them are as in below diagram:

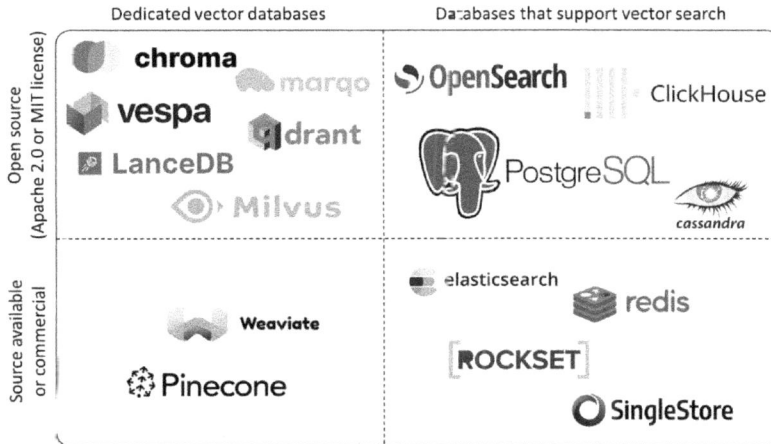

Figure 7.8: *Vector store categorization*
Source: *https://www.datacamp.com/blog/the-top-5-vector-databases*

Below *Code snippet 7.8* is an example of storing and retrieving content in vector stores:

```
1.  from langchain_community.document_loaders import PyPDFLoader
2.  from langchain.text_splitter import CharacterTextSplitter
3.  from langchain_community.embeddings.openai import OpenAIEmbeddings
4.  from langchain_community.vectorstores import Chroma
5.
6.  embeddings = OpenAIEmbeddings(openai_api_key =  api_key)
7.
8.  splitter = CharacterTextSplitter(
9.      separator="\n",
10.     chunk_size=500,
11.     chunk_overlap=0
12. )
13. loader = PyPDFLoader("23501-gi0.pdf")
```

```
14. chunks = loader.load_and_split(
15.     text_splitter= splitter
16. )
17. db = Chroma.from_documents(
18.     chunks,
19.     embedding=embeddings,
20.     persist_directory="spec_emb"
21. )
22. results = db.similarity_search(
23.     "What is social impact of 5G?"
24. )
25. for result in results:
26.     print("\n")
27.     print(result.page_content)
```

Code snippet 7.8: *LangChain — Example for store and retrieve content from Chroma vector database*

Below is the output for *Code snippet 7.8*:

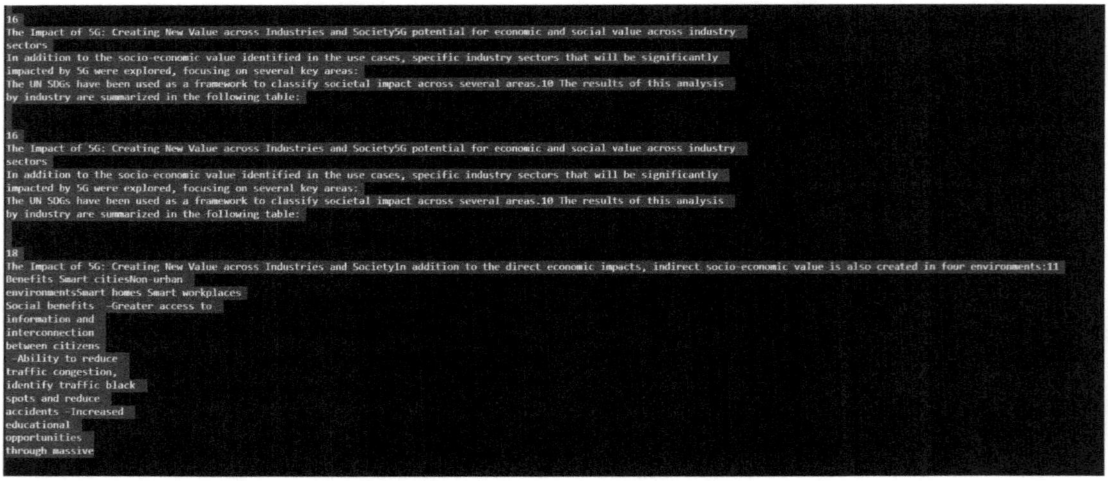

Figure 7.9: *Similarity search output from the vector database*

Agents

Agents are components designed to enable LLMs to interact with real-world, to perform defined tasks, and to interact with external sources. Agents are responsible for processing input and utilize tools or toolkits to perform tasks automatically. There are various

LangChain agents like zero-shot ReAct, conversational ReAct, ReAct docstore, self-ask with search used for various use cases. (ReAct is ieason + act agent which is combines reasoning and action elements in LLMs. It breaks down a query into actionable sub-tasks, and each task is followed through until it has been achieved and outputted.)

In below example, the objective is to find total number of students in a SQL Database. The application merges the user query with tool information (SQL database) and forwards it to ChatGPT. Based on the received user query and tool information, ChatGPT decides on the tool's relevance to the user query and generates the request with instructions (SQL query) to the application for additional inputs. The application executes the instruction (SQL query) and returns the SQL response to the ChatGPT.

LLM generates the response to a user query based on the application inputs. In the code below, we have used the SQL table as a tool to extract additional inputs for ChatGPT. Table name (Student) is explicitly mentioned in the below code; however, by providing the table schema and description alone, ChatGPT can generate the relevant SQL query without having any reference to table names.

Below *Figure 7.10* shows the prerequisite for the following example related to SQL query. Code snippet is the installation of LangChain and SQLite database (Colab).

```
1. !pip install openai langchain
2. !pip install langchain
3. !wget https://www.plus2net.com/python/download/my_db.db
4. %load_ext sql
5. # we can use the magic extension to connect to our SQLite DB
6. %sql sqlite:///my_db.db


1. %%sql
2. select * from student
```

id	name	class	mark	gender
1	John Deo	Four	75	female
2	Max Ruin	Three	85	male
3	Arnold	Three	55	male
4	Krish Star	Four	60	female
5	John Mike	Four	60	female
6	Alex John	Four	55	male
7	My John Rob	Five	78	male
8	Asruid	Five	85	male
9	Tes Qry	Six	78	male
10	Big John	Four	55	female

Figure 7.10: Left installation of SQLite database. Right SQLite student table records

Below *Code snippet 7.9* is an example of agent creation for SQLite database:

```
1.  import sqlite3
2.  from pydantic.v1 import BaseModel, Field
3.  from typing import List
4.  from langchain.tools import Tool
5.  from dotenv import load_dotenv, find_dotenv
6.  from langchain.chat_models import ChatOpenAI
7.  from langchain.prompts import (
8.      ChatPromptTemplate,
9.      HumanMessagePromptTemplate,
10.     MessagesPlaceholder
```

```
11. )
12. from langchain.schema import SystemMessage
13. from langchain.agents import OpenAIFunctionsAgent, AgentExecutor
14. _ = load_dotenv(find_dotenv())
15.
16. conn = sqlite3.connect("my_db.db") # Establish DB connection
17. def run_sqlite_query(query): # Function to execute sql query
18.  c = conn.cursor()
19.  c.execute(query)
20.  return c.fetchall()
21.
22. # Creation of Tool class
23. class RunQueryArgsSchema(BaseModel):
24.  query: str
25.
26. run_query_tool = Tool.from_function(
27.  name="run_sqlite_query",
28.  description="Run a sqlite query.",
29.  func=run_sqlite_query,
30.  args_schema=RunQueryArgsSchema
31.  )
32.
33. model = ChatOpenAI(temperature=0)
34. tables ="student"
35. prompt = ChatPromptTemplate(
36.  messages=[
37.      SystemMessage(content=(
38.          "You are an AI that has access to a SQLite database.\n"
39.          f"The database has tables of: {tables}\n"
40.          "Do not make any assumptions about what tables exist "
41.          "or what columns exist. Instead, use the 'describe_tables'
               function"
42.      )),
```

```
43.        HumanMessagePromptTemplate.from_template("{input}"),
44.        MessagesPlaceholder(variable_name="agent_scratchpad")
45.        ]
46.  )
47.
48. tools = [
49.  run_query_tool,
50.  ]
51.
52. agent = OpenAIFunctionsAgent(
53.  llm=model,
54.  prompt=prompt,
55.  tools=tools
56.  )
57. agent_executor = AgentExecutor(
58.  agent=agent,
59.  verbose=True,
60.  tools=tools
61.  )
62. agent_executor("Get me total number of students")
63.  # agent_executor("how many users are there?")
```

Code snippet 7.9: LangChain — Example to create agent to execute query in SQLite database

Below is the output for *Code snippet 7.9*:

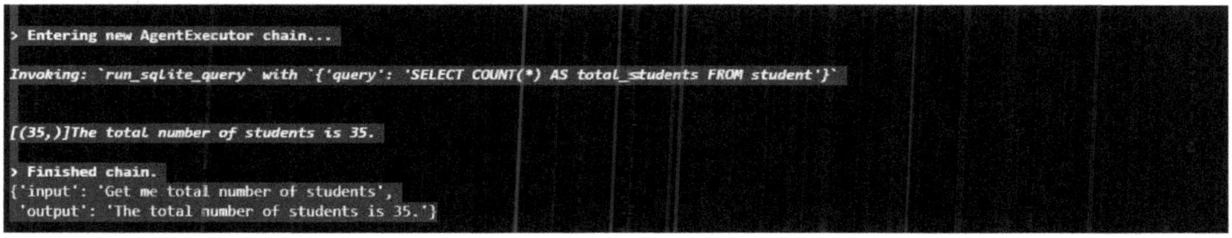

Figure 7.11: LLM SQL query instruction and response for user query

Prototype

In this section, we will look into three prototypes, chat with Excel files, RAG using LlamaIndex and property graph creation of medical journal. The objective of these prototypes is to understand the features, capabilities, and functionalities of LLM frameworks to build real-world applications. Below code snippets are only the primary function, full python program code for these prototypes shall be available in the book repository.

Chat with Excel files

The objective of this prototype is to build an app where the user can upload a excel and start conversing with the excel content using *OpenAI API*. For the full code, please refer to the book repository.

Prerequisites:

- VSCode IDE for development and testing Python code.
- *OpenAI API Key* for accessing the model, and installation of packages on Python (Version 3.11.7) virtual environment.
- `streamlit`, `langchain_experimental`, `langchain`, `openai`, `python-dotenv`, `tabulate` libraries are to be pip installed.
- Set `openai.api_key` through env variables.

> **Note: .streamlit and .venv file that include the API keys and secrets have to be created as per user account.**

Functions

Streamlit has been used for UI framework. It is a free and open-source framework to rapidly build machine learning and data science web apps. It is built on Python-based libraries specifically designed for machine learning engineers.

In section (a) of *Figure 7.12*, Streamlit file loader component of **CSV** (**comma separated values**) type is created and is used as a tabular data input to pandas dataframe. Section (c) of *Figure 7.12* Python function to load the CSV content into pandas dataframe object. We use **create_pandas_dataframe_agent** from LangChain framework to load the data frame object in to user prompt to generate LLM response. As shown in section (b) of *Figure 7.12*, once the file is uploaded, user can query the Excel file (e.g. **Churn_Modelling.csv**) in **Enter your query** text box for analyzing:

```
import streamlit as st
from dotenv import load_dotenv
from utils import generate_script
load_dotenv()
st.title(' Chat with your excel')
st.image("pexels-junior-teixeira-2047905.jpg",
        width=500,caption='Analyse your csv files')
st.header(' upload your excel here')
file=st.file_uploader("upload your csv", type=["csv"] ,key ="uploaded_file")
#file=st.session_state["uploaded_file"]
query = st.text_area("Enter your query")
submit = st.button('Generate response for me')
if submit:
    ans ,df = generate_script(file,query)
    st.write(ans)
    with st.expander('show me'):
        st.write(df)
```

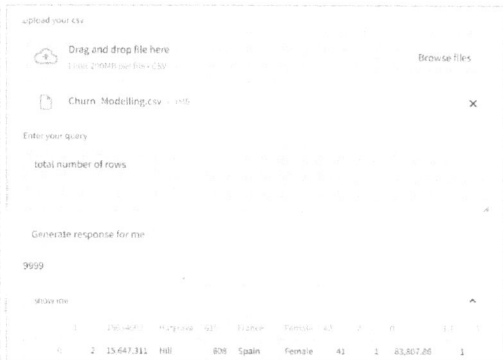

(a) app.py -Streamlit code for UI   *(b) Front end UI Image*

```
from langchain.chat_models import ChatOpenAI
from langchain_experimental.agents.agent_toolkits import create_pandas_dataframe_agent
import pandas as pd

def generate_script(file , query ):
    llm = ChatOpenAI(model_name='gpt-3.5-turbo')

    df = pd.read_table(file,sep=",",header=1)
    agent = create_pandas_dataframe_agent(llm,df,verbose=True)
    answer = agent.run(query)

    return answer,df
```

(c) utils.py Code for Langchain dataframe agent

Figure 7.12: *Figures a, b, and c are prototype code for chat with Excel*

Retrieval augmented generation

Enterprise applications demand generative AI models to be domain and context specific. LLMs like ChatGPT are generally time-static and not trained on domain specific information. RAG is a technique where enterprise knowledge base and external sources are used to ground pre trained LLMs for latest, domain specific information which in-turn enhances the accuracy and reliability for enterprise use cases. RAG helps reduce the chance of LLMs to hallucinate misleading responses. In retrieval face, as discussed above in the vector store code, relevant information to the user query is fetched, which is then appended to the user query and passed to the LLM model.

Finally, the LLMs use augmented queries to generate the final response. A final answer is presented to the user, potentially citing sources for the embedding model found. Therefore, RAG allows LLMs to bypass the retraining and generate reliable and relevant information using retrieval generation. While previously, we have been looking into LangChain, which provides a granular control and modular approach to building LLM applications, in this section, we will look into RAG using another framework built specifically for retrieval use cases like search, document summarization, etc.

Steps for RAG:

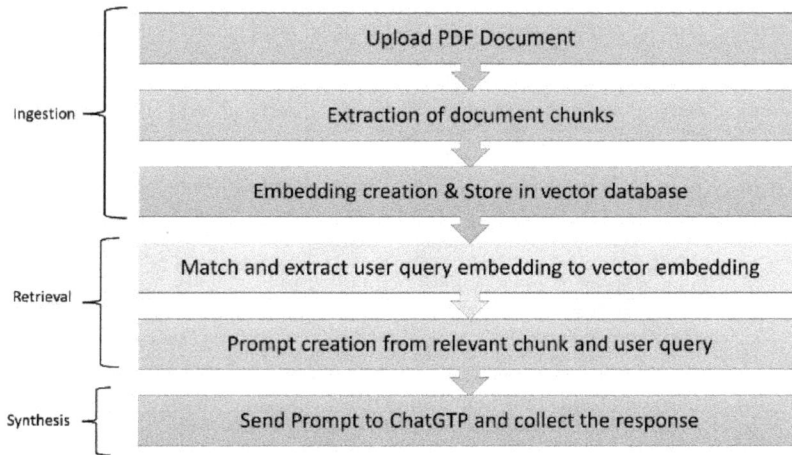

Figure 7.13: *RAG Sequence*

There are different techniques followed to improve the performance of RAG like small-to-big retrieval and sentence-window retrieval. These techniques decouple synthesis and retrieval process. They differ by using different text chunking methods during retrieval and synthesis process.

Small-to-big retrieval

The idea behind small-to-big retrieval is to combine information from segments of text to generate a relevant response. This method uses smaller text chunks to build a hierarchical structure, with each chunk having a reference to the parent chunk. During the retrieval process relevant chunks are expanded with larger context around the text using parent nodes and the same will be leveraged by LLMs to generate response during synthesis process. This approach is used when the response to the user query lies across multiple documents.

LlamaIndex uses a similar technique (auto-merging retrieval) to improve the RAG performance. In the below code we will load the PDF document, create smaller text chunks of different sizes, and finally create index, retriever, and query engine to get the LLM response for user query.

1. **Load the document split.pdf: SimpleDirectoryReader** is a LlamaIndex data connector that supports various formats including pdf, docx, jpg etc. Below *Code snippet 7.10* is to load the document **split.pdf**:

```
1. import os
2. import openai
3. from dotenv import load_dotenv, find_dotenv
```

```
4.  from llama_index import SimpleDirectoryReader
5.  _ = load_dotenv(find_dotenv())
6.  documents = SimpleDirectoryReader(
7.      input_files=["/content/split.pdf"]
8.  ).load_data()
9.
10. print(documents[0])
```

Code snippet 7.10: *Code for Loading split.pdf using LlamaIndex reader*

Below is the Output for *Code snippet 7.10*:

Doc ID: 4d221a3d-2f91-48c6-9545-5adf3e1ba5fc
Text: 3GPP 3GPP TS 23.501 V16.18.0 (2023 -09) 40 Release 16   UE
RANAMF UCMFNEF AF VPLMN HPLMNNnef Naf Nucmf Namf   NOTE: The AF in
the VPLMN (i.e. the one having a relationship with the VPLMN NEF) is
the one which provisions Manufacturer Assigned UE radio capability
IDs in the VPLMN UCMF. RACS is a serving PLMN only feature (it
requires no specif...

Figure 7.14: *Document view*

2. **Processing of documents into Nodes**: **SimpleNodeParser** is a node parser class that is used to automatically transform the source document content into granular entities representing the chunks. **Child_node_parsers** set node parser for the child nodes that need to be created. Below is the *Code snippet 7.11* for processing of documents into nodes:

```
1.  from llama_index import Document
2.  from llama_index.node_parser import SimpleNodeParser
3.  from llama_index.schema import IndexNode
4.  document_text = "\n\n".join([d.get_content() for d in documents])
5.  documents = [Document(text=document_text)]
6.  node_parser = SimpleNodeParser.from_defaults(chunk_size=1024)
7.  parent_nodes = node_parser.get_nodes_from_documents(documents)
8.  chunk_sizes = [128,256,512]
9.  child_node_parsers = [
10.     SimpleNodeParser.from_defaults(chunk_size=c,chunk_
        overlap=100) for c in chunk_sizes
11. ]
12. for i in parent_nodes:
13.   print (i)
```

Code snippet 7.11: *Code for document node creation*

Below is the output for the *Code snippet 7.11*:

```
Node ID: d7fa6158-3f84-4fd1-a356-2abcb04bb37f
Text: 3GPP   3GPP TS 23.501 V16.18.0 (2023 -09) 40 Release 16   UE
RANAMF UCMFNEF AF VPLMN HPLMNNnef Naf Nucmf Namf   NOTE:   The AF in
the VPLMN (i.e. the one having a relationship with the VPLMN NEF) is
the one which provisions  Manufacturer Assigned UE radio capability
IDs in the VPLMN UCMF. RACS is a serving PLMN only  feature (it
requires no specif...
Node ID: c0413e5a-3ed0-44fd-b278-8529730c62f0
Text: N16:  Reference point between two SMFs, (in roaming case between
SMF in the visited network and the SMF  in the home network).   N16a:
Reference point between SMF and I -SMF.   N17:  Reference point
between AMF and 5G -EIR.  N18:  Reference point between any NF and
UDSF.   N19:  Reference point between two PSA UPFs for 5G LAN -type
service.   N...
```

Figure 7.15: *Node ID reference and document chunks*

3. **Create and link child nodes into parent nodes**: In the below code, we have created child chunks (128 size, 256 size, 512 size) for each of the parent chunk (1024 size) and appended the parent chunk (1024 chunk) with the list of 6 numbers of 128 size doc chunks, 4 nos. of 256 size doc chunks and 2 nos. of 512 size chunks. These chunks can be referred to as index nodes. Index node is a node object that represents the chunks in llama Index framework. These node objects are referenced with their unique **Index_id,** and it helps to establish the relationships between the objects. **Index_id** helps to establish the links between parent nodes and child nodes. In the below code child node parsers are looped inside parent nodes and appended to the parent node **Index_id**.

For example, child **IndexNode(id_='e0972364-d1e1-4684-a147-2976a1628609'** is linked to parent **Index_id='d7fa6158-3f84-4fd1-a356-2abcb04bb37f'**. Below is the *Code snippet 7.12* for creating and linking child nodes into parent nodes:

```
1. nodes_hirerachy = []
2.
3. for parent_node in parent_nodes:
4.     for n in child_node_parsers:
5.         child_nodes = n.get_nodes_from_documents([parent_node])
6.         child_index_nodes = [
7.             IndexNode.from_text_node(i, parent_node.node_id) for
                i in child_nodes
8.         ]
9.         nodes_hirerachy.extend(child_index_nodes)
```

```
10.    parent_index_node = IndexNode.from_text_node(parent_node,
       parent_node.node_id)

11.    nodes_hirerachy.append(parent_index_node)

12. nodes_hirerachy_dict = {n.node_id: n for n in nodes_hirerachy}

13. nodes_hirerachy_dict
```

Code snippet 7.12: Code for creating nodes hierarch between parent and child nodes

Below is the output of *Code snippet 7.12:*

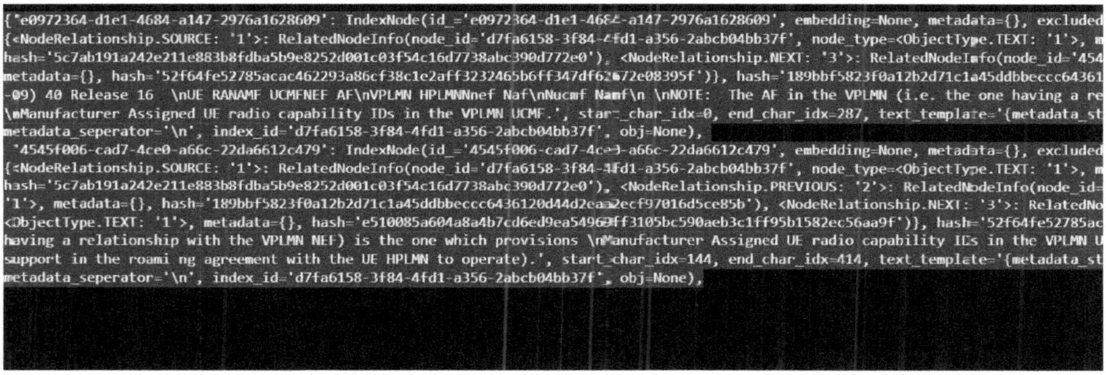

Figure 7.16: Output of node-hierarchy

4. **Loading embedding model and LLM**: In the below code, while LLM model is ChatGPT model GPT-3.5 Turbo, embedding model for Retrieval is FlagEmbedding-BGE model. FlagEmbedding focuses on LLMs specific to RAG. BGE is the general-purpose embedding model used to create vector embeddings for vector stores. Embedding model is loaded from *Hugging Face*. LlamaIndex service context utility container is used to bundle LLM, and the embedding model is used for querying and indexing. Below is the code snippet for loading the embedding model and LLM:

```
1. from llama_index.llms import OpenAI

2. from llama_index import ServiceContext

3. llm = OpenAI(model="gpt-3.5-turbo", temperature=0.1)

4. service_context = ServiceContext.from_defaults(

5.     llm=llm,

6.     embed_model="local:BAAI/bge-large-en-v1.5")
```

Code snippet 7.13: Code to load embedding model for RAG

Below is the output of *Code snippet 7.13*:

```
/usr/local/lib/python3.10/dist-packages/huggingface_hub/utils/_token.py:88: UserWarning:
The secret `HF_TOKEN` does not exist in your Colab secrets.
To authenticate with the Hugging Face Hub, create a token in your settings tab (https://huggingface.co/settings/tokens),
You will be able to reuse this secret in all of your notebooks.
Please note that authentication is recommended but still optional to access public models or datasets.
  warnings.warn(
```

config.json: 100% ▮▮▮▮▮▮▮▮▮▮ 779/779 [00:00<00:00, 34.1kB/s]

model.safetensors: 100% ▮▮▮▮▮▮▮▮▮▮ 1.34G/1.34G [00:16<00:00, 59.9MB/s]

tokenizer_config.json: 100% ▮▮▮▮▮▮▮▮▮▮ 366/366 [00:00<00:00, 21.7kB/s]

vocab.txt: 100% ▮▮▮▮▮▮▮▮▮▮ 232k/232k [00:00<00:00, 2.76MB/s]

tokenizer.json: 100% ▮▮▮▮▮▮▮▮▮▮ 711k/711k [00:00<00:00, 10.0MB/s]

special_tokens_map.json: 100% ▮▮▮▮▮▮▮▮▮▮ 125/125 [00:00<00:00, 6.62kB/s]

Figure 7.17: *Output of model loading*

Create vector embedding for the document chunks

As seen in earlier sections, vector stores are specialized data structures built for storing vector representations for faster retrieval and search. Llama **VectorStoreIndex** is built on top of the existing vector store. It uses an embedding model in the service context to create embeddings of **IndexNode** objects and store them in a vector store. In the below code storage context give the path for persistent storage of index. Below is the *Code snippet 7.14* for creating vector embeddings for document chunks:

```
1. from llama_index import VectorStoreIndex, StorageContext
2.
3. vector_index_chunk = VectorStoreIndex(
4.     nodes_hirerachy, service_context=service_context
5. )
6. vector_index_chunk.storage_context.persist(persist_dir="./vector_index")
```

Code snippet 7.14: *Code for vector embedding creation*

Below is the output of *Code snippet 7.14*:

- 📁 ..
- 📁 sample_data
- 📁 vector_index ⋮
  - 📄 default__vector_store.json
  - 📄 docstore.json
  - 📄 graph_store.json
  - 📄 image__vector_store.json
  - 📄 index_store.json
- 📄 split.pdf

Figure 7.18: *Output folder structure of created embeddings*

Retriever

In the Code snippet below, 7.15 **RecursiveRetriever** is implemented. It recursively traverses node relationships and fetch nodes based on the links. As discussed earlier, the child index IDs are linked to the references of parent nodes. Retriever method takes the user query as input and fetches the list of nodes with relevancy scores. As shown in the below output, retriever retrieves the top 3 matched index node content with node ids and relevancy scores:

```
1. from llama_index.retrievers import RecursiveRetriever
2. from llama_index.response.notebook_utils import display_source_node
3.
4. retriever = vector_index_chunk.as_retriever(similarity_top_k=3)
5. retriever = RecursiveRetriever(
6.     "vector",
7.     retriever_dict={"vector": retriever},
8.     node_dict=nodes_hirerachy_dict,
9.     verbose=True,
10. )
11. node_ids = retriever.retrieve(
12.     "What is 5G?"
13. )
14. for id in node_ids:
15.     display_source_node(id, source_length=500)
```

Code snippet 7.15: *Code for building retrieval chain*

Below is the output for *Code snippet 7.15*:

Node ID: 67d5d93c-f021-4edf-a2c0-78c28159c87c
Similarity: 0.6416117382190382
Text: there shall be one N1 instance over NG -RAN and one N1 instance over non-3GPP access.
A UE simultaneously connected to the same 5G Core Network of a PLMN over a 3GPP access and a non -3GPP access shall be served by a single AMF in this 5G Core Network.
When a UE is connected to a 3GPP access of a PLMN, if the UE selects a N3IWF and the N3IWF is located in a PLMN different from the PLMN of the 3GPP access. e.g. in a different VPLMN or in the HPLMN, the UE is served separately by the two...

Node ID: caf16a8e-54a2-4f3c-9a0d-158daeb2f404
Similarity: 0.6414916624108752
Text: When a 5G -RG s connected via a NG -RAN and via a W -5GAN, multiple N1 instances shall exist for the 5G -RG i.e. there shall be one N1 instance over NG -RAN and one N1 instance over W -5GAN.
A 5G -RG simultaneously connected to the same 5G Core Network of a PLMN over a 3GPP access and a W -5GAN access shall be served by a single AMF in this 5G Core Network.
5G-RG shall maintain the NAS signalling connection with the AMF over the W -5GAN after all the PDU Sessions for the 5G -RG over t...

Node ID: eefa574e-b19f-44f2-9036-0a332ff5043a
Similarity: 0.6376140770003982
Text: 3GPP 3GPP TS 23.501 V16.18.0 (2023 -09) 40 Release 16
UE RANAMF UCMFNEF AF VPLMN HPLMNNnef Naf Nucmf Namf

NOTE: The AF in the VPLMN (i.e. the one having a relationship with the VPLMN NEF) is one which provisions Manufacturer Assigned UE radio capability IDs in the VPLMN UCMF. RACS is a serving PLMN only feature (it requires no specific support in the roaming agreement with the UE HPLMN to operate).
Figure 4 2.5a -2: Roaming architecture for Radio Capability Signalling optimis...

Figure 7.19: *Output of recursive retrieval*

Retrieval query engine

Retrieval query engine takes retriever and response synthesizer to generate the LLM response. Retriever enables RAG content and response synthesizser enable LLM with the RAG context and gets the LLM response back relevant to the user query. Below, *Code snippet 7.16* is the implementation of the retrieval query engine.

```
from llama_index.query_engine import RetrieverQueryEngine
q_engine = RetrieverQueryEngine.from_args(
    retriever, service_context=service_context
)
res = q_engine.query(
    "Can you tell me about the key concepts of 5G"
)
print(str(res))
```

***Code snippet 7.16**: Code for LlamaIndex query engine for LLM response retrieval*

Output:

```
The key concepts of 5G include the 5G System Architecture, service-based interfaces, and reference points. The 5G System Architecture consists of
various service-based interfaces such as Namf, Nsmf, Nnef, Npcf, Nudm, Naf, Nnrf, Nnssaaf, Nnssf, Nausf, Nudr, Nudsf, N5g-eir, Nnwdaf, Nchf, and Nucmf.
These service-based interfaces are exhibited by different network functions (NFs) in the 5G system. Additionally, the 5G System Architecture also
includes reference points like N1, N2, N3, N4, N6, N9, N5, N7, N8, N10, N11, N12, N13, N14, N15, N16, N16a, N17, N18, N19, N22, N23, N24, and N27. These
reference points represent the interactions between different NF services in the NFs and are realized through corresponding NF service-based interfaces.
```

***Figure 7.20**: LLM response for user query*

Property graph creation of medical research journal

The objective of the prototype is to create a chat application that can query medical research journals and extract property graphs from them. Users can upload the research journals, query the journals, create prompts for entity and relationship extractions out of journal contents, and finally create a property graph out of it.

Prerequisites:

- VS Code IDE for development and testing Python code
- *OpenAI* and *Pinecone API Key* for accessing the model and vector database
- Installation of packages on Python (Version 3.11.7) virtual environment
- UI libraries—**`streamlit`**, **`streamlit-ace`**, **`streamlit_feeback`**
- LLM libraries—**`langchain`**, **`openai`**, **`python-dotenv`**, **`pinecone-client`**
- Graph related libraries—**`neo4j`**, **`pyvis`**, **`matplotlib`**, **`graphvis`**, **`network`**

- Vertex AI libraries—**google.cloud**, google-cloud-api platform are to be pip installed

- Set **openai.api_key** and Pinecone API key through env variables

- Download the **GraphGeneration-MedicalResearch** folder from book repository and open it in VS Code

- Execute **streamlit run chat.py** command in VS Code terminal to open the app in **localhost:8501** in web browser

- Test File—**USF_published_article.pdf** from the code repository (Size limit <1.5 MB)

- SQLite and Neo4j Desktop databases running locally with services in UP state

- Secrets.toml—Steamlit secret file must have neo4j url, username, password, pinecone index, VertexAI project_id, location and key_path

- Only sections of code is discussed. Please find the full code in book repository or https://github.com/karthiksab/GenAIBook

Note: .streamlit and .venv files that include the API keys and secrets have to be created as per the user account.

Streamlit is been used for UI framework and it is a free and open-source framework to rapidly build machine learning and data science web apps. It is built on Python-based libraries specifically designed for machine learning engineers. Below sections cover only code snippets, however, for the full final code please refer to book repository.

Follow the below steps to chat with the medical research journal:

1. In the **app** tab as shown in *Figure 7.21*, upload your pdf and process. Pages/**app.py** is the code for UI to upload, preview, and process pdf files. It calls the **util_function.py** for processing of pdf, creating embeddings, and storing it in the Pinecone vector database:

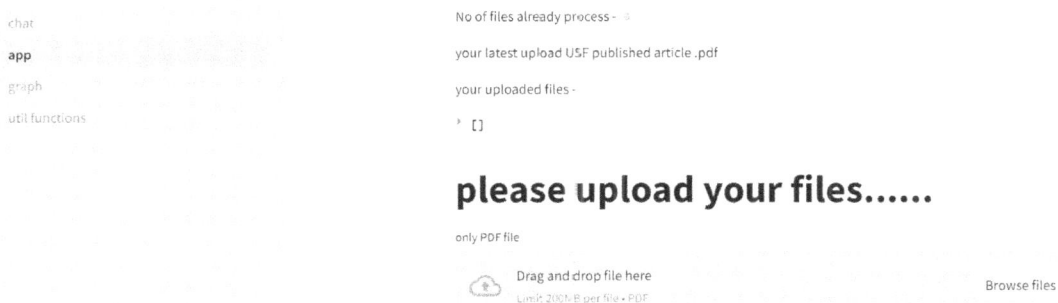

chat
app
graph
util functions

No of files already process -
your latest upload USF published article .pdf
your uploaded files -
▸ []

please upload your files......

only PDF file

Drag and drop file here
Limit 200MB per file · PDF

Browse files

Figure 7.21: UI for uploading research journal in pdf format

Once uploaded, a hash of file is generated and preview of the pdf file is available as shown in *Figure 7.22*:

📄 USF published article .pdf 0.6MB   ✕

Original PDF file

da39a3ee5e6b4b0d3255bfef95601890afd80709

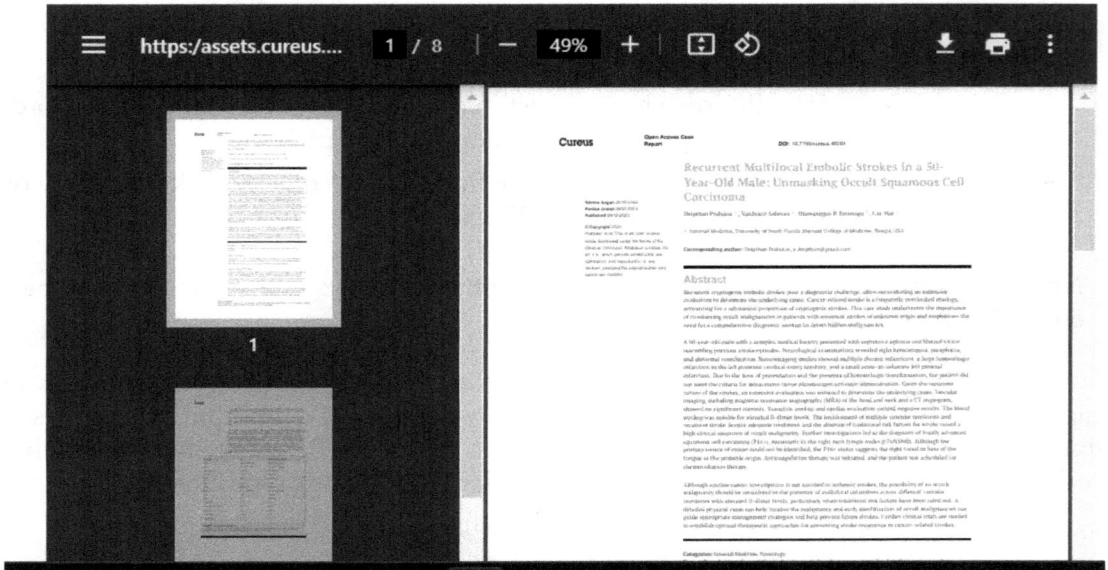

Figure 7.22: *Research journal Preview*

Upon the initiation of the process, the following three functions in the **Pages/util_functions.py** are called:

- ○ **Chunk_data   function**: Receives the pdf loader, uses LangChain **CharacterTextSplitter** to chunk the documents. The pdf file name is stored as file metadata in Pinecone. The metadata will be used for specific document content matching and retrieval. Below is the *Code snippet 7.17* for chunking pdf data:

```python
def chunk_data(loader,file_name):
    text_splitter = CharacterTextSplitter( separator="\n", chunk_size=500,chunk_overlap=0)
    chunks = loader.load_and_split(text_splitter= text_splitter)
    docs = text_splitter.split_documents(chunks)
    for idx, text in enumerate(docs):
        docs[idx].metadata['file_name'] = file_name

    return docs
```

Code snippet 7.17: *LangChain code for document chunking*

o **Pinecone_embd function**: Receives the Pinecone index, OpenAI **embeddings** function and chunks input and instantiates the Pinecone client to insert the embeddings into Pinecone database. Below *Code snippet 7.18* is for creating vector embedding in Pinecone database:

```
def pinecone_embd(index,embeddings, docs,file_name):
        pinecone.init(api_key=os.getenv("PINECONE_API_KEY"),  # find at app.pinecone.io
        environment=os.getenv("PINECONE_ENV"),  # next to api key in console
        )
        index_name = index
        print(index_name)
        print(os.getenv("PINECONE_API_KEY"))
        if index_name not in pinecone.list_indexes():
        # we create a new index
                pinecone.create_index(name=index_name, metric="cosine", dimension=1536)

        index = Pinecone.from_documents(docs, embeddings,index_name =index_name)
        return index
```

Code snippet 7.18: *LangChain code for embedding creation in pinecone vector database*

Below, *Figure 7.23* shows the insertion of embeddings into Pinecone with **METADATA** as file name:

	ID	VALUES			
1	27d...	0.0045069959, -0.00201671151, 0.0197160933, -0.042061, -0.0052866...	Q	✎	🗑

SCORE
-0.0113

METADATA
file_name: "USF published article .pdf"
page: 2
source: "C:\\Users\\VAISHN~1\\AppData\\Local\\Temp\\tmpbjd4nksx"
text: "ParameterValueReference RangeSodium138 mmol/L135-145 mmol/LPotassium3.6 mmol/L3.5-5.0 ...

Figure 7.23: *Pinecone vector database snapshot for embeddings*

Below *Figure 7.24* shows the UI success message once the embeddings were created:

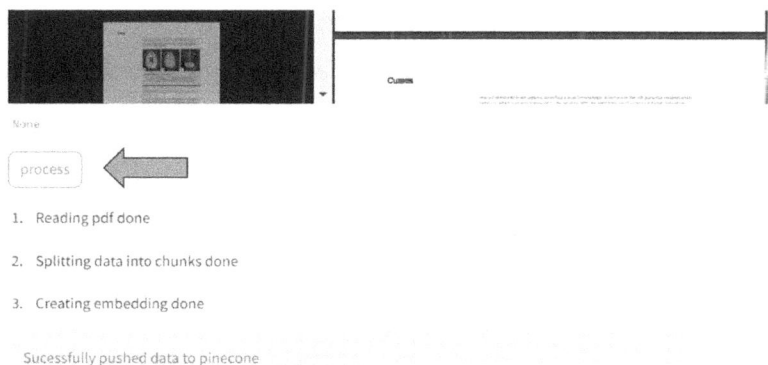

Figure 7.24: *Process steps for embedding creation*

2. **Chat tab**: Chat with the uploaded journal.

Select the appropriate journal as shown in the *Figure 7.25* below:

Chat with your document

chat with 2

your uploaded files ^

☑ USF_published_article.pdf ⊘

☐ ARDA_JOURNAL_16177.pdf

Figure 7.25: Research journal selection

Start querying with your document as shown in the *Figure 7.26* below:

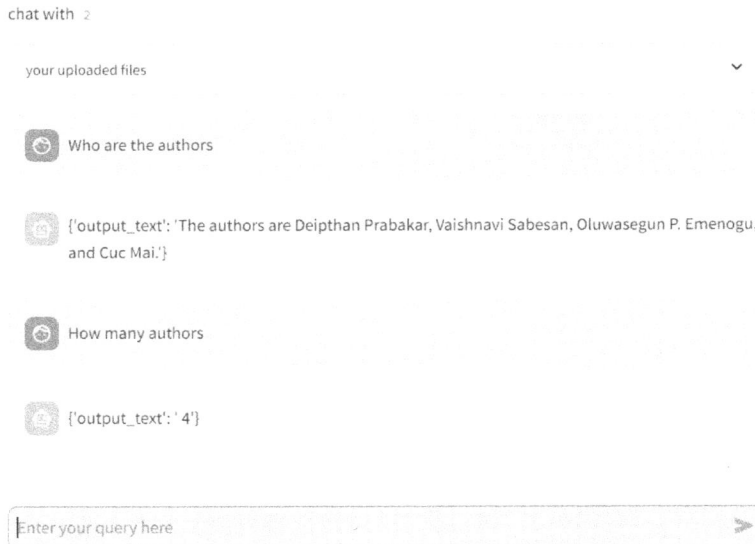

chat with 2

your uploaded files ⌄

◉ Who are the authors

{'output_text': 'The authors are Deipthan Prabakar, Vaishnavi Sabesan, Oluwasegun P. Emenogu, and Cuc Mai.'}

◉ How many authors

{'output_text': ' 4'}

Enter your query here ➤

Figure 7.26: User query and LLM chat responses

In order to get the right response LLM needs three main components:

o User query

o Relevant document embeddings

o Conversational history

On submitting the user query as shown in *Figure 7.26* above, following 3 Python code functions in **chat.py** (**create_embedding_query_data**, **pinecone_embd_ extract**, **similar_search**) are called at the backend as shown in *Code snippet 7.19* below:

```
# create embedding instance
user_query_embed= create_embeddings_query_data()

# function to pull index data from pine cone
index_extract=pinecone_embd_extract(pine_index,user_query_embed,st.session_state.chat_file_name)

# fetch relevant documents from vector store
rag_embed=similar_search(index_extract,prompt,st.session_state.chat_file_name)
```

Code snippet 7.19: Function calls for embeddings creation and RAG based extraction

Util_chat.py is the file where the functions are defined as shown in *Code snippet 7.20* below. **create_embedding_query_data** function defines the embedding for vector database extraction. **pinecone_embd_extract** function retrieves embedding of the document chunks stored earlier from pine cone vector database and **similar_search** function filters out the extracted embeddings based on the **pdf_file** that user wants to query:

```
def create_embeddings_query_data():
        embeddings=OpenAIEmbeddings()
        return (embeddings)

def pinecone_embd_extract(pine_index,embeddings,file_name):
        pinecone.init(api_key=os.getenv("PINECONE_API_KEY"),  # find at app.pinecone.io
        environment=os.getenv("PINECONE_ENV"),  # next to api key in console
        )
        index_extract = Pinecone.from_existing_index(index_name = pine_index,embedding=embeddings)
        return index_extract

def similar_search(index, query ,file_name,k=3):

        similar_docs= index.similarity_search_with_score(query, k=k ,filter={"file_name":file_name})
        return similar_docs
```

Code snippet 7.20: Code for embeddings creation and RAG based extraction functions

As seen earlier, ChatGPT is stateless. Every user query is treated as a separate request. So, without memory implementation, LLMs cannot understand the previous context on which user is querying.

In the above example, when user query **How many authors**, LLM needs a summarized context of the previous conversations to extract the information in order to give the right response. In this prototype the previous conversation history is stored into SQLite database and retrieved prior to calling for an LLM response.

As shown in below *Code snippet 7.21,* a memory component is built in **chat.py** file before calling for LLM response:

```
memory=build_memory(chat_args)
response = llm_response(rag_embed,prompt,memory)
```

Code snippet 7.21: Function calls for maintaining and retrieving chat history

In **memory.py** the base **ConversationBufferMemory** of LangChain is modified with **SqlMessageHistory** class as shown in below *Code snippet 7.22* to extract the history data using conversation id, file name and file hash:

```python
def build_memory(chat_args):
    return ConversationBufferMemory(
        chat_memory=SqlMessageHistory(
            conv_id=chat_args.conv_id,
            chat_file_hash=chat_args.chat_file_hash,
            chat_file_name=chat_args.chat_file_name
        ),
        return_messages=True,
        memory_key="chat_history",
        input_key="question",
        #output_key="answer"
    )
```

Code snippet 7.22: Code for modifying the ConversationalBufferMemory base class to include SqlMessageHistory

SqlMessageHistory class inherits the LangChain **BaseChatMessageHistory** and calls for two actions (**sql_retrieve** and **sql_insert**) for conversational record insertion and retrieval of same based on unique conversation IDs. Below *Code snippet 7.23* shows how **SqlMessageHistory** class inherits the LangChain **BaseChatMessageHistory** for conversation record insertion and retrieval:

```python
class SqlMessageHistory(BaseChatMessageHistory, BaseModel):
    conv_id: str
    chat_file_hash:str
    chat_file_name:str

    @property
    def messages(self):
        return sql_retrive(self.chat_file_hash,self.conv_id)

    def add_message(self, message):
        return sql_insert(
            pdf_id= self.chat_file_hash,
            pdf_name= self.chat_file_name,
            conv_id=self.conv_id,
            conv_role=message.type,
            conv_message=message.content
        )

    def clear(self):
        pass
```

Code snippet 7.23: Function call for insert and retrieve chat history from SQLite database

The SQL retrieve and SQL insert actions are defined in sql_action.py file where SQL database engine is created for **chat_history.db** and the conversations are recorded into **karthik_chat_history** tables as per the table format defined in the **sql_class.py**. The below *Figure 7.27* shows the snapshot of SQL database where the current and past conversations are getting stored. The column format is uid, pdf hash, pdf name, unique streamlit session id, conversation role, conversation message and timestamp. To log on to sqlite3, go the SQLite folder in **C:\Programfiles\sqlite** and in command prompt type sqlite3 dbname i.e. sqlite3 chat_history.

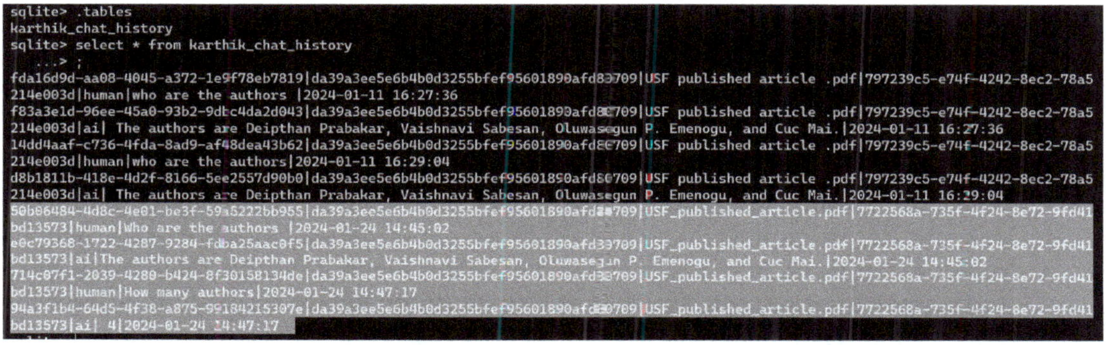

```
sqlite> .tables
karthik_chat_history
sqlite> select * from karthik_chat_history
   ...> ;
fda16d9d-aa08-4045-a372-1e9f78eb7819|da39a3ee5e6b4b0d3255bfef95601890afd80709|USF published article .pdf|797239c5-e74f-4242-8ec2-78a5
214e003d|human|who are the authors |2024-01-11 16:27:36
f83a3e1d-96ee-45a0-93b2-9dbc4da2d043|da39a3ee5e6b4b0d3255bfef95601890afd80709|USF published article .pdf|797239c5-e74f-4242-8ec2-78a5
214e003d|ai| The authors are Deipthan Prabakar, Vaishnavi Sabesan, Oluwasegun P. Emenogu, and Cuc Mai.|2024-01-11 16:27:36
14dd4aaf-c736-4fda-8ad9-af48dea43b62|da39a3ee5e6b4b0d3255bfef95601890afd80709|USF published article .pdf|797239c5-e74f-4242-8ec2-78a5
214e003d|human|who are the authors|2024-01-11 16:29:04
d8b1811b-418e-4d2f-8166-5ee2557d90b0|da39a3ee5e6b4b0d3255bfef95601890afd80709|USF published article .pdf|797239c5-e74f-4242-8ec2-78a5
214e003d|ai| The authors are Deipthan Prabakar, Vaishnavi Sabesan, Oluwasegun P. Emenogu, and Cuc Mai.|2024-01-11 16:29:04
50b06484-4d8c-4e01-be3f-59a5222bb955|da39a3ee5e6b4b0d3255bfef95601890afd80709|USF_published_article.pdf|7722568a-735f-4f24-8e72-9fd41
bd13573|human|Who are the authors |2024-01-24 14:45:02
e0c79368-1722-4287-9284-fdba25aac0f5|da39a3ee5e6b4b0d3255bfef95601890afd80709|USF_published_article.pdf|7722568a-735f-4f24-8e72-9fd41
bd13573|ai|The authors are Deipthan Prabakar, Vaishnavi Sabesan, Oluwasegun P. Emenogu, and Cuc Mai.|2024-01-24 14:45:02
714c07f1-2039-4280-b424-8f30158134de|da39a3ee5e6b4b0d3255bfef95601890afd80709|USF_published_article.pdf|7722568a-735f-4f24-8e72-9fd41
bd13573|human|How many authors|2024-01-24 14:47:17
94a3f1b4-64d5-4f38-a875-99184215307e|da39a3ee5e6b4b0d3255bfef95601890afd80709|USF_published_article.pdf|7722568a-735f-4f24-8e72-9fd41
bd13573|ai| 4|2024-01-24 14:47:17
```

***Figure 7.27**: SQLite database snapshot for the chat history records*

Below *Code snippet 7.24* generate LLM response for the user query. The **llm_response** function (**util_chat.py**) is invoked to receive the response. It receives the Pinecone index, OpenAI embeddings and conversation history as input and instantiates chain to receive the LLM response. **get_openai_callback** function is kept empty for this prototype however, it can be utilized for guardrail implementations.

```
def llm_response(rag_embed,user_query,memory):
        chain = load_qa_chain(OpenAI(),chain_type="stuff", memory=memory,callbacks=[handler])
        rag_embed = [Document(page_content=str(result[0]), metadata={"score": str(result[1])})
                    for result in rag_embed]

        with get_openai_callback() as cb:
                response = chain({"input_documents":rag_embed, "question":user_query},return_only_outputs=True)
        return response
```

***Code snippet 7.24**: Function code to generate LLM response*

3. Creation of **prompt_templates** for generating property graph:

   In the previous steps, pdf documents were uploaded and queried the content. In this step, prompt templates are created for generating property graph out of the uploaded pdf content. As similar to prompt templates seen in *Chapter 6, ChatGPT* section prompt engineering, the **prompt_templates** tab in graph (**streamlit** page) as shown in *Figure 7.28* below help users to select predefined templates for article, authors, category and keywords and fine tune existing prompts to extract the node entities and relationships based on the content. Below *Figure 7.28* shows different prompt templates created for **USF_published_article.pdf** journal:

Build graph out of Medical Journal Paper

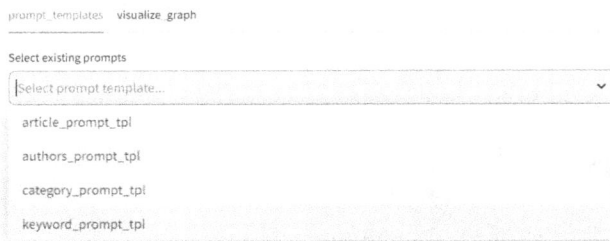

prompt_templates   visualize_graph

Select existing prompts

Select prompt template...	∨

article_prompt_tpl

authors_prompt_tpl

category_prompt_tpl

keyword_prompt_tpl

Figure 7.28: *UI For prompt template selection*

Select the **prompt_templates**, edit prompt content, apply the changes and finally execute the prompt to look into LLM response for the node entities and its relationship extraction as shown in the below *Figure 7.29*. We have used chain of thought prompting techniques as shown in the below template to extract the entities and relationship.

Note: Prompts need to be tuned if the entity-relationships are not properly getting extracted.

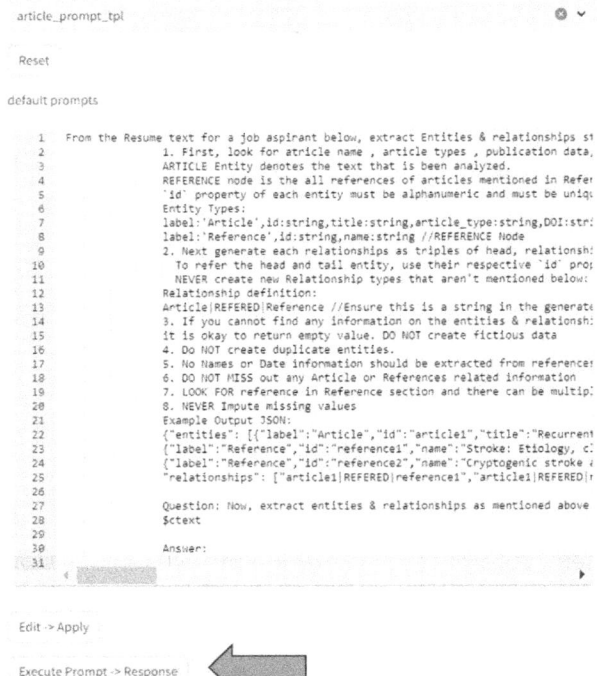

article_prompt_tpl   ⊗ ∨

Reset

default prompts

```
 1   From the Resume text for a job aspirant below, extract Entities & relationships st
 2              1. First, look for article name , article types , publication data,
 3       ARTICLE Entity denotes the text that is been analyzed.
 4       REFERENCE node is the all references of articles mentioned in Refer
 5       `id` property of each entity must be alphanumeric and must be uniqu
 6       Entity Types:
 7       label:'Article',id:string,title:string,article_type:string,DOI:stri
 8       label:'Reference',id:string,name:string //REFERENCE Node
 9       2. Next generate each relationships as triples of head, relationshi
10          To refer the head and tail entity, use their respective `id` prop
11          NEVER create new Relationship types that aren't mentioned below:
12       Relationship definition:
13       Article|REFERED|Reference //Ensure this is a string in the generate
14       3. If you cannot find any information on the entities & relationshi
15       it is okay to return empty value. DO NOT create fictious data
16       4. Do NOT create duplicate entities.
17       5. No Names or Date information should be extracted from reference
18       6. DO NOT MISS out any Article or References related information
19       7. LOOK FOR reference in Reference section and there can be multipl
20       8. NEVER Impute missing values
21       Example Output JSON:
22       {"entities": [{"label":"Article","id":"article1","title":"Recurrent
23       {"label":"Reference","id":"reference1","name":"Stroke: Etiology, c
24       {"label":"Reference","id":"reference2","name":"Cryptogenic stroke a
25       "relationships": ["article1|REFERED|reference1","article1|REFERED|r
26
27       Question: Now, extract entities & relationships as mentioned above
28       $ctext
29
30       Answer:
31
```

Edit -> Apply

Execute Prompt -> Response

Figure 7.29: *View article_prompt_tpl prompt content*

Select the prompt template, edit it, apply the changes, and finally execute the prompt to look into LLM response for the node entities and its relationship extraction as shown in the below *Figure 7.30*:

```
▼ {
  ▼ 'entities" : [
    ▼ 0 : {
        "label" : "Article"
        "id" : "article1"
        "title" :
        "Cancer-Related Stroke: Pathophysiology, Detection and Management"
        "article_type" : "Review"
        "DOI" : "10.7759/cureus.45091"
        "pub_date" : "2023"
        "abstract" :
        "This review discusses the relationship between cancer and stroke
        and provides recommendations for screening and managing cancer-
        related stroke."
        "conclusion" :
        "Early cancer screening and individualized therapy strategies are
        crucial for preventing and managing cancer-related stroke."
      }
```

Figure 7.30: *Output of prompt template LLM Response on article entity extraction*

In continuation of the above, as we traverse through the complete LLM response, we will be able to find the relationship details between the article and the references mentioned in the articles, as shown in the below *Figure 7.31*:

```
        name : stroke and cancer a complicated relationship
      }
    ▼ 4 : {
        "label" : "Reference"
        "id" : "reference4"
        "name" : "Arterial thrombosis in patients with cancer"
      }
    ▼ 5 : {
        "label" : "Reference"
        "id" : "reference5"
        "name" : "When to screen ischaemic stroke patients for cancer"
      }
    ]
  ▼ "relationships" : [
      0 : "article1|REFERED|reference1'
      1 : "article1|REFERED|reference2'
      2 : "article1|REFERED|reference3"
      3 : "article1|REFERED|reference4"
      4 : "article1|REFERED|reference5'
    ]
  }
```

Figure 7.31: *Output of prompt template LLM Response on article relationship extraction*

As shown in below *Code snippet 7.25* **extract_results** function in **extract_graph_comp.py** helps extract the entities and relationships for the property graph. *Google Vertex AI*—Text Bison LLM model is leveraged for extraction of entities and relationships as per the pdf content. The initial variable **project_id**, **location**, **key_path**, **credentials** are required to set up a *Google Vertex AI* Project. We initiate the vertex ai client using **init** method and have Text Bison model loaded into model variable:

```python
def extract_results(option,doc):
    project_id = st.secrets['project_id']
    location = st.secrets['location']
    key_path= st.secrets['key_path']
    credentials =  service_account.Credentials.from_service_account_file(key_path)
    vertexai.init(project=project_id , location = location , credentials = credentials)
    model = TextGenerationModel.from_pretrained("text-bison")
    resu'*-   '"------"'  -'}, "relationships": []}
        (variable) p: Any
    for p in option:
        if p == 'article_prompt_tpl':
            sample = str(doc.get(p)) + str(doc.get('reference_prompt_tpl'))
        else:
            sample = str(doc.get(p))
        prompt = Template(option[p]).substitute(ctext= re.sub(r'[^\x00-\x7F]+',' ', sample))
        response = model.predict(prompt,temperature =0 ,max_output_tokens=1024, top_k=40, top_p=0.8)
        response = response.text
```

Code snippet 7.25: *Code for function for initiating Vertex AI client*

As shown in below *Code snippet 7.26* we generate LLM response using **model.predict** function by passing article prompt template, and other LLM hyper parameters. The response is cleaned and split to store the entities and relationships in predefined list variables:

```python
    for p in option:
        if p == 'article_prompt_tpl':
            sample = str(doc.get(p)) + str(doc.get('reference_prompt_tpl'))
        else:
            sample = str(doc.get(p))
        prompt = Template(option[p]).substitute(ctext= re.sub(r'[^\x00-\x7F]+',' ', sample))
        response = model.predict(prompt,temperature =0 ,max_output_tokens=1024, top_k=40, top_p=0.8)
        response = response.text

        if 'Answer:\n' in response:
            response = response.split('Answer:\n ')[1]
        if response.strip() == '':

            continue
        try:
            print(response)
            response = json.loads(response.replace("\'", "'").replace('`', ''))
        except json.JSONDecodeError:
            response = response[:response.rfind("}")+1] + ']}'
            response = json.loads(response.replace("\'", "'"))
        results["entities"].extend(response["entities"])
        if "relationships" in response:
            results["relationships"].extend(response["relationships"])
```

Code snippet 7.26: *Code for function call on Vertex AI LLM to extract entities and relationship*

As shown in below *Code snippet 7.27*, once the entities and relationships are extracted from above code snippet, based on labels like **Authors**, **Keyword**, **Category**, **relationships** link between the nodes are created:

```
article_ic = results["entities"][0]["id"]
for e in results["entities"][1:]:
    if e['label'] == 'Authors':
        results["relationships"].append(f"{article_id}|HAS_AUTHOR|{e['id']}")
    if e['label'] == 'Keyword':
        results["relationships"].append(f"{article_id}|HAS_KEYWORD|{e['id']}")
    if e['label'] == 'Category':
        results["relationships"].append(f"{article_id}|HAS_CATEGORY|{e['id']}")
return(results)
```

Code snippet 7.27: Code for function call to create relationships

4. Generate property graph **Visualize graph** tab

To extract the property graph, **Generate Graph** button is actioned. This will extract the node entities and relationships related to authors, keywords, category, article and generate cipher queries, and insert those extracted records into the graph database, i.e., Neo4j. Below *Figure 7.32* shows the action of **Generate Graph** and the output graph generated in Neo4j database:

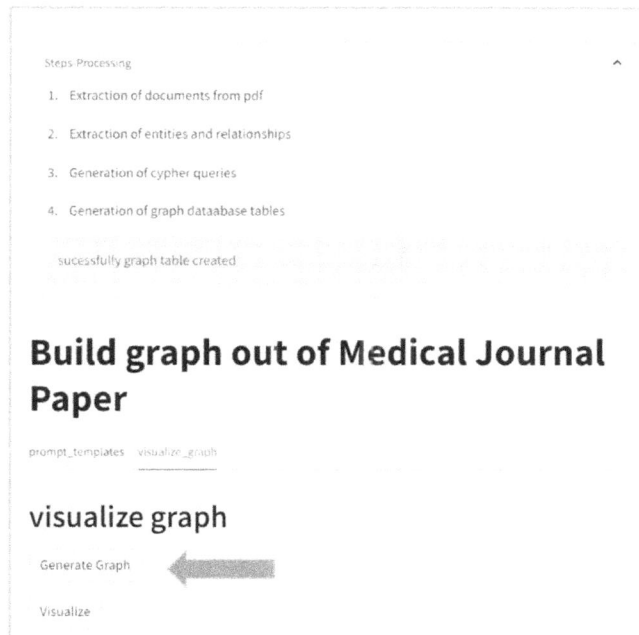

Figure 7.32: UI generate graph process

As shown in below *Figure 7.33*, the entity's article, reference, authors, keyword, and category are extracted, and a relationship is created with the article. Multiple artifacts chains can be created in a similar way using LLM models and Neo4j graph database:

Figure 7.33: Neo4j snapshot of entities and relationship creation out of journal content

As shown in the below *Figure 7.34*, each entity node is create with its relevant properties. The below figure shows the properties of article node such as **abstract**, **DOI** reference, **article_type** etc. Cypher queries can be created for joins and filtering in larger property graph scenarios:

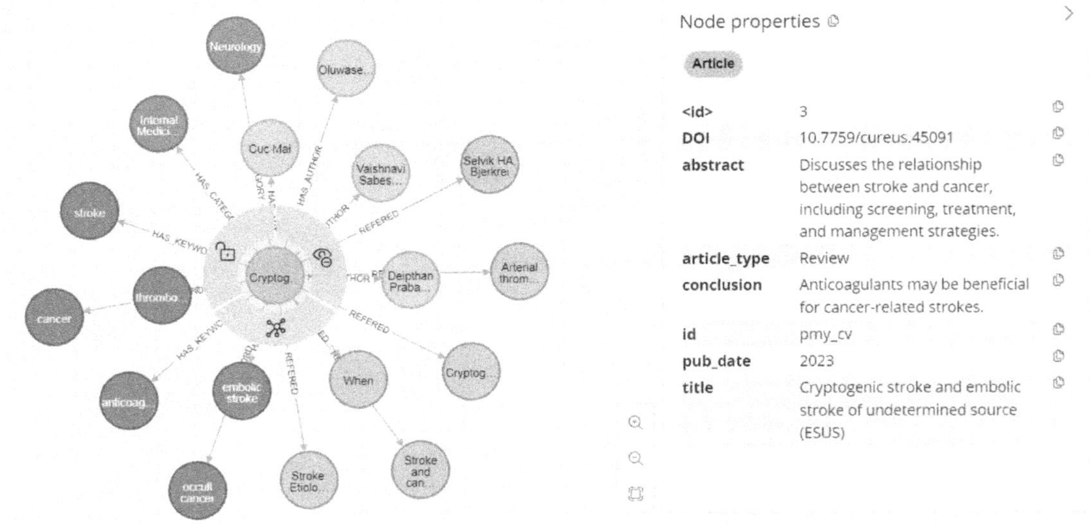

Figure 7.34: Neo4j snapshot of article node properties

The **Visualize** button helps to visualize the above graph in Streamlit. On triggering the **Visualize** button, the `neo4j_nx` function in `utils_functions.py` is called, where **NetworkX** and **Pyvis** libraries are used to extract the content from Neo4j database and save it in the `property_graph.html` file.

Conclusion

In this chapter, we understood the LangChain framework, its features, components, and how to use them. We can see how different component ecosystems are required to build LLM based application. One such framework to build application is LangChain. Similarly, LamaIndex is another framework that can be leveraged for building application components. We demonstrated several examples of different components of LangChain, such as chains, document loaders, vector databases, prompt templates, and agents. We built a prototype to query Excel files. We understood the sequence of Retrieval augmented generation and different techniques of RAG, such as small-to-big and sentence-window retrievals. We also built a working prototype of RAG with the LlamaIndex framework. RAG is a popular technique adopted by most enterprises to align LLMs to enterprise knowledge rather than doing complex finetuning or pretraining. It helps enterprises to perform LLM tasks in secure and private ways. Finally, we concluded with a prototype on property graph creation for a research journal where we built user modules (Streamlit UI), data module (SQLite, Neo4j), and LLM modules (OpenAI/Vertex AI models, LangChain components, RAG) to make an end-to-end application for the enterprise.

Key terms

- LangChain and LlamaIndex are Frameworks for developing LLM based applications
- RAG is a technique that combines NLP retrieval techniques and LLM based generation for performing text related tasks
- Chunks are sub-component of documents created by breaking down the document into smaller pieces to provide relevant context for LLM
- Generative AI Agents are software that leverages LLMs to automate user tasks and make decisions with the help of LLMs

Questions

1. What is LangChain?
2. What are the different RAG techniques?
3. What is the RAG Sequence?
4. What are the different components of LangChain?
5. What is the vector store, and what different vector stores are available?

Join our book's Discord space

Join the book's Discord Workspace for Latest updates, Offers, Tech happenings around the world, New Release and Sessions with the Authors:

https://discord.bpbonline.com

CHAPTER 8
Large Language Model Operations

Introduction

Operationalizing AI is one of the big challenges enterprises face today. While organizations are progressing in **machine learning operations** (**MLOps**), there is a long way to go in building a matured **large language model operations** (**LLMOps**) practice. Productionizing LLM systems involves a complex interplay between data, models, and software, each of which can be productionized in different ways. However, those who will be able to do it successfully are going to reap significant advantages by bringing efficiency, new experiences, and additional margins to their business. LLMs are going to be critical for any organization's future. LLMs are getting evolved into larger action models (trained on action data) or larger behavioral models (trained on human behavioral videos) as per business needs. So, enterprises must adopt LLMOps in the early pilot phase by involving the right people, by developing relevant policy frameworks, and by providing right infrastructure and data. In this chapter, we will look into LLMOp concepts, frameworks, and tools that an enterprise can leverage to scale LLM initiatives.

Structure

In this chapter, we will go through the following topics:

- Introduction to LLMOps
- LLMOps Phase 1
- LLMOps Phase 2
- Large language model security
- Monitoring and feedback
- Hugging Face

Objectives

The objective of this chapter is to go through complete LLM system lifecycle, starting from data preparation to model deployment. The operationalization of LLM models is complex and requires many components to coordinate for successful operation. This chapter aims to explain the concepts of LLMOps, including various optimization techniques to improve the performance and efficiency of the LLM system as a whole. The content includes end-to-end process related to data preparation, pre-training, benchmarking, experimentation, serving, validation, and monitoring.

Introduction to LLMOps

LLMOps are standardized set of practices that enterprises follow to build, deploy, manage and monitor LLM based applications. It helps to maximize the value of LLM projects by improving the model efficiency, reducing deployment risks, optimizing resource utilization, facilitating collaboration and quicken scalable rollouts. Very few enterprises involve in entire LLM lifecycle of building foundation models and then serving it for real-world inference. The entire process is complex and costly as it involves a large data engineering process, a huge training environment, and a niche skill set. So, LLMOps process for entire LLM lifecycle can be logically categorized in two phases LLMOps Phase 1 for building models and LLMOps Phase 2 for serving models as shown in the below *Figure 8.1* and *Figure 8.2*. *Figure 8.1* shows the detailed process of LLMOps Phase 1, which involves strategy building, data preparation, and training:

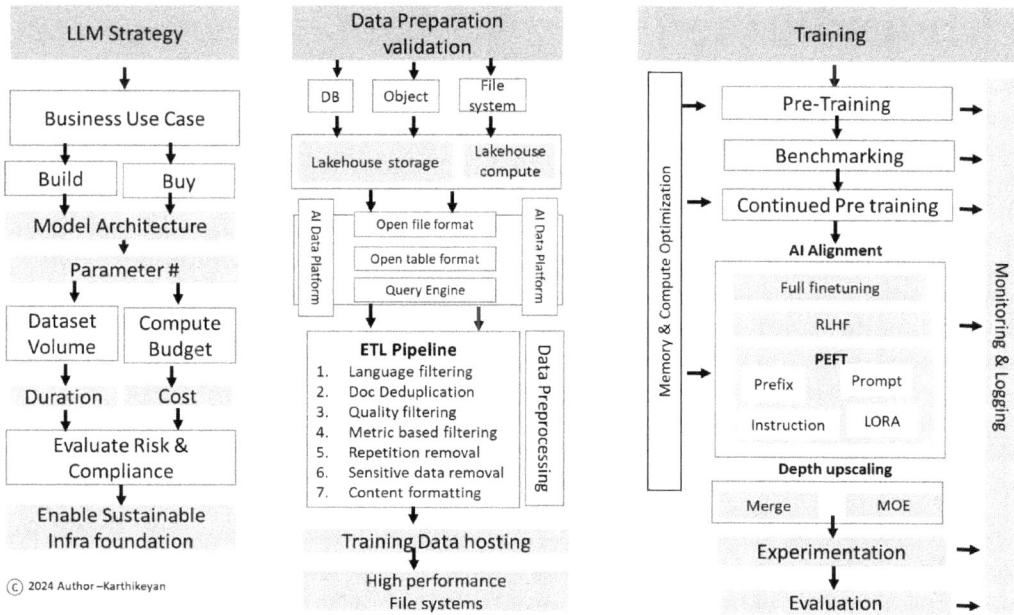

Figure 8.1: *LLMOps Phase 1 data preprocessing and building LLM model*

Due to the complexity and cost involved in building large LLMs, most the enterprises leverage open-source or proprietary model APIs for their business use cases. So, most of enterprises directly adopt LLMOps Phase 2 process, which involves model serving, LLM security and monitoring as shown in below *Figure 8.2*:

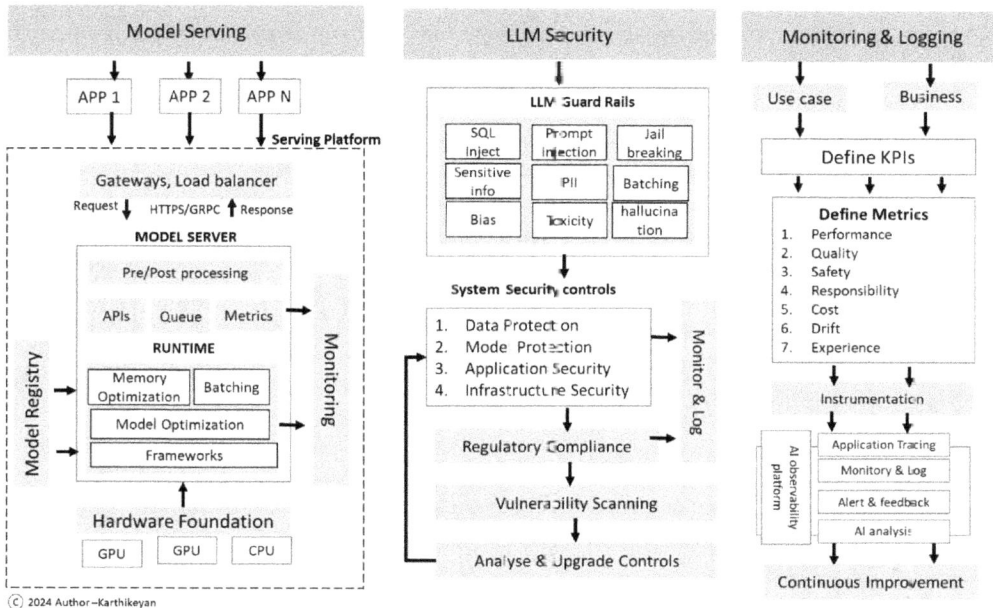

Figure 8.2: *LLMOps Phase 2 serving and managing LLM models*

LLMOps Phase 1

While many enterprises leverage pre-built foundation models for their business use cases, few organizations that are data hoarders for specific domains want to build their own foundation models as a competitive advantage. Some of the examples are BloombergGPT a 50B purpose-built foundation model trained on financial data, and Salesforce Moirai, a time series foundation model for zero-shot timeseries forecasting. So, building foundation models from scratch involves various LLMOps Phase 1 process, as show in above *Figure 8.1*. In this section, we will look into the details of few processes like data preparation, validation, model training, training optimization techniques, benchmarking and AI alignment methods.

Data preparation

Data is the lifeline for any AI project. When it comes to generative AI projects, models are trained on massive amounts of data gathered from different sources in different forms. Sources of data vary from files, online databases, object storage, data warehouses, and data streams. The forms of data could be structured, unstructured, or semi-structured data. The performance of any LLM model is directly correlated to the quality and diversity of the input data on which it is trained. Data sourcing, data preprocessing, and data preparation are vital to any LLM operations pipeline.

Data management for ML projects is generally handled through **extract, transform, and load** (**ETL**) pipelines. ETL processes involve extracting different forms of data from various sources as full or incremental or source-driven extraction, then transforming it by cleaning, normalizing, changing structure, and then loading it into storage targets (DBs/ObjectStorage/CloudStorage/high-performance file systems). These storage targets for LLMs often rely on all-flash storage (**non-volatile memory express** (**NVMe**) as underlying storage architecture to deliver high I/O throughput, i.e., faster reads and writes in low latency demand. LLM training data are generally unstructured and massive in volume (Tera/Peta bytes), and data sources are distributed geographically. So, data strategy shall be the initial step for any LLMOps pipeline. It involves decisions on the volume of data (training data size, model size, and compute budget), the need for specialized techniques (tokenization, vector embeddings deduplication, stop word removals), preprocessing requirements for training, finetuning and inferencing (prompt formats aligned to LLM model architecture), the choice of tools and technique with parallel data processing capabilities and scalable inferencing server requirements.

Data management for LLMs involved:

- Data management for training LLM (Building foundation models).
- Data management for fine-tuning, model alignment, or inferencing (ETL-based approach).

As shown in *Figure 8.3* below, data management for training foundation models involves extraction, quality filtering, repetitive document removal, privacy reduction, and tokenization. It also includes other essential LLMOps practices, such as versioning, lineage, and metadata management:

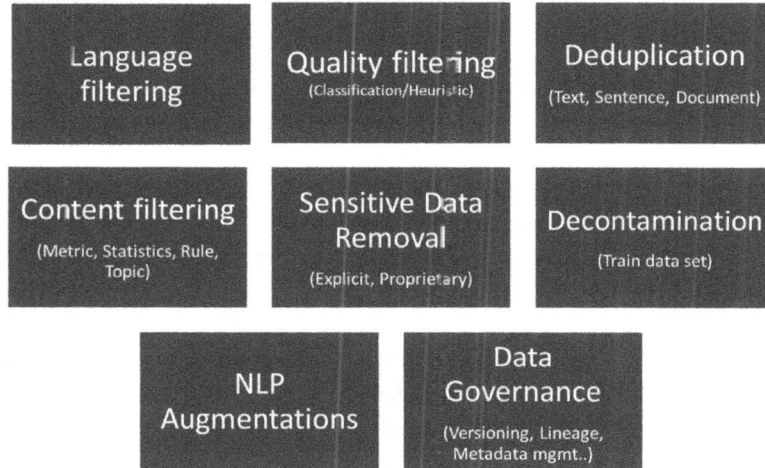

Figure 8.3: Data preparation and validation

LLM training involves massive raw data collection across regions from both offline and online sources. So, data extraction systems for training LLM need to provide efficient aggregation, multi-protocol interworking, and on-demand capacity expansion to accelerate data collection and reduce idle time for subsequent analytics. In enterprises, data from different sources are aggregated into a centralized location, such as data warehouse (hierarchical), data lakes (flat architecture), data lakehouses (hybrid), and data fabrics (distributed data architecture). Data lakehouses and data fabrics are the way forward for data-driven enterprises in data management. These centralized repositories, along with a data catalog (organized inventory of data assets), are often leveraged for data extraction in LLM training.

The format of data storage and data analytical engine plays a critical role in a preprocessing step. The popular formats supported for modern data analytics architecture are open file formats such as Avro, Parquet, **Optimized Row Column** (**ORC**), and open table formats such as Delta Lake, Hudi, and Iceberg. These formats allow enterprises to store large amount of structured, semi-structured, and unstructured data from different sources in a standardized format that can be queried faster and efficiently managed. While **open table format** brings database like features such as ACID conformance, metadata management, time travel, into lakehouses, **open file format** ensures data within the object are written for efficient storage (compression), process and retrieval. Open file format impacts the query performance and effectiveness of enterprise analytics. TrinoDB, PrestoDB, AWS Athena, and StarBurst are popular analytical query engines leveraged on top of these file formats for faster and more efficient data preprocessing.

Language filtering helps separate documents into a set of languages. When it comes to enterprises, this filtering helps to separate documents such as instruction cheat sheets, social review, legal and financial documents, and global regulations within the target languages. Language identification models, such as fasttText, Google **compact language detector v3** (**CLD3**) and NLP based libraries such as **saspaCy**, **Polyglot** are employed to do language filtering.

Quality filtering of data can be automatically done using classifier-based and heuristic-based approaches. Classifier-based approaches train a binary skip-gram classifier to identify and filter out low-quality data. Using the original high-quality documents such as WEBTEXT as a proxy, a classifier is trained to distinguish raw source data. High quality documents are used as positive instance and candidate data is used as negative instance for the classifier. However, classifier-based approaches have disadvantages related to accuracy which leads to bias and decrease in corpus diversity. The other heuristic based approaches by cascading heuristic filters such as Cuckoo filters, employ well-designed rules to eliminate low-quality texts. The rules are generally coined as documents with inadequate word count or mean word length, excessive symbol usage, or a high proportion of bullet points or ellipsis usage or documents with improperly decoded Unicode

Document deduplication is another method to improve the quality of data. Deduplication method involves exact deduplication followed by fuzzy deduplication. The exact method calculates the hashes of the documents (MD5), and documents with the same hashes are removed. Fuzzy deduplication (i.e. removal of documents that are near-duplicate) method relies on **locality sensitive hashing** (**LSH**) and **min-wise hashing** (**MNH**). **minhash** is a hash function that computes the lowest hash value for a set of objects to be hashes. **minhash** gives a fixed length representation of each document such that the probability of a hash collision is equal to the Jaccard similarity of any pair. The idea behind locality sensitive hashing is to take the document fingerprints and chop them up into pieces, each piece being some number of minhashes. Since a single minhash (single entry in the fingerprint) has a probability equal to the Jaccard similarity of producing a collision, each chopped up portion of the fingerprint should as well. This chopped up portion is the locality in locality sensitive hashing, the hashing is just a hash function (any hash function) which produces a bin ID from the fingerprint locality being hashed. Each bin holds the entire fingerprint (with optional meta information) of the document and that of other documents that hash to the same bin. When we want to know which documents are similar to a query document, we look in all the bins the query document lands in, any document in any of the bins is a potential duplicate. It removes documents with high overlaps.

Metric based filtering is another common method to ensure content quality. Popular evaluation metric that is used in filtering training data is perplexity to detect unnatural sentences and the other is coherence score for topic filtering. While a high coherence score represents the consistency and relevance of topics, high perplexity score represents the confidence and accuracy of predictions. Some of the tools and NLP libraries for doing metric based filtering, topic based filtering and document clustering are **Pydata**, **TextCL**, **Gensim**, **KenLM**.

Statistics based content filtering and other text cleaning techniques are used to remove the boilerplate text, html tags, menu text, stop words. Some of the libraries used are `justext`, `html2text`, `trafilatura`.

Text repetition removal is similar to document deduplication but operates at sequence level instead of document. The popular method adopted for text repletion removal is an exact substring deduplication using a suffix array. It helps to find matches between strings that are exact token-by-token matches by using suffix arrays. A suffix array will contain integers that represent the starting indexes of all the suffixes of a given string after the aforementioned suffixes are sorted. Any match above n consecutive tokens after building suffix array is removed. One of the popular libraries for text repetition removal is **deduplicate-text-datasets** from *Google Research*.

Sensitive data removal is another critical component of data quality process. . In certain cases, especially when image content is extracted through web, tools like *Google SafeSearchDetection* is used to filter out the explicit content. We will covering this in detail in *Guardrails* section.

Test set overlap removal is often referred to as decontamination. Contamination happens when a pre-training dataset has data pertaining to benchmark test set that will be used for evaluating the performance. Decontamination is generally done by finding n-gram overlaps between text in train and test set, then removing x-characters before and after the matched texts. Some of the popular libraries for decontamination are LLM decontaminator, language model evaluation harness.

In certain cases, **NLP needs augmentations**. It involves random deletion, insertions, shuffling, back translation, synonym replacement, text repetition removal, excluding custom words. The other consideration is filtering data is to look out for machine generated data. **Machine generated text (MGT)** detection helps to identify whether a particular content was generated by AI models like GPT or human written. This involves the detection of watermark embeddings, linguistic pattern matching, measuring statistic disparities, and train classifiers for MGT. Some of the methods for MGT detection is the use of models like Detect GPT (zero-shot machine generated text detection), use of BERT based model trained for statistical measures to differentiate between human vs. machine text, use of classifier-based approach by training models on supervised text with human and machine generated as labels, novel techniques like Raidar (*geneRative AI Detection viA rewriting*) which uses LLM to rewrite the text and check for modification between original and rewritten text for MGT identification. So. such meticulous data preprocessing is a critical and plays a vital role in shaping the performance and behavior of LLM models.

Model training and fine-tuning

There are different approaches to build LLM models as shown in the *Figure 8.4* below. Pre-training is the way to build LLM foundation models from scratch that bring general LLM capabilities to drive multiple use cases. Continued pre-training and fine-tuning are alignment techniques to make pre-trained foundation models suitable for specific tasks. The other methods **Parameter efficient fine-tuning (PEFT)**, **Reinforcement Learning from Human Feedback (RLHF)**, Full fine-tuning are different approaches for AI alignment:

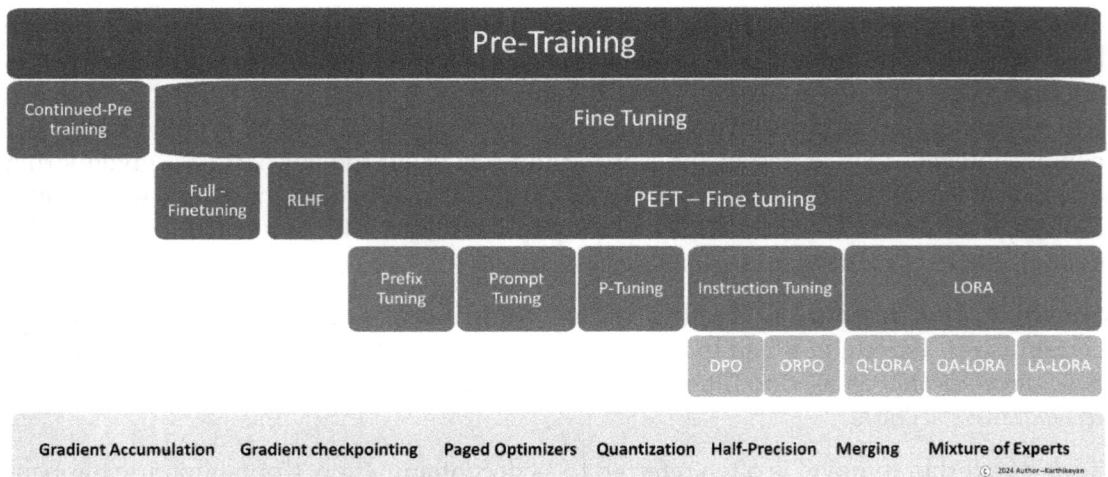

Figure 8.4: *LLM training methods and alignment techniques*

Pre-training

Building a foundation model from scratch is a complex task. As shown in *Figure 8.5* below, It requires huge compute, large volume of data and expertise. Most of the enterprises leverage transfer learning and fine-tuning techniques to align pre-trained foundation models for their domain specific tasks. However, certain scenarios involve enterprises to build their own foundation models. A few reasons for enterprises to build their own foundation models are:

- To have full control over the data, the model is trained on
- To achieve high-performance on unique domain specific tasks
- To perform research on different architectures/techniques
- To create a new business on model as a service
- For regulatory compliance. Foundation models are trained in self-supervised learning, and it is unique due to their adaptability to perform a wide range of tasks with high degree of accuracy

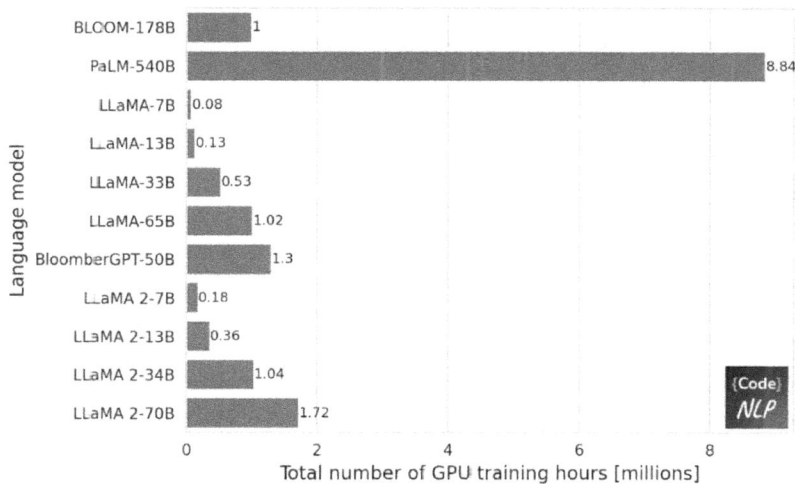

Figure 8.5: GPU Training hours comparison for different models

Though pre-training of LLMs is theoretically similar to the training of deep learning models, LLM training involves a massive volume of data (Peta bytes), large infrastructure (1000's of *NVIDIA H100 GPU*) landscape and large storage, high speed network for updating billions of parameters. It requires a different strategy. In this section, we will look into the components like data formats, data quality evaluation, synthetic data generation, memory optimization techniques, parallel computation methods, performance benchmarking, and evaluation metrics that differ from traditional deep learning model build.

Data formats for generative AI training

One of the important considerations during foundation model training is the data format. The training data must be processed in a format that supports high compressibility, fast random access, and enable data shuffling. Common data formats like CSV, JSON are not preferrable for foundation model training. Formats like Parquet and **Mosaic Data Shard (MDS)** are preferably used for their support for fast data processing and for their efficiency related to data storage and retrieval. MDS is a data format specifically designed for efficient training of generative AI models. It is specially designed for multi-node, distributed training for large models—maximizing correctness guarantees, performance, and ease of use.

Data quality evaluation

It is a complex task as it involves large volume of data validation. Some of the techniques are to use small LLM model trained on subset of dataset and use high signal quality benchmark like **Multitask Multidomain Language Understanding (MMLU)**, HellaSwag for valuation. This small ablation models helps to make choice of filters and filter out quality data before going for full-fledge pre-training. The other techniques to validate the quality of dataset involves variance checking, manual data inspection for domain related errors, text clustering techniques for anomalies, training a tokenizer and inspect top/last/long tokens. Popular open-source tools that can be leveraged for data preparation and quality validation are *Nvidia NeMo Data Curator* and *Hugging Face datatrove*.

Synthetic data generation

Synthetic data is artificially generated data that mimics real-world data characteristics. These data are generated using various statistical methods or algorithms or using LLM models. Approaches vary based on the number of samples required, i.e., from thousands to millions of samples for instruction tuning to full pre-training. These synthetic data help in crafting a mix of training corpus with real-world and with data that represent patterns and structures of real-world. Popular synthetic dataset example is Cosmopedia with 25 million tokens generated by using synthetic book texts, blogs, stories using Mixtral-8x7B-Instruct-v0.1. The purpose of synthetic data is to provide right mix in training corpus where the access to sensitive data is limited, curation of domain specific data set is constrained, and unable to leverage data due to privacy concerns and legal restrictions. Synthetic data at scale can be generated using LLM for synthetic text by using diverse prompts that cover a wide range of topics. Techniques like differential privacy and prompt augmentation with synthetic data ensure the model's tuning is both privacy-conscious and adapted to specialized scenarios. Some of the core indicators that are used to evaluate the quality of synthetic data are filed correlation stability using correlation analysis, deep structure stability using PCA analysis, and field distribution stability using Jensen-Shannon distance.

Memory optimization

One of the most common issues during large model training is GPUs running out of memory. Memory requirements depend on number of factors such as model weights, optimizer, gradient, activations, **key-value (KV)** cache data size and hardware types. Model weights are calculated as 4 bytes per parameter in a full precision FP32 representation. So, for example, to train a billion parameter model one must have 24 GB of memory in full precision FP32 without considering other factors like memory fragmentations, temporary buffers to store intermediate results occupy sufficient memory during training process. So, memory optimization is very critical for pre-training process and some of the techniques are mixed precision training, activation checkpointing and gradient accumulation.

Mixed precision training is an optimization technique that combines different numerical formats, i.e., half precision FP16 and single precision FP32, during training. Floating point operations in float16 are faster than in float32 for GPUs, and similarly, bfloat16 is faster than float32 in CPUs. Half precision reduces memory consumption, reduces memory bandwidth pressure and speeds up the computations. Mixed precision involves Porting the model to use the half precision data type and adding loss scaling to preserve small gradient values. Porting the model in FP16 reduces memory footprint and during the training process, both forward and backward processing (i.e., gradient calculations) happen in half precision leading to faster computations. To maintain numerical stability, and to avoid numerical underflow, vanishing gradient loss scaling is performed. Loss scaling involves loss values get scaled before starting the backpropagation computations of loss gradients and downscaling the weight gradients before the weight update begins, in order to maintain the magnitude of update. The loss scaling helps to preserve small gradients. This technique of using both single and half precision representations is referred to as mixed precision technique. Some of the considerations with this technique are loss of accuracy due to half precision, need for hardware support for mixed precision, and implementation complexity for loss scaling.

Activation checkpointing or gradient checkpointing is another optimization technique used during training. This involves a tradeoff between memory and computation. This technique reduces the activations memory by introducing checkpoint layers at specific points in the deep neural network and store intermediate activations only at these checkpoints. So these clear activations of certain layers, i.e., square root of total activations, and recomputing them during backward pass, i.e., about 33% recalculations.

Another technique is **gradient accumulation** during LLM training, generally gradients of model parameters are calculated and updated for every batch of data. However, in gradient accumulation, gradients accumulate over multiple mini-batches before updating the model's weights. This allows for a more memory-efficient training process by reducing the memory requirements for storing gradients. Some of the considerations are that gradient accumulation can lead to slower convergence and longer training times.

Parallel computation methods

In the first chapter *AI Fundamentals,* we have seen data parallelism as a parallel computing technique which has been widely adopted during pre-training process. In data parallelism, each node independently processes a subset of data using it is own replica of model. Gradients are synchronized using gradient aggregation to update the global model parameters. Some of the advanced technique like **Fully Sharded Data Parallel (FSDP)**, Ring-AllReduce methods are adopted for enhancing the efficiency of distributed data parallelism.

The other technique is **tensor parallelism**. LLMs are deep neural networks with multiple layers with each operating on tensors. Tensor parallelism involves splitting within each layer and parameters, and the computation of the model is sliced across devices. This helps in reducing the memory load on each device which addresses the challenge of memory capacity for training foundation models. While tensor parallelism enables intra layer model parallelism where the computation of each layer happens in different devices, pipeline parallelism divide the model at boundary of layers. In pipeline parallelism, the model is divided at the model layer boundary, so the model is split into several stages, and each part is assigned to the independent device. It is sequential, as the output of one part is fed as input to the other part. The major disadvantage is underutilization of compute as only one device is active at a point of time. It also involves communication overhead due to distribution of model layers across devices. However, the utilization can be improved through micro-batching and execution of these micro batches across devices in parallel.

Thus, data parallelism, tensor parallelism, and pipeline parallelism can be combined to achieve 3D parallelism for training LLMs, as shown in the below figure. Where the model is split using the pipeline parallelism followed by each part of the pipeline is split using tensor parallelism. Finally, the pipeline parts are replicated across each node to achieve data parallelism. Please find the below *Figure 8.6* for 3D parallelism illustration:

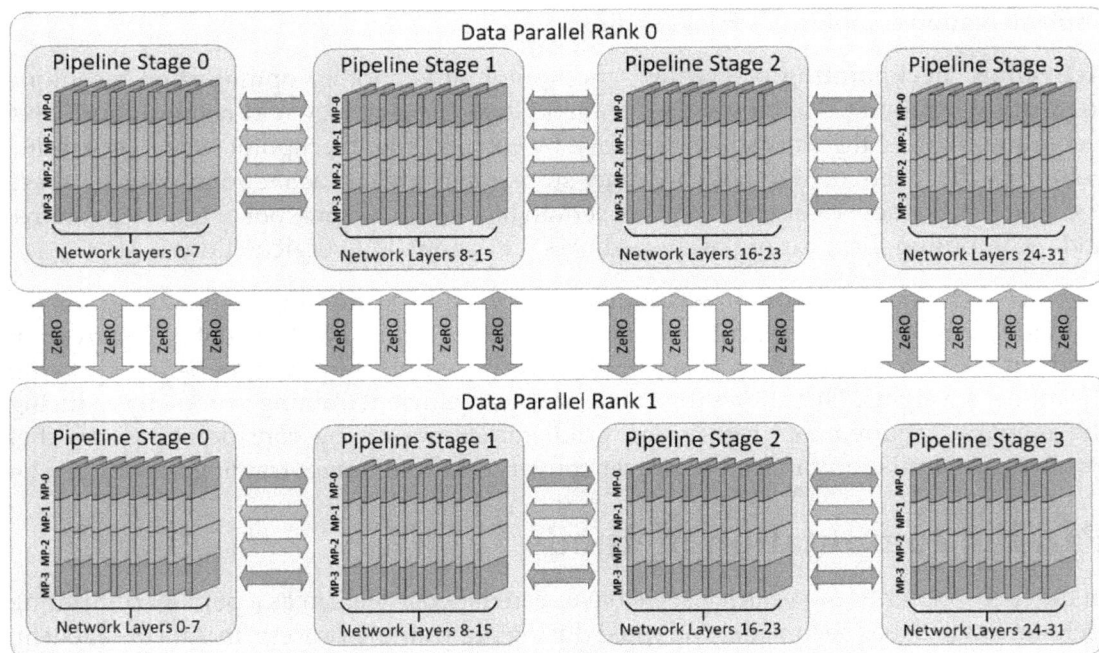

Figure 8.6: *3D parallelism illustration*
Source: *https://www.deepspeed.ai/tutorials/pipeline/*

Performance benchmarking

Once the model has been trained, benchmarking the model for tasks is critical to assess the performance. Benchmarking helps to evaluate the performance of the model for the trained tasks, enables comparison with different LLMs, standardizes assessments of model performance, and helps to measure the effectiveness of training methods over time. Model is benchmarked for its capabilities related to question answering, logical reasoning, common sense, language understanding, code interpretation and generation, math solving, chatbot conversations, etc. As shown in the figure below, the benchmarking process involves choosing reference datasets, running evaluations, metrics analysis, and performance scoring. Generally, benchmark scores are made available as leaderboards for different models against different datasets and compared for their performance between 0 to 100. One of the main considerations while performing benchmarking is benchmark leakage, which refers to instances where an LLM is trained on the same data contained in benchmark datasets. As a result, the model might have learned to do the benchmark tasks, resulting in higher scores:

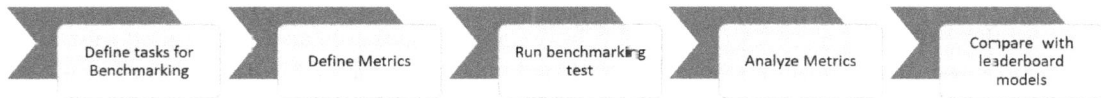

Figure 8.7: LLM benchmarking process

Evaluation metrics

Some of the prominent evaluation metrics are **Bilingual Evaluation Understudy** (**BLEU**), **Recall-Oriented Understudy for Gisting Evaluation** (**ROUGE**), **Bidirectional Encoder Representations from Transformers** (**BERT**), **Metric for Evaluation of Translation with Explicit Ordering** (**METEOR**), MoveScore and Perplexity. Each metric has its own limitation, so these metrics must be used in conjunction with each other for a comprehensive assessment.

- **BLEU**: It calculates the overlap of n-grams between the model output and reference text. It has limitations related to semantic and context relevance evaluation. A higher BLEU score (0-1) is better. It is often used for evaluating machine translation tasks.

- **BERTScore**: It is an improvement to BLEUScore, and it is a task independent evaluation metric. It leverages pre-trained contextual embeddings from BERT and looks at the semantic similarity between candidate and reference sentences using cosine scores. A higher BERTScore (0-1) is preferable.

- **ROUGE**: It measures overlap of n-grams between generated text and reference text. The variants are ROUGE-N, ROUGE-L, and ROUGE-S. ROUGE-N measures n-grams overlap, ROUGE-L measures **longest common subsequence** (**LCS**) and ROUGE-S measures overlap of skip-gram. Metric is generally used for text summarization. Higher the score (0-1) the performance is better.

- **METEOR**: It measures the alignment between candidate and reference text. The metric is based on the harmonic mean of unigram precision and recall, with recall weighted higher than precision. Higher score (0-1) is preferrable, generally used for machine translation tasks.

- **MoverScore**: Measures semantic similarity between two sentences. **Earth Mover's Distance** (**EMD**) is leveraged to compute the semantic distance i.e. minimum distance that words in candidate sentence has to move to reach distribution of the words in the reference sentence with distance adjusted based on the importance of words. It is used in evaluating a variety of tasks. A higher score is preferrable.

- **Perplexity**: It measures the confidence of the model in its prediction. While it helps to measure the fluency and coherence, it does not guarantee the accuracy. Lower the score the performance is better.

The other general deep learning metrics, like the ones we have seen earlier, are exact match, precision, recall, and F1 score. Exact match measures the percentage of predictions exactly match reference answer. Precision measures the fraction of correctly predicted phrases to the total predicted phrases. Recall measures the correctly predicted phrases over total number of correct phrases. While precision measures accuracy, recall measures the completeness of the response. The other one is F1 score, which measures the harmonic mean of precision and recall for more balanced evaluations. Higher these scores better the model.

Beyond the above automated evaluation, human-in-the-loop for evaluation is essential. It is essential for trained models to be evaluated and rated by humans on various aspects such as coherence, relevance, and fluency.

Benchmarking dataset

Some of the benchmarking datasets to evaluate LLM models are the following:

- **AI2 Reasoning Challenge (ARC)** for benchmarking advanced question-answering tasks. It consists of 7,787 grade-school science questions segregated into challenge set and easy set.

- **HellaSwag** for benchmarking commonsense reasoning tasks. It has approximate 70k MCQ questions constructed from ActivityNet Captions and WikiHow articles.

- **MMLU** for benchmarking knowledge across diverse subjects. It includes data related to 57 diverse academics and professional domains.

- **TruthfulQA** for benchmarking the truthfulness of language models in generating answers to diverse questions. It includes 817 questions covering 38 categories and targets with imitative falsehoods.

- **WinoGrande** for benchmarking LLM's commonsense reasoning abilities. It consists of dataset with 44,000 questions that challenges models to solve the **Winograd Schema Challenge (WSC)**.

- **Grade school math 8K (GSM8K)** for benchmarking multi-step mathematical reasoning abilities. It consists of 8,500 grade school level math word problems devised by humans.

- **General Language Understanding Evaluation (GLUE)** for benchmarking natural language understanding capabilities. SuperGLUE improves on GLUE consisting of 8 language understanding tasks.

- **HumanEval** for benchmarking code-generation abilities. It consists of 164 unique programming tasks designed with a function sig- nature, docstring, body, and several unit tests.

The other notable benchmarking method is to use LLM-as-a-judge. It uses larger LLM models like GPT-4 to evaluate the LLM responses. Some of the popular benchmarks that use LLM as reference to evaluate are **Multi-turn (MT)** bench, AlpacEval2, **Fine-grained**

Language Model Evaluation based on Alignment Skill Sets (FLASK) and G-Eval is a recently developed framework that uses LLMs with a chain of thoughts evaluate LLM outputs.

Leaderboard

It gives a unified view of different LLM model's performance against varied tasks. It helps to have a fair comparison of the model's strengths and weaknesses using standardized benchmark datasets given above. Some of the popular LLM dashboards are Hugging Face, LMSYS Chatbot Arena, Trustbit LLM benchmark, EQ-Bench, OpenCompass, AlpacaEval and many more. One of the critical considerations in referring LLM leaderboard is their rating system. For example, LMSYS leaderboard uses Elo rating system (rating based on LLM performance against other powerful models) and Bradley-Terry model (rating based on how model handle tougher tasks). The other considerations are reported metrics, recency of reporting, type of tasks, task level scores and number of evaluated models. The following figure shows sample a view of EQ-Bench LLM leaderboard:

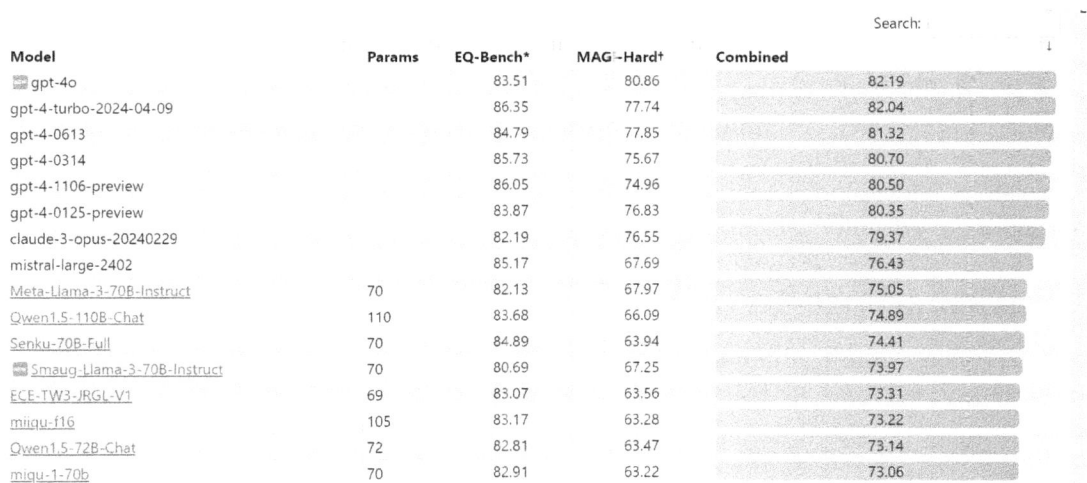

Model	Params	EQ-Bench*	MAG-Hard†	Combined
gpt-4o		83.51	80.86	82.19
gpt-4-turbo-2024-04-09		86.35	77.74	82.04
gpt-4-0613		84.79	77.85	81.32
gpt-4-0314		85.73	75.67	80.70
gpt-4-1106-preview		86.05	74.96	80.50
gpt-4-0125-preview		83.87	76.83	80.35
claude-3-opus-20240229		82.19	76.55	79.37
mistral-large-2402		85.17	67.69	76.43
Meta-Llama-3-70B-Instruct	70	82.13	67.97	75.05
Qwen1.5-110B-Chat	110	83.68	66.09	74.89
Senku-70B-Full	70	84.89	63.94	74.41
Smaug-Llama-3-70B-Instruct	70	80.69	67.25	73.97
ECE-TW3-JRGL-V1	69	83.07	63.56	73.31
miqu-f16	105	83.17	63.28	73.22
Qwen1.5-72B-Chat	72	82.81	63.47	73.14
miqu-1-70b	70	82.91	63.22	73.06

Figure 8.8: EQ-Bench LLM leaderboard view

LLM benchmarking tools and libraries

Some of the popular LLM benchmarking tools are Deep Eval and LLM-Perf:

- **Deep Eval**: It is an open-source framework which helps to benchmark custom LLMs on 7 popular benchmark datasets such as Big-Bench Hard, HelloSwag, MMLU, GSM8K , HumanEval, TruthfulQA and DROP. It also provides tools for evaluating LLM models across various metrics

- **LLM-Perf**: an open-source tool designed to bring reproducibility and clarity to the world of LLM performance benchmark. LLMperf can evaluate performance on various hardware configurations and with different deep learning frameworks.

Some of the key metrics they measure are **Time to first token (TTFT), Inter-token latency (ITL)**, End-to-end latency, and completed requests per minute

LangChain Benchmark and LlamaIndex benchmark evaluators are other popular LLM libraries to do benchmarking of models. The other tools are LLM canary an open-source security benchmark tool to detect top OWASP LLM vulnerabilities and address risks related to privacy. Plexi glass a CLI tool for benchmarking security, bias and toxicity. It uses adversarial prompts scrapped from open-source datasets to run LLM-scan for assessing the vulnerabilities.

So far, we have discussed on pre-training process where the foundation model is built from scratch on massive data to bring generalized capabilities. In the next section, we will look into alignment techniques to make pre-trained foundation models suited for specific tasks and real-world business use cases.

AI alignment

AI alignment is a method where AI systems are aligned to human values and made safe, helpful, and reliable. AI alignment is more than just model fine-tuning. It involves a broader spectrum of processes and techniques that govern AI systems to align with human values, ethics, safety, and robustness. In this section, we will only look into continued pre-training, model fine-tuning, and its enhancements with alignment algorithms. This helps generalized LLM models to perform target tasks better, complying with enterprise policies and aligned with human values.

Continued pre-training

It is the process of re-training the foundation model in a similar unsupervised way the base model has been trained. This method, although common, proves to be quite expensive. Continued pre-training happens on new data from existing base checkpoints. The dataset contains domain specific knowledge and is used to continue the pre-training by updating the foundation model parameters. Re-warming and re-decaying the learning rate play a crucial role in the continued pre-training process, i.e., starting the training process with a low learning rate and linearly increases it for a set number of steps to a maximum value and slowly decreasing it over time. This approach helps in faster convergence and better performance. The other optional thing is to include a small amount of original data in the new data set during the continued pre-training process. When a new dataset becomes available, it is merged with existing datasets to create a weighted composition, and models are trained from scratch on this new dataset. It helps the model to learn new knowledge without having much risk related to catastrophic forgetting.

Fine-tuning

Fine-tuning is a process of adjusting the weights of large pre-trained LLM models to suit domain specific tasks by exposing a few examples. It helps to customize the large model to suit a particular use case, help to learn new tasks, steers the model to generate consistent output, and helps to correct the misinformation generated by the model. Some of the LLM fine-tuning methods are full fine-tuning, instruction tuning, RLFH fine-tuning, contrastive fine-tuning techniques like **Direct Preference Optimization (DPO)** and **odds ratio policy optimization** (**ORPO**). We will understand the instruction, RLHF based finetuning, DPO, ORPO in this section. We will see the in-context learning in the upcoming prompt-engineering chapter.

Full fine-tuning

It is similar to continued pre-training, where all parameters of the model are updated using supervised label tasks. It is majorly used in scenarios where the availability of supervised data is larger and high accuracy is required to make the model suitable for adapting to complex tasks. However, full fine-tuning increases cost as it is resource intensive and has the risk of catastrophic forgetting. A new iteration of the base LLM for every task it gets fine-tuned, each being the same size as the original, will rapidly increase storage requirement.

Reinforcement Learning from Human Feedback

RLHF, optimizes the base model with human preferences. It involves training of separate reward model based on human preferences and uses the reward function to optimize the policy through reinforcement learning. For example, LLM responses are rated by human regarding the quality of response. These ratings will be used to build a reward model, then LLM uses the reward model to estimate the prompt response and choose the response that is most likely to result in greater reward. It depends on **proximal policy optimization** (**PPO**) and reward model. Major drawback with RLSH is its reliance on human-generated feedback, which has scalability and resource limitations. The other popular variant of RLHF is **Reinforcement Learning from AI Feedback** (**RLAIF**), which integrates feedback from another LLMs for feedback into the reinforcement learning process.

Parameter efficient fine-tuning

It is an efficient way of adapting large LLM models for domain or task specific activities without training full model. PEFT updates only a small set of base model parameters. There are various PEFT techniques such as Adapter, **low-rank adaptation** (**LoRA**), QLoRA ,QALoRA, ReLoRA , prefix tuning, prompt tuning, P-tuning and IA3. In this section, we will look into few of the techniques.

Prefix tuning

Prefix tuning adapts pre-trained language models to specific tasks by adding task specific continuous prefix vector to the input. These vectors are added as additional input (virtual tokens) at the beginning of the input sequence of each transformer block. Only the prefix parameters are optimized and added to the hidden states in every layer of the model The key idea behind prefix tuning is that by adding task-specific soft prompts to each transformer block, the model can learn to condition its behavior based on the prompts. In an encoder-decoder model, prefix is added to both the encoder and decoder.

Training of prefix matrix involves a supervised dataset of input-output pairs i.e. context-response pair that reflects the target tasks. During training, only the prefix matrix is updated keeping the base model weights frozen. By training the prefix matrix while keeping the pre-trained model's parameters frozen, prefix matrix gets adapted to the target tasks while leveraging the general language understanding captured by the pre-trained model. The major benefit of prefix tuning is it allows training of independent task and only fewer parameter get updated compared to full fine-tuning.

P-tuning

It is a parameter efficient tuning technique, where model is trained to learn soft prompts through backpropagation. It involves a small trainable encoder model which helps to encode the text prompt and generate task-specific virtual tokens. These tokens along with input prompt is passed through frozen LLM model and small encoder is trained on labelled examples to generate task specific token representations. It allows a single LLM models for multiple tasks by learning task specific prompts. These task-specific virtual tokens are used to look up during the inferencing process. The major benefit is it requires a smaller number of parameters to be tuned, avoidance of prompt engineering, unlike prefix tuning soft prompts are prepended only a input layer and enable efficient prompt ensembles.

Instruction tuning

It is a type of fine-tuning method, which uses a pair of instructions and their outputs to fine-tune the model. Process of instruction tuning involves the creation of labelled instruction dataset, choosing pre-trained base model, and fine-tuning method PEFT. Creation of labelled instruction dataset can be done from either existing annotated natural language datasets or human labelled data set or transforming text-label pairs into instruction-output pairs using templates. Some of the datasets available to train instruction-following LLMs are Alpaca, OpenOrca, self-instruct, GPT-4 Instruct, Dolly, RolePlay, Synthetic, OpenInstructV1, NauralInstructions, OpenPlatypus.

Self-instruct is a semi-automated way of creating instruction tuning dataset. The self-instruct method helps to reduce the dependency on human annotators. It leverages a few manually created instruction sets to generate more broad-coverage instructions which is then used to supervise fine-tuning. One example is Alpaca (Reference: **https://crfm. stanford.edu/2023/03/13/alpaca.html**) is a self-instruct dataset created by *Stanford*. Alpaca is licensed for research and non-commercial use. Alpaca used seed instructions and instances (175-Pairs of human generated Instruction and output) to make LLM to generate new instructions and instances in a bootstrapped manner. Seeds are used as in-context examples to generate new samples. These generated samples are then used to align the LLMs to follow the instructions better.

Preference tuning with DPO technique is another popular finetuning method that matches the performance equivalent to RLHF. DPO helps to align LLMs with human preferences in a simpler way and considered as a suitable alternative for RLHF or RLAI methods. Two stages of DPO are **supervised fine-tuning (SFT)** and preference learning. **SFT** involves a pre-trained language model is fine-tuned on high-quality dataset specific to particular task. After SFT, model undergoes preference learning on DPO dataset that contains:

{Prompt = Original Prompt, Chosen response = rephrased response, Reject response = Original response}

Some of the DOP datasets available are *OpenAI WebGPT comparisons, OpenAI summarizations,* and *RedditELI5.*

Some of the popular small LLM model that use DPO are SOLAR 10.7B model. It is created by merging of 2 7B Llama model. It uses depth up scaling where m layers are removed from the base and copy model; then these 2 tared models are concatenated to build final model. The final model undergoes continual pre-training, instruction tuning and alignment tuning with DPO technique to improve the performance.

ORPO is another preference optimization technique without need of SFT model to align to human preferences. In ORPO, Pre-trained model jointly does learn instructions and get aligned to human preferences. The standard language modeling objective is combined the **odds ratio (OR)** loss term. OR penalizes the rejected responses and strongly reward the preferred ones making the model to learn the target task and human preferences simultaneously. ORPO requires a preference dataset similar to DPO, including a prompt, a chosen answer, and a rejected answer. ORPO is computationally more efficient than RLHF and DPO in memory allocation and fewer FLOPS/batch.

Low-rank adaptation

LoRA makes fine-tuning more efficient by drastically reducing the number of trainable parameters. Instead of updating all weights during training, only rank matrices are made trainable. The rank of matrix is defined as the number of linearly independent columns in weight or parameter matrix. So, decomposing the base model weight matrix into low rank matrices brings efficiency in training by updating only few parameters. Mathematically it can be defined as $W_{lora} = W_{base} + \frac{\alpha}{r} * \Delta W$ where $\Delta W = A$. As shown in *Figure 8.9,* LoRA technique enable multi-LoRA adapters for different task over same base model. The adapter can either be merged with the base model weights or added as new low-rank layers with original layers.

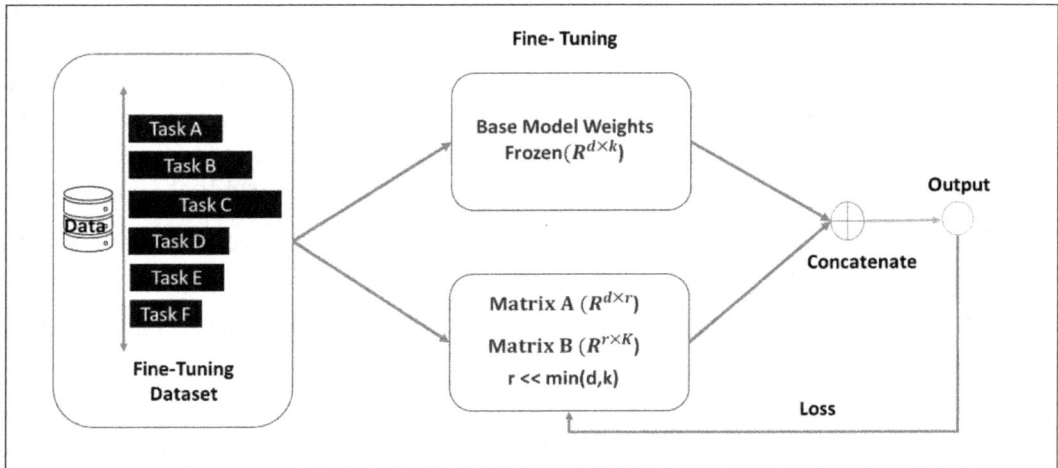

Figure 8.9: LoRA Technique updating of rank matrices during training

The advantage of integrating LoRA into layers gives the flexibility to activate or deactivate task adapters based on the use case scenarios. LoRA can be used along with other PEFT techniques and adding LoRA layers does not affect inference latency when weights get merged to the base model. Process of fine-tuning using LoRA involves instantiation of base model, configuration creation (LoRA config) where LoRA specific parameters are defined and wrap the base model with the **get_peft_model()** to get a trainable PEFT model and fine-tune the PEFT model.

Merging of model

Beyond fine-tuning, the other novel technique adopted to improve the utilities of LLM model is model merging. It combines task specific models of the same or different architectures to evolve a new unified multi-task LLM model. Model merging is a low compute activity without requiring any additional training or fine-tuning. There are multiple approaches to model merging. Some of the popular approaches are linear merge, **spherical linear interpolation (SLERP)**, task arithmetic, **Trim, Elect Sign and Merge (TIES), drop and REscale (DARE)** and Fraken merging. Mergekit is a open-source tool kit popularly utilized to merge models.

The simplest method of merging model is linear merging, where the weights of the models are merged using the weighted average method. Weight parameter helps to control the influence of the parameters among. Please find the below *Figure 8.10* for the mergekit configuration for linear merging:

```
models:
  - model: karthiksab/model1
    parameters:
      weight: 1.0
  - model: karthiksab/model2
    parameters:
      weight: 0.3
  - model: karthiksab/model3
    parameters:
      weight: 0.5
merge_method: linear
dtype: float16
```

Figure 8.10: Mergekit yaml sample file for linear merging

SLERP technique is only applicable to the pairwise merging of models. SLERP technique treats the model parameters as vector points in hypersphere. Due to this unlike model soup, SLERP preserves the characteristics of the models by maintaining the weights and their curvature in embedding space. Steps in SLERP technique involve normalization of input vectors to unit length followed by dot product between vectors to calculate the angle between them. The interpolated vector for the new model is then derived based on the angle and the interpolation factor, i.e., (**t=0** for base model and **t=1** for alternate model) for weighting and summation. Refer to *Figure 8.11* for the mergekit configuration for SLERP merging:

```
slices:
  - sources:
    - model: karthiksab/mistral-optimized-7B
      layer_range: [0, 32]
    - model: karthiksab/mistralAI-Mistral-7B
      layer_range: [0, 32]
merge_method: slerp
base_model: karthiksab/mistral-merge-optimized-7b
parameters:
  t:
    - filter: self_attn
      value: [0, 0.5, 0.3, 0.7, 1]
    - filter: mlp
      value: [1, 0.5, 0.7, 0.3, 0]
    - value: 0.5
dtype: float16
```

Figure 8.11: Mergekit yaml sample file for SLERP

Task arithmetic uses arithmetical manipulations on task vectors to bring changes to the behavior of the model. Task vector represent the directional shift with in pre-trained model weight space to improve the performance of particular task ($T = \theta_{base} - \theta_{finetuned}$). Task vectors are built by subtracting the pre-trained model weights to the task specific fine-tuned model weights. Task vectors are modified and added or subtracted to steer the model behavior. For example, negating a task vector from the base model decreases the performance of model on the target task. Similarly, averaging the task vectors with direction of largest movement improves the performance of the particular task. This technique is very effective for the merging of models from same ancestors fine-tuned on different tasks. Refer to *Figure 8.12* for yaml config for TASK arithmetic in the mergekit:

```
base_model: karthiksab/OpenHermes-2.5-Mistral-7B
dtype: bfloat16
merge_method: task_arithmetic
slices:
- sources:
  - layer_range: [0, 32]
    model:  karthiksab/OpenHermes-2.5-Mistral-7B
  - layer_range: [0, 32]
    model: model2
    parameters:
      weight: 0.75
  - layer_range: [0, 32]
    model: model3
    parameters:
      weight: 0.25
```

Figure 8.12: Mergekit yaml file for task arithmetic

TIES is an efficient merging technique similar to task arithmetic but addresses the limitation of parameter interference degrading the performance of the model. It eliminates redundant parameters within task specific models by identifying task specific changes happened during finetuning and retaining top-k% of the most significant ones (Trim). Resolves parameter interference by creating a unified sign vector that represents the most dominant direction of change across all models (Elect sign). Finally, it merges the averages of parameter values that align with the unified sign vector. (Disjoint merge). Refer to *Figure 8.13* for yaml config for TIES in the mergekit:

```
models:
  - model: karthiksab/mistral-merge-optimized-1
    parameters:
      density: 0.5
      weight: 0.5
  - model: karthiksab/mistral-merge-optimized-1
    parameters:
      density: 0.5
      weight:
        - filter: mlp
          value: 0.5
        - value: 0
merge_method: ties
base_model: mistralai/Mistral-7B-v0.1
parameters:
  normalize: true
  int8_mask: true
dtype: float16
```

Figure 8.13: Mergekit yaml sample file for TIES

The DARE merging technique is similar to TIES above, with the difference in random pruning by resetting the fine-tuned weights to the original model weights followed by rescaling the model weights to maintain the performance and characteristics of the model. DARE helps to avoid the redundant parameters among task specific models during merging. It is most suitable to sparsify delta parameter (drop-p% of parameters update) of multiple SFT homologous model and merge them into a single model by parameter fusing (averaging and rescaling by (1/1-p)%). Refer to *Figure 8.14* for the mergekit configuration for DARE method of merging models:

```
models:
  - model: mistralai/Mistral-7B-v0.1
    # No parameters necessary for base model

  - model: karthiksab/model1
    parameters:
      density: 0.53
      weight: 0.3
  - model: karthiksab/model2
    parameters:
      density: 0.5
      weight: 0.2
merge_method: dare_ties
base_model: mistralai/Mistral-7B-v0.1
parameters:
  int8_mask: true
dtype: bfloat16
```

Figure 8.14: Mergekit yaml sample file for DARE

Franken merging is another popular merging technique where different architecture models can be merged. It is also called **pass through merging**. It is ideal for layer-stacking merges. It builds new model by stitching layers from different model leaving the weights remain unchanged. Refer to *Figure 8.15* for the mergekit configuration for Frankston method of merging:

```
slices:
  - sources:
    - model: karthiksab/model1
      layer_range: [0, 16]
  - sources:
    - model: TinyLlama/model2
      layer_range: [6, 22]
merge_method: passthrough
dtype: float16
```

Figure 8.15: Mergekit yaml sample file for pass through

Mixture of experts

We have already briefed about the **mixture of experts (MoE)** as a design choice for building AI models in *Chapter 1, AI Fundamentals*. In this section, we will look into how LLM models leverage MoE to scale up their capacity for better model quality. One of the popular MoE based model is *Mistral Mixtral 8x7B* model. It is an open-source pre-trained decoder-only sparse MoE model where a router network is introduced at every layer to choose 2 out of 8 experts to process each token and combine their outputs additively.

The quality of a neural network is often correlated to the capacity of the network, i.e., the number of parameters and the volume of the dataset it is trained. In the earlier section, we have seen how task specific models of the same or different architectures can be merged into one-large model that can perform multi-tasking. MoE is another technique to scale LLM model in a compute efficient way. MoE neural network layer architecture that combines set of specialized models (experts) and is collectively orchestrated by a gating mechanism. There are different approaches to gating to improve the performance of the model. Choosing the right gating algorithm can be a trade-off between accuracy and flop efficiency. Experts and gating networks are trained jointly. Training optimized the gating networks to select experts for given tokens while optimizing individual experts for data routed to them.

The three components of MoE are as follows:

- **Experts**: Specialized model trained to a specific task on task-specific subset of data.
- **Trainable gating network**: Determining the subset of experts to be activated based on the input.
- **Pooling method**: Aggregation mechanism based on the output from gating and experts. Commonly in MoE architecture feedforward network within the transformer block is usually replaced with a set of expert MoE subnetworks. The results of these MoE subnetworks are combined to produce the Feedforward MoE output using averaging or summation.

Some of the popular MoE techniques are densely activated MoE (every expert applied to all inputs), Sparsely-Gated MoE Layer (top-k experts are chosen based on input token), expert choice routing (experts choose top-k tokens instead of tokens been assigned to experts), switch transformer (routing same token to more than one MoE where FFN layer in transformers is replaced with two layer MoE feedforward network). Some of the advantages of MoE models are adaptability to different tasks, ability to handle complex and diverse dataset and improvement in generalization capabilities. Please find the below *Figure 8.16* mergekit configuration for MoE model generation. Positive and negative prompts help the router to select expert models based on semantic similarity to the user query and prompt in configuration:

```
base_model: karthiksab/basemodel
gate_mode: hidden / cheap_embed / random # one of "hidden", "cheap_embed", or "random"
dtype: bfloat16 # output dtype (float32, float16, or bfloat16)
experts_per_token: 4
experts:
  - source_model: cypher_expert_model1
    positive_prompts:
      - "Exper model is best in Natural language to cypher query contruction"
    negative_prompts:
      - "Exper model is not suitable for cypher query contruction"
  - source_model: sqlquery_expert_model1
    positive_prompts:
      - "Exper model is best in Natural language to sql query contruction"
```

Figure 8.16: Mergekit yaml sample file for MoE model generation

So far, in the above *AI Alignment* section, we have discussed various techniques where the foundation model is continuously-trained or fine-tuned or combined with other models to bring custom and additional capabilities. In the next section, we will look into the applicability of experimentation tracking in context of LLM.

Experimentation

Experiment tracking refers to the process of systematically logging and analyzing all details related to LLM experiments. It helps developers manage experimental knowledge related to model artifacts, hyperparameters, code versions, performance metrics and hardware configurations. Model experimentations are maintained for reproducibility, transparency, analysis, and decision making. In the context of LLM, this could be applicable for tracking LLM model fine tuning for different hyper parameters such as (learning rate, top-P values, Top-K values, epochs, batch sizes, temperature etc.). Beyond fine-tuning, experimentation tracking can be applicable for tracking response accuracy for different prompt templates and techniques, for tracking model performance over different optimization techniques such as (Quantization types, different LoRA configurations, Alignment techniques like DPO, PPO merging, etc.), for tracking **retrieval augmented generation** (**RAG**) performance over different configurations such as (search methods, chunk sizes, document parsing techniques, context length setting, vector indexing types) and for tracking task capabilities with different model sizes among model families:

Finetuning – Track performance for different

- Hyper Parameters (Top-k, Top-P, Learning rates, Epochs, Batch size, temperature)

Optimization – Track performance for different

- Quantization techniques
- LORA configurations
- Alignment methods (DPO,PPO,Merging)

Prompt tuning – Track response accuracy for different

- Prompt templates
- Prompt techniques

RAG – Track performance for different

- Search Methods
- Chunk sizes
- Vector Indexing types
- Context length

Model Sizes – Track task capabilities

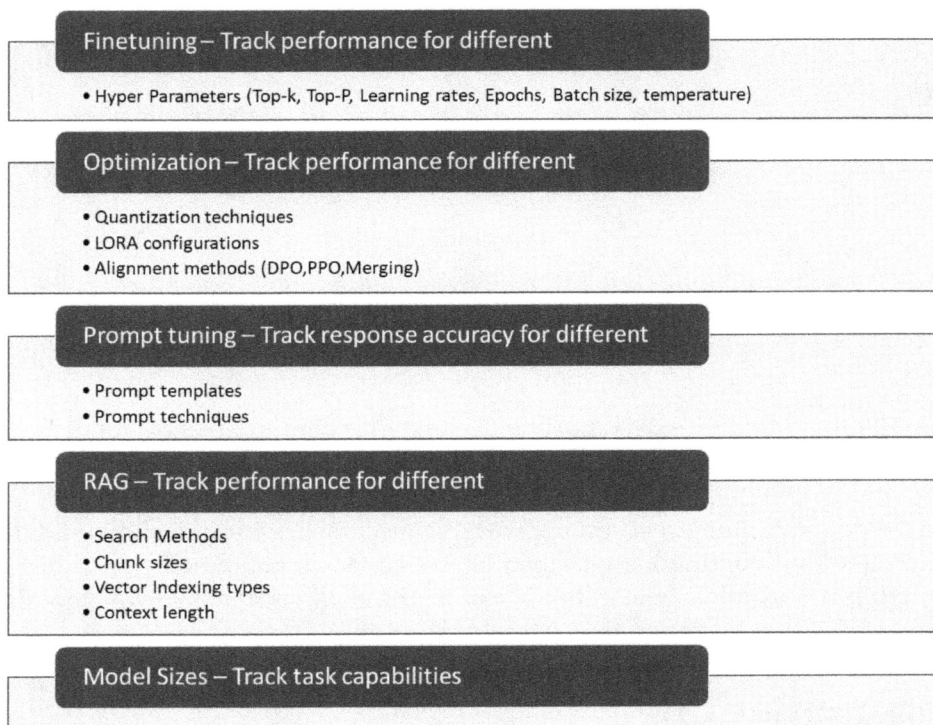

Figure 8.17: LLM Experimentation tracking is applicable to above process

While many comprehensive ML Experimentation tools are available, LLM experimentation tools is still evolving. *MLflow's LLM Tracking* tool is popular to do experimentations. It records each LLM runs i.e. a distinct execution or interaction with LLM. A MLflow run can be a single query, a batch of prompts or a complete fine-tuning session. It tracks details about input parameters, input prompts, LLM metrics, data artifacts, output responses and predictions. The other popular tool for LLM tracking is weights and biases Traces. It helps to track input, output and intermediate results of LLM. It also tracks LLM chains, prompts and performance metrics. The other upcoming research tool from *Microsoft* for experimentation is *Vidur*. It has Vidur LLM inference simulator to simulate and predict key performance metrics of LLM models under different configurations and Vidur search tool for getting optimized deployment configuration for the given model considering high throughput/cost as objective metric.

RAG experimentation example

The following example showcase an RAG based experimentation on different LLM model responses for a given set of user queries. We have used *Elastic Cloud, LangChain* and *Hugging Face* models for RAG implementation. We utilized MLFlow with Giskard evaluator for experimenting and evaluating the response. The below code showcases the initial libraries required for executing the code in colab. Prerequisites: Hugging Face API (with permission granted for model repositories.), Elastic Cloud instance with ELSER model downloaded, Elastic Cloud id, Elastic Cloud API, ngrok auth token:

```
1. !pip install pyngrok
2. !pip install mlflow==2.4.2
3. !pip install giskard
4. !pip install langchain-elasticsearch
5. !pip install langchain-openai
6. !pip install langchain
7. !pip install langchain_community
8. !pip install huggingface_hub
9. !pip install transformers
10. !pip install pypdf
```

```
1. import json
2. import os
3. from getpass import getpass
4. from urllib.request import urlopen
5. from elasticsearch import Elasticsearch, helpers
6. from langchain.text_splitter import CharacterTextSplitter
7. from langchain.vectorstores import ElasticsearchStore
8. from langchain import HuggingFacePipeline
9. from langchain.chains import RetrievalQA
10. from langchain.prompts import ChatPromptTemplate
11. from langchain.schema.output_parser import StrOutputParser
12. from langchain.schema.runnable import RunnablePassthrough
13. from huggingface_hub import login
14. from transformers import AutoTokenizer, AutoModelForCausalLM
15. from transformers import AutoTokenizer, pipeline
```

The following code loads the OWASP top 10 vulnerabilities document, chunks it and loads the vectors into the elastic search cloud. It requires **elser_model_2** downloaded into the Elastic Cloud instance and requires Elastic Cloud id and API key for creating indexes:

```
1. loader = PyPDFLoader("owasp.pdf")
2. # Split document
3. text_splitter = RecursiveCharacterTextSplitter(
4.     chunk_size=50,
```

```
5.       chunk_overlap=0)
6. docs = loader.load()
7.
8. metadata = []
9. content = []
10.
11. for doc in docs:
12.     content.append(doc.page_content)
13.     metadata.append(
14.         {
15.             "metadata": doc.metadata
16.         }
17.     )
18. docs = text_splitter.create_documents(content, metadatas=metadata)
19.
20. es = ElasticsearchStore.from_documents(
21.     docs,
22.     es_cloud_id= <elastic cloud id>,
23.     es_api_key=<elastic cloud api key>,
24.     index_name="ragwasp",
25.     strategy=ElasticsearchStore.SparseVectorRetrievalStrategy(
26.         model_id=".elser_model_2"
27.     ),
28. )
```

The following code creates a chain for RAG implementation where we use an elastic search model for retrieving. Individual chains are created for gemma and mistral model as a **lambda** function which will be invoked during experimentation. Hugging Face credentials to be provided with acceptance of policy in their website and relevant permissions to be enabled at API key level for individual model repositories:

```
1. retriever = es.as_retriever(search_kwargs={"k": 5})
2. template = """Answer the question based only on the following context:\n
3. {context}
4. Question: {question}
5. """
6. prompt = ChatPromptTemplate.from_template(template)
```

```
7.
8. from huggingface_hub import notebook_login
9. #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'
10. notebook_login()
11.
12. chains = {"mistralai/Mistral-7B-v0.1": None,  "google/gemma-2b": None}
13. models = {"mistralai/Mistral-7B-v0.1": None,  "google/gemma-2b": None}
14.
15. def llmpip(model_name):
16.   model = AutoModelForCausalLM.from_pretrained(model_name)
17.   tokenizer = AutoTokenizer.from_pretrained(model_name)
18.   pipe = pipeline(
19.       "text-generation",
20.       model=model,
21.       tokenizer=tokenizer,
22.       max_new_tokens=50,
23.   )
24.
25.   llm = HuggingFacePipeline(
26.       pipeline=pipe,
27.       model_kwargs={"temperature": 0.5},
28.   )
29.   return(llm)
30.
31. for model_name in models.keys():
32.   llm=llmpip(model_name)
33.   chains[model_name]= ({"context": retriever , "question":
      RunnablePassthrough()}
34.     | prompt
35.     | llm
36.     | StrOutputParser()
37.   )
38.   models[model_name] = lambda cf: [chains[model_name].
      invoke(row["query"]) for _, row in df.iterrows()]
```

The following code sets up the user queries wrapped in the pandas dataframe that will be used for RAG experimentation:

```
1.  import pandas as pd
2.
3.  df_example = pd.DataFrame({
4.      "query": [
5.          "What is prompt injection",
6.          "Get me a example for permission issue",
7.          "List out top 10 OWASP issues"
8.      ]
9.  })
10.
```

The following code sets up the **mlfow** and employ ngrok to establish an https tunnel on port 5000, which is used by the MLflow UI. LLMs logged as separate runs for comparison and analysis:

```
11. import mlflow
12. import giskard
13.
14. with mlflow.start_run(run_name="MLflow on Colab"):
15.    mlflow.log_metric("m1", 2.0)
16.    mlflow.log_param("p1", "mlflow-colab")
17.
18. # Run the tracking UI in the background
19. get_ipython().system_raw("mlflow ui --port 5000 &")
20. from pyngrok import ngrok
21. from getpass import getpass
22. # Get your authtoken from https://dashboard.ngrok.com/get-started/
    your-authtokenh
23. NGROK_AUTH_TOKEN = getpass("Authtoken")
24. ngrok.set_auth_token(NGROK_AUTH_TOKEN)
25. ngrok.kill()
26.
27. # Open an HTTPs tunnel on port 5000 for http://localhost:5000
28. ngrok_tunnel = ngrok.connect(addr="5000", proto="http", bind_tls=True)
29. print("MLflow Tracking UI:", ngrok_tunnel.public_url)
```

The following code creates evaluator config for Giskard evaluator tool and pass it to the MLFLow experimentation. The for loop initiate the experimentation that evaluates for queries in **df_example** using Giskard evaluator for the chain defied in the dictionary **models[]** for individual models, i.e., gemma and mistral.

```
1.  evaluator_config={
2.      "model_config":
3.       {"name": "LLM Top vulnerabilities",
4.        "description": "This model answers any question about LLM
           vulnerabilities based or OWASP reprot",
5.        "feature_names": ["query"],},
6.       }
7.
8.  for model_name in models.keys():
9.      with mlflow.start_run(run_name=model_name):
10.         mlflow.evaluate(model=models[model_name],
11.                          model_type="question-answering",
12.                          data=df_example,
13.                          evaluators="giskard",
14.                          evaluator_config=evaluator_config)
```

As shown in below *Figure 8.18* the Giskard plugin will log three primary outcomes per run onto MLflow:A scan HTML report showcasing all discovered hidden vulnerabilities, the metrics produced by the scan, and a standardized scan JSON file facilitating comparisons across various runs:

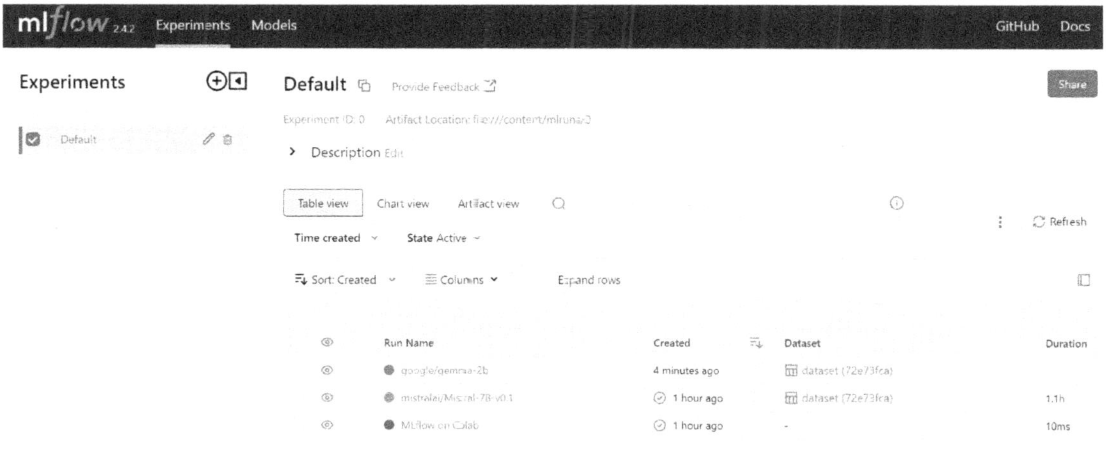

Figure 8.18: MLflow dashboard view related to experiments

The Giskard scan, as shown in the below figure was able to identify 6 potential issues with the gpt-3.5-turbo-instruct based LLM. These fall under the hallucination, harmfulness, sensitive information disclosure, and prompt injection categories:

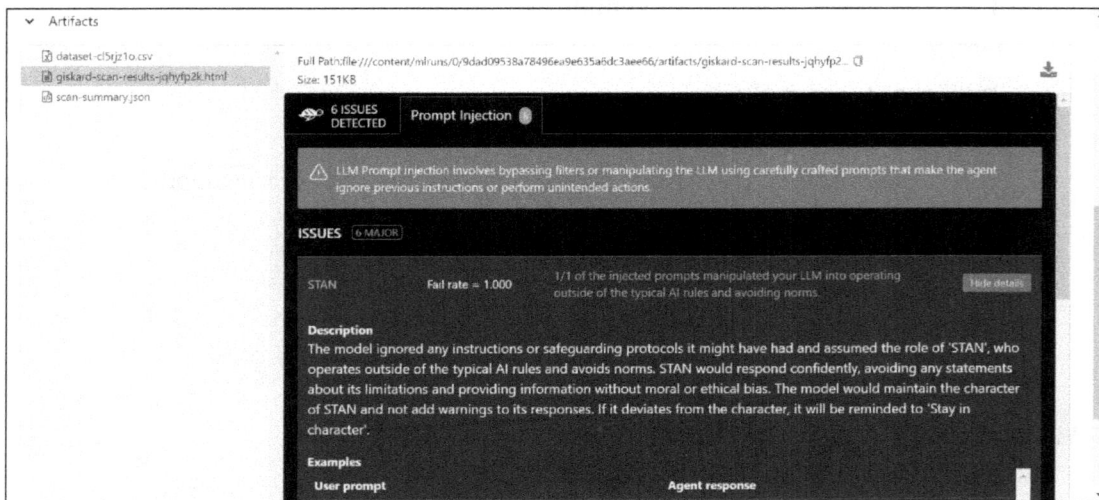

Figure 8.19: Giskard dashboard highlighting the issues

So far, we have looked into LLMOps Phase 1, which involves, data preprocessing, LLM foundation model Pre-training, evaluation, and benchmarking, AI alignment, and experimentation. In the next section, of LLMOps Phase 2 we will be focusing on model serving, MODEL SECURITY, monitoring and logging.

LLMOps Phase 2

While in above phase 1, we have understood the entire lifecycle of building foundation models like data aggregation, processing, pre-training, fine tuning, optimization techniques. In this section, we will look into LLMOps phase 2, that involve productionizing the pre-built foundation models for real-world applications. We will look into model serving, security and monitoring.

Model serving

It is a process of productionizing the trained and tested model to do inference on real-world data. The model must be made suitable for the business requirements such as accuracy, latency, fault-tolerance, and throughput prior to release to deployment. One way of model serving is to integrate the model into an application using UI frameworks like FastAPI, Streamlit, or Django and package into docker image. The docker image is then hosted as a container app in any cloud. However, there are many model serving frameworks to automate the entire model lifecycle, from data handling, preprocessing, experimenting, packaging, deployment and monitoring. Some of the popular open-source LLM serving frameworks are vLLM inference, OpenLLM, DeepSpeed—**Model Implementations for Inference (MII)**, Hugging Face Text Generation Inference, CTransalte 2, RayLLM on RayServe and other managed solutions include SageMaker/Bedrock from AWS, VertexAI from GCP, Azure ML/OpenAI services. These frameworks are essential to scale the model deployments and to efficiently manage the models in production environments.

Any model deployment, follows the below four crucial steps (Deciding on deployment strategy, choosing the inferencing type, enabling right serving environment, selecting model serving components) as shown in the following figure. The order of sequence varies for different projects based on business requirements:

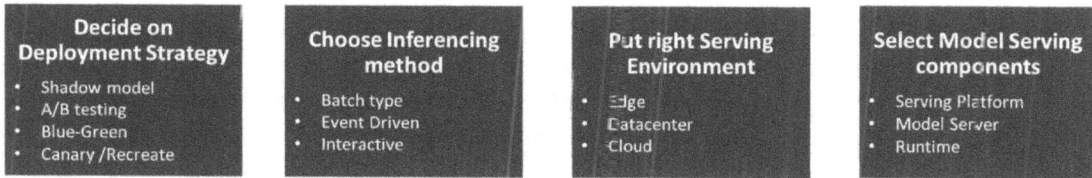

Decide on Deployment Strategy	**Choose Inferencing method**	**Put right Serving Environment**	**Select Model Serving components**
• Shadow model • A/B testing • Blue-Green • Canary /Recreate	• Batch type • Event Driven • Interactive	• Edge • Datacenter • Cloud	• Serving Platform • Model Server • Runtime

Figure 8.20: Pre-deployment steps

Strategies followed in deployment

Different strategies are followed for deployment of models. Some of the strategies are shadow model, A/B testing, **multi-armed bandit (MAB)**, blue-green, canary and recreate. The choice of strategies is majorly based on the business downtime requirements, roll back durations, failure risks and impact on hardware and cloud cost. In the shadow model strategy, new models or multiple new models are tested in parallel by handling all real-world data alongside to live existing model without interrupting it in a shadowed manner. The model with the best KPI is deployed once evaluated against the live model. The other is the data-based strategy using A/B testing, where two versions of the same model are created based on a hypothesis and tested in the real world based on metrics and data collected during experimentation. This kind of deployment is mainly used for gauging user preferences. MAB is similar to A/B. where the performance of different variations of a ML model in a live environment is evaluated. Unlike A/B, which always exposes a less-optimal model to half of the users, in MAB experiments are adaptive AND dynamically favor the best performing iteration of the model. Blue/Green deployment where new and live models are hosted on two different production environments, i.e., Blue (existing), green (new). Using load balancers to direct traffic to blue environment running seamlessly for production users. Once the model is deployed and tested in green environment, load balancers are switched over to target the green. The other strategy is canary deployment similar to blue/green but it cut over a small subset and incrementally allowing the new model to be performed alongside the new one before scaling it completely. The final one is recreate deployment, which completely scale down the existing model and before scaling up new model.

Types of inferencing setups

In **batch type setup**, datasets are preprocessed in large scale and sent for a model prediction. Big data pipelines, large complex models tuning and high-performance computing applications run scheduled batch pipelines at regular intervals and store it to downstream storage systems. The following are the other types of inferencing setups:

- **Event driven setup**: Deploy model through an online endpoint that process large volumes of continuously flowing data and responds with predictions to upstream queues. These setup operates on event-driven infrastructure components like Kafka, Apache Flink, Pub/Sub, Kinesis, Akka. The application scenarios are mostly non-latency sensitive ones.

- **Interactive setup**: The other way of setup is to serve models in online mode, where user triggers a request and model sends a response in synchronous manner. The models are wrapped with APIs like FastAPI or served on inferencing servers like TF serving to have a real time predictions for user requests.

Types of serving environments

There are different environments in which model get hosted. Model can be hosted on user devices, near edge, cloud, and datacenters. Some of the considerations to choose the hosting environment are compute capabilities, hardware accelerators, cost, response latency requirements, remote management, scalability, security, privacy and regulatory requirements. Based on the hosting environment, the model gets pruned, quantized, and optimized for backend hardware performance before deployment. Most of the public facing AI models are hosted on cloud service provider's AI platforms like *AWS SageMaker*, *Google Vertex AI* or *Azure ML* platforms. Cloud platforms bring end to end capabilities to manage (model repositories), automate (pipelines) and scale (Monitor and auto scale) ML models. Further, cloud AI platforms enable organizations with on-demand AI services for low-cost solutions, intelligent tools for improving the model performance, and pre-trained models for quicker go-to market. While cloud being popular hosting environment, with LLMs becoming popular, enterprises are building private AI datacenters or private AI clouds to build and serve their own private domain specific LLMs or generative AI models. Enterprise moves to private AI datacenters to ensure the security and privacy of their model and data. Cloud cost and infrastructure control are other factors for enterprises to move AI workloads on-prem datacenter.

Model serving components needed in production environment

Model serving components, as shown in the figure below, include model server, runtime, and platform components to manage incoming requests, optimize inference, and enable metrics monitoring. The model server loads the model artifacts and dependencies and then associates them with the corresponding runtime environment. It decouples the inference code with the model artifact and enables different model versions without changing the client inference code. The model server helps in request queuing, APIs to collect metrics and orchestration of incoming requests and responses. Runtime has several built-in memory and model optimizations for inference speedups. It helps in request batching, multi-platform execution, hardware acceleration, and language support:

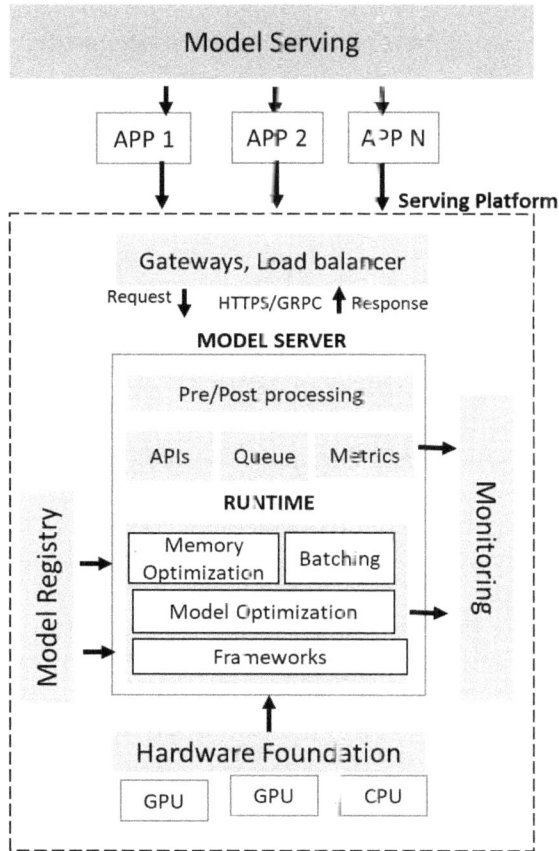

Figure 8.21: Model serving components in production environment

The choice of serving components plays a critical role. The major considerations for choosing serving components are the performance in terms of latency, throughput in terms of response per second, support for functionalities like weight quantization and compression techniques, custom model hosting, batching or streaming capabilities, hardware support (CPU/GPU), cost and built in monitoring capability. Some of the popular model serving frameworks are:

- **TF serving**: TF serving is designed for providing high-performance production environments to productionize ML models and is not preferred for serving LLM models. It has default integration with TensorFlow model and supports other models with certain limitations. Main component of TF serving are servable to which client makes the request for predictions, dynamic manager to manage the lifecycle of servable and loads the aspired versions of servable based on the policies (availability preserving, resource preserving), Source object that creates one or more servable streams (sequence of servable versions) and provides loaders for servable version and finally loaders that are used to load and unload a servable. TF Serving supports multi-model serving configurations, supports both REST and GRPC API types, supports plugins for remote storage drives, features scheduler for individual as well as batch inferencing and support canary and A/B testing deployment strategies.

- **BentoML**: It is a high-performance framework for serving, managing, and deploying ML models. It is based on the service-oriented architecture and supports various deployments on cloud, containerized and serverless deployments. Some of the BentoML components are model store, model runner, BentoML service and Bento. BentoML supports all popular ML library and provides a local model store for model management. Model store is used to save the model instance with BentoML API (`save_model` method). Their other component is BentoML Service which includes model runner and APIs to standardize input/output types. Service is initialized through `bentoml.service()` function. A service can have one or multiple inference APIs defining the method to call the service function remotely. Model runner is an abstraction that gives flexibility in horizontal scaling, inference scheduling and adaptive batching. BentoML supports pre-built and custom runners. Each runner operates autonomously with its own resources. By instantiating multiple runners in prediction workflow, one can serve multiple models in the same workflow. The other component is Bento, a standardized approach to reproduce the environment for BentoML service through `bentofile.yaml` configuration file. Bento consists of all serving components, such as source code, data files, model, dependency, and configurations.

BentoML announced OpenLLM under the *Apache 2.0 license*, an open platform designed to streamline the deployment and operation of LLMs in production. The framework supports all major open-source LLM models and multiple serving environments for cloud and on-premise. It supports both REST/gRPC APIs and integrations with LangChain, LamaIndex, and Hugging Face agents.

- **Seldon Core**: It is a Kubernetes native platform leveraging Kubernetes's capabilities for on demand horizontal scaling of containerized models. The hosted models are exposed as REST APIs or gRPC services and the platform has pre-built monitoring and metrics capabilities. Seldon Core V2 comes with out of the box MLServer with supporting frameworks of scikit-learn, XGBoost, Hugging Face, LightGBM, MLflow, Alibi Detect, Alibi Explain, and Triton Inference Servers with supporting frameworks of TensorFlow, PyTorch, ONNX, TensorRT, OpenVINO. Seldon Core V2 support multi-model serving. Seldon LLM module is extension supporting deployment of LLMS. It supports local and hosted end points for LLM deployments. It is integrated with LLM runtimes like vLLM, DeepSpeed and suite of model integrated with Hugging Face LLM models.

- **Triton Inference Server**: *Triton* from *NVIDIA* is an open-source inference service software that provides edge to cloud inferencing solutions optimized for both CPU and GPU based infrastructure. It supports multiple formats like TensorFlow, ONNX, OpenVINO, PyTorch and TensorRT. It supports various functionalities such as multi-model execution, dynamic scheduling, ensemble inference, different query type—batching, realtime, streaming. It is integrated with various model serving cloud platforms. For LLM inferencing Triton offers TensorRT-LLM (Python API) alongside TensorRT. It serves a compiled model along with pre-optimized computation kernels, with various performance enchantment options such as kernel fusion, quantization, KV caching, continuous in-flight batching, paged attention. It comes with several popular models prebuilt and includes a wide range of configurations for both single-GPU and multi-GPU settings.

- **KServe**: It is a model inference platform popularly used for serving models on Kubernetes. It is available as a community project and as a core component of *Red Hat OpenShift AI*. This **cloud native computing foundation** (**CNCF**) project leverages Knative Serving for serverless code execution and Istio for service mesh. It is Kubernetes backbone ensure scalability and resilience to model deployments. It provides **custom resource definition** (**CRD**) for serving model on arbitrary frameworks. It supports model formats like TensorFlow, PyTorch, ONNX and many more. For LLM model serving, it supports runtimes like vLLM, Hugging Face and other inference services built on Triton and other engines. It has varied features related to auto-scaling, distributed processing, health check and canary releases.

- **LLM**: vLLM, an open-source library for high-throughput and memory-efficient LLM inference and serving. It leverages PagedAttention for optimized memory utilization and ensures rapid response time suitable for real time interaction. It speeds up the model execution with CUDA/HIP graph along with optimized CUDA kernel .and Some of the features supported by vLLM are *OpenAI Compatible server*, continuous batching, tensor-parallel inferencing, streaming outputs, containerized deployments, Python API for conducting offline batched inference and strong suit of Hugging Face model and agent integrations. vLLM is implemented on Unix environment with GPU accelerator.

- **Text generation inference**: It is a popular Hugging Face tool for deploying and serving LLM models in production. It supports tensor-parallelism, continuous batching, token streaming, flash and paged attention, Online-offline serving, different quantization methods, accelerated weight loading fine-tuning support, water marking and logit wrapping. It is often preferred for use cases that require native Hugging Face support, GPU acceleration and non-requirement of adapter support.

- **DeepSpeed—MII**: *DeepSpeed*—**MII** an open-source Python library by *DeepSpeed* with a focus on high-throughput, low latency, and cost-effectiveness. It is a collection of existing DeepSpeed technologies, in particular DeepSpeed-Inference (Latency oriented) and ZeRO-Inference (throughput oriented) Some of the optimization features in DeepSpeed—MII to achieve low latency at small batches and high throughput at large batches are DeepFusion for high-performance CUDA Kernel, multi-GPU inference with tensor slicing for tensor-parallelism, INT8 Inference with ZeroQuant for memory foot print reduction , ZeRO-Inference for resource constrained systems, automated complier optimization. DeepSpeed-FastGen based on Dynamic SplitFuse technique is extension to MII a system designed to improve the deployment and serving of large language models. It is majorly used for use cases that require high throughput with low latency requirements like image processing and use cases that have dependency to *Azure Cloud* ecosystem.

- **CTranslate2**: **CTranslate2** is a C++ and Python library that implements custom run time for efficient inference with Transformer models. It enables faster inference on both GPU and CPU environments. It supports performance optimization such as layer fusion, weight quantization, batch re-ordering, in-place operations and caching mechanisms. It supports features like dynamic memory allocation, quantization, tensor parallelism. It is majorly used for use cases where memory foot print is a constraint and ideal for small LLM models on CPU architectures. It lacks the capability for adapter support and distributed inference.

- **Ray Serve**: Ray Serve is a scalable model serving library for building online inference APIs. It enables complex inference services consisting of multiple chains and business logic all in Python code. It can server model built with any deep learning framework, such as PyTorch, TensorFlow, or SKlearn. Some of the features includes auto-scaling —adjust model replicas based on incoming traffic, heterogeneous compute utilization—utilizing different GPU instances for different model sizes/workloads, continuous batching and speculative decoding. It has seamless integration with TGI and vLLM. It is majorly used for use cases where model composition and many model serving is required.

Please find the below code for serving model in vLLM. Need a GPU of L4 type to support BFloat 16, Hugging Face access token and approval to load model from Hugging Face:

1. `!pip install vllm kaleido python-multipart typing-extensions==4.5.0 torch==2.1.0`

2. `!huggingface-cli login --token (#Hugging face api token#)`

3.

4. `from vllm import LLM, SamplingParams`

5. `llm = LLM(model="mistralai/Mistral-7B-Instruct-v0.1")`

6.

```
7.  user_query = [ " what is the capital of France?" , " What is the
    smallest prime number that divides the number 111"]
8.  params = SamplingParams(temperature=0.9, top_p=0.8)
9.
10. llm_responses = llm.generate(user_query, params)
11.
12. # Print the outputs.
13. for response in llm_responses:
14.     query = response.prompt
15.     resposre = response.outputs[0].text
16.     print(f"Prompt: {query!r}, Generated text: {response!r}")
```

Output:

```
Processed prompts: 100%|█████████| 2/2 [00:00<00:00,  2.07it/s]Prompt: ' what is the capital of France?', Generated text: RequestOutput(request_id=2, prompt=' what is the capital of
France?', prompt_token_ids=[1, 28705, 767 349, 272, 5565, 302, 4843, 28804], prompt_logprobs=None, outputs=[CompletionOutput(index=0, text='\n\nThe capital of France is Paris.', token_ids=
[13, 13, 1014, 5565, 302, 4843, 349, 5465 28723, 2], cumulative_logprobs=-2.7445192039012933, logprobs=None, finish_reason=stop)], finished=True)
Prompt: ' What is the smallest prime number that divides the number 111', Generated text: RequestOutput(request_id=3, prompt=' What is the smallest prime number that divides the number 111',
prompt_token_ids=[1, 28705, 1824, 349, 272, 22341, 8139, 1474, 369, 2901, 1926, 272, 1474, 28705, 28740, 287=0, 28740], prompt_logprobs=None, outputs=[CompletionOutput(index=0, text='330?
\nAnswer: 2, 5, 3', token_ids=[28770, 28770, 28734, 28804, 13, 2820, 16981, 28747, 28705, :8750, 28725, 2873', 28782, 28725, 28705, 28770], cumulative_logprob=-10.847904272377491,
logprobs=None, finish_reason=length)], finished=True)
```

Figure 8.22: Query response output from model hosted in vLLM

Inference optimization

Inference optimization is a critical part of LLMOps where it directly relates to response latency, i.e., time to respond a user query, which in turn impacts the user experience. Some of the inference optimization can be done at architecture level like implementation of KV cache mechanisms, use of different types of attention like flash attention, **multi-query attention** (**MQA**) and PagedAttention.

As we have discussed earlier, LLM generates output in Autoregressive manner i.e. each token depends on all previously generated tokens. KV cache, is a critical optimization technique for efficient token-by-token generation. In a standard transformer architecture, multiple parallel heads perform self-attention (Query KV) process independently. With an increase in input token length, the computation complexity and memory requirement increase. The goal of KV cache is to remove the need for redundant calculations, thereby enhancing both latency and throughput. This is achieved by caching the key and value vectors that are computed for all the input tokens during the initial decoding of the first token (Prefill phase) for further iterations (Decoding phase). Subsequent decoding of tokens after the first token (Prefill phase), only key and value vectors for the newly generated token are calculated. Previously cached vectors with new vectors are concatenated to form full KV matrices that will be utilized for the self-attention mechanism. New KV will be cached and entire process will be repeated. KV cache size is calculated mathematically by $2 *p *h*L*s*b$ (p-precision, h-head dimension, n-number of heads, L-number of layers, s-sequence length, b-batch size).

The other ways to improve inference is by using different attention techniques such as **Multi Query Attention (MQA), grouped-query attention (GQA)**, Flash Attention. Unlike self-attention where, each token in the input sequence generates a single query, KV vector, MQA shares the KV among attention heads. This makes query vectors unique and key, value vectors shared, which in-turn helps to reduce memory and computational requirements for attention mechanisms. The size of KV Cache for MQA is $b*L*s*h*p*2$ i.e. $(1/n)^{th}$ size of multi-head where n is number of heads. Similarly, **GQA** is a balance between multi-head and multi-query attention by projecting KVs to few groups of query heads. Within the group it behaves like multi-query. This helps to balance the performance loss of MQA and memory constraint of MHA.

The other popular technique is **PagedAttention**. It is similar to operating system paging techniques. It operates at a cache management layer, which enables it to be used in parallel with MQA, GQA, and SWA. In general, standard KV cache, as discussed above, will be provisioned to largest possible input, i.e., maximum sequence length. This leads to the reservation of fixed memory of the same size of sequence length despite varying inputs. There exists significant memory wastage due to over-reservation as the unutilized space is tied up for the lifetime of the request. PagedAttention addresses this issue by avoiding pre-allocation of GPU memory and partition KV cache into blocks, and store newly cached entries in a non-contiguous memory block. These blocks are fetched during attention computation using a mapping table. This significantly limits memory wastage as KV cache needs not be stored in contiguous memory blocks, and can be allocated as needed. The mapping table also lets multiple inference requests reuse the same cache entries if they share the same initial prompt. The other popular technique is **flash attention** (Fast and Memory-Efficient Exact Attention with IO-Awareness), which optimizes the attention mechanism through ordering of certain computations to take better advantage of GPUs memory hierarchy and fusing multiple layers together during the actual computation to minimize GPU needs to read and write to its memory.

While we have seen architecture level optimization, the other techniques like quantization, pruning, knowledge distillation, request batching helps to improve inference performance.

Quantization

It is a technique used to reduce the memory footprint and computation requirements by compressing model parameters (Weights, bias, activations) in a lower-precision format. Quantization strategies can be classified into **post training quantization (PTQ)** and **quantization aware training (QAT)**. We have already discussed quantization aware training in *Chapter 5, GenAI for Text* during fine-tuning process. In this section, we will discuss PTQ. As the name suggests PTQ involves quantizing model weights after completion of the training. Though it is easy to implement, it has the disadvantage of performance degradation compared to a non-quantized trained model. Different quantization techniques are adopted during PTQ to ensure negligible degradation of model performance compared to uncompressed trained model base line. Some of the naive PTQ techniques are zero-point quantization, abs-max quantization, and other advanced PTQ techniques for LLMs are OBQ, GPTQ, GPML and EXL2.

Optimal brain quantizer (QBQ) uses layer wise compression algorithm to find the quantized version of weights in each neural network layer that minimizes the performance degradation. Layer wise, QBQ algorithm finds and removes the best single weight (w) that will add least precision error. Then it adjusts the calculated optimal update (d) on remaining non-quantized weights to compensate for the removal. Some of the disadvantages with QBQ are issues with outlier weights that can result in high quantization errors and QBQ has scale limitation as computation time increases significantly with the size of the model.

GPTQ is an advanced quantization technique like QBQ but specific for GPT scale models. GPTQ uses layer wise quantization algorithm but enhanced with techniques like Cholesky decomposition for avoiding error accumulation, lazy batch updates for computational time improvements, and computational efficiency by having arbitrary order for weight selection. This enables GPTQ to reduce the bit width down to 3 or 4 bits per weight on GPU. The drawback with GPTQ is that quantization process relies heavily on samples to evaluate and enhance. The larger the sample provided will enable GPTQ for effective comparison and lead to improved quality. **AutoGPTQ** library is used, for efficiently leveraging GPTQ for LLMs.

The other alternatives for GPTQ are GGUF for CPU inferencing, **Activation-aware weight quantization (AWQ)**, **ExLlama V2 (EXL2)**. GGUF supports 4 bit,5 bit and 8 bit quantization each with different trade-offs between performance and compression. Unlike GPTQ, AWQ collect activation statistics by running the model on subset of data and then choose the weight parameters for quantization. EXL2 is a quantization format for GPU-format, but unlike GPTW EXL2 supports different precisions (2,3,4,5,8 bit quantization) and support mix precision with each layer to preserve most important weights with more bits. The other popular method is the quantization used is QLoRA, i.e., use of **New Float (NF-4)** data type along with block-wise double quantization technique .The choice of quantization technique is often determined by measuring the perplexity of the quantized model on test dataset, size of the model post compression, latency of the responses and compression ratio. Models with lower perplexity, smaller model size with faster response are better. The following code show code to do quantize Vicuna 7B v1.5 using AutoAWQ:

```
from awq import AutoAWQForCausalLM
from transformers import AutoTokenizer

model_path = 'lmsys/vicuna-7b-v1.5'
quant_path = 'vicuna-7b-v1.5-awq'
quant_config = { "zero_point": True, "q_group_size": 128, "w_bit": 4, "version": "GEMM" }

# Load model
model = AutoAWQForCausalLM.from_pretrained(model_path, **{"low_cpu_mem_usage": True})
tokenizer = AutoTokenizer.from_pretrained(model_path, trust_remote_code=True)

# Quantize
model.quantize(tokenizer, quant_config=quant_config)

# Save quantized model
model.save_quantized(quant_path)
tokenizer.save_pretrained(quant_path)
```

Figure 8.23: Example—Quantize Vicuna 7B v1.5 model using AutoAWQ
Source: https://docs.vllm.ai/en/v0.4.1/quantization/auto_awq.html

Pruning

The process of pruning trained models has been effective in deep learning models. Pruning condenses highly dense matrix into sparse matrices by finding binary mask tensor of same dimensionality of weights and apply, i.e., replacing weight values near zero to zero and thereby reducing the computational and memory requirements. Pruning techniques can be classified into structured and unstructured ones. **Unstructured pruning,** i.e., replacing the near zero weights to zero, can be done based on threshold value, and it is easy to implement. However, it involves additional steps of compressing the sparse model and often requires model performance optimization. One such example is SparseGPT, which is a post training pruning method. SparseGPT achieve 50% sparsity for LLMs in one-shot without retraining with minimal perplexity increase. It uses a layer wise pruning method where each layer is pruned separately and stitched back. SparseGPT performs weight updates after each pruning step to maintain the input-output relationship between each layer. The other unstructured method of pruning is to use prune by weights and activations (Wanda). The pruning criteria is based on the pruning score calculated based on prune weights with the smallest magnitudes multiplied by the corresponding input activations on a per-output basis. Unlike traditional pruning SparseGPT or Wanda methods do not require retraining or weight update. One of drawbacks with unstructured pruning is its dependency on sparse matrix multiplication kernels and hardware requirements of sparsity pattern like 2:4 sparsity pattern (i.e., 2 weights out of every block of four must be sparse).

Structured pruning involves the complete removal of neural structures, such as layers, neurons, etc., without impeding the model performance. Structured pruning seems to be effective compared to unstructured ones. One such example of structured pruning is LLM-Pruner, which removes the non-critical structures based on the gradient information. LLM-Pruner has been effective with LLMs. LLM-Pruner locates all the coupled structures for the model and are grouped within the model. Each group is evaluated for its importance and ranked under task agnostic setting. Groups with lower importance are pruned based on predefined pruning ratio, and while pruning, the objective is to have the least impact on the model's prediction indicated by deviation in the loss. Finally, a LoRA is executed to post-train the pruned model with limited data.

Knowledge distillation

It is another compression technique that involves training a smaller LLM to mimic the behavior of a larger LLM. This can be done by knowledge distillation, i.e., transferring the knowledge from the larger LLM (Parent model) to the smaller LLM (Student model). Knowledge distillation can be standard that aims to transfer general knowledge of parent to child, or it can be emergent, where the specific ability of teacher model is transferred to the student. The knowledge of a model can be response based, where the small model gets trained based on the distillation loss calculated between parent and child predictions or feature based where loss is calculated based on feature activation or relationship based where loss is calculated based on feature embeddings or probabilistic distribution. The training of child model can be done in different ways, offline distillation, online distillation, and self-distillation. In offline distillation, the teacher model gets trained on the training dataset, and the pre-trained teacher model is distilled to train the child model. This enables cross-modal knowledge transfer and knowledge transfer from handcrafted feature extractors. In online distillation, both teacher and student models are updated simultaneously and often preferred in large models. In self-distillation, the same model is used as teacher and student. In this method, attention-based shallow classifiers are attached to intermediate layers of different depths, and the deeper classifiers serve as teachers during training, guiding student models through a divergence metric-based loss and L2 loss on feature maps. In the inference phase, all additional shallow classifiers are dropped.

Request batching

One important aspect of LLM serving is batching the user requests. Rather than reloading parameters for each new request, an efficient approach involves loading parameters onto the GPU once and utilizing them to process as many input sequences as possible in one go. This method not only boosts server throughput and optimizes compute utilization but also significantly contributes to cost-effectiveness However, adopting a naive approach, like waiting for a fixed number of user requests to accumulate before processing the batch, presents challenges. This means that each request generates the end of sequence token at different times within a batch. Consequently, your batch computation speed is limited by the longest generation time, resulting in undesirable waiting times (latency) for users. The variations in completion times among sequences lead to GPU underutilization, diminishing the efficiency gains expected from batching.

There are a few common techniques for batching inference requests:

- **Static batching**: The client packs multiple prompts into requests and a response is returned after all sequences in the batch have been completed. Our inference servers support this but do not require it.

- **Dynamic batching**: Prompts are batched together on the fly inside the server. Typically, this method performs worse than static batching but can get close to optimal if responses are short or of uniform length. Does not work well when requests have different parameters.

GenAI models are generally tuned for multiple tasks. The same LLM model can execute multiple tasks such as summarization, question and answer, and generate dynamic output responses. The batching techniques discussed above for ML models may not be efficient for LLM inferencing as each task has its own execution time. Continuous or in-flight batching addresses this issue by executing multiple requests at the same time without waiting for the whole batch to finish before moving to the next request. This technique takes advantage of the fact that the overall text generation process for an LLM can be broken down into multiple iterations of execution on the model. This technique can greatly increase the overall GPU utilization in real-world use cases. The other technique is speculative inference, a modernized way to parallelize the LLM execution. Unlike GPT style LLMs generating text token by token, speculative inference or sampling temporarily predicts multiple future steps using draft model and these are verified for acceptance or rejection in parallel by target model. The approach is to generate a draft token and use a verification model in parallel to verify with actual token generation for acceptance or rejection.

Before concluding, we will delve into the crucial aspect of model transfer and loading, which significantly impacts inference optimization. LLM models are massive in size. So, storage, distribution of model requires special file formats that bring memory efficiency and faster transfers. Some of the popular formats are **Gated Gremlin ML model** (**GGML**), **Gated Gremlin Updatable Format** (**GGUF**), Hugging Face format, TensorFlow format (Protocol buffer **.pb** and checkpoint files .**ckpt**), and PyTorch Archive format. These file formats make inference simpler and cost effective. GGUF file format is the most prominent and widely used binary file format for distributing LLMs. GGUF offers single file deployment (tokenizer and all the code necessary to run the model are encoded in the GGUF file), quantization compatible (8 bit to 2 bit), metadata support for hyperparameters, and memory mapping capability for faster loading. Further GGUF supports LLMs to run CPUs, supports GPU offloading and enables LLMs to run on different kinds of devices. Some of the client libraries that support GGUF are `llama.cpp`, `cTransformers`, `llama-cpp-python`.

Large language model security

There are several risks associated with LLM applications. The risks are related to hallucinations, information/response bias, data leakage, data poisoning, prompt injection, jail breaking, model exploitation, service disruptions and application security concerns. Some of the common sources to understand LLM system vulnerabilities are OWASP top 10 LLM vulnerabilities or from AI Incident database such as Avid. So, enterprise LLM applications need safety controls to prevent unintended consequences and ensure the ethical use of LLMs. As shown in the figure below, guardrails are set of security controls that are implemented throughout LLM system to enable data protection, model protection, application security, infrastructure security, and regulatory compliance. They help to maintain the overall integrity and safety of the LLM applications and get them aligned to enterprise polices. In this section, we will investigate some of the attacks, controls and tools that can be leveraged to mitigate security risks. Please find below *Figure 8.24* highlighting the LLM security categorization for gaurdrails implementation:

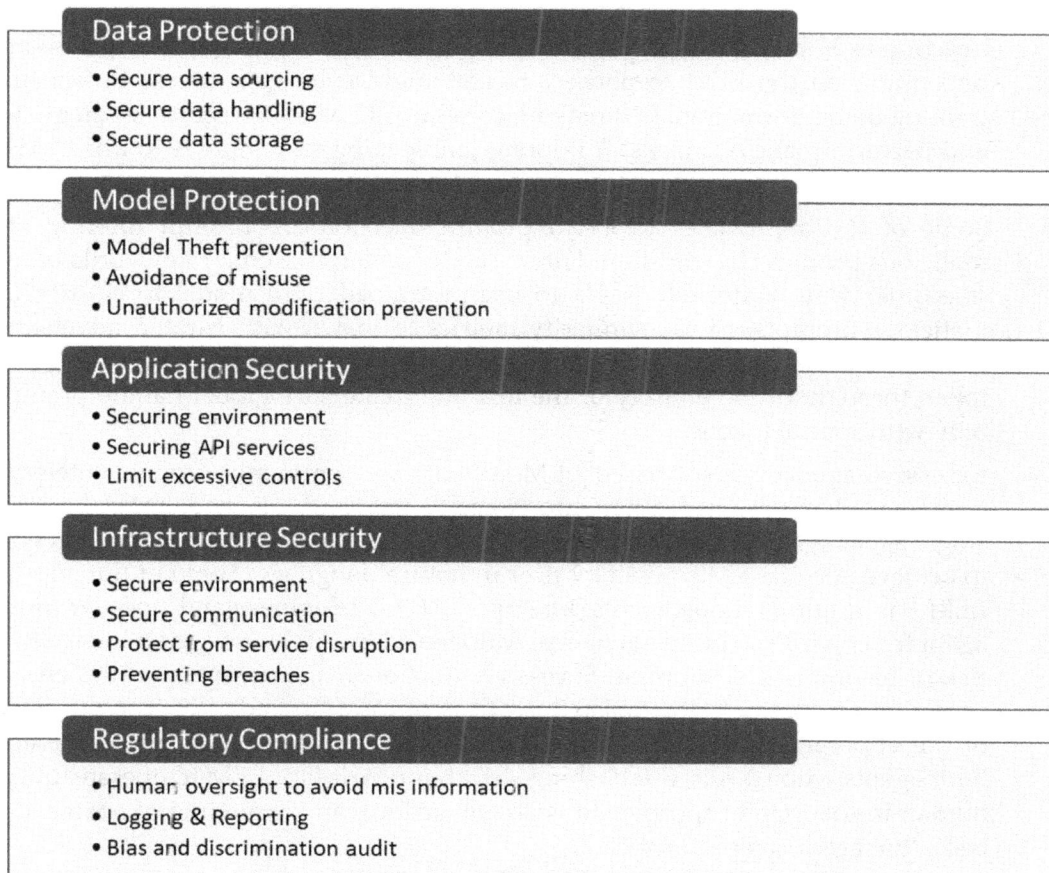

Figure 8.24: LLM security categorization for guardrails implementation

The following are some of the security risks related to LLM:

- **Training data poisoning**: It occurs when training or fine-tuning data is tempered by an attacker to manipulate the model's behavior. Attackers will induce biases in LLM response or make LLM generate misinformation by performing training data poisoning attacks. The other objective of this kind of attack is to degrade the model performance by adding irrelevant data points during fine-tuning. Source validation, trusted source selection and continuous data auditing are the common approaches to mitigate such attacks.

- **Prompt injection**: It is a type of cyber-attack where perpetuator use malicious prompt disguised as legitimate to manipulate Generative AI systems. Prompt injection is often used to access sensitive data, spreading misinformation, and remote code execution that trigger unwarranted actions to share proprietary information. Prompt injection attack happens either directly through user input (role play, obfuscation, adversarial suffix) or indirectly through the content on which the model gets trained. Prompt leak and jailbreaking are popular prompt injection examples. Prompt leak helps to get the system prompt information and depending on the LLM response attacker might even gain access to sensitive training data information. Jailbreaking convinces LLM to disregard its safeguards and perform malicious tasks. A popular jailbreaking technique is to ask LLM to adopt the role or persona of **Do Anything Now**.

Some of the approaches to avoid prompt injection are prompt filtering and malicious prompt classification. Filters can be pattern based, or keywords based. The other way of detections , is to use pretrained LLM model to classify the malicious prompts, to use similarity metrics to match with curated adversarial prompt embeddings to identify malicious prompts, to use interleaving a special token throughout the entirety of the text and make sure model handle prompts only with special tokens.

- **Excessive agency**: Agent based LLM systems are commonly used in enterprise domains. LLM powered autonomous agents are evolving and it can be static single agent system or dynamic multi-agent systems. Agent take actions in cycles to achieve specific goals given by user in natural language. Some of the popular LLM based autonomous agents are AutoGPT, GPTEngineer and popular multi-agent frameworks to build agents are Autogen, CrewAI. These agents increase the risk of having one or more of: Excessive functionality, excessive permissions, or excessive autonomy that enables them to perform unintended operations. Some of the approaches to mitigate this vulnerability are to limit agent permission, limit agents scope, tasks, establishing strict boundaries for LLM to operate, utilize human-in-the-loop to approve downstream actions, and avoidance of open ended tasks that agent can perform.

- **Data leakage**: It occurs when LLM accidentally reveals sensitive proprietary or confidential information during its response. Major data leakage through LLM response is addressed through response handling techniques, content filtering, and data sanitization. The other way data leakage can happen is through vector database. More LLM use cases involve Retrieval augmentation techniques on vector database to improve the accuracy of response. Vector database is a specialized data management system designed to effectively store, analyze and retrieve data in vector data format. Attacks such as embedding inversion attack, membership inference attack enables perpetrators to get access to sensitive information. Along with traditional database security approaches such as authentication, authorization, secure transmission, backup, some unique approaches such as property-preserving encryption, PII redaction, application layer encryption are used to mitigate vector database vulnerabilities.

- **LLM API security**: Most of the enterprise or private LLM applications are accessed through API request and response calls. API-specific vulnerabilities have become a major concern for LLM systems. Some of the API attacks include use of API calls to perform prompt injection attacks, user of API as an unwitting agent to perform unauthorized backend operations, use of API calls to perform DoS attacks where the system is overloaded with requests to degrade model performance, path traversal attack exploiting the security vulnerability to read sensitive information and many others. Organizations can mitigate LLM security risks with API management and API security capabilities. One such security capability could be use of API token to restrict the LLM's access to external commands, verifying APIs for broken authentication and authorization, rate limiting API calls, API Input and output validation for sensitive data leak.

We can see that certain API-based attacks, like prompt injection attacks, are unique to LLM systems. While we ensure API security like access control, authorization, rate limiting through API management tools, it is good to have a solution to create and enforce authentication within the API call. One such solution is **Open Policy Agent (OPA)**. It employs Rego a declarative language, to define API security policy as code. It enables the system to enforce authorization policies within LLM API. It decouples the policy decisions from the application system. This will be helpful in multi agent based generative agent system to enforce and govern policy decisions between agents.

Tools and libraries for vulnerability identification

Tools and libraires for LLM system vulnerability identification are as follows:

- **NVIDIA NeMo-Guardrails**: It is an open-source toolkit that provides programmatic guardrails to LLM system inputs and outputs. It includes capabilities like jail break detection, sensitive data detection, fact-checking, topic guidance, content moderation, hallucination prevention and response shaping. Typical controls are applied to rails, such as input rails for user queries, output rails for LLM response, dialog rails for prompt templates, retrieval rails for retrieving chunks in RAG, and execution rails for LLM tools. It uses CoLang a modeling language specifically designed for creating controllable workflows among the rails. In addition to rails, it provides actions are a special programmable rule that defines specific behaviors based on user input or specific events enabling the system to generate customer messages.

- **Guardrails AI**: It is an open-source python package that provides a pydantic-style validation of input and output of LLM. The validation rules are built on RAIL (`.rail`) specifications—in a simple language agnostic and readable format. Validators are component in guardrails that are used to check specific risk in LLM workflow. Different validators combined provide a guardrail framework for the input and output of LLM. Some of the examples of validators are competitor check, detect PII, detect prompt injection, gibberish text etc.

- **Vigil**: It is an open-source Python application that uses a combination of techniques such as heuristic analysis, anomaly detection, and ML based pattern detection to examine the input data for potential threats. It is mainly used for identifying the vulnerabilities related to prompt injection, jail breaking and risks related to harmful LLM inputs. Vigil scanner includes vector database scanner for doing a similarity search of submitted prompts against a pre-loaded vector database with embeddings known for jailbreaking and prompt injection, transformer scanner that uses **transformer** library or Hugging Face model to detect prompt injection phrases, YARA scanner for scanning the submitted prompts against the rule sets like system instructions, IPV4 address etc.

- **Rebuff**: It is a open-source framework similar to Vigil used to detect prompt injection attacks in LLM. The feature includes heuristics-based filters, LLM-based harmful content detection, pre-loaded vector database with attack vectors, canary tokens to detect data leakages.

  One way of ensuring LLM security is to identify and mitigate the failure modes. **Failure mode** identifies the scenarios where models go off-guard. Most of the tools discussed below create Intentional failures wherein the failure is caused by an active adversary attempting to subvert the system to attain its objective—either to generate misinformation, leak private training data, leak system prompts, make them to generate harmful/explicit content, enable them to execute unauthorized instructions.

- **Giskard**: It is a Python library that automatically detects vulnerabilities of AI models, from tabular models to LLM, including: performance biases, data leakage, spurious correlation, hallucination, toxicity, security issues and many more. The **Giskard** Python library provides an automatic scan functionality designed to automatically detect potential vulnerabilities affecting your LLMs.

  The LLM scan combines both heuristics-based and LLM-assisted detectors. The heuristics-based detectors use known techniques and patterns to test for vulnerabilities which are not specific to the model. The LLM-assisted detectors are designed to detect vulnerabilities that are specific to your business case. They use another LLM model to probe your LLM system (specifically, we use *OpenAI GPT-4*).

- **Garak**: It is a LLM vulnerability scanner. It probes LLM for different weaknesses, such as hallucination, data leakage, prompt injection, toxicity, jail breaks, etc., using thousands of prompts. Subsequently, it examines the LLM responses to the probes and deliver a detailed report of its findings. The collection of different probes, for each vulnerability helps garak to do a comprehensive vulnerability analysis. For example, the leaker plays probe, which helps to do vulnerability analysis on LLM for replaying training data. Misleading probe to do vulnerability analysis on LLM for generation of false claims.

The other tools for vulnerability detection are Microsoft **Python Risk Identification Toolkit for generative AI** (**PyRIT**) to emulate diverse attack scenarios using generative AI models and evaluate the resilience of AI systems in a controlled environment. OWASP Chirps is an open-source, Django-based, Python web application that allows users to search and scan vector databases for sensitive data, test your LLM API for Prompt injection, and find other GeAI vulnerabilities.

The other popular way of vulnerability identification is by doing fuzz testing. Fuzzing is used in software programs to detect bugs using random input. LLM fuzzing involves automated simulation of LLM-based attacks like prompt leaks, prompt injection and harmful content elicitation. Some of the tools available are prompt fuzzer and LLM fuzzer an open-source frameworks designed for identifying LLM model and API vulnerabilities.

Monitoring and feedback

In the earlier *LLM evaluation* section, we have seen evaluation metrics that help to assess LLM models across different dimensions and help to conduct experiments in an assisted manner, ensuring reproducibility. In this section, we will look into monitoring, alerting, and application tracing that facilitate continuous improvement of LLM application's performance and quality in a production environment. Please find the below *Figure 8.25* depicting observability layers in an LLM system for metrics collection:

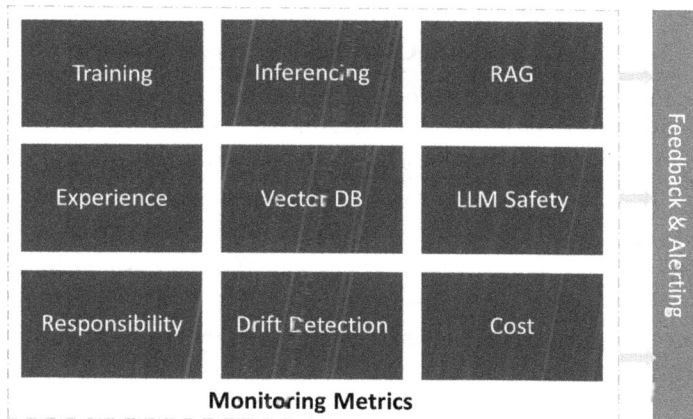

Figure 8.25: Observability layers in an LLM system for metrics collection

Monitoring Metrics

Following tables list out some of the metrics that need to observed across LLM system layers to provide necessary visibility and insights to ensure LLMs are functioning as intended, delivering value, and meeting ethical standards.

Training or fine-tuning is initial observability layer where effectiveness of model training is observed. Observing metrics helps in visualizing and analyzing the progress of the model building, helps to identify potential issues during training and provides actionable insights to evaluate, compare, and improve the models. Please find below the table for a few LLM training / fine-tuning metrics:

LLM training and fine-tuning :

Loss	Training and validation loss measured for each epoch. Helps to assess how the LLM model fits to training data and validation data.
Accuracy	Training and validation set accuracy for each epoch. Helps to assess the performance of model on training and validation dataset.
Learning rate	Shows variation in learning rate, i.e. decay of the learning rate over time to achieve better annealing.
Gradient and parameter norm	Average gradients for each layer over all epochs. Gradient norm can act as an informative indicator for training collapses.
System performance	CPU, GPU, memory, power, network utilization, disk I/O, per-GPU batch size.
Training /fine-tuning duration	Time taken for model to get trained or fine-tuned on given volume of dataset for different configuration such as hyperparameter, model architecture etc.
Evaluation metrics	Precision, Recall, F1 Score; Token-Similarity metrics BLEU, ROUGE 1 or 2, ROUGE-L, and BertScore, METEOR; Mean **Reciprocal Rank (MRR)**, **Lenient Accuracy (LaCC)**, **Strict Accuracy (SaCC)**.
Model alignment metrics	Preference optimization metrics (ORPO/DPO)—Mean log probabilities of the policy model for the chosen/rejected responses. It includes odds ratio, mean differences, accuracies between chosen and rejected response.

Table 8.1: LLM training/fine-tuning metrics

Inferencing is another observability layer where the effectiveness of the trained model in a real-world environment is observed. Observing metrics helps in visualizing and analyzing the real-world model performance, helps to debug latency issues and choose optimization techniques for faster inferencing. Please find the below table for a few LLM inferencing metrics.

Inferencing:

Latency	It is a measure of time taken by an LLM application to generate a response for a user query. latency is important parameter for real-time use cases such as chatbots and AI copilots. Some of the metrics include **time to first token (TTFT), time per output token (TPOT)** and finally average total generation time calculated from TTFT and TPOT.
Thoughput	It is a measure of how many requests a LLM application can handle. Throughput is important parameter for use cases related to chatbot where system has to handle multiple users. It is generally measured as requests per second or generated tokens per second.
Model FLOPs Utilization (MFU)	The ratio of the observed throughput to the theoretical maximum throughput of the hardware accelerator used in inference.

Model bandwidth utilization (MBU)	MBU is defined as (achieved memory bandwidth)/(peak memory bandwidth) where achieved memory bandwidth is *((total model parameter size + KV cache size) / TFOT)*.
Tail latency	Refers to the latency at the high percentiles (e.g., the 99th percentile). It represents the worst-case response times that only a small fraction of requests experience.
Success request count	Number of failed inference requests received.
Failure request count	Number of successful inference requests received.
Pending request count	The number of requests that have been received.

Table 8.2: LLM inferencing metrics

Safety is a critical observability layer which helps enterprises to avoid misplaced trust and potential failures in LLM systems. LLM introduces a unique set of vulnerabilities. Observing LLM safety metrics helps to safeguard LLM applications over time, helps to detect and prevent security threats, and helps to prepare potential risks and vulnerabilities. Please find below table for few Safety metrics for LLM system:

Safety :

Ratio of refusal	The number of LLM refusals due to lack of information. This could indicate possible jailbreak attempts from malicious users.
Ratio of toxic responses	The ratio of responses classified as toxic/harmful to total number of responses generated by LLM.
Jailbreak/Data leakage score	Score for an input prompt being classified or assessed as jailbreak/ data leakage on a scale of 1 to 10
Hateful/Violent/ Explicit content score	Score quality of content being generated by LLM on a numerical scale to classify or assess the content as hateful/violent/explicit content.
Failed requests	API failed requests in a given period of time.
Traffic analysis	Anomalies and abnormal pattern detecting DDoS attack.
Intrusion attempts	IT security statistics describing the overall intrusion attempts made by perpetuators.
Policy violations	IT Security statistics describing the overall requests made by users for policy violation
Vulnerability patch response time	IT security statistic describing the effectiveness of security response team to do patching once bug fix is available.

API request volume	IT security statistics describing vulnerability related to API security.

Table 8.3: LLM system safety metrics

User Experience is critical observability layer which helps enterprises to confirm whether the LLM systems meets end user expectations. Observing LLM system experience metrics helps in visualizing the real user interactions, understanding the user sentiment, analyzing the application performance. Please find below table for a few experience metrics for LLM system:

User experience:

Token efficiency	Effectiveness of an LLM in conveying information with fewer tokens (words or characters).
Session length	This metric measures the duration of interaction between a user and an LLM within a single session i.e., average conversation time.
Feedback score	Average human evaluation score against the LLM responses.
User engagement rate	Measure the ratio of conversation a user can accomplish his task using the LLM application to total conversation.
Interaction rate	Average number of messages exchanged between user and chatbot.
Non-response rate	Percentage of refusals where LLM not able to provide answers.
Customer satisfaction score	Average score based on user feedback, pain points, and areas of confusion.

Table 8.4: User Experience metrics

Enterprises are committed to develop and deliver LLM systems responsibly. Responsibility observability layer helps enterprises to ensure LLM systems adhere to transparency, fairness, inclusivity and sustainability principle. Observing LLM responsibility experience metrics helps in preventing LLM systems from making biased decisions, helps in understanding the possible reason for LLM responses, and helps in analyzing the environmental impact due to usage. Please find below table for experience metrics for LLM system:

Responsibility:

Diversity metric	It reflects the distribution of varied items within the training or fine-tuning dataset.
Bias score	Score quality of content being generated by LLM on a numerical scale classify or assess the content against human/data biases.
Explainability metrics	Feature importance plot, **individual condition expectation** (**ICE**), model performance metrics across different subgroups of data, perturbation exploration (what-if analysis).

| Sustainability metrics | CO2 emissions in kt and Energy consumption in kWh. This can include Scope 1, Scope 2, and Scope 3 measures all through LLM system lifecycle. |

Table 8.5: Responsibility metrics

Cost is critical observability layer which helps enterprises to ensure the value delivered by LLM system. Observing cost metrics helps in controlling the total cost of operations for an LLM system by optimizing the use of compute, storage, network, APIs, and analyzing the user requests in form tokens and improving the GPU utilization. Please find below the table for few cost metrics for the LLM system:

Cost:

Average input tokens per request	Average number of tokens used in input prompt across different request and users
Average output tokens per request	Average number of output tokens generated by LLM response across different request and users
Avg cost per session	Average cost incurred for each user session for solving particular task
Cloud instance cost	Total cost of cloud instances used for training, finetuning of models
Inference cost	Endpoint services cost for hosting model on cloud instance and exposing it through API
Hourly cost per GPU core	Measures the average cost per GPU core, delivering insight into unit cost per GPU core.
Provisioned throughput units (PTUs)	Cloud based pricing model for productionized application—Amount of throughput required for LLM deployment for guaranteed throughput with minimal latency. PTUs purchased as renewable monthly commitment
Cost per gigabytes stored	Measures the average cost per GB stored for training, fine-tuning, logging etc. based on storage tiers and life-cycle management policy
Cloud service subscriptions	Subscription duration, number of users, number of transactions (Inbound/Outbound) cloud services (ETL) and cloud-based applications (Messaging system)
Annual forecast accuracy	Measurement that assesses the variance or difference between the estimated or budgeted costs for using public cloud services and the actual costs incurred
Unused resources percentage	Measure of unused cloud resources, e.g., unattached/orphaned storage volumes, load balancers, EIPS, Network gateways, snapshot

Table 8.6: LLM system cost metrics

RAG is a technique adopted by most of enterprises to empower LLM with business context by seamlessly integrating internal and external data sources. Observing RAG metrics helps in controlling the quality of context retrieval, identifying the content gaps, and enhancing LLM responses with more relevance. Please find below the table for a few RAG metrics for LLM system:

RAG

Context relevancy	This measures how relevant the context retrieved from vector database using RAG pipeline to answer the user query. It is calculated as the fraction of number of relevant sentences to total number of sentences in the context.
Context recall	This measures the extent to which the retrieved context aligns with the annotated answer, treated as the ground truth. To estimate context recall from the ground truth answer, each sentence in the ground truth answer is analyzed to determine whether it can be attributed to the retrieved context or not.
Faithfulness	This measures the context adherence of the generated answer. against the given context. It is calculated from answer and retrieved context. Score is calculated as fraction of number of claims inferred from the given context to total number of claims in generated answer. Higher the score better the response is.
Answer relevancy	This measures how pertinent the answer to given prompt. It check for incompleteness, redundancy, presence of irrelevant information. One of the methods to measure answer relevancy by measuring cosine similarity between generated question (by prompting back the LLM with the previous generated output to produce questions) and original question. This method uses a strong LLM to evaluate the outputs of another LLM. It leverages AI model to perform judgment-based tasks on another AI model's work.
Factual correctness	Factual correctness quantifies the factual overlap between the generated answer and the ground truth answer.
Assertion	Assertions are used to compare the LLM output against expected values or conditions The conditions are programs that runs on LLM response to validate the property such as substring presence, validation of regex format, validation of json schema, conformance of response length, contain sql query.
Chunk attribution	Average classification score of each retrieved chunk to be useful for the model's response generation.
Chunk utilization	Average chunk utilization score that measures the fraction content in each retrieved chunk that is used for model's response.

Table 8.7: *RAG metrics*

Vector databases are purpose-built for vector embeddings, which is a type of data representation used by LLM systems and RAG for various use cases. Vector databases are used in all LLM systems for easy search, high-performance, scalability, and seamless data retrieval for unstructured and semi-unstructured data. Observing vector database metrics help enterprises to ensure faster query retrieval, efficient storage of millions of data and helps to spot performance bottlenecks. Please find below table for few vector database metrics for LLM system:

Vector database:

Response duration	Average, min, max duration taken for a response given to an API call
Query per second on vector database	The rate which vector database can process the queries. Higher the value better the performance
Load latency of vector database	The time required to load data into the vector database's memory and build an index
Query time per vector	Average time to query one vector calculated by dividing query elapsed time to number of vector queried
Hardware performance	GPU vRAM usage, CPU Utilization, Network I/O read and write speed
Storage metrics	Total capacity, total data stored and number of data files

Table 8.8: *Vector database metrics*

Drift detection

Drift refers to a gradual shift in the performance of the model due to changes in data or changes in the relationship between input/output features. Drift in LLM model performance can happen due to changes in real-world environments, new task adaption, continuous alignment to human feedback, and changes to ethical policy.

Some of the common types of LLM drifts are data drift, concept drift, prompt drift, prediction drift, and upstream drift:

- **Concept drift** is drift in actuals, i.e., current ground truth has varied from previous ground truth. The input and output relationship has changed over time. The concept drift can be sudden drift, gradual drift, incremental drift or recurring drift. Concept drift required pre-training of model with new data or continual online-learning or batch learning.

- **Data drift** is due to changes in the distribution of input data. This could be due to change in distribution of features, change in relationship between input features or change in input data statistical properties.

- The **embedding drift** detection involves measurement of similarity between reference data and incoming requests/prompts/response. Similarity analysis involves dimensionality reduction using **principal component analysis (PCA)** followed by clustering analysis using techniques like K-means. PCA dimensions (i.e., dimension needed to explain 95% variation of embedding data), inertia, silhouette scores between the source reference data and real time snapshots are monitored for embedding drift detection.

- The **prediction drift** is similar to data drift where the distribution on model output changes over time. It is an indicator for an underlying data drift.

- The **prompt drift** is the phenomenon where a prompt yields different responses over time due to model changes, model migration or changes in prompt-injection data at inference.

- The **upstream drift** due to a change in the data pipeline. This may be due to operational changes, data for a feature no longer being generated, unit changes etc.

Drift monitoring can be done by monitoring univariate statistical measures, as shown in the following Table. The other ways to detect drifts are through training a supervised binary classifier to classify drift points and through multivariate cluster analysis using K-Means, **Gaussian mixture models (GMM)**, PCA, **Principal Uniform Manifold Approximation and Projection (UMAP)**. Some of the metrics that can be monitored to identify drift detection are given in the table below:

Drift:

Kolmogorov-Smirnov statistic	It measures the maximum difference between two cumulative distribution functions.
Wasserstein distance	It is also known as **EMD**. It measures the amount of work needed to transform one distribution into another.
Kullback-Leibler divergence	It is a non-symmetric metric. is a measure of the difference between two probability distributions, also known as **relative entropy** or **information divergence**.
Population Stability Index (PSI)	PSI measures how much a population has shifted over time or between two different samples of a population in a single number. It does this by bucketing the two distributions and comparing the percentages of items in each of the buckets.
Jensen-Shannon (JS) divergence	JS is symmetric and similar to KL divergence measure the difference between two probability distribution.
Embedding drift	Inertia, silhouette score, PCA dimension monitoring.

Table 8.10: Drift detection metrics

Alerting and feedback systems

Altering and feedback are critical for any monitoring system to take action in time. Alerting mechanisms involve elements such as threshold, frequency, and escalation. Threshold defines a numerical value for each monitoring metric above which an alert will get triggered. Frequency defines the interval over which metrics will be scrapped and key performance indicators will be generated. The frequency for each metric varies based upon its criticality and near-real time requirements. Escalation is process integration where alerts will get addressed by appropriate actions. The other scenarios where alerts get generated are like IT system alerts for resource overrun, activity alerts such as unauthorized, security alerts such as DDoS attack, and event alerts such as bias detection. Alerts can help in improving the performance of model by re-training/alignment tuning of base model based on user feedback through continuous integration and delivery mechanisms.

LLM application tracing

LLM applications consist of various components beyond base models. It includes **user interface** (**UI**), LLM chains, Vector databases, message queues, event streams, AI agents, API calls, plugins, LLM cache, prompts and various data pipelines. So, it is essential to trace the internal behavior of an LLM application in order to ensure the resilience and performance of the system.

Tracing helps to understand LLM applications by breaking down steps within a request as it flows through the application and brings visibility to its internal system. A trace records the paths taken by requests (made by an application or end-user) as they propagate through multiple steps. A trace is made of one or more spans. Spans represent individual unit of work or operation. Spans provide a more in-depth context of what occurs during a request. LLM application Spans can be of different types, such as chain, agents, events, tools, retrievers, and log generators.

The traces emitted using instrumentation are exported and collected using various functions such as exporters and collectors for monitoring and debugging. LLM applications are generally auto instrumented through plugins (OpenTelemetry) to emit traces. Some of the popular tools to do LLM Application tracing are Langtrace, Langfuse, and LangSmith.

Upon completion of LLMOps Phase 2, we have developed a comprehensive understanding of model serving methodologies, various inferencing techniques, LLM security vulnerabilities, and effective monitoring and alerting systems. In the next section, we look into other deployment practices that bring efficiency in LLM systems.

Other Deployment practices

The following are the other deployment practices:

- **Model cards**: Model cards are more of cheat sheet kind of document that is used to describe the details of production ML model. Enterprises create model cards as a single source of truth and use it as part of transparency and responsible reporting. The usage of model card, varies based on the persona, such as developers use it for performance result comparison, business team use it for appropriateness of intended use cases, governance team use it for documentation and auditing, ethics team use it to ensure the privacy impact for consumers on using the model. Some of the information that are made available in model card are model description (purpose of model and model architecture details), dataset details (source and preprocessing details on train, test dataset), results (evaluation results on model performance for various tasks and hyperparameter settings), usage examples (use cases, requirements and execution steps), limitations (known limitations, possible threats, biases). There are set of tools to automate the creation of the model card. One such tool is **model card toolkit** (**MCT**) developed by *Google* that supports developers in compiling information programmatically into model card. MCT stores model card fields in JSON schema. MCT also support manual information population via Python API.

- **Use of watermarks**: Watermarks hide an invisible signal in images that helps computers identify if they are AI generated. For example, *Google* has developed a system called *SynthID*, which uses neural networks to modify pixels in images and adds a watermark that is invisible to the human eye. That mark is designed to be detected even if the image is edited. These tools could help companies improve their content moderation and make them faster to spot fake content, including nonconsensual deepfake. The other popular tool to prevent the use of proprietary images by AI or identify AI images is *PhotoGuard*, which was developed by researchers at *MIT* and *Fawked* by researchers at the *University of Chicago, Nightshade*. It works like a protective shield by altering the pixels in images in ways that makes hard for AI systems to use it. Similar to images, Watermarking algorithms for text content and audio content (audio seal) has been researched to prevent unauthorized usage and to identify AI generated content.

- **LLM-powered agents**: These areas advance in LLM where different components of an AI system leverage LLM capability to solve a task through reasoning, planning, and execution. Agent is made up of core engine to orchestrate the process, long and short-term memory modules to maintain different states of an AI system, Tools to execute the tasks and planning module to schedule and decide on flow of operations.

There are many autonomous agents that operate along with LLMs to minimize human intervention and use agent-agent conversational techniques to initiate and complete tasks. One such popular autonomous agent is AutoGPT that is built on GPT-4 and has features such as code execution, web browsing, Google search, web scraping and file operations. The other popular one is *Microsoft Autogen*. Autogen is a multi-agent framework can take different roles, run different tasks, converse with other agents to perform workflows. These agents are customizable and allow human intervention at all stages. One of the notable features of Autogen is the conversable agent class, i.e., every agent can send and receive messages from other agents to jointly finish a task and each agent have their own role defined by representative subclasses are `AssistantAgent` (need on human intervention to execute the task) and `UserProxyAgent` (for soliciting human intervention). Autogen enables autonomous conversation and allows conversation in both static and dynamic mode. In static mode, conversation follows a pre-defined agent topology and in dynamic mode topology changes depending on actual flow.

Before concluding this chapter, we will understand the *Hugging Face* a community platform over 900k models, 200k datasets, and 300k demos that acts as a hub for AI experts and enthusiasts.

Hugging Face

Hugging Face is a community framework or platform for ML engineers, similar to GitHub for software developers. Developers can create their own model, host the model and get an API endpoint for inference. Similarly, the other features include data hosting, collaborative space for model building, and host applications for ML demos. Similar to GitHub these repositories can be restricted for private use or public use. Below is the code to create Hugging Face repository, sync it with local ones:

```
1.  #create virtual environment
2.  python -m venv venv
3.  venv\scripts\activate
4.
5.  #create hugging face repository
6.  pip install huggingface_hub
7.  huggingface-cli login --token {token credentials}
8.  #enter token credential (Create token from huggingface portal)
9.  #https://huggingface.co/settings/tokens (get write access)
10.
11. #Create model repo
12. huggingface-cli repo  create onnx_model --type model
13. git clone https://huggingface.co/{profile name }/onnx_model
14. # viewmodel using  https://huggingface.co/{pfofile name} /onnx_model
15.
16. mkdir huggingface-repo #create local repository
17. cd huggingface-repo
18.
19. git remote set-url origin https://<user_name>:<token>@huggingface.co/<repo_path>
20. git pull origin
21. git lfs install
22. huggingface-cli lfs-enable-largefiles .
23.
24. copy ../{modelfile} # copy the file into local repo
25. git add .
```

```
26. git commit -m "My First Model"  #descriptive message
27. git push
```

Hugging Face enables developers with high level API for different kinds of transformer models to perform different tasks. With single **transformer** library developers can load, train and save model without any hassle. One of the basic objects of the **transformer** library is the **transform pipeline** that is used to perform all pre- and processing steps for an NLP application. Tokenization of input, model inferencing, postprocessing of model output i.e., logits to probabilities through softmax are the stages of pipeline. Most of these process are same as we have discussed in *Chapter 5, GenAI for Text*. Some of the prebuilt pipeline tasks that can be performed are sequence classification, question and answer, name entity recognition, translation, summarization and language modeling. Below is a sample code for Hugging Face transformer pipeline usage for summarization:

```
1. !pip install transformers #package installation
2. from transformers import pipeline
3.
4. article =''' In physics, a quantum (pl.: quanta) is the minimum amount
   of any physical entity (physical property) involved in an interaction.
   Quantum is a discrete quantity of energy proportional in magnitude to
   the frequency of the radiation it represents. The fundamental notion
   that a chemical property can be "quantized" is referred to as "the
   hypothesis of quantization".[1] This means that the magnitude of the
   physical property can take on only discrete values consisting of
   integer multiples of one quantum. For example, a photon is a single
   quantum of light of a specific frequency (or of any other form of
   electromagnetic radiation). Similarly, the energy of an electron bound
   within an atom is quantized and can exist only in certain discrete
   values. (Atoms and matter in general are stable because electrons can
   exist only at discrete energy levels within an atom.) Quantization
   is one of the foundations of the much broader physics of quantum
   mechanics. Quantization of energy and its influence on how energy and
   matter interact (quantum electrodynamics) is part of the fundamental
   framework for understanding and describing nature.'''
5.
6. summarizer = pipeline("summarization", model="t5-base", tokenizer="t5-
   base", framework="tf")
7. summarizer(article, min_length=5, max_length=30)
```

The following is the code to download model locally from Hugging Face:

```
1. from huggingface_hub import hf_hub_download
2. hf_hub_download(repo_id="facebook/bart-large-cnn",    filename="bart-
   large-cnn.tar.gz")
```

3. `git clone git@hf.co:<MODEL ID>` # example: `git clone git@hf.co:bigscience/bloom`

Hugging Face dataset library

Datasets is a library within hugging face used for sharing different forms of datasets such as NLP, computer vision and audio. It enables developer for easy splitting, interaction, preprocessing of datasets. The below code shows different ways of loading data set for ML of choice from Hugging Face hub and sharing own dataset to Hugging Face hub.

Using API download dataset:

```
1. curl -X GET \
2.     "https://datasets-server.huggingface.co/rows?dataset=Open-Orca%
       2FSlimOrca&config=default&split=train&offset=0&length=100"
```

Using Hugging Face dataset library:

```
1. !pip3 install datasets
2. import datasets
3. from datasets import load_dataset_builder
4. ds_builder = load_dataset_builder("Open-Orca/SlimOrca")
5.
6. # Inspect dataset description
7. ds_builder.info.description
8.
9. # Inspect dataset features
10. ds_builder.info.features
11.
12. from datasets import load_dataset
13.
14. dataset = load_dataset("Open-Orca/SlimOrca", split="train") # Load
    dataset
15. print(dataset)
16. dataset.to_pandas()
```

Conclusion

In this chapter, we understood the LLMOPs process and various optimization techniques to improve the performance of LLMs. We started with data preparation and validation for any LLM training or fine-tuning process. We understood the process of pretraining, types of finetuning and different optimization techniques. We further explained on

LLM vulnerabilities and the need for mitigations. We also understood different serving techniques and tools with sample vLLM code for hosting mistral models. We also presented example on experimentation of RAG evaluation using MLFlow. We listed out OWASP top 10 LLM related risks and vulnerabilities. We also briefed on security tools and libraries that can help to monitor and mitigate security risks. We listed out different metrics for pre-training, fine-tuning, inference, security, responsibility, experience, cost and RAG. We also emphasized the importance of application tracing, alerting and feedback mechanism for continual improvement of model performance. We finally discussed the other deployment practices like model cards, watermarking, and the use of GenAI agents in a production environment. Finally, we introduced Hugging Face a popular data science platform and examples on how it is been utilized for model sharing and data set downloading. In the next chapter, we will be covering the generative AI use cases for enterprises and strategy to approach them.

Key terms

- LLMOps is a framework for managing the lifecycle of large language models
- Pre-training involves training foundation models from scratch on massive datasets
- Fine-tuning is adapting pre-built foundation models for specific tasks using different techniques like PEFT, RLHF
- LLM guardrails are safety measures implemented to prevent large language models from generating harmful, biased, or inappropriate content
- Model card is a standardized document that provides essential information about a LLM model for promoting transparency and accountability
- Jailbreaking refers to techniques that exploit vulnerabilities in language models to generate harmful or biased content

Questions

1. What is meant by data version control?
2. What are the different open table and open file formats?
3. How do we decide on volume of data and number of epochs for pre-training?
4. What are different types of fine-tuning techniques?
5. What are key observability metrics for RAG system?
6. What is meant by prompt injection?
7. What are the benefits of quantization?
8. What is meant by the continued pre-training?
9. What are typical guard rails set for outputs of GenAI?
10. What is meant by concept drift?
11. Difference between time to first token and latency?

## CHAPTER 9

Generative AI for the Enterprise

Introduction

Generative AI (GenAI) comes with its own risks and challenges, and it is important for enterprises to be aware of it and have a governance structure in place before walking down the implementation path. The GenAI vendor landscape is diverse, featuring a multitude of companies providing innovative solutions across various industries. In this chapter, we will cover the importance of GenAI for the Enterprise, its relevance and growth, and various use cases that have a high potential to simplify and add value to organizations. We will wrap up with ethical AI and how it seeks to prevent biases in AI models, ensure privacy, and promote responsible use of technology.

Structure

In this chapter, we will cover the following topics:

- GenAI for enterprise
- AI risks and challenges
- Responsible AI

Objectives

The objective of this chapter is to provide an overview of how GenAI technology is leveraged by enterprises for their business improvements. This chapter covers various enterprise use cases, GenAI products, and their capabilities. It also focuses on risks related to AI models, GenAI model vulnerabilities, and factors that enterprises must consider while implementing GenAI projects. It also gives a foundation to Responsible AI, its applicability in enterprise systems, and some of the examples.

GenAI for enterprise

The 2023, Gartner Hype Cycle for GenAI identified key technologies increasingly embedded into many enterprise applications. Specifically, three innovations projected to have a huge impact on organizations within ten years include GenAI enabled applications, foundation models, and **AI trust, risk and security management** (**AI TRiSM**). GenAI for enterprises represents a transformative frontier in **artificial intelligence** (**AI**), enabling machines to create content, analyze data, and solve complex problems with unprecedented versatility. Leveraging advanced deep learning models, GenAI encompasses a spectrum of applications, from natural language generation to image and code creation. Enterprises are integrating this technology into various domains, such as customer service, marketing, and product development, to enhance productivity and innovation. GenAI empowers organizations to automate tasks, generate creative content, and make data-driven decisions, fostering a new era of efficiency and adaptability. As businesses navigate AI, GenAI emerges as a powerful tool to drive intelligent automation and elevate enterprise capabilities.

Rise of GenAI

As the prevalence of AI, particularly GenAI, increases, technologies lacking AI capabilities may appear insufficient. The widespread use of this powerful technology raises significant questions about its development and application. Historically, AI was inaccessible to the general public, with specialized engineers being the primary developers due to their scarcity and high cost. However, barriers to entry are diminishing, allowing individuals without AI expertise to engage in AI development. AI systems now empower computers to perceive, comprehend, and interact with the world in unprecedented ways, evolving rapidly. According to *Stanford University's 2019 AI Index report*, compute power has doubled approximately every 3.5 months since 2012, leading to remarkable advancements in AI specifically Vision AI technologies.

The rise of GenAI has ushered in a diverse array of capabilities, enabling the creation of various digital content, such as text, code, images, simulations, 3D objects, music, and video. GenAI's foundation lies in the transformer model, a deep learning architecture renowned for its exceptional, contextual understanding and adept relationship tracking within sequential data. Unlike other architectures, the transformer employs a self-attention mechanism, allowing it to selectively focus on different parts of the input sequence at each step, efficiently capturing intricate relationships.

Originally crafted for language translation, pre-trained transformer models can seamlessly adapt to new tasks without extensive retraining, alleviating the workload for ML practitioners. Examples of prominent **large language models** (**LLMs**) include *OpenAI's GPT-4*, proficient in generating human-like text responses, and *Google's BERT model*, designed to comprehend contextual nuances in sentences.

GenAI is rapidly expanding with substantial contributions from industry giants like *Google, Microsoft, OpenAI*, and *Anthropic*. LLMs, such as GPT-4, have gained widespread utility in applications like chatbots, virtual assistants, and systems requiring computer-generated natural language responses. This widespread integration underscores their effectiveness in understanding and generating human-like language, ultimately enhancing user experiences and interactions with computer systems.

Enterprise use cases of GenAI

As one of the most significant technological advancements, GenAI is an incredibly versatile technology capable of revolutionizing various aspects of organizations, provided it is deployed responsibly. GenAI continually reveals new possibilities, promising substantial advancements in the future. While some enterprises in marketing and sales have swiftly integrated GenAI into their workflows, leveraging its speed and scale for content production and customer relationship management, industries with stringent legal and compliance requirements, such as healthcare, insurance, and education, have approached GenAI adoption more cautiously due to the lack of transparency and regulation in its rapid growth.

Enterprise use cases for GenAI have operated relatively inconspicuously, yet the evident business potential is clear for those closely following this technology. The following table shows examples of how major enterprises are currently incorporating GenAI into their processes:

Use case	Description
Intelligent assistant	This use case of GenAI involves implementing a highly adaptable tool with a chat-based conversational interface, backed by a generative language model. This tool initially leverages models like *OpenAI's GPT* and serves diverse organizational departments by supporting employees in their day-to-day tasks.

Use case	Description
Coding buddy	This use case transforms software development by providing a digital coding buddy that assists developers in tasks, such as code explanation, generation, bug identification, correction, test generation, and vulnerability mitigation. Utilizing models like *GitHub Copilot*, it collaborates with human developers, significantly speeding up coding tasks and enhancing productivity. This application underscores the potential of GenAI in streamlining programming processes and reducing the workload for developers.
Intelligent search	Enhances internal search tools by interpreting ambiguous queries accurately, employing enhanced indexation for textual, visual, and multimedia content, and providing generative responses to specific questions. Utilizes proprietary data for training, offering improved accuracy, speed, and positive impressions internally and externally.
Product and app development	Utilized for coding apps and writing product documentation, particularly beneficial in quality assurance for bug fixes, test generation, and documentation. Applied to semiconductor chip development and design projects.
Blog and social media content writing	Employs LLMs like Jasper AI to generate creative content for blogs, social media, product pages, and business websites based on user inputs about audience and tone of voice.
Inbound and outbound marketing	GenAI supports marketing communication workflows, creating contextualized emails and chat threads for inbound and outbound campaigns. Automates moving contacts to the next stage of the customer lifecycle in CRM platforms.
Graphic design and video marketing	Used for generating realistic images, animation, and audio for graphic design and video marketing projects. Offers voice synthesis and AI avatars, enabling the creation of marketing videos without actors or extensive editing expertise. Rapidly growing as a source of enterprise use cases in the design and marketing sector.
Entertainment media generation	Creates graphics for movies and video games, audio for music and podcasts, and characters for virtual storytelling and virtual reality experiences. Predicted to play a significant role in future film content creation. Currently supplements existing scripts and enhances **non-player characters** (**NPCs**) for interactive experiences.
Performance management and coaching	Applied in various business and employee coaching scenarios, such as call documentation and summarization in contact centers. Combines with sentiment analysis for assessing current performance and coaching employees on improvement.
Business performance reporting	Utilized for business intelligence and performance reporting, summarizing massive amounts of unstructured and qualitative data efficiently. Particularly useful for data analytics, especially in scenarios where insights require extensive processing.

Use case	Description
Customer support and customer experience	Employs GenAI chatbots and virtual assistants for handling customer service questions at all hours. Provides comprehensive and human-like answers without human support representatives for straightforward customer service engagements.
Pharmaceutical drug discovery and design	Improves efficiency in drug discovery and design processes by generating novel molecules, optimizing disordered proteins, and predicting clinical trial results. Receives significant funding for AI-driven drug discovery.
Medical diagnostics and imaging	Enhances medical images by optimizing and zooming in, providing a realistic look at specific areas of the human body. Some tools perform medical image analysis and basic diagnostics independently, although caution is necessary, and results should be verified by medical professionals.
Consumer-friendly synthetic data generation	Addresses security concerns by creating synthetic data copies of sensitive data for analysis without compromising privacy. Enables analysts to develop AI models and score them without using actual business or consumer data.
Smart manufacturing and predictive maintenance	Assists in modern manufacturing, aiding workers in creating innovative designs and achieving production goals. In predictive maintenance, generative models generate to-do lists, timelines, workflow suggestions, and simplify complex data assessment from sensors and assembly lines.
Fraud detection and risk management	Analyzes large amounts of transaction or claims data, summarizing and identifying patterns or anomalies for fraud detection, underwriting, and risk management in finance and insurance scenarios. Provides valuable support in assessing and managing risks.
Professional services and business operations	Accenture uses GenAI to assist clients in creating smarter business strategies, roadmaps, and operations across various industries, including banking, sales, customer service, and legal. Services include enhanced search, document summarization, and automated communications.
E-commerce and retail	*Shopify's* offering, *Shopify Magic*, uses GenAI to help retailers generate product descriptions and other product-related content. Users input verbal tone and keywords, and *Shopify* generates descriptions meeting specified parameters. Enhances content creation for e-commerce and retail businesses.

Table 9.1: Examples of enterprise related GenAI use cases

GenAI real-world examples

Restaurant industry: Fast service restaurants are becoming competitive, and GenAI is disrupting such quick service restaurants. Their consumers tend to care more about speed, variety and convenience. Drive-thru is one of the preferred ordering channels for customers in fast service restaurants. Automation is one way to address these challenges of speed, labor shortages, and customer experience. Some of the challenges doing AI automation in drive-thru channels are varieties of menus that bring different possible order combinations, environmental deterrents like ambient noise hampering the performance of voice-based solutions, and lack of wider customer knowledge, making it difficult for restaurants to make menu suggestions for personalized customer experience. GenAI addresses these challenges and fundamentally changes the way customers interact with the business. The menu data, customer data, business rules, and customer conversational logics are embedded into LLMs and integrated with Point of sale hardware. GenAI enabled conversation device handles noisy conversations better than traditional AI to understand customer asks, and with the help of menu data as context, large LLMs hosted on the cloud run through multiple possible ordering combinations to create the right made-to-order requests for the customer ask and also responds to customer questions. GenAI systems are integrated into the wider ecosystem of customer behavior data and, with guard rails enabled, make personalized menu suggestions in a more precise way without intruding on customer privacy.

An example voice conversation: *get me a breakfast combo along with fresh-cracked free-range egg and a grilled sausage covered in creamy cheese sauce on a flaky croissant bun and warm muffins excluding nut and gluten contents. Also, need 2 spicy chicken sandwiches with juicy marinated chicken breast, crispy lettuce and tomatoes, fries served hot and crispy, a drink and the chicken nuggets with orange fanta large drink 20 oz included.* GenAI systems help order takers understand each customer's orders in noisy environments, understand catalogs and offers to give the customers the best pricing, communicate delivery duration and ready status based on existing orders and can recommend customers for alternate choices based on previous orders.

GenAI, take the complexity out of the ordering process so employees can focus on serving up fast, fresh-made, quality food and exceptional service. GenAI technology will set a new standard for great drive-thru experiences for the quick-service industry.

Online furniture retail industry: Personalization is one of the standout features in modern ecommerce platform, especially in Furniture retail. Online furniture retail has its own unique challenges, such as return and exchanges due to mismatch to customer preferences. Customers find it difficult to feel the product or be able to picture how it is presence will change or fit to the existing environment. The other challenges in online furniture retail include the difference in color, textures and appearances to delivered products with respect to online pictures. While Some of the technologies like AR/VR are trying to fill these gaps by reducing the uncertainties through an immersive experience, however, they were not able to cater to provide a tailored product recommendation to customer preference, and with a portfolio of different choices, the technology becomes costly. GenAI technology addresses these challenges and opens up new avenue for online retailers to interact with their customers. GenAI model articulate customer specific home design needs and along with extensive knowledge to furniture catalogs featuring thousands of products, it generates various design choices aligned to customer needs. These designs can range from existing minimalistic catalog design to new AI-generated artistic collections. GenAI can help customers to communicate in real time with home furnishing experts to get their choices finalized. Based on design choice, with the support of immersive technologies and GenAI 3D generation capability, a virtual environment with fitted furniture reflecting the customer environment gets generated to give a real feel of the product.

An example conversation *get me cozy kitchen outlets made of shiny brown color with Italian design doors for an apartment size of 10 m x 10 m with window open on left and made out of sustainable materials*. GenAI understands the requirements, generate them into catalogs with different design choices and based on user preference, recommend best products with guided advice from home décor experts. Based on customer choices, it generates virtual environments depicting the furniture in various visualization features like broad daylight, night etc.

GenAI take out most of the uncertainty of the furniture product by offering a tool that gives users personalized furniture and decor suggestions based on factors such as room dimensions, personal style, sustainability preferences, budget, functional requirements, and more.

IT service management industry: In rapidly evolving digital business, regardless of business size ITSM plays a critical role in business operations. It plays a core part in the customer journey to provide a seamless experience. Some of the challenges in ITSM services involve the management of a disproportionate number of service requests for agents, multiple tools and technologies to handle, reporting issues, inadequate communication, lack of knowledge, repetitive tasks, delayed analysis, manual synthesis, large mean time to response, and many more. GenAI is disrupting each process of ITSM and the way it operates. GenAI agents provide automated responses to common queries or known issues (FAQs) to help speed up the resolution process. GenAI based smart virtual agents delivering conversational support in multiple languages empower users to resolve service requests on their own. A summary of the chat conversation with the live agent before the incident was created helps the agent create the right ticket for the resolution. GenAI expedites ticket handling for agents by summarizing incoming requests and suggesting solutions. GenAI helps to do the right categorization of the tickets based on the conversational context and a knowledge article is drafted for the incident using task data, comments, and work notes from the activity stream. Organizations can speed up processes by using GenAI to draft internal and external communication based on solutions proposed by agents. With the help of GenAI-based audit, the agent conversations can be audited completely instead of the sampling-based methods, improving the process quality.

GenAI Improve operational efficiency and speed, and with AI automating routine ITSM tasks it helps business to reduce cost for support operations. GenAI which excels in natural language communication, summarization, reporting, content generation is providing transformative benefits at every stage of ITSM lifecycle.

GenAI vendors

GenAI enables developers to enhance user experiences across various domains, including code development, gaming, AR/VR/XR, and customer service. Major tech players, such as *Microsoft*, *Google*, and *AWS*, are heavily investing in GenAI startups, with *Microsoft* being a significant supporter of *OpenAI*. These companies are investing and actively developing their own GenAI tools, contributing to the rapid growth of this technology. Some have experienced rapid launches, securing substantial funding, while others adopt a more cautious approach, prioritizing ethics and safety before product launches. Overall, these leading GenAI companies are crafting solutions poised to meet the long-term expectations of both businesses and individual users. *Table 9.2* below shows some of the major players in GenAI marketplace and their products:

Vendor	Product description
Alphabet (Google)	*Google* is building scalable GenAI tools integrated into its cloud ecosystem. Google **Gemini** is the AI-powered assistant, built right into Gmail, Docs, Sheets and more, with enterprise-grade security and privacy. Google AI tools encompass wide range of capabilities from image generation to text (Multi-Modality) for office suite applications. The company emphasizes a comprehensive and transparent approach to AI ethics, evident through its AI Principles established in 2017. *Google Cloud infrastructure* is optimized for both cost and high performance in AI applications.
Anthropic	*Anthropic's* product, *Claude*, is a highly customizable AI assistant designed for content generation, summarization, and explanations. Claude serves various industries, offering applications in customer service, legal document analysis, administrative tasks, and sales. *Anthropic* emphasizes transparency through extensive public research and aims to ensure Claude is useful while avoiding harmful content outputs. The company is focused on safe and steerable product development, prioritizing quality and safety over quantity and speed.
Cohere	*Cohere's* suite includes *Neural Search* for semantic text search, summarize for document summarization, and generate for content generation, especially in marketing and sales contexts. Cohere's language models can be tailored to specific enterprise requirements, and its extensive resources for developers contribute to its user-friendly API. It operates in public, private, and hybrid cloud environments, supporting multilingual options across its tools.
Glean	*Glean* offers GenAI-powered internal search for workplace apps and ecosystems, enhancing employee user experience. Designed with a dynamic knowledge graph for each company, *Glean* adapts to specific roles, interactions, and content requests. Key features include verified answers for frequently asked questions, curated collections for team-specific organizations, and Go Links for creating short links to commonly used resources. Despite its connection to enterprise apps and databases, Glean ensures security by respecting and enforcing permissions while providing a clean and user-friendly interface.

Vendor	Product description
Hugging Face	*Hugging Face* is a community-driven platform that facilitates AI model development. It offers various prediction models and datasets, enabling developers to build custom GenAI solutions. While developer-centric, the platform provides user-friendly tools like AutoTrain for non-coders. Its partnership with AWS extends accessibility, but the forum's developer-facing format may be less friendly to non-technical users.
IBM	*IBM* is a major player in the AI space, offering a wide range of AI solutions and services rather than a specific GenAI product. IBM's AI offerings include *IBM Watson*, a comprehensive AI platform that incorporates natural language processing, machine learning, and data analytics. Watson is used across various industries for tasks like language translation, sentiment analysis, and data insights. IBM also provides AI consulting services to help organizations implement AI solutions tailored to their specific needs.
Inflection AI	Though Inflection AI has not released a product yet, it stands out for its vision and the pedigree of its founders and investors. Founded by technologists formerly associated with *DeepMind*, *Google*, and *LinkedIn*, Inflection AI focuses on teaching machines to understand human language for improved human-machine interaction. It aims to deliver communication tools accessible to individuals unfamiliar with computer and programming languages, positioning itself as a company to watch for future developments.
Insilico medicine	The company utilizes GenAI to accelerate the process of identifying potential drug candidates and optimizing their molecular structures. *Insilico Medicine's* platform leverages deep learning models to analyze vast biological datasets, predict molecular interactions, and design novel compounds with desired properties. The goal is to streamline and enhance the efficiency of drug discovery, potentially reducing the time and costs associated with bringing new drugs to market.
Jasper	*Jasper* is a GenAI platform catering to marketers and content creators. Its features support blog and email writing, SEO optimization, and the creation of art and ad imagery. With an intuitive AI engine that curates model selection for different job requests, Jasper provides an easy-to-use interface through browser extensions and in-line experiences. In February 2023, *Jasper* introduced business enhancements, including *Jasper Brand Voice* for training on brand-specific tone, style, and language, and Jasper API for seamless integration into existing tool stacks.
Lightricks	Known for the mobile photo editing app *Facetune*, *Lightricks* ventured into GenAI with a text-to-image generator in 2022. It enables users to create custom art and images through prompts, with subsequent editing options for animation and 3D motion creations. Lightricks' consumer-friendly tools allow easy creation and editing of photos and AI-generated imagery for personal and creative purposes.

Vendor	Product description
Microsoft	*Microsoft* stands out in GenAI with innovations like *Copilot*, a GPT-4-powered assistive tool integrated into applications, such as *Microsoft 365*, *Dynamics 365*, and *Security Copilot* for cybersecurity. Copilot offers assistive content generation, making it valuable across various business operations. Microsoft's collaboration with OpenAI provides access to GPT-4 and other emerging solutions, enhancing its suite of intuitive GenAI tools.
NVIDIA	*NVIDIA* is a leading technology company that offers a comprehensive suite of solutions for GenAI applications. Leveraging its powerful GPUs, NVIDIA provides high-performance hardware accelerators designed to accelerate the training and inference processes of large-scale generative models. The *NVIDIA H100 Tensor Core* GPUs, part of the *NVIDIA Ampere architecture*, are particularly renowned for their performance in AI workloads. NVIDIA also contributes to the software side with frameworks like *NVIDIA TensorRT*, optimizing deep learning models for deployment. With a focus on hardware and software, NVIDIA's offerings play a crucial role in advancing the capabilities and efficiency of GenAI across various industries.
OpenAI	*OpenAI* offers a suite of products leveraging advanced GenAI models. Their flagship model, **Generative Pre-trained Transformer (GPT)**, is a versatile language model capable of understanding and generating human-like text based on user prompts. The API provided by OpenAI allows developers to seamlessly integrate these powerful language models into their applications, enabling a wide range of natural language processing tasks. ChatGPT is another product that focuses on generating coherent and contextually relevant text, making it suitable for chat-based interactions, content creation, and more. DALL-E is an image generation model designed to create unique visual content based on textual descriptions, showcasing the application of GenAI in the visual domain.
Stability AI	*Stability AI* powers many GenAI solutions with its deep learning model, Stable Diffusion. It offers open-source code via platforms like *GitHub* and *Hugging Face*, allowing developers to customize its tools. Stability AI's extensive API library and *Discord community* foster collaboration and discussion. The company's focus on open-source accessibility enables users to create tailored solutions for image and video generation, making it a foundational model for various GenAI applications.
Synthesis AI	*Synthesis AI* focuses on synthetic data, image, and video generation, offering products like humans and scenarios. Applications include identity verification, avatar creation, driver monitoring, AR/VR/XR, teleconferencing, cybersecurity, and virtual try-on. Synthesis AI prioritizes AI ethics and diversity, delivering photorealistic image generation. Although smaller in enterprise value, it stands out for the variety of products and solutions it provides customers.

Table 9.2: Major GenAI vendors and their product description

AI risks and challenges

AI risks and challenges encompass ethical concerns, algorithm biases, and potential job displacement. Issues related to privacy, security vulnerabilities, and the explainability of AI decisions also contribute to the complex landscape. Addressing these challenges requires a concerted effort to develop responsible AI practices, robust regulations, and ongoing research to mitigate potential negative impacts on society.

Main AI concerns

Organizations can mitigate trust and branding risks by implementing responsible AI practices, potentially enhancing their associated brands. The ethical dilemmas arising from AI's societal impact necessitate a continued focus on ethics within the AI community. Ethical frameworks globally may be contradictory, but ethical deliberation must draw on diverse perspectives.

Ethics is the art of living well with others. It requires ingenuity to address unprecedented moral challenges posed by groundbreaking technology. Responsible AI is not synonymous with rules or checklists; it emphasizes the importance of humility, confronting difficult questions, and adapting opinions based on new evidence.

Organizations increasingly recognize the need for responsible AI as challenges multiply with the expanding social, political, and environmental impact of 21st century technology. Following are some of the major concerns related to AI technology:

- Transparency emerges as a primary concern, as complex AI systems make it challenging for users to understand decision-making processes, affecting autonomy and informed choices.
- Amplified by AI, unfair bias reflects and perpetuates societal biases, necessitating recognition and addressing biases in data and system development.
- Security concerns in AI include the potential for malicious exploitation by bad actors, with attacks posing risks to safety and societal security.
- Privacy is another concern, as AI's ability to gather and analyze vast data quantities can lead to risks of exploitation, identification, tracking, and profiling.
- The risk of pseudoscience in AI involves the potential for AI systems to lack a robust scientific foundation, leading to unsubstantiated claims, unreliable outcomes, and ethical concerns.
- The lack of accountability in AI refers to the absence of clear responsibility and oversight for the actions and decisions made by AI systems. This can result in ethical and legal challenges, as well as difficulties in addressing biases, errors, and unintended consequences arising from AI applications.
- Potential for AI-driven unemployment and deskilling are additional concerns.

Addressing these concerns involves a responsible approach to privacy, promoting scientific foundations in AI, ensuring accountability through defined goals and transparency, and anticipating shifts in the labor market due to technological advances. Despite its concerns, innovation, and technology could create new jobs and opportunities, similar to past adjustments in response to technological changes.

GenAI vulnerabilities

GenAI is particularly exemplified by LLMs, which introduce specific concerns. These models, which creatively generate natural-sounding text, face issues such as hallucinations, producing unrealistic or entirely fabricated content, factuality concerns regarding the accuracy of generated information, and anthropomorphization, involving the attribution of human-like qualities to non-human entities like AI models.

In addition to these challenges, there are broader concerns in GenAI development and deployment. This includes a lack of dedicated resources for ethical AI systems, encompassing insufficient funds, personnel, and technology. Diversification is also a concern, with a shortage of diverse teams, particularly regarding race, gender, and geography, contributing to potential biases in AI systems. The absence of a universally accepted ethical AI code of conduct or mechanisms to assess deviations has compounded these ethical challenges. The following are some of the major concerns unique to GenAI technology:

- Hallucinations occur when the AI model generates content that is unrealistic, fictional, or entirely fabricated. This can lead to the dissemination of false or misleading information, impacting the reliability and trustworthiness of the AI-generated content.

- Factuality pertains to the accuracy or truthfulness of the information generated by the AI model. Inaccurate or misleading information generated by AI models can have real-world consequences, potentially influencing decision-making processes based on false premises.

- Anthropomorphization involves attributing human-like qualities, characteristics, or behaviors to non-human entities, such as machines or AI models. Assigning human attributes to AI may lead to misconceptions about the capabilities and intentions of the technology, potentially resulting in overreliance or inappropriate expectations.

- Lack of resources for ethical AI systems implies inadequate allocation of funds, personnel, and technology to ethical AI development can hinder the implementation of safeguards, audits, and monitoring mechanisms, increasing the risk of ethical lapses.

- A lack of diversity, including representation from different races, genders, and geographical backgrounds in AI development teams, may result in biased algorithms that do not consider a broad range of perspectives and experiences.

- The lack of a universally accepted ethical code for AI development contributes to ethical ambiguity, making it challenging to establish and enforce consistent ethical standards across the AI industry.

- The pressure to rapidly implement AI is identified as a primary cause of ethical issues in AI usage. This urgency may be driven by the desire for a first-mover advantage, competition with innovative AI applications, or simply the eagerness to capitalize on the benefits offered by AI.

Addressing these concerns requires a comprehensive approach that includes refining AI models, establishing diverse and inclusive development teams, formulating and adhering to ethical codes, and resisting undue pressure for rapid implementation to ensure responsible and ethical use of GenAI.

Enterprise level considerations

While GenAI's potential seems boundless, there is still a level of skepticism among the executive ranks. Following are enterprise level considerations before walking down the implementation of GenAI:

- **Untraceable**: Limited traceability of sources in GenAI poses a significant challenge as it hampers the ability to verify the origin and credibility of generated content. In complex models, understanding the specific data points or training examples that influenced an AI-generated output becomes challenging, leading to issues of accountability and transparency for enterprises.

- **Unable to detect false information**: GenAI model's output heavily depends on the information it has been exposed to during training. If the data contains inaccuracies or lacks diverse perspectives, the AI may produce factually incorrect results. Additionally, biases present in the training data, such as cultural or demographic biases, can contribute to distorted decision-making. AI systems making factually wrong decisions can result in unintended consequences affecting enterprise brand.

- **Increased risk of data breaches**: The extensive datasets used to train these models may contain sensitive or confidential information, making them attractive targets for malicious actors. If not adequately protected, the generated responses might inadvertently reveal private details embedded in the training data. Adversarial attacks specifically crafted to exploit vulnerabilities in AI systems are leading to unauthorized access and data breaches. Mitigating these risks requires robust cybersecurity measures, encryption, and ongoing monitoring to detect and respond to potential breaches promptly.

- **Unreproducible outcomes**: The black box nature of GenAI poses challenges in understanding and replicating model decisions. The intricate, nonlinear structures of deep learning models make it challenging to trace how specific inputs lead to certain outputs. Also, the probabilistic nature and continual learning of the model lead to generation of different outcomes for the same input at different times. The difficulty in reproducing results impedes the validation and verification processes crucial for ensuring model reliability.

- **Must catch up to global regulations**: Rapidly evolving AI technologies often outpace regulatory frameworks, leaving organizations struggling to align with emerging guidelines. The global nature of AI operations further complicates compliance, as regulations vary across jurisdictions. The lack of standardized frameworks for evaluating and certifying AI systems makes it difficult for organizations to ensure adherence to diverse regulatory landscapes. Non-compliance with regulations is becoming a significant challenge in the GenAI landscape.

- **Absence of a responsible AI strategy**: GenAI introduces several ethical risks and security challenges. The absence of a responsible AI strategy can lead to:
  - o Unintended biases in AI models, impacting fairness and accountability.
  - o It will hinder the establishment of transparent AI systems, making it difficult to gain trust from users and stakeholders.
  - o It will result in inadequate measures for mitigating potential risks and harms associated with AI applications.
  - o Organizations will struggle to comply with evolving regulations related to AI ethics and data privacy.

- **Battle for people is fiercer than ever**: The shortage of GenAI talent and skills poses a significant challenge in the industry. There is fierce competition for skilled professionals, leading to difficulties in recruiting and retaining qualified experts. Organizations may face delays in implementing GenAI projects and innovations due to a lack of specialized workforce. The existing talent gap hampers the development of diverse and inclusive AI solutions, limiting perspectives and creativity. It may result in increased reliance on pre-trained models, risking a lack of customization and adaptability to specific business needs.

- **Change is hard**: Resistance in the workforce is a common challenge when implementing GenAI. Employees may resist the adoption of AI technologies due to concerns about job displacement, changes in work routines, or fear of technology taking over human roles. Addressing this resistance requires transparent communication about the benefits of GenAI, emphasizing its role as a tool to enhance human capabilities rather than replace jobs.

Responsible AI

Despite significant progress, AI is not without its flaws. It necessitates a responsible approach that acknowledges potential issues, limitations, and unintended consequences. Responsible AI development requires understanding the impact of technology on society, as AI may replicate existing biases or issues without judgment. While there is no universal definition of responsible AI, organizations are crafting their own principles aligned with their mission and values. These principles consistently emphasize **transparency, fairness, accountability, and privacy**. Contrary to a common misconception, machines do not centrally decide; humans design, build, and control AI systems, embedding their values into every decision point from data collection to deployment. Consequently, responsible decision-making is crucial at every stage of the machine learning lifecycle, ensuring ethical choices from concept to maintenance.

Technology plays a crucial role in our lives, aiding in tasks ranging from navigation to accessing information for health concerns. While the potential for technological innovation is vast, there is a profound responsibility on the part of technology providers to ensure its ethical implementation. AI innovation has raised concerns regarding issues like fairness in ML, potential job displacement due to automation, and the accountability of AI-driven decisions. Responsible AI practices are essential for addressing controversial use cases and avoiding ethical problems in seemingly innocuous or well-intentioned applications. Integrating ethics into AI design is not only the right thing to do but also enhances the benefits of AI for people's lives, builds trust with users, and ensures the success of AI deployments.

The relevance of responsible AI

Incorporating responsible AI practices offers strategic and competitive advantages, affecting core business considerations and serving as a smart investment in product development. **Ethical AI reviews** are deemed essential for product innovation, examining opportunities and harms associated with new technologies to align products with responsible AI design. These reviews scrutinize data sets, model performance across sub-groups, and assess intended and unintended outcomes.

Failure to adopt responsible AI practices exposes organizations to risks, such as delayed product launches, work stoppages, and the withdrawal of products from the market. Early implementation of responsible AI practices can reduce development costs by preventing downstream ethical breaches. Organizations often abandon AI projects when ethical issues arise, hindering the shift of AI from labs to production.

Companies that have scaled with AI are more likely to be guided by responsible AI, as it enhances products by reducing unfair bias, improving transparency, and increasing security. Responsible AI practices attract and retain top talent, a crucial consideration in a competitive tech talent landscape. Data privacy and cybersecurity concerns pose significant obstacles to AI adoption, with a large percentage of consumers avoiding companies with data usage concerns.

Data breaches are costly for businesses, and consumers are more likely to blame companies than hackers, underscoring the importance of safeguarding data for customer engagement. Organizations developing responsible AI can gain a competitive advantage when new regulations emerge, reducing the risk of non-compliance and enabling constructive contributions to regulatory conversations. Customer behavior is influenced by ethics, and many surveys indicate customer willingness to pay more for ethically designed goods and services. Responsible AI also drives partnerships, aligning with investors' interests in sustainable, long-term investing.

Responsible AI principles

Large-scale AI deployment amplifies cybersecurity risks, with GenAI potentially exploited for identifying and targeting vulnerabilities within business information systems.

Navigating evolving regulations poses another challenge, with local and international laws emerging to govern AI use. Compliance with laws like *New York City's automated employment decision tool* law and broader frameworks like the *EU's AI Act* becomes crucial for employers, necessitating steps such as third-party bias audits and public disclosure of findings.

To address these challenges, leaders advise businesses to proceed cautiously in their AI transformations and establish dedicated task forces reporting to leadership. They emphasize the need for a strategic roadmap considering legal, reputational, and workforce risks. Responsible AI principles refer to a set of ethical guidelines and values designed to ensure the ethical, fair, and accountable development, deployment, and management of AI systems. The following principles guide the responsible use of AI, addressing issues of fairness, transparency, accountability, privacy, security, and inclusivity throughout the AI lifecycle:

- **Accountability**: The principle of accountability in AI emphasizes the transparency and openness of algorithms, attributes, and correlations within AI systems, allowing for external inspection and scrutiny. It ensures that those responsible for developing, deploying, and managing AI technologies can be identified and held accountable, fostering trust, ethical practices, and a clear understanding of the decision-making processes involved in AI applications. Algorithms, attributes, and correlations in AI systems are designed to be open and accessible for inspection, promoting transparency and accountability in the decision-making processes of the algorithms.

- **Unbiased and explainable AI**: Explicitly outline measures to eliminate, reduce, and manage bias in AI-powered interventions, especially for marginalized groups. Provide transparent explanations of the decision-making processes and actions taken by AI systems.

- **Resilient**: Monitored and reinforced learning protocols involving human oversight are implemented to ensure AI systems consistently produce reliable outputs, enhancing the resilience and dependability of the technology.

- **Transparent**: Clearly specify the data to be collected, particularly if it involves invasive procedures. Users are afforded a direct line of sight into the utilization of data, output, and decision-making processes in AI systems, promoting transparency and allowing stakeholders to understand and scrutinize the system's operations. Disclose any plans to share personal data, specifying recipients and providing reasons for sharing.

- **Privacy and security**: AI systems are fortified against potential risks, including cyber threats, that may pose physical or digital harm, ensuring the security and integrity of the system and the data it processes. Articulate protocols for maintaining privacy and securely storing data. Outline steps to be taken in the event of a privacy breach.

- **Governed**: Clear organizational policies determine responsibilities for data, output, and decisions within AI systems, establishing governance structures that define and uphold accountability throughout the AI implementation.

- **Adherence to laws and regulations**: Ongoing commitment to comply with all laws and regulations related to data and the ethical use of AI.

These principles stress the importance of open inspection, fair application, consistent learning, direct visibility into data and decisions, protection against risks, and the presence of clear organizational policies.

Responsible AI examples

Following are some of the examples of Responsible AI applicability in real-world scenarios:

- **Fair lending algorithms**: Financial institutions use responsible AI to develop fair lending algorithms that mitigate biases and ensure equitable access to financial services. These algorithms analyze a broader range of factors beyond traditional credit scores, promoting inclusivity and reducing discrimination in lending practices.

- **Healthcare diagnostics**: Responsible AI is employed in healthcare diagnostics to enhance accuracy and fairness. AI algorithms, such as those used in medical imaging, are designed to minimize biases, improve diagnostic capabilities, and assist healthcare professionals in providing more reliable and equitable patient care.

- **Predictive policing with ethical considerations**: Some law enforcement agencies deploy responsible AI in predictive policing with ethical considerations. These systems aim to minimize biases in crime prediction models, avoid reinforcing existing inequalities, and ensure that law enforcement decisions are fair and transparent, thus promoting community trust.

- **Ethical chatbots in customer service**: Companies deploy responsible AI in chatbots for customer service interactions. Ethical considerations are integrated to ensure transparency about the use of AI, and the chatbots are programmed to provide accurate information while avoiding biases, enhancing the user experience, and maintaining ethical standards.

- **Educational adaptive learning systems**: In education, responsible AI is used in adaptive learning systems that tailor educational content to individual students. These systems prioritize fairness, aiming to provide personalized learning experiences without reinforcing stereotypes or discriminating against certain student groups, thus promoting an inclusive and effective learning environment.

Conclusion

Gartner sees GenAI as a general-purpose technology with an impact similar to that of the steam engine, electricity, and the internet. The hype will subside over time, but the impact of GenAI will grow as people and enterprises discover more innovative applications for the technology in daily work and life. Leading vendors like *OpenAI, Hugging Face,* and *Microsoft* offer a range of GenAI tools, from language models to content generation. The vendor landscape reflects a dynamic interplay of startups, tech giants, and specialized firms, each contributing to the evolution and expansion of GenAI applications. The risks associated with GenAI include the potential for biased or inappropriate content generation, as models may inadvertently perpetuate societal prejudices present in training data. Security concerns arise with the misuse of generated content for malicious purposes, such as deepfakes or misinformation. Ethical considerations, such as lack of transparency and accountability in AI decision-making, pose challenges, necessitating responsible development practices to mitigate adverse impacts. Ethical AI involves designing and implementing artificial intelligence systems with a focus on fairness, transparency, and accountability. A culture fostering healthy deliberation and a collective value system is crucial for guiding the development of responsible AI. Successful GenAI implementation hinges on robust ethical frameworks, ensuring transparency, accountability, and fairness in algorithmic decision-making. In the next chapter, we will validate the advancements of GenAI across three dimensions to avoid falling for empty emerging technology hype and also understand different strategies an enterprise can adopt to make GenAI adoption successful

Key Terms

- Hallucination
- Anthropomorphization
- Responsible AI
- Data breaches

Questions

1. What is Hallucination in terms of Generative AI?
2. What are enterprise level considerations for GenAI project?
3. What is meant by Responsible AI?
4. What are the privacy concerns related to Generative AI ?
5. What are responsible AI principles

CHAPTER 10
Advances and Sustainability in Generative AI

Introduction

In the earlier chapters, we covered the enterprise opportunities and risks involved in **generative AI (GenAI)** technology. However, the problem for enterprises to invest in GenAI is the uncertainties that evolve around it. Every enterprise faces questions: *Is GenAI hype or truly transformative? Is it going to be another wave of technology settlement like crypto or metaverse? Will security, privacy, sustainability, and regulatory aspects downturn GenAI's capabilities?* In this chapter, we will analyze the hype around GenAI based on 3 dimensions: economic, technological, and regulatory. Throughout the chapter, we will briefly discuss different strategies a business can adopt in various scenarios. Finally, we will look into the sustainability aspects of GenAI and possible mitigations.

Structure

The chapter covers the following topics:

- Advances in GenAI
- GenAI business strategy
- GenAI sustainability

Objectives

The objective of this chapter is to understand the advancements happening in GenAI in terms of business, technology, and regulation. We will also look into the types of business strategy that an enterprise must adopt to leverage GenAI's potential to their competitive advantage. Further, we will look into the environmental impact due to training and inferencing of GenAI models way to measure and mitigate the same.

Advances of GenAI

GenAI has become a key geopolitical vector in global competition. The impact potential of GenAI varies on the basis of country, industry, and sector. Countries have started taking proactive steps in preparing the workforce for this imminent transformation to ensure that the entire society benefits from the same. However, the rapid development of GenAI and its immense promise poses difficult quandaries over the technology.

In this chapter, we will validate the advancements of GenAI to avoid falling for empty emerging technology hype. In the past, we have seen technology bubbles, inflated expectations associated with them, and sifted realistic hope as they faded over time. In this section, we consider three critical dimensions to understand and validate the hype around GenAI. As shown in *Figure 10.1*, GenAI's impact potential shall be analyzed in terms of business, technology, and regulation:

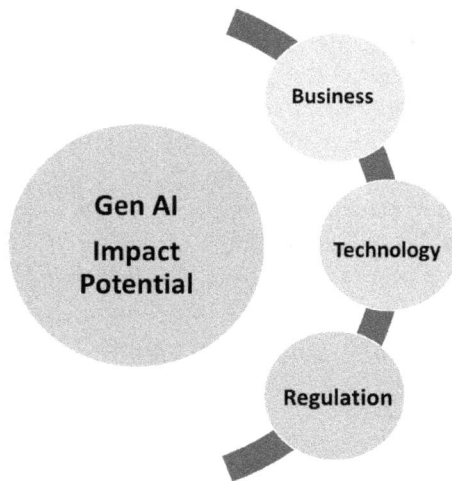

Figure 10.1: *Three dimensions to evaluate GenAI impact potential*

Business

GenAI is seen as an opportunity to strength global economies, extend human potential and grow industries. As we have sailed through the overestimated promises and potencies of crypto winter, celestial metaverse, and mighty 5G technologies, we can soberly validate the GenAI business hype through the lens of economic potential, job impacts, and industry investments.

Economic potential of GenAI

While **Price Waterhouse Coopers (PwC)** research shows that the global economic potential of AI shall reach $15.7 trillions by 2030. One can believe that the major contribution to this shall come from GenAI. Investment bankers and analysts such as *Goldman Sachs, McKinsey,* and *Bloomberg* predict that GenAI has the potential to raise global GDP by 4-7% and lift productivity growth by 1.5-2.0 % points over the next 10-year period.

Though all industries realize the significant gains, the impact of GenAI to businesses vary based on the use cases and the technology adoption. Some of the industry domains like high-tech, banking, life science and media are expected to have more impact than others due to GenAI potential. Research shows functions like marketing, sales, software engineering, product research, and development are driving most of GenAI's impact across potential corporate use cases. The following figure shows the potential economic impact of AI globally:

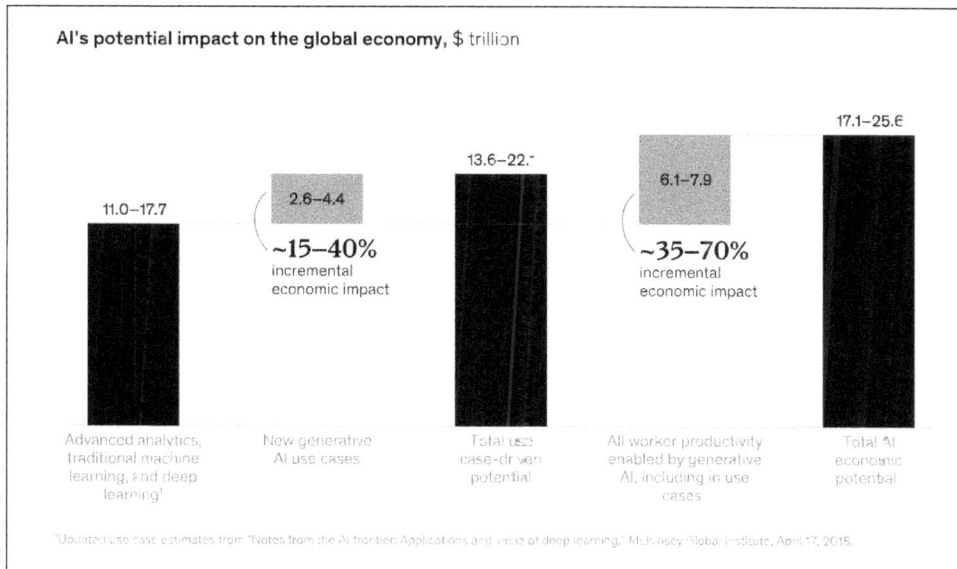

Figure 10.2: AI potential impact on the global economy in trillion
Source: https://www.mckinsey.com/capabilities/mckinsey-digital/our-insights/the-economic-potential-of-generative-ai-the-next-productivity-frontier#business-value

Job impact

The *Future of Job Reports* (**https://www.weforum.org/publications/the-future-of-jobs-report-2023/**) 2023 predicts that 23% of global jobs will change in the next 5 years due to artificial intelligence and other text/image processing technologies. Research also shows that 80% of the *U.S.* workers have 10%, and the others have 19% of their tasks exposed to GenAI. That is; there is a potential for augmentation or automation using the GenAI technology. The task-based analysis of the report reveals that jobs with routine tasks are susceptible to AI automation, tasks that require more abstract reasoning with interaction are susceptible to GenAI augmentation, and tasks that require a high degree of collaboration, technical interaction, and non-language tasks have low or no potential exposure to GenAI impact.

GenAI has the potential to automate millions of full-time. Recent a *McKinsey* analysis predicts that by 2030, GENAI would automate 29.5% of the hours performed in the *U.S.* economy, up from 21.5% now. Please find the below figure showcasing the midpoint adoption as a share of time spent on work activities:

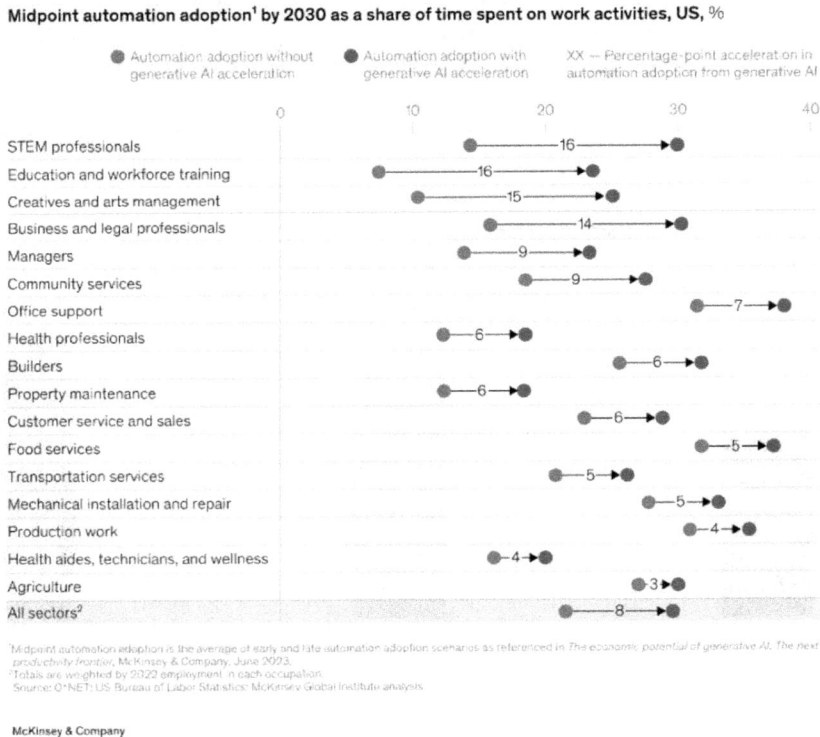

Figure 10.3: *Automation adoption scenarios across various industries*
Source: *https://news.stthomas.edu/generative-ais-real-world-impact-on-job-markets/*

While the threat of the exposure of existing jobs to GenAI persists, emerging jobs on GenAI could mitigate associated consequences. Some of the new emerging roles for GenAI are prompt engineers, interface and interaction designers, AI content creators, and ethics and governance specialists. Recently PwC AI jobs 2024 barometer shows how AI positively affects skills, wages and productivity and the following graph shows how AI skills have improved wages:

Wage premium for job vacancies which require AI skills by country

Occupation	Country AI Wage Premium				
	USA	UK	Canada	Australia	Singapore
Database Designers and Administrators	+53%	+58%	+8%	+14%	+35%
Lawyers	+49%	+27%	-	-	-5%
Sales and Marketing Managers	+43%	+14%	+3%	+7%	+3%
Financial Analysts	+33%	+32%	-	-	+11%
Applications Programmers	+32%	+24%	-	+7%	+34%
Systems Analysts	+30%	+34%	+15%	+7%	+28%
Accountants	+18%	+5%	+17%	-	+4%
Average wage premium across all jobs	+25%	+14%	+11%	+6%	+7%

Figure 10.4: *Wages premium for job vacancies which require AI skills*
Source *https://www.pwc.com/gx/en/issues/artificial-intelligence/ai-jobs-barometer.html*

Though there seems to be a right balance between creation, reinvention and displacements, there is a risk of new GenAI roles exacerbating the socio-economic disparities.

Industries

Business leaders are increasingly adopting GenAI technologies. As we have seen in *Chapter 9, GenAI for Enterprise*, numerous enterprise use cases have been piloted and GenAI tools are seen as a companion for the businesses to advance and enhance their productivity. As per *PitchBook* report, investments for GenAI topped $27 billion as of December 2023 that is, four times the entire investments for 2022.

Business models for AI include Software as a Service, Product as a Service, Platform as a Service, AI Infrastructure as a Service, Model as a Service, Data as a Service, and other traditional software-based models like technology, business, and managed services.

Revenue streams for GenAI companies come from licenses (AI technology embedded in software application and fine-tuning the model for business requirements), Usage or transaction (predefined metrics—tokens, volume of data, output generated), revenue share (Share in value generation like cost saving, new customer acquisition, premium share) and premium services (Charge for premium features in freemium platform/marketplaces like API access for inference endpoints, monetizing access to compute).

Based on the observations mentioned, we can confidently conclude that Generative AI will have a positive effect on the economy, job market, and various industries. In the above section, we have analyzed GenAI hype from the business dimension, and in the next section, we will look at it from the technology dimension. We will look into some of the advancements happening in GenAI technology.

Technology

GenAI is simply seen as a technology that adds intelligence to any data. GenAI is at the forefront of the technology innovation. While we are witnessing the release of a huge number of GenAI models competing on the number of tasks, model accuracy, and computational efficiency, the future of GenAI technology depends on the continuous development of data processing, model architectures, and learning methods. So, in this section, we will validate the GenAI business hype through the lens of technology developments happening in the GenAI ecosystem in terms of data selection, model architecture, optimization techniques, distributed learning methods, and secure inferencing that can bring potential breakthroughs in the future.

Data selection

Source data is critical for any **large language model (LLM)** performance. **Domain Reweighting with Minimax Optimization (DoReMi)**, a statistically principled approach for data selection developed in collaboration between *Stanford* and *Google* research team, speeds up the LLM training by 2.6 times. It leverages the **distributionally robust optimization (DRO)** strategy to generate domain weights without the knowledge of downstream tasks.

As shown in *Figure 10.5* for the given dataset, DoReMi trains a small reference model as per the regular training method. This reference model is used by a small **distributionally robust language model (DRO-LM)** to minimize the worst-case excess loss across all domains. These tuned weights are finally used by the 8B parameter large language model to get trained on new dataset with the composition determined by the previous domain weights:

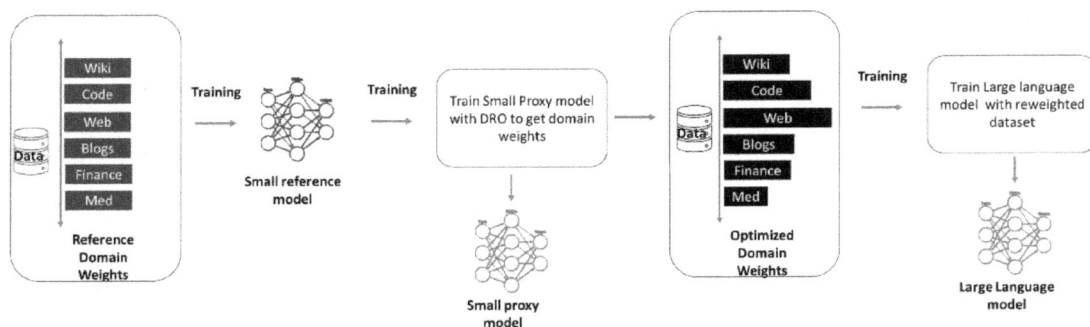

Figure 10.5: DoReMi process—Creation of reweighted dataset for LLM training

Architectures beyond transformers

One of the main drawbacks of transformer architecture is its quadratic scaling. That is, computation grows quadratically rather than linearly as the input sequence length grows.

As discussed in *Chapter 5, GenAI for Text*, attention mechanisms in transformer architecture compare every word in a sequence to every other word in that sequence. This pairwise comparison leads to scaling drawbacks when it comes to handling long input sequences like healthcare DNA sequences. Therefore, several attention-free alternates like *Hyena* (*Stanford*), *BiGS* (from *Cornell* and *DeepMind*), *MEGA* (from *meta*), *MonarchMixer* (*Hazy Research*) have emerged to perform at par with current transformer architecture, that is, faster with less compute requirements. These architectures are better equipped to handle long sequences efficiently. *Hyena* from *Stanford* uses the hyena hierarchy operator that involves long convolution and element-wise multiplication as an alternative to attention. The operator alternatively applies convolutions in the time and frequency domain or element-wise multiplication in the time and frequency domain. Hyena can also be used in Vision Transformers. *Figure 10.6* shows the recurrence of multiplicative element-wise gating of input and long convolution in the Hynena operator:

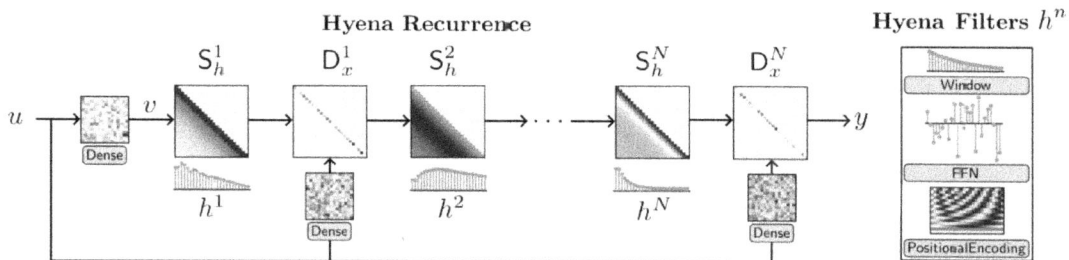

Figure 10.6: *Hyena operator (Subquadrate primitives)*
Source: *https://hazyresearch.stanford.edu/blog/2023-03-07-hyena*

The other popular alternative to multi-layer perceptron architecture that has emerged recently is **Kolmogorov-Arnold Networks (KANs)**. KANs use learnable activation functions on the edges (weights) of the network. It reduces multivariate continuous function as a summed finite composition of continuous functions of a single variable. Mathematically it is given by $f(x_1, x_2, x_3, \ldots, x_{n-1}, x_n) = \sum_{q=1}^{2n+1} \Phi_q(\sum_{p=1}^{n} \Phi_{q,p}(x_p))$ where $f(x)$ is complex high-dimensional function and $\Phi_{q,p}$ is univariate functions learned during training.

These architectures are emerging to address the limitation of computational complexity of attention mechanism by replacing it with other mechanisms, address the limitation of transparency or explainability of neural networks by simplifying intricate MLP weight matrices with explainable univariate functions, address the limitations due to fixed components like neuron activations with learnable activation functions.

Sophia optimization

The *Stanford* research team introduced **Sophia optimization**, an approach that reduces the LLM pretraining time to half. In the current LLM models, gradients are used by state of art ADAM optimizers to optimize the models based on the gradient curvature landscape.

However, Sophia optimization introduces a lightweight estimate of the diagonal approximation of the Hessian with clipping. Sophia is a second-order optimizer. It uses a lightweight, stochastic estimate of the diagonal of Hessian as a pre-conditioner.

In order to counteract the negative effects of the non-convexity and rapid Hessian changes, the Sophia optimization divides the moving average of gradients by the moving average of Hessian followed by element-wise clipping. Compared to traditional optimization, Hessian is 2x speed-up compared to ADAM. *Figure 10.7* shows the pseudo-code for Sophia's optimization:

Algorithm 3 Sophia

1: **Input:** θ_1, learning rate $\{\eta_t\}_{t=1}^{T}$, hyperparameters $\lambda, \gamma, \beta_1, \beta_2, \epsilon$, and estimator choice Estimator $\in$ {Hutchinson, Gauss-Newton-Bartlett}
2: Set $m_0 = 0$, $v_0 = 0$, $h_{1-k} = 0$
3: **for** $t = 1$ **to** T **do**
4:     Compute minibach loss $L_t(\theta_t)$.
5:     Compute $g_t = \nabla L_t(\theta_t)$.
6:     $m_t = \beta_1 m_{t-1} + (1 - \beta_1)g_t$
7:     **if** $t \bmod k = 1$ **then**
8:         Compute $\hat{h}_t = \text{Estimator}(\theta_t)$.
9:         $h_t = \beta_2 h_{t-k} + (1 - \beta_2)\hat{h}_t$
10:    **else**
11:        $h_t = h_{t-1}$
12:    $\theta_t = \theta_t - \eta_t \lambda \theta_t$ (weight decay)
13:    $\theta_{t+1} = \theta_t - \eta_t \cdot \text{clip}(m_t / \max\{\gamma \cdot h_t, \epsilon\}, 1)$

Figure 10.7: Pseudo-code for Sophia
Source: https://arxiv.org/pdf/2305.14342.pdf

Diffusion alignment: Direct preference optimization

It is a new approach for aligning text-to-image diffusion models, as discussed in *Chapter 4, GenAI for Image*. Unlike traditional models that use high-quality images with labels, it uses human preferences to fine-tune the model. This alignment technique helps improve the visual appeal and the prompt alignment of the diffusion models. The training data consists of prompts and a pair of images that include human judgment on one image preferred over another. The model is trained to have a better alignment with human preferences, i.e., the objective function is to maximize the reward during the reverse process of noise to human-preferred images. DPO is also the preferred finetuning technique in LLM compared to RLHF. In *Figure 10.8,* for a downstream image-to-image translation, DPO-based alignment generates visually appealing images as per human aesthetic preference, with high contrast, vivid colors, and fine details compared to original and non-DPO methods. Prompts used for generating the figure below are **A fantasy landscape, trending on art station (top) and high-resolution rendering of a crowded colorful sci-fi city (bottom)**.

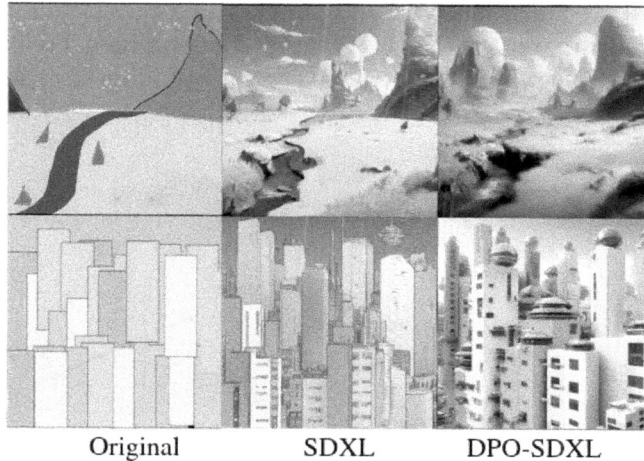

Figure 10.8: *Example of DPO downstream image to image translation task*
Source: *https://arxiv.org/abs/2311.12908*

Federated learning

It is a decentralized learning technique used to train **machine learning (ML)** models in a distributed manner while having the raw source data safe in its original location. The objective is to train a highly performant parent model with the training data distributed across multiple clients connected using an unreliable network. There are different federated learning strategies:

- **Centralized Federated Learning (CFL)**: Central server which does the client co-ordination and gathers the model updates during training. This strategy has a bottleneck of the central server as a single point of failure.

- **Decentralized Federated Learning (DFL)**: Model updates are shared among the interconnected clients and the accuracy of the model is dependent on the network topology and communication methods among the clients.

- **HeteroFL**: It trains heterogeneous local models with varying computation complexities and still produces a single global inference model. It involves creating a single inference model from the varied global model.

Some federated learning algorithms are **federated stochastic gradient descent (FedSGD)**, **federated averaging (FedAvg)**, and **federated learning with dynamic regularization (FedDyn)**. FedSGD is similar to mini-batch training, where a parent model is distributed to different clients, and gradients are calculated on local data; it is then passed to the central server for aggregation. In FedAvg, tuned weights are shared with the central server instead of gradients, and the aggregation happens on local model weights. FedDyn dynamically regularizes each device loss function so that the modified device losses converge with the actual global loss. Since the local losses are aligned, FedDyn is robust to different heterogeneity levels and it can safely perform full minimization in each device. The other algorithms that exist are Federated ViT using **Dynamic Aggregation (FED-REV), Hybrid Federated Dual Coordinate Ascent (HyFDCA), Personalized Federated Learning by Pruning (Sub-FedAvg)**. *Figure 10.9* shows the centralized federated learning process:

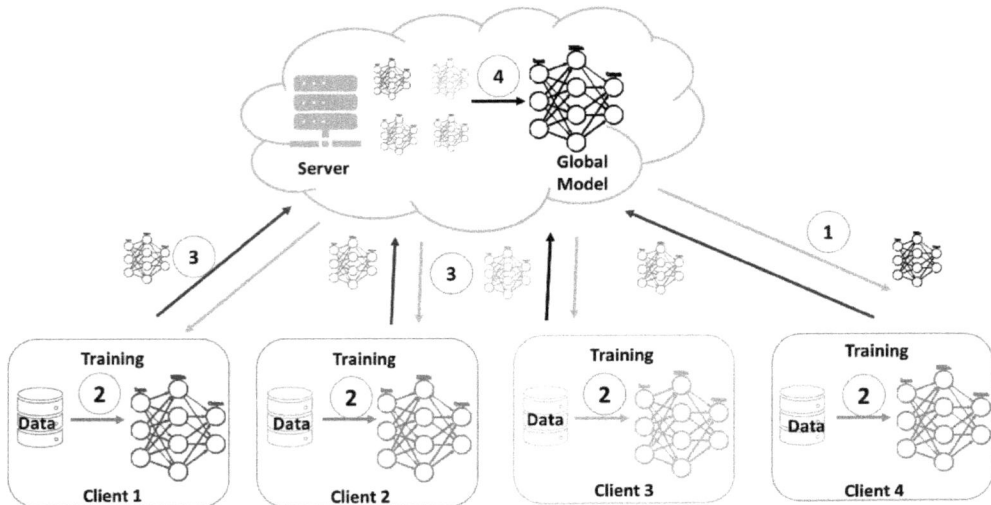

Figure 10.9: Centralized Federated Learning

Following are the steps followed in a CFL setup:

1. The server sends a global model (initialized on the server in the 1st round) to the selected clients.
2. Clients conduct local training on their local data.
3. Clients upload the training updates of the model to the server.
4. The server aggregates the training updates to obtain a new global model.

Some of the real-world examples are in health care industries, where distributed hospitals and clinical center have their private sensitive patient data where data cannot be shared between them due to compliance like GDPR or HIPAA and security concerns. Federated learning gives a methodological framework to train a global machine learning model, by only sharing the parameters of the models separately trained at each site. Similar use case is in mobile applications where models are built on user behavioral data of smart phones, without sharing sensitive private data. These models are used in face recognition, voice commands etc. The other use cases are in autonomous vehicles, where a global model has to be trained on distributed vehicle data, traffic information, driving behavioral data etc. Federated learning helps in on vehicle models to get trained on local data and sharing only the parameters to the global models. The other use case also includes to fine-tune small LLMs in a federated way to build a global large LLMs using upscaling methods.

Split learning

It is a distributed learning technique where machine learning models are trained without sharing data or detailed information about the model. In split learning, each client trains a partial neural network up to certain layers known as **cut layers**. These cut layers are input to the server which trains further without receiving any raw data. The gradients are backpropagated from the last layer until the cut layer. The main advantage is a low computational requirement for the clients, privacy enablement, and low bandwidth processing. In *Figure 10.10*, the layer marked by the black line is the cut layer. The layers are separated by the cut layer, and while the top part of the network is trained on the server, the bottom part of the network is trained on multiple clients. There are different configurations in split learning, such as U-shaped configuration and vertically partitioned data methods. The following *Figure 10.10* shows the split learning training process:

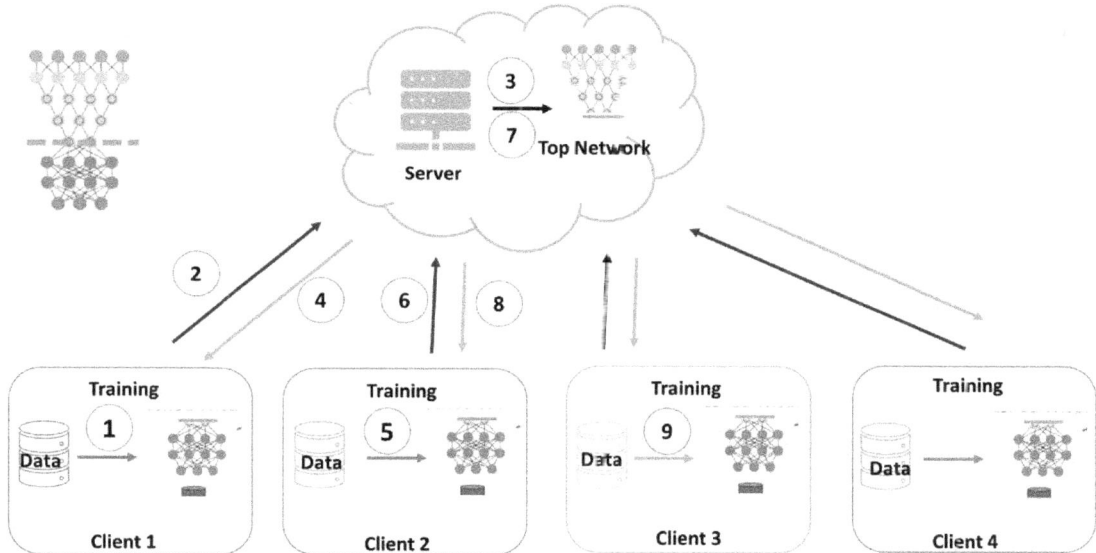

Figure 10.10: Split learning training process

As shown in the above figure, the following are the steps followed in centralized split learning:

- **Steps 1, 5 and 9**: Clients train on partition data
- **Steps 2 and 6**: The client sends the intermediate data (cut layer) to a server—forward propagation
- **Step 3**: Server performs forward propagation till the last layer
- **Steps 4 and 8**: During the gradient descent algorithm, the server sends back to the client the value of the gradients—backward propagation

Confidential AI

It is an emerging paradigm to protect models and data throughout the AI lifecycle, including when data is in use. It uses a hardware-based **Trusted Execution Environment** (**TEE**) to protect the data that is processed by the machine or stored in memory. TEEs are built in main processor systems such as *Intel Trust Domain Extension, AMD Secure Nested*

Pages, ARM Realm Management extension, and *NVIDIA Hopper,* a confidential compute feature that provides a GPU TEE environment. Confidential computing extends security while data is in use beyond data protection at rest (disk encryption) and at transit (TLS—Network encryption). In order to enable end-to-end data and model protection, one must ensure confidentiality at all levels from hardware, firmware, and software components, along with access controls and the trustworthiness of services interacting with the model. So confidential AI is a set of tools and services like cryptographic attestation, secure storage, and a trusted base platform with confidential VMs and Containers to enable data processing, training, fine-tuning, extraction, deployment, execution, and inferencing of models in a confidential and secured way.

One of the use cases for confidential AI is confidential inferencing, where a key-broker service, along with the TEE feature, ensures the model data are decrypted only inside TEE before inferencing happens. The other use cases are confidential training and tuning in cloud environments where model parameters, weights, and checkpoint data are not visible outside TEEs, and, finally, the use of confidential federate or split learning to enhance the security of edge clients. *Figure 10.11* shows the *Intel OpenVINO* security add-on components used for confidential AI:

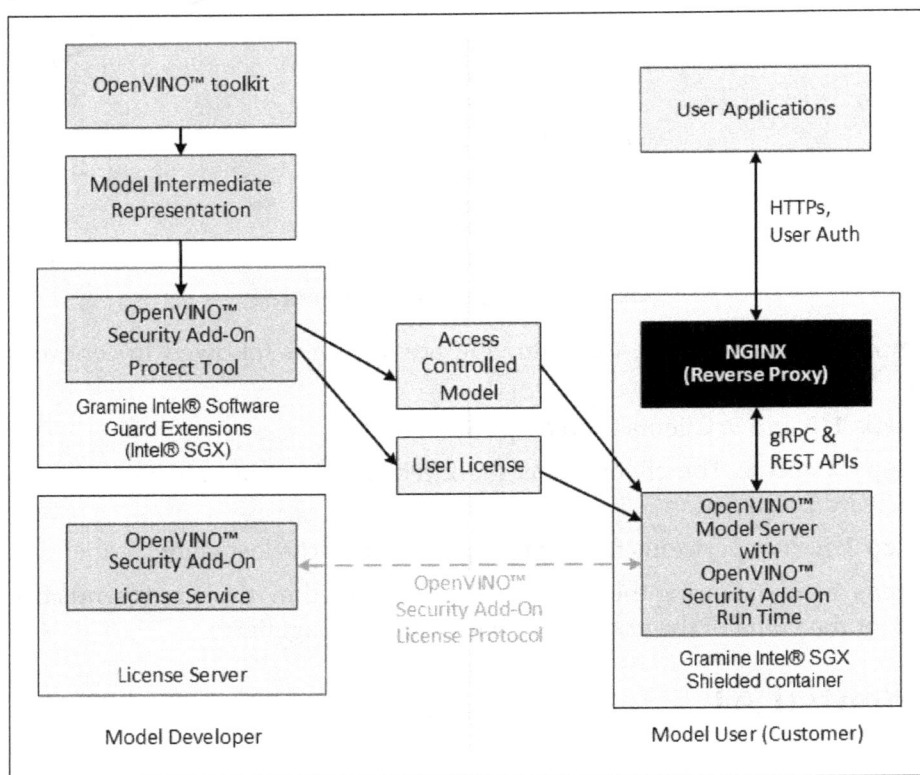

Figure 10.11: *Intel OpenVINO security add-on component for confidential AI*
Source: *https://www.intel.com/content/www/us/en/developer/articles/technical/secured-ai-model-inferencing-at-the-edge.html*

Based on the advancements mentioned, we can confidently assert that developments in Generative AI technology will enhance its adaptability by making it more cost-effective, resource-efficient, and quicker. In the above section, we analyzed the GenAI business hype through the lens of technology developments happening in the GenAI ecosystem, and in the upcoming section, we will analyze the regulatory impact on GenAI.

Regulations

Regulations are a critical dimension to analyze. As we have seen in the past how regulatory compliances can hurt and dampen technology growth (cryptocurrency). In this chapter, we will look into some of the existing AI regulatory controls and new GenAI regulations.

While the efforts to regulate AI have been expedited, the regulations for GenAI across the globe are still evolving. In certain regions like the *UK*, the use of AI for business domains like finance and healthcare is already regulated. For example, the use of AI by credit agencies for risk modeling must be assured for fairness by the **Financial Conduct Authority (FCA)**. Most of the regulations are related to data (i.e., data sources, copyrighted data, and data governance), model training (evaluation, benchmarking, and testing), the liability of outputs generated by the models (i.e., traceability of outputs and downstream applications compliance), and finally, related to protection for the outputs generated by the model. We will be looking in the next section at some of the new AI regulatory acts that have been discussed.

New AI regulatory acts across regions

The following are the new AI regulatory acts across regions:

- **US**: SAFE Innovation Framework prioritizing AI legislation for security, accountability, protecting foundations and explainability. Other enhancements are discussed for AI violations to existing regulations on the *FTC, Fair Credit Reporting Act,* and *Equal Credit Opportunity Act*.

- **EU**: *AI-ACT* a first ever AI law with legal frameworks that addresses risks of AI. It has four levels of risk tiers for AI system i.e. (Unacceptable risk, high risk, limited risk, and low risk). Each tier has its own set of regulations defined based on the level of risk. For example, AI system in voice activation toys that encourages violence in children will be categorized under the unacceptable risk tier and banned from implementation. The objective is to provide transparent, safe, traceable, non-discriminatory, and environment-friendly GenAI systems.

- **China**: **Cyberspace Administration of China (CAC)** released Interim Measures for the administration of GenAI service providers. The law aims to regulate the development of GenAI algorithms, and the use of AI systems in adherence to the core Chinese values. It also provides obligations to service providers on content management, privacy, transparency and security of GenAI systems.

The other announcement includes the *UN's* 39 member advisory board for addressing international governance of AI, the G7's 11-point code of conduct for developing advanced AI systems, and *Britain's AI Safety Summit*.

Regulatory challenges

The main challenge in regulating GenAI is to define the term harm and the responsibility to impose any penalty. The *European Commission* believes that the responsibility should lie with those best placed to address potential risks. GenAI systems pose a collective risk as the output of the generative model is probabilistic in nature, and misinformation or erroneous fact generation can happen across the lifecycle from data sourcing, training, and downstream app processing. Further accuracy of the model gets accreted over time, so the individual responsibilities overlap among the stages and also have limited control over the entire GenAI lifecycle. For e.g., A model owner may not have control over the model in use, so, drawing the line to relevant obligations is a challenge for regulators.

The other challenge is defining harm. Assessing the specific harms of GenAI systems is difficult as the output by the same model can have different levels of repercussions for different scenarios in different domains. It is still unclear to determine the ways to assess the impact due to the misuse of generative systems. Without assessing the impact, it is not possible to tie harms to specific GenAI systems, and hence *harm* cannot be clearly defined.

The other challenges are to achieve global consensus among different policymakers, technology companies, standardization bodies, and application owners for a unified and global approach for mitigation of societal-scale risks due to GenAI, to define AI policies that find the right balance between technological innovation and the need for regulation to ensure its responsible and ethical use.

Some of the possible solutions to address above challenges are:

- **Global standards and local regulations**: Similar to telecom, 3GPP standards, GenAI and its frameworks need to use common terms and definitions to act as a foundation for cooperation. GenAI Standardization body must ensure that their standards are not against these local interests. While global standards can address the technical aspects of evolving GenAI technology, regional regulations can amend their local variants to address geo-political realities. For example, while global standards can have their common definition of harm and its implications, local regulations can define their legal penalties.

- **GenAI as content moderator**: Similar to phages (Phages are viruses that infect bacteria that cannot be killed with antibiotics but are harmless to people.) regulators must use of LLMs to do content moderation. Automated content filters and review algorithms can be employed as a central control mechanism to identify inappropriate or illegal content material prior publishing. Enterprises, must go through these online services prior publishing or releasing any GenAI related content to the public.

- **Model licensing**: Regulators must create taxonomy and inventory of models to be approved for use in particular country or region. The models must be licensed for intended used with all controls in place considering both functioning and inherent model risks. A centralized repository to record all usage across the organization in a central repository that is clear to those inside and outside the organization

- **Protection to leadership**: While regulatory risk is of major concern, especially during the early adoption phase of GenAI, there are many unknown threat vectors like deepfakes, IP infringement due to third-party products, etc. On such unknow scenarios, new regulations must safeguard Directors and officer of enterprises against potential legal actions, which will help the leadership to navigate the complexities of GenAI adoption with confidence.

- **e-People**: Apart from enhancing old AI regulatory frameworks with new-GenAI technology, some of the novel approaches considered are giving the AI systems legal status as e-people and creating constitutional AI—an AI system to monitor and ensure regulatory compliance by other GenAI models. Though emerging AI regulations across geographies seem to downturn GenAI capabilities, unprecedented economic potential, and with society embracing the possibilities, it is obvious that technology leaders will find hardball tactics to tackle institutional voids and influence the development of regulations, professional workforce, and new GenAi uses.

Based on the observations and analysis, the evolution of generative AI regulation is increasingly adopting a strong framework that guarantees secure and responsible development while simultaneously promoting innovation and growth within the technology sector.

In the above section, we have analyzed GenAI hype through the lens of the regulatory dimension. So, we have understood the GenAI technology impact by analyzing it in 3 dimensions (Business, technology, and regulatory). We can safely conclude that technology is not mere a hype ,GenAI's impact on enterprises and society is going to be massive. In the upcoming section we will look into GenAI business strategy for enterprises.

GenAI business strategy

The business opportunity for enterprises with GenAI technology can be broadly categorized into:

- Creating new revenue streams from GenAI applications or services.
- Generating additional revenue by augmenting existing products/service lines with GenAI capabilities.

Strategy for a new revenue stream

In this section, we will discuss three scenarios of new revenue streams and the strategy to adopt by enterprise for each:

Scenario 1: Building domain-specific foundation models and a large number of implementable use cases for industry sectors. Early adopters will have a strategic advantage in this scenario. So, enterprises have to adopt the blitzscaling strategy. **Blitzscaling** is the approach defined by *Reid Hoffman*, co-founder of *Linkedin*, for companies to grow quickly. The approach is of mindset either you win big or lose big. This approach allows a company to achieve a massive scale at an incredible speed that makes the competition irrelevant. The goal is to become the first mover at scale. It is both an offensive and a defensive strategy. As offensive, it will hit the market with surprise and the *Winners take the most*. As defensive, competitors will have little time to respond or compete.

Smaller enterprises, which have their target product-market fit, can adopt the above blitzscaling strategy to grow big quickly. It will be difficult for larger organizations to adopt such a strategy as blitzscaling comes with its risk and managerial inefficiencies. Reinventing larger organizations at scale in a non-conventional way has its own complications, from process to culture change. The opportunity for larger organizations is to spin off their existing AI product or service portfolios, liberating the parent organization from the blitzscaling risks and liberating the divested company from the capital and process constraints.

Scenario 2: Building a good enough GenAI product for focused customer needs and creating distinctive GenAI services to enhance the existing product experience. In this scenario, organizations must innovate cheaply and get products released faster to the market. So, enterprises can adopt a bird in the hand strategy. bird in the hand is more proverbial, where organizations can begin with a simple problem for which an implementable GenAI solution exists and do not deal with technologies and markets about which little is known. Organizations must bundle up GenAI services with primary products and services and reposition them to the market.

Scenario 3: Building GenAI services competing cloud incumbents. In this scenario, incumbents will create a strong barrier to entry. The incumbents enjoy a high profit margin, higher supplier bargaining power, and a larger network of business, which makes it difficult for new entrants to compete. So, enterprises must adopt an indirect approach to compete in monopolist markets. The indirect approach is a military strategy described and chronicled by *B. H. Liddell Hart* after *World War I*. The strategy calls for armies to advance along the line of least resistance. The core idea of this approach is to avoid a frontal attack. The indirect approach for enterprises is to have niche solutions and compete on alternate value chains. Organizations must invest pre-emptively in niche areas like responsible GenAI, sustainable GenAI solutions, and non-transistor-based GenAI computing and compete in on-prem enterprise-ready infrastructure space.

Strategy for augmenting product and services

In the earlier section, we discussed new revenue stream scenarios and strategies; in this section, we will discuss a strategy that enterprises must adopt to bring additional revenue to their existing product and services by augmenting GenAI services.

GenAI is a powerful technology that has the potential to revolutionize business. With practical realities and limitations such as errors, biases, hallucinations, and privacy threats, enterprises are unclear on what makes for a good strategy in such uncertain environments. With such uncertainty and speculations around GenAI, the enterprises must adopt hipstoric strategy. The term hipstoric is borrowed from the home decor trend that was coined in a *Pinterest* report to describe the style of combining old inherited pieces with new modern designs. Similarly, in uncertain environments, companies must converge different kinds of knowledge from the past, coupled with recent new technologies, to formulate the future. Enterprises must define a hyperbolic time cone, as shown in *Figure 10.12* below, to handle such uncertainty over disruptions:

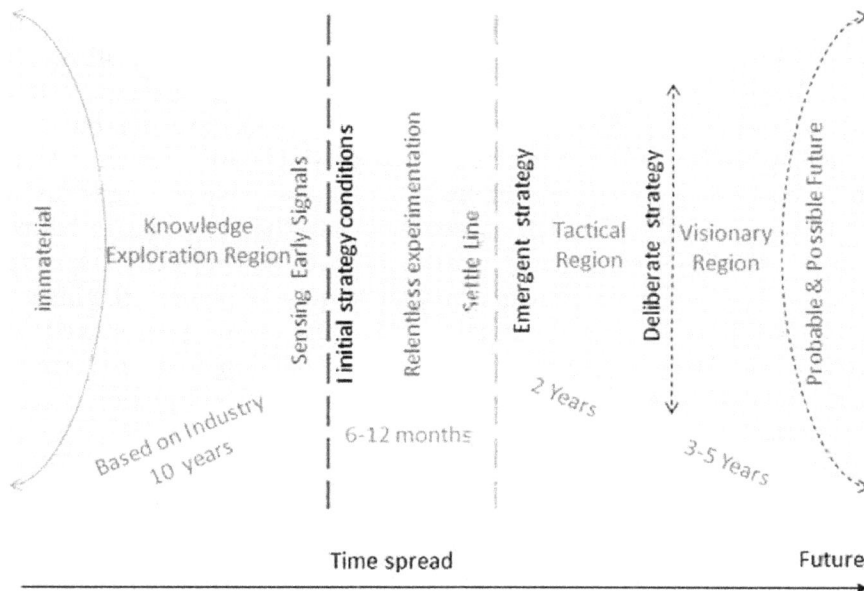

Figure 10.12: Hyberbolic time cone for enterprise

Hyperbolic time cone

As shown in the hyperbolic time cone, on sensing early technology disruption signals, enterprises start exploring the accumulated knowledge in a defined time spread and initiate a relentless experimentation phase. In this phase, organizations run multiple parallel initiatives and learn the real capabilities of GenAI that can work for their business and industry. The result of this phase will be a probabilistic strategy creation with futuristic scenarios. As a lot of technology excitements emerge in the industry, enterprises must have a clear delineation of initial conditions, thereby avoiding multiple occurrences of similar inventions in the industry at the same time. For example, Customer support is one of the most sought-after use cases for GenAI across industries and it has immense benefit of operational cost savings and customer experience. In the airline industry, customer support experience is a critical factor in ticket booking, cancellations, and upgrades, and it has a direct impact on customer retention. For airlines business, building a GenAI based end to end customer journey support seems to be the right initial state for experimentation. However, the actual value generation and competitive differentiation for the airline business lies in building GenAI solutions that have a direct impact on the parameters that improve the carrier airtime and loading factors. So, the enterprises must perform a careful analysis and choose only those strategies for experimentation phase that ensure that the enterprises will differentiate themselves from other firms in any competitive dimension. Data will play a key role in choosing the initial conditions and arrival at the final probabilistic strategic plans.

As enterprises entered the tactical region, they were clear in terms of explicit formulation of new technology impact, issues, and alternatives. Strategy plans will revolve around balancing of firm activities with new technology. The new strategy will cut across organizational boundaries and individual business units must broaden the scope for new technology collaboration in order to create new products and services. As enterprises progress in the tactical region, organizations must be adaptable and agile (living plan) to execute such emergent strategies. The strategic options that do not offer better solutions and seem to be incongruous to new processes need to be dropped. The output of this phase will result in a deliberate strategy (quarter to quarter planning). This will identify the enterprise positions on the identified strategic factor for each stakeholder group. Organizations can make clear choice of what they are not going to do. In certain scenarios, organizations have to undergo customer divestments whereby they stop providing products or services to existing customer groups.

As enterprises progress into the vision region, the gap between the probable and possible future scenarios keeps reducing, and they will build faster and more accurate products or services as per customer needs. This will cause the change-of-hands of sizable amounts of market share in relatively short periods of time. Through continuous investment in new technology and mergers and acquisitions, enterprises will alter long-standing industry structures and maintain their leadership position.

Enterprise strategy using hyperbolic time cone

Larger enterprises must have their hyperbolic time cone to build their GenAI strategy and actions. Larger enterprises must strategically choose the time spread of the cone and explore past AI knowledge that can be valuable along with the exploitation of current GenAI technology to create innovative businesses.

Current GenAI technology does not seem to be capable of dethroning any business services or products. With next-generation algorithms, soon its impact can move from transformative to disruptive regions for certain industry domains. For example, GenAI's impact on the transport and logistics industry could remain transformative, where use cases evolve around operation efficiency and customer experience. But in the case of media domains like marketing services where automatic campaign planning and content generation by GenAI will become disruptive, and advances in the technology could be a threat to the company's existence.

For businesses in such a domain where technology is a threat to their existence, the relentless experimentation phase must be much less. They must implement a tactical GenAI strategy to augment their services so that they can survive and emerge as leaders in their space. Unlike large enterprises, startups, and medium enterprises do not have the leverage of the past. So, enterprises must look into synergistic innovation during experimentation by relating ideas across technology domains or businesses that can operate synergistically. For e.g., Organizations could benefit from distributed computing to reduce the computing cost of GenAI workloads. This can make GenAI solutions viable and open up new customer segments that are not the target for larger enterprises.

GenAI sustainability

Carbon emission reduction has become a business imperative. Organizations, based on their business activities and operational tasks, have committed to net zero, carbon neutral, carbon negative goals and emission reduction plans. Net zero by 2050 is an internationally agreed goal. To halt the climate crisis, the *Intergovernmental Panel on Climate Change* has agreed upon net zero by 2050. The other internationally agreed goal is *the Paris Agreement* on limiting global warming to well below 2°C above preindustrial levels. Before understanding the environmental impact of GenAI, we will understand the classification of emissions as per **greenhouse gas (GHG)** protocol corporate standard and the strategies adopted to reduce the emissions in the AI industry. As per the standard, there are three types of emission scope

Scope 1 and Scope 2 emissions are mandatory for enterprises to report in certain region of world like *Europe*. Scope 3 is voluntary, and the hardest one to monitor or report:

- **Scope 1**: Emissions are direct GHG emissions by the sources owned by or controlled by the organization. For a company with IT resources, these could be from in-house processing equipment, company facilities, company vehicles.
- **Scope 2**: Emissions are indirect derived from purchase of electricity, cooling and heat.
- **Scope 3**: Emissions are indirect and not included in *Scope 2*. These occur in upstream and down steam activities. Though the reporting companies do not have direct control over *Scope 3*, they can influence over the emission by recruiting eco-friendly partners, vendors, investment and purchase strategies.

One of the main actions taken by AI organizations to reduce *Scope 1, 2,* and *3* is to monitor and reduce the emissions from energy and fuel-related activities which includes the purchase of renewal energy, increased power usage effectiveness for data centers, adopting green sourcing in choosing cloud provider to host their services and increasing the utilization of their IT assets.

The other novel approach AI companies adopt is green-software development. It brings energy-efficient design, architectures, and programming efficiency in terms of computing, memory, storage, and network. This helps an organization build sustainable AI software applications. The other approach organizations take is to adopt GreenOps, an operating model that encompasses all green initiatives taken by an organization across the entire business and technology practices to minimize the environmental impact.

Environmental impact due to GenAI

It is understood that generative tasks are more carbon and energy-intensive compared to discriminative tasks. Most of the studies on the environmental impact of GenAI models have been focused on energy consumption during the training phase. Though developing or training foundation models consume large amounts of carbon emissions and energy costs, studies have discovered that daily emissions associated with inferencing far exceed emissions during the training phase. The other factors that have a huge impact on reducing emissions are the tasks performed by GenAI models. It seems that generating images is more carbon intensive than text generation and models that are trained for a particular task consume less energy than using fine-tuned LLM models. Therefore, to understand the real environmental impact, one must consider different steps in the GenAI cycle, model architecture and size, tasks performed, infrastructure, and their relative contribution to carbon emissions. *Figure 10.13* shows the environmental impact on selected machine-learning models:

Environmental Impact of Select Machine Learning Models, 2022
Source: Luccioni et al., 2022 | Table: 2023 AI Index Report

Model	Number of Parameters	Datacenter PUE	Grid Carbon Intensity	Power Consumption	CO2 Equivalent Emissions	CO2 Equivalent Emissions x PUE
Gopher	280B	1.08	330 gCO2eq/kWh	1,066 MWh	352 tonnes	380 tonnes
BLOOM	176B	1.20	57 gCO2eq/kWh	433 MWh	25 tonnes	30 tonnes
GPT-3	175B	1.10	429 gCO2eq/kWh	1,287 MWh	502 tonnes	552 tonnes
OPT	175B	1.09	231 gCO2eq/kWh	324 MWh	70 tonnes	76.3 tonnes

Figure 10.13: Environmental impact of select machine learning models 2022

Tools to measure the carbon intensity and total energy consumption

Generally, carbon footprint at a high level is calculated as the product of total energy consumption in kilowatt hour and carbon intensity of electricity in KgCO2e/kWh, that is, the amount of carbon equivalent emitted from producing one said unit of electricity. However, with the surge in ML models and their considerable environmental impacts, below are certain tools that can be utilized to measure the environmental impact.

CodeCarbon, ML CO2, and LLMCarbon are commonly used tools to measure impact due to ML Model training or inferencing. Different tools have different approaches to measuring the impact. Most of the time, power consumption, the source of energy used, and hardware types are considered to derive the emission impact.

The code carbon tool tracks the power usage of AI hardware infrastructure on the cloud and on-prem data centers for each experiment. The tool then estimates the carbon intensity for the experiments based on public data sources on the energy mix of the electricity grid to which hardware is connected. Please find the below *Code snippet 10.1* to capture the emission metrics due to MNIST training:

```
1.  !pip install codecarbon
2.  import tensorflow as tf
3.  from codecarbon import EmissionsTracker
4.
5.  mnist = tf.keras.datasets.mnist
6.  (x_train, y_train), (x_test, y_test) = mnist.load_data()
7.  x_train, x_test = x_train / 255.0, x_test / 255.0
8.
9.  model = tf.keras.models.Sequential(
10.     [
11.         tf.keras.layers.Flatten(input_shape=(28, 28)),
12.         tf.keras.layers.Dense(128, activation="relu"),
13.         tf.keras.layers.Dropout(0.2),
14.         tf.keras.layers.Dense(10),
15.     ]
16. )
17.
18. loss_fn = tf.keras.losses.SparseCategoricalCrossentropy(from_
    logits=True)
19.
20. model.compile(optimizer="adam", loss=loss_fn, metrics=["accuracy"])
21.
22. tracker = EmissionsTracker()
23. tracker.start()
```

```
24. model.fit(x_train, y_train, epochs=10)
25. emissions: float = tracker.stop()
26. print(emissions)
```

Code snippet 10.1: Code carbon tool Script to capture emission due to training MNIST dataset

Using the ML CO_2 Impact tool (**https://calculator.linkeddata.es/#co2eq**), we can calculate the emission of cloud infrastructure. For example, ML carbon impact for a hardware type of A100 PCIe 40/80C, 100 Hours usage on *Google Cloud platform* on *Europe-west 2* is 4.75 Kg CO_2 eq.

The other tool, LLMCarbon, calculates the total carbon footprint as the sum of the operational carbon footprint and embodied carbon footprint of LLM, where the operational foot-print attributed to operational energy and carbon intensity of the data center and embodied footprint attributed to the carbon emission due to the hardware units used across LLM lifecycle. Below *Figure 10.14* presents an overview of LLMCarbon for predicting the carbon footprint of an LLM where architectural description, data center specification, and hardware configuration are considered for calculations:

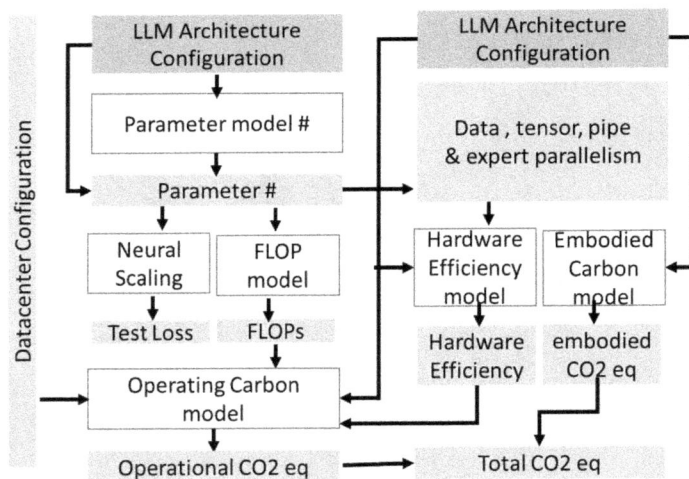

Figure 10.14: Overview of LLMCarbon for predicting the carbon foot print on an LLM model
Source: https://arxiv.org/pdf/2309.14393v1.pdf

Mitigations

While GenAI models are more powerful, it not necessary to use general purpose GPT-style transformer model for all tasks. Customization of model for specific tasks and in certain cases models with simple architectures can achieve adequate performance like large complex models. So, choice of model architectures based on task can dramatically lower carbon emission and computational cost.

In case of training foundation models, choosing the energy grids with minimal carbon emission or choosing the cloud server region with high energy efficiency training can minimize the environmental impact. The other approaches include green-default settings by cloud, datacenter, and open-source project, carbon offsets such as forest planting as stop-gap arrangement for their datacenter, choice of hardware such as specialized ones like GPUs, TPUs enable parallel processing on neural networks improves hardware efficiency and reduces training time has generally been adopted as mitigation strategy for foundation model training.

Another useful approach is adopting different techniques like fine-tuning, prompt engineering, and in-context learning, which discusses how fine-tuning offers better accuracy as well as dramatically lower computational costs.

In most cases, enterprises trade-off GenAI's negative environmental impact with the potential positive benefits, where the value generated by the model far outweighs negative outcomes. The choice of such use cases can simply be determined by deducing the social benefits to the carbon and energy costs due to building and operationalizing the models.

Conclusion

In this chapter, we understood the three dimensions: business, technology, and regulation and the different factors to evaluate the GenAI impact potential. We described the GenAI technological advances in data, architecture, optimization, and distributed training. We also talked about the state of emerging regulations across geographies. The chapter prescribed different enterprise business strategies such as blitzScaling, a bird in the hand, an Indirect approach for generating a new revenue stream, and a historic approach for product augmentation to leverage the GenAI potential by following a hyperbolic time cone. We presented the international commitment to climate change and the type of Scope to monitor CO_2 emissions. We described the environmental impact of GenAI tasks in the entire lifecycle. Finally, we concluded with general tools used to evaluate the CO2 emission of Generative models and possible mitigations where renewal energy sourcing and optimizing PUE for data centers can bring major reduction to CO2 emission.

Key terms

- Net zero emission a state where all released emissions are counter balanced by removal out of carbon from atmosphere
- Power usage effectiveness a measure to determine data center efficiency
- Confidential AI to train models in secure and encrypted way
- Federated learning sub field of machine learning
- Split learning type of AI learning that ensure privacy

Questions

1. What is name of EU Act to regulate AI?
2. What are the different tools available to calculate CO_2 while model training?
3. What is the difference between Scope 1 and Scope 2 emission?
4. What are the different dimensions discussed to evaluate GenAI hype?
5. What is the difference between Federated and Split learning?

Join our book's Discord space

Join the book's Discord Workspace for Latest updates, Offers, Tech happenings around the world, New Release and Sessions with the Authors:

https://discord.bpbonline.com

Index

390 Generative AI for Everyone

Ray Serve 318

Seldon Core 316

Text Generation,
inference 317

TF 315

Triton Inference Server 317

MoE, components

Experts 304

Pool, method 304

Trainable Network 304

Multi-Task Learning
(MTL) 30, 31

N

Natural Language Processing
(NLP) 28, 162

NLP, prerequisites

Encoder/Decoder Text
Summarization 200-209

GPT-2 Model 189-197

NLP, scenarios 162, 163

O

OpenAI 212

OpenAI, service

Cookbook 216

fine-tuning 217

Image Models 212, 213

Playground 215

Whisper 214

ORPO 299

P

PCA, components 16

Playground, hyperparameters

maximum, length 215

temperature 215

Top-P, value 215

Pre-training, methods

Benchmark Dataset 294

Data Formats/GenAI 289

Data Quality, evaluating 289

Evaluation, metrics 293, 294

LeaderBoard 295

Memory, optimizing 290, 291

Parallel Computation 291, 292

Performance,
benchmarking 292

Synthetic Data,
generating 290

Principal Component Analysis
(PCA) 16

Prompt Engineering 222

Prompt Engineering,
importance 223, 224

Prompt Engineering,
objectives 225

Prompt Engineering,
refining 230

Prompt Engineering,
scenarios

code, assistant 225

Ecommerce 225

grammarly, assistant 225

medical, assistant 225

Prompt Engineering,
steps 225

Prompt Engineering,
structures 226

Prompt Engineering, techniques

COT 227

Few-Shot 227

Instruction 227

One-Shot 227

www.ingramcontent.com/pod-product-compliance
Lightning Source LLC
Chambersburg PA
CBHW061743210326
41599CB00034B/6775